STUDY GUIDE FOR BAUMOL, BLINDER, AND SCARTH'S

ECONOMICS

PRINCIPLES AND POLICY

Canadian Edition

Craig Swan / William M. Scarth

University of Minnesota   McMaster University

Academic Press Canada

Toronto

Canadian Cataloguing in Publication Data

Swan, Craig.
    Study guide for Baumol, Blinder, and Scarth's
Economics, principles and policy, Canadian edition

Supplement to: Baumol, William J.   Economics,
principles and policy.   Canadian ed.
ISBN 0-7747-3044-7

1. Economics.   2. Economics—Problems, exercises,
etc.   I. Scarth, William M., 1946-   II. Baumol, William J.
Economics, principles and policy.   Canadian ed.
III. Title.

HB171.5.B3222 1985   330   C85-099305-9

Printed in Canada

Introduction

This study guide is designed to be used with *Economics: Principles and Policy*, Canadian Edition, by William J. Baumol, Alan S. Blinder, and William M. Scarth. This guide is not meant to be a substitute for the basic textbook; rather, experience has shown that conscientious use of a supplemental aid such as this can lead to greater learning and understanding of the course material. It might also improve your grade.

The chapters in this book parallel those in *Economics: Principles and Policy*, Canadian Edition. Each chapter here is a review of the material covered in the textbook chapters. You should first read and study each chapter in the textbook and then use the corresponding chapter in this book. "Use" is the correct verb, as each chapter in this book is designed for your *active* participation.

The material with which you will be working is organized into the following elements.

LEARNING OBJECTIVES

Each chapter starts with a set of behavioural learning objectives. These indicate the things you should be able to do upon completing each chapter.

IMPORTANT TERMS AND CONCEPTS

As one of the learning objectives for each chapter states, you should be able to "define, understand, and use correctly" the terms and concepts that are listed in this section. They parallel the Concepts for Review listed at the end of the text chapter. Being able to *define* these terms is likely to be important for your grade. But to really *understand* what they mean, rather than to temporarily memorize their definition, is even better. The ultimate test of your understanding will be your ability to *use correctly* the terms and concepts in real-life situations.

CHAPTER REVIEW

Each review section has a summary discussion of the major points of each chapter. The reviews are designed to be used actively. Frequently you will need to supply the appropriate missing term or to choose between pairs of alternative words. Some of the missing words are quite specific and can be found in the list of important terms and concepts. At other times the answers are less clear-cut, as the following hypothetical example illustrates: "If people expect inflation at higher rates than before, nominal interest rates are likely to _____."
Any of the following would be correct answers: increase, rise, go up. In cases like this, do not get concerned if the answer you choose is different from the one in the back of the book.

BASIC EXERCISE

Most chapters have one or more exercises that are designed for you to use as a check on your understanding of a basic principle discussed in the chapter. Many of the exercises use simple arithmetic or geometry. While getting the correct answers is one measure of understanding, do not mistake the arithmetic manipulations for the economic content of the problems. A hand calculator may make the arithmetic less burdensome.

SELF-TESTS FOR UNDERSTANDING

Each chapter has a set of multiple choice and true-false questions for you to use as a further check on your understanding. It is important to know not only what the correct answers are but also why other answers are wrong. Especially when considering the true-false questions, be sure you understand why the false statements are false.

APPENDIX

Eleven of the 42 chapters in the text contain appendices, which generally are designed to supplement the chapter content with material that is either a bit more difficult or that offers further exposition of a particular economic concept. There is material in this guide for each appendix in the text. In some cases the review material for the appendix parallels that for the chapter, including learning objectives, important terms and concepts, and so forth. In other cases, the appendix material is reviewed here in the form of an additional exercise designed to illustrate the principles discussed in the appendix.

SUPPLEMENTARY EXERCISE

Many chapters end with a supplementary exercise, which may be either an additional mathematical exercise or some suggestions that will allow you to use what you have learned in real-world situations. Some of the exercises use more advanced mathematics. Since many of these exercises review the material in the Basic Exercise, they illustrate how economists use mathematics and are included for those students with appropriate training. The most important thing is to understand the economic principles that underlie the Basic Exercise, something that does not depend upon advanced mathematics.

Being introduced to economics for the first time should be exciting and fun. For many of you it is likely to be hard work, but hard work does not have to be dull and uninteresting. Do not look for a pat set of answers with universal applicability. Economics does not offer answers but rather a way of looking at the world and thinking systematically about issues. John Maynard Keynes said:

> The theory of economics does not furnish a body of settled conclusions immediately applicable to policy. It is a method rather than a doctrine, an apparatus of the mind, a technique of thinking, which helps its possessor to draw correct conclusions.

Bertrand Russell, the distinguished British philosopher and mathematician, had considered studying economics but decided it was too easy. The Nobel prize-winning physicist Max Planck also considered studying economics but decided it was too hard. Whether, like Russell, you find economics easy or, like Planck, you find it hard, we trust that with the use of this guide you will find it relevant and exciting!

Craig Swan
William Scarth

Contents

I

What Is
Economics
All About?

What Is Economics?

1

LEARNING OBJECTIVES

After completing the material in this chapter you should be able to:

- define, understand, and use correctly the terms and concepts listed below.
- explain the role of abstraction, or simplification, in economic theory.
- explain the role of theory as a guide to understanding real-world phenomena.
- explain why imperfect information and value judgments will always mean that economics cannot provide definitive answers to all social problems.

IMPORTANT TERMS AND CONCEPTS

Voluntary exchanges
Comparative advantage
Productivity
Externalities
Correlation versus causation
Model
Rationality
Opportunity Cost
Marginal analysis
Marginal costs
Abstraction and generalization
Theory

CHAPTER REVIEW

Chapter 1 has two objectives: It introduces some of the types of problems economists concern themselves with, offering 12 important Ideas for Beyond the Final Exam; and it discusses the methods of economic analysis, in particular the role of theory in economics.

The problems discussed in the first part of the chapter have been chosen specifically to illustrate 12 basic economic issues to be remembered beyond the final exam. You should not only read this material now, but make sure to re-examine the list at the end of the course. Understanding the economic principles that underlie these 12 basic issues is the real final examination in economics as contrasted with the final examination for this course.

The methods of economic inquiry are perhaps best described as "eclectic," meaning that they are drawn from many sources according to their usefulness to the subject matter. Economists borrow from all the social sciences in order to theorize about human behaviour. They borrow from mathematics in order to express those theories concisely. And, finally, they borrow from statistics in order to make inferences from real world data about hypotheses suggested by economic theory.

Economists are interested in understanding human behaviour not only for its own sake, but also because of the policy implications of this knowledge. How can we know what to expect from changes resulting from public policy or business decisions unless we understand why people behave the way they do? As an example of all this, consider the 12 ideas discussed in the first part of this chapter. Each idea derives from economic theory. As you will learn, each idea also offers important insights into actual historical experience and is an important guide to the evaluation of future changes.

As in other scientific disciplines, theory in economics is an abstraction, or simplification, of innumerable complex relationships in the real world. When thinking about some aspects of behaviour, say a family's spending decisions or why the price of wheat fluctuates so much, economists will build a model that attempts to explain the behaviour under examination. The elements of the model are derived from economic theory. Economists study the model to see what hypotheses, or predictions, are suggested by the model. These can then be checked against real-world data. An economist's model will typically be built not with hammer and nails, but with pencil, paper, and computers. The appropriate degree of abstraction for an economic model is, to a large extent, determined by the problem at hand and is not something that one can specify in advance for all problems.

An important part of most economic models is the assumption that people's behaviour is *rational*.

(1) Economists use the assumption of rationality to characterize (*ends*/*means*), not _____ . People's ultimate desires are determined by their own preferences. Economists do not make judgments about the rationality or irrationality of these preferences. But given these desires, economists usually assume that people act in an efficient and rational manner to satisfy these desires, subject of course to the information and resources available to them.

Economists clearly believe that they can make a significant contribution to the discussion and resolution of many important social issues. It is hoped that by the time you finish this course you will agree with this belief. At the same time you should realize that the contribution of economics is that it offers a way of looking at questions rather than a comprehensive set of answers to all questions. Economists will always have differences of

(2) opinion when it comes to final policy recommendations because of incomplete _____ and different

_____ judgments.

SELF-TEST FOR UNDERSTANDING

Circle T or F for True or False as appropriate.

1. Economic models are no good unless they include all the detail that characterizes the real world. T F

2. Material in this text will reveal to you the true answer to many important social problems. T F

3. Economists use the concept of rationality to characterize the means people use to achieve objectives, rather than the objectives themselves. T F

4. Opportunity cost is measured by considering the next best alternative. T F

5. Economists' policy prescriptions will always differ because of incomplete information and different value judgments. T F

6. Theory and practical policy have nothing to do with each other. T F

SUPPLEMENTARY EXERCISE

In recent years the Banca Nazionale del Lavoro in Rome has been publishing a series of recollections and reflections by distinguished economists on their professional experiences. If your college or university library receives the *Banca Nazionale del Lavoro Quarterly Review*, read what some of these authors have to say about their lives as economists. The December 1983 issue contains reflections by William J. Baumol.

The Use and Misuse of Graphs

LEARNING OBJECTIVES

After completing the material in this chapter you should be able to:

- define, understand, and use correctly the terms and concepts listed below.
- interpret various graphs:
    use a two-variable graph to determine what combinations of variables go together.
    use a three-variable graph to determine what combinations of the X and Y variables are consistent with the same value for the Z variable.
    use a time-series graph to determine how a variable of interest has changed over time.
- construct two-variable, three-variable, and time-series graphs given appropriate data.
- compute the slope of a straight line and explain what it measures.
- explain how to compute the slope of a curved line.
- explain how a 45° line can divide a graph into two regions, one in which the Y variable exceeds the X variable, and another in which the X variable exceeds the Y variable.

- explain the implication of each of the following:
    failure to adjust variables for changes in prices and/or population
    omitting the origin
    the use of different units
    the use of short time periods with unique features

IMPORTANT TERMS AND CONCEPTS

Two-variable diagram
Horizontal and vertical axes
Origin (of a graph)
Slope of a straight (or a curved) line
Negative, positive, zero, and infinite slope
Tangent to a curve
Y-intercept
Ray through the origin
45° line
Contour map
Time-series graph

CHAPTER REVIEW

Economists like to draw pictures, primarily various types of *graphs*. Your textbook and this study guide also make extensive use of graphs. There is nothing very difficult about graphs, but being sure you understand them from the beginning will help you avoid mistakes later on.

All the graphs we will be using start with two straight lines defining the edges of the graph, one on the bottom and one on the left side. These edges will usually have labels to indicate what is being measured in

(1)   both the vertical and horizontal directions. The line on the bottom is called the (*horizontal/vertical*) axis, and the

line running up the side is called the _____ axis. The point at which the two lines meet

is called the _____ . The variable measured along the horizontal axis is often called the *X* variable, while the term *Y* variable is often used to refer to the variable measured along the vertical axis.

Some graphs show the magnitude of something at different points in time, say gross national product, university enrollment, or average grades of university students. Such a graph will measure time along the horizontal axis and

(2)   dollars, people, or average grades along the vertical axis. This sort of graph is called a _____

_____ graph.

One does not always have to measure time along the horizontal axis. One could draw a picture plotting any two variables by measuring one variable on one axis and another variable on the other axis. Figure 2–1 is a two-variable diagram plotting expenditures on alcoholic beverages and ministers' salaries. Does this graph imply that wealthier clergy are responsible for more drinking or does it imply that more drinking in general is increasing the demand for, and hence the salaries of, clergy? Most likely neither interpretation is correct; just because you can plot two variables together does not mean that one caused the other.

Many of the two-variable diagrams that you will encounter in introductory economics use *straight lines*, primarily for simplicity. An important characteristic of a straight line is its *slope*, which is measured by comparing differences between any two points. Specifically one measures the slope of a straight line by dividing the

(3)   (*horizontal/vertical*) change by the corresponding _____ change as we move to the right along the line. One can use the changes between any two points to compute the slope because the slope of a

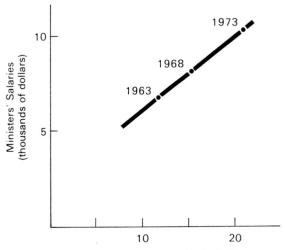

FIGURE 2–1

MINISTERS' SALARIES AND
EXPENDITURES ON ALCOHOL

Source: National Council of Churches of Christ in the U.S.A.;
U.S. Commerce Department.

straight line is _____. If the straight line shows that both the horizontal and vertical variables increase together, then the line is said to have a (*positive/negative*) slope; that is, as we move to the right the line slopes (*up/down*). If one variable decreases as the other variable increases, then the line is said to have a

_____ slope. A line with a zero slope shows _____ change in the *Y* variable as the *X* variable changes.

There is a special type of straight line that passes through the origin of a graph. This is called a

(4) _____ through the origin. Its slope is measured in exactly the same way as the slope of any other straight line. A special type of ray is one that connects all points where the vertical and horizontal variables are equal. If the vertical and horizontal variables are measured in the same units, then this line has a slope

of +1 and is called the _____ line.

Like straight lines, curved lines also have slopes, but the slope of a curved line is not constant. We measure the slope of a curved line at any point by the slope of one straight line that just touches, or is

(5) _____ to, the curved line at the point of interest.

A third type of graph is used by economists as well as cartographers. Such a graph can represent three

(6) dimensions on a diagram with only two axes by the use of _____ lines. A traditional application of such a graph in economics is a diagram that measures different inputs along the horizontal and vertical axes and then uses contour lines to show what different combinations of inputs can be used to produce the same amount of output.

BASIC EXERCISES

These exercises are designed to give you practice working with graphs and economic data.

1. Reading Graphs
   The demand curve in Figure 2-2 represents the demand by colleges and universities for new Ph.D. economists in 1979.
   a. What quantity would colleges and universities have demanded if they had had to pay a salary of $18 000?

   _____.

   b. What does the graph tell us would have happened to the quantity demanded if salaries had been only $14 000? The quantity would have (*increased/decreased*) to

   _____.

   c. What would have happened to the quantity demanded if salaries were $20 000? It would have (*increased/decreased*) to

   _____.

2. Growth Trends
   a. Look at Table 2-1, which has data on personal income after taxes. The data clearly show that between 1950 and 1980 aggregate personal income after taxes increased fourteenfold (192.3 ÷ 13.3 = 14.46). Do you agree that individuals in 1980 were this much richer than they were in

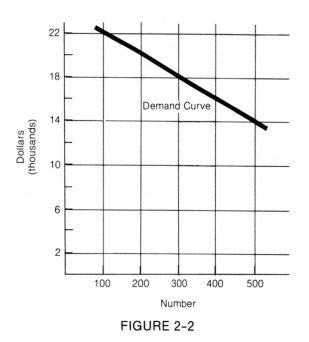

FIGURE 2-2

THE DEMAND FOR NEW Ph.D. ECONOMISTS

Source: This figure is based on research reported by W. L. Hansen *et. al.,* ''Forecasting the Market for New Ph.D. Economists,'' *American Economic Review,* March 1980, pp. 49–63 and data provided by Professor Francis Boddy.

TABLE 2-1

Year	Aggregate Personal Income After Taxes (billions of dollars)	Population (millions)	Income per Capita	Price Index (1971 = 1.000)	Real Income per Capita (1971 prices)
1950	13.3	13.7	_____	.548	_____
1960	26.6	17.9	_____	.721	_____
1970	54.0	21.4	_____	.969	_____
1980	192.3	23.9	_____	2.223	_____

Source: Statistics Canada.

1950? Could they buy 14 times as many goods and services as they could in 1950?

b. For each year in Table 2-1, divide aggregate income by the corresponding data for population to compute income per capita instead of aggregate income. Rather than a fourteenfold increase, per capita income in 1980 was only

_____ times its 1950 level.

c. For each year divide income per capita by the corresponding price level to compute income per capita in constant prices. The figures in the last column of Table 2-1 will tell us how per capita purchasing power, or real income, has changed since 1950. (The appendix to Chapter 6 contains

more information about how a price index is constructed and what can be done with it.) In 1980, per capita purchasing power was

_____ times its 1950 level.

3. Dangers of Omitting the Origin

a. Figure 2-3 suggests that, for the economy depicted, the battle against inflation had been won by the fall of Year 1. Use the Graph in Figure 2-4 to redraw the figure including the origin. Which figure gives a more accurate picture of inflation? Why?

b. It is not always clear how one should measure economic data. In Figure 2-3 inflation is measured as the percentage change in the

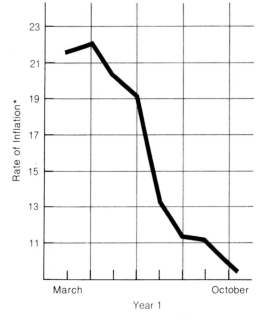

FIGURE 2-3

*Percentage change in consumer price index over preceding three months, multiplied by four for annual rate.

Consumer Price Index over the previous three months expressed at an annual rate. Table 2-2 reports data on consumer prices. Use these data to compute inflation over a twelve-month period and plot those data in Figure 2-4. What does it suggest about the battle against inflation?

c. You might enjoy reading "The Consumer Price Index: Measuring Inflation and Causing It," by Robert J. Gordon, *The Public Interest*, Spring 1981, pp. 112-34.

TABLE 2-2

	Consumer Price Index		
	Year 1	Year 2	Inflation*
March	209.1	239.8	_____
April	211.5	242.5	_____
May	214.1	244.9	_____
June	216.6	247.6	_____
July	218.9	247.8	_____
August	221.1	249.4	_____
September	223.2	251.7	_____
October	225.4	253.9	_____

*For each month, inflation = [(Price Index Year 2 ÷ Price Index Year 1) - 1] × 100; e.g., for March, inflation = [(239.8 ÷ 209.1) - 1] × 100 = 14.7.

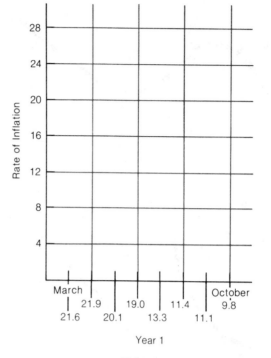

FIGURE 2-4

SELF-TESTS FOR UNDERSTANDING

Test A

Circle the correct answer.

1. Referring to parts (1), (2), (3), and (4) of Figure 2-5, determine which line has a(n)

positive slope	negative slope	zero slope	infinite slope
a. (1)	a. (1)	a. (1)	a. (1)
b. (2)	b. (2)	b. (2)	b. (2)
c. (3)	c. (3)	c. (3)	c. (3)
d. (4)	d. (4)	d. (4)	d. (4)

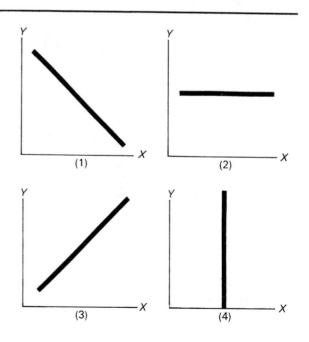

FIGURE 2-5

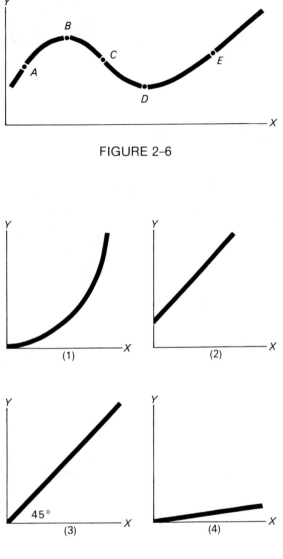

FIGURE 2-6

FIGURE 2-7

know that for the X and Y combination associated with this point,

   a. the X variable is greater than the Y variable.
   b. a line from the origin through this point will be a ray and will have a slope greater than +1.
   c. the Y variable is greater than the X variable.
   d. the slope of the point is less than 1.

4. The slope of a curved line is
   a. the same at all points on the line.
   b. found by dividing the value of the Y variable by the value of the X variable.
   c. found by determining the slope of a straight line tangent to the curved line at the point of interest.
   d. always positive.

5. Referring to parts (1), (2), (3), and (4) of Figure 2-7, determine which part(s) show a ray through the origin.
   a. (2)
   b. (1) and (3)
   c. (1) and (4)
   d. (3) and (4)

Test B

Circle T or F for True or False as appropriate.

1. The slope of a line measures the value of the Y variable when the X variable is equal to zero.   **T F**

2. The slope of a straight line is the same at all points on the line.   **T F**

3. A negative slope means that the Y variable decreases when the X variable increases.   **T F**

4. A time-series graph can be used to show what combinations of the X and Y variables are associated with a given value of a third variable.   **T F**

5. Omitting the origin from a time-series graph can exaggerate the magnitude of increases and decreases.   **T F**

6. A straight line that has a Y-intercept of zero is also called a ray through the origin.   **T F**

7. All rays through the origin have the same slope.   **T F**

8. If X and Y are measured in the same units, then a 45° line is a ray through the origin with a slope of +1.   **T F**

2. Referring to Figure 2-6, determine at which point the curved line has a(n)

positive slope	negative slope	zero slope	infinite slope
a. A	a. A	a. A	a. A
b. B	b. B	b. B	b. B
c. C	c. C	c. C	c. C
d. D	d. E	d. E	d. None

3. If X and Y are measured in the same units, and we consider a point that lies below a 45° line, then we

9. If *X* and *Y* are measured in the same units, then any point above a 45° line is a point at which the *X* variable is greater than the *Y* variable. **T F**

10. The use of short periods for a time-series graph may be misleading in that they record behaviour that is unique to that particular period. **T F**

The Economic Problem

3

LEARNING OBJECTIVES

After completing the material in this chapter you should be able to:

- define, understand, and use correctly the terms and concepts listed below.
- explain why the true cost of any decision is its opportunity cost.
- draw a production possibilities frontier for a firm or for the economy.
- explain how information about the production possibility frontier contains information about the opportunity cost of alternative output combinations.
- explain how an economy can shift its production possibilities frontier.
- explain the link between market prices and opportunity cost.
- explain why specialized resources mean that a firm's or economy's production possibilities frontier is likely to bow outward.

- explain why specialization and division of labour is likely to require the use of markets.
- describe the three co-ordination tasks that every economy must confront.

IMPORTANT TERMS AND CONCEPTS

Scarcity
Choice
Opportunity cost
Production possibilities frontier
Principle of increasing costs
Investment goods
Efficiency
Specialization
Division of labour
Exchange
Market system
Three co-ordination tasks

CHAPTER REVIEW

The issue of scarcity and the related necessity to make choices are fundamental concerns of economics. This chapter is an introduction to these issues. They have already been implicitly introduced in many of the 12 Ideas for Beyond the Final Exam, and they will reappear many times throughout the text.

(1) The importance of *choice* starts with the fact that virtually all resources are ___limited___. No individual can do or buy everything in the world. Most people's desires exceed their incomes and, even for the very rich, there are only 24 hours in a day. Everyone makes choices all the time. Similarly, firms, educational institutions, and government agencies make choices between what kinds of outputs to produce and what combination of inputs to use. The example of a farmer choosing between planting wheat and soybeans is a traditional one. Governments, for instance, must make choices between raising taxes and reducing public services.

What is a good way to make choices? The obvious answer is to consider the available alternatives.

(2) Economists call these forgone alternatives the ___opportunity cost___ of a decision. For example, imagine it is the night before the first midterm in Introductory Economics, an examination that will cover Chapters 1–6, and here you are only on Chapter 3. A friend suggests a night at the movies and even offers to buy your ticket so "it won't cost you anything." Do you agree that the evening won't cost anything? (What will you be giving up?)

Economists also like to talk about the choices available to the economy as a whole. At first the idea of choices for the economy may sound a bit strange. It may be easiest to imagine such choices being made by the central planning bureau of an eastern European economy. Even though there is no central planning bureau for the Canadian economy, it is useful to think of opportunities available to the Canadian economy. The opportunities selected result from the combined spending and production decisions of all citizens, firms, and governments.

The *production possibilities frontier* is a useful diagram for representing the choices available to a firm or an economy. The frontier will tend to slope downward to the right because resources are

(3) (*scarce/specialized*). The frontier will tend to bow out because most resources are ___specialized___. For any one year the resources available to an economy—the number of workers, factories, and machines, and the state of technology—are essentially fixed. Over time, an economy can choose to increase its resources if it chooses to produce (*more/less*) consumption goods and ___more___ investment goods. Similarly, technological advancements are more likely if an economy devotes (*more/fewer*) resources to research and development. In terms of a frontier showing possible combinations of consumption and investment goods, the true cost of faster economic growth is given by the forgone output of ___consumption___ goods.

Opportunity cost is the best measure of the true cost of any decision. For an economy as a whole, with choices represented by a production possibilities frontier, the opportunity cost of changing the composition of

(4) output is given by the ___slope___ of the production possibilities frontier.

As an economy produces more and more of one good, say, missiles, the opportunity cost of further

(5) increases is likely to (*increase/decrease*). This change in opportunity cost is an illustration of the principle of ___increasing___ cost and is a result of the fact that most resources are (*scarce/specialized*).

For given amounts of all but one good, the production possibilities frontier for an economy measures the maximum amount of the remaining good that can be produced. Thus the production possibilities frontier defines maximum outputs. There is, of course, no guarantee that the economy will operate at a point that is

(6) on the frontier. If there is unemployment, then the economy is operating (*on/inside*) the frontier. If a firm or economy operates inside its production possibilities frontier, it is said to be ___inefficient___; that is, with the same resources the firm or the economy could have produced more of some commodities.

All economies must answer three important questions:
1. How can we use resources efficiently to produce on the production possibilities frontier?
2. What combinations of output shall we produce; that is, where on the frontier shall we produce?
3. How shall we distribute what is produced?

(7) The Canadian economy answers these questions through the use of markets and prices. If markets are functioning well, then money prices (*will/will not*) be a good guide to opportunity costs. Problems arise when markets do not function well and when items do not have explicit price tags.

BASIC EXERCISE

1. This exercise is designed to explore more fully some of the implications of the production possibilities frontier for an economy. Figure 3-1 shows the production possibilities frontier for the economy of Laurentian, which produces only bread and automobiles.

   a. If all resources are devoted to the production of bread. Laurentian can produce

   _____56,000_____ loaves of bread. In order to produce 1000 cars, the opportunity cost in

   terms of bread is _____4000_____ loaves. To produce another 1000 cars, the opportunity

   cost (*rises*/falls) to _____12,000_____ loaves. As long as the production possibilities frontier continues to curve downward, the opportunity costs of increased automobile output will (*continue to rise*/start to fall). These changes are the result, not of scarce

   resources per se, but of _specialized_ resources. (You might try drawing a production possibilities frontier with constant opportunity cost. Can you convince yourself that it should be a straight line?)

   b. Find the output combination of 2500 automobiles and 32,000 loaves on Figure 3-1. Label this point *A*. Is it a feasible combination

   for Laurentian? Label the output combination 1500 automobiles and 40,000 loaves *B*. Is this combination feasible? Finally, label the output combination 1000 automobiles and 52,000 loaves *C*. Is this combination feasible? We can conclude that the feasible output combinations for Laurentian are (*on*/*inside*/outside) the production possibilities frontier.

   c. An output combination is inefficient if it is possible to produce more of one or both goods. Which, if any, of the output combinations identified in Question b is an inefficient

   combination? _____B_____. Show that this point is inefficient by shading in all the feasible points showing more of one or both goods.

SELF-TESTS FOR UNDERSTANDING

Test A

Circle the correct answer.

1. Economists define opportunity cost as
   a. the dollar price of goods and services.
   b. the hidden cost imposed by inflation.
   c. the value of the next best alternative use that is not chosen.
   d. the *time* you must spend shopping.
2. Referring to Figure 3-1, determine which of the following output combinations would represent an efficient use of resources.
   a. 1000 automobiles and 30,000 loaves of bread.
   b. 1500 automobiles and 40,000 loaves of bread.
   c. 2000 automobiles and 44,000 loaves of bread.
   d. 2500 automobiles and 28,000 loaves of bread.
3. Consider the output combination 2000 automobiles and 40,000 loaves of bread in Figure 3-1. The principle of increasing cost
   a. works only for increases in the output of automobiles (i.e., movements along the frontier to the right).
   b. works only for increases in the output of bread (i.e., movements along the frontier to the left).
   c. works for movements in either direction.
   d. refers to shifts in, not movements along, the frontier.
4. The fact that resources are scarce implies that the production possibility frontier will
   a. have a negative slope.
   b. be a straight line.

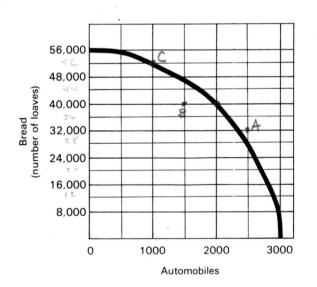

FIGURE 3-1

c. shift out over time.

d. bow out from the origin.

5. Which of the following statements imply that production possibilities frontiers are likely to be curved, rather than straight, lines?

   a. Ultimately all resources are scarce.

   b. Most resources are more productive in certain uses than in others.

   c. Unemployment is a more serious problem for some social groups than for others.

   d. Economists are notoriously poor at drawing straight lines.

6. Which of the following implies a shift in the production possibilities frontier for a shoe firm?

   a. Raising all prices by 10 percent.

   b. Borrowing money to hire more workers and buying more machines.

   c. Changing the composition of output toward more women's shoes and fewer men's shoes.

   d. Expanding the advertising budget.

7. Consider a production possibility frontier showing alternative combinations of corn and computers that can be produced in Cimonoce, a small island economy in the South Pacific. The opportunity cost of more computers should be measured in terms of

   a. the slope of the production possibility frontier.

   b. the X-intercept of the production possibility frontier.

   c. the Y-intercept of the production possibility frontier.

   d. the area under the production possibility frontier.

8. Which of the following would not shift an economy's production possibility frontier?

   a. A doubling of the labour force.

   b. A doubling of the number of machines.

   c. A doubling of the money supply.

   d. More advanced technology.

9. A rational decision is one that

   a. will win a majority if put to a vote.

   b. is supported unanimously.

   c. best serves the objectives of the decision-maker.

   d. is supported by the *Globe and Mail*.

Test B

Circle T or F for True or False as appropriate.

1. There can never be any real scarcity of manufactured goods as we can always produce more. T **F**

2. Market prices are always a good measure of opportunity cost. T **F**

3. The principle of increasing costs is a reflection of the fact that most productive resources tend to be best at producing a limited number of things. **T** F

4. An economy can shift its production possibilities frontier outward by the process of economic growth. **T** F

5. Because they have the power to tax, governments do not need to make choices. T **F**

6. The existence of specialized resources means that a firm's production possibilities frontier will be a straight line. T **F**

7. The existence of widespread unemployment means that an economy is operating inside its production possibilities frontier. **T** F

8. When an economy is using its resources efficiently it will end up somewhere on its production possibilities frontier. **T** F

9. Because they are non-profit organizations, colleges and universities do not have to make choices. T **F**

10. A sudden increase in the number of dollar bills will shift the economy's production possibilities frontier. T **F**

SUPPLEMENTARY EXERCISES

1. **The Cost of University or College**

   Those of you who are paying your own way through university may not need to be reminded that the opportunity cost of your lost wages is an important part of the cost of your education. You can estimate the cost of your education as follows: Estimate what you could earn if instead of attending classes and studying you used those hours to work. Add to this estimate your direct outlays on tuition, books, and any differential living expenses incurred because you go to school. (Why only differential living expenses?) (You might enjoy reading "College: The Dumbest Investment of All" in the September 1974 issue of *Esquire*.)

2. **The Cost of Children**

   Bob and Jane both took Sociology 1 last year. As part of the course they were asked to compute the cost of raising a child. Bob estimated the cost as $90,000; an average of $2000 a year in increased family expenditures for the first 12 years, then $3000 a year for the next 6 years, and finally 4 years of university at $12,000 per year. Jane also was enrolled in Econ 1. She estimated the cost as $170,000. She started with all the same outlays that Bob did but also included $20,000 a year for four years as the opportunity cost of the parent who stayed at home to care for the child. Which calculation do you think is a more accurate reflection of the cost of raising a child? What would be the cost of a second child?

3. Consider an economy with a production possibilities frontier between cars (C) and tanks (T) given by

$$C = 2.5L^2 + 5K^2 - 0.3T^2$$

where L is the size of the labour force (200 people) and K is the number of machines, which is also 200.

a. What is the maximum number of cars that can be produced? The maximum number of tanks?
b. Draw a graph of the production possibilities frontier.
c. Is this frontier consistent with the principle of increasing costs?
d. What is the opportunity cost of more tanks when 10 tanks are produced? 50 tanks? 200 tanks?
e. Find a mathematical expression for the opportunity cost of tanks in terms of cars. Is this mathematical expression consistent with the principle of increasing cost?

Supply and Demand: An Initial Look

4

After completing the material in this chapter you should be able to:

- define, understand, and use correctly the terms and concepts listed below.
- draw a demand curve, given appropriate information on possible prices and the associated quantity demanded.
- draw a supply curve, given appropriate information on possible prices and the associated quantity supplied.
- explain why demand curves usually slope downward and supply curves usually slope upward.
- determine the equilibrium price and quantity, given a demand and supply curve.
- explain what forces will tend to move market prices and quantities toward their equilibrium values.
- analyse the impacts on both prices and quantities of changes that shift either the demand curve or the supply curve or both.
- distinguish between a shift in and a movement along either the demand or supply curve.

- explain the likely consequences of government interference with market-determined prices.

IMPORTANT TERMS AND CONCEPTS

Demand schedule
Demand curve
Supply schedule
Supply curve
Supply-demand diagram
Shortage
Surplus
Equilibrium price and quantity
Equilibrium
Shifts in versus movements along supply and demand curves
Price ceiling
Price floor
Exchange rate

CHAPTER REVIEW

Along with scarcity and the need for choice, *demand* and *supply analysis* is a fundamental idea that pervades all of economics. After studying this chapter, look back at the list of the 12 Ideas for Beyond the Final Exam in Chapter 1 and see how many of these concern the "law" of supply and demand.

Economists use a *demand curve* as a useful summary of the factors influencing people's demand for different commodities. A demand curve shows how the quantity demanded of some good changes as the

(1) _____ of that good changes, holding all other things constant. A demand curve usually has a (*negative/positive*) slope, indicating that as the price of a good declines people will demand (*more/less*) of it. A particular quantity demanded is represented by a single point on the demand curve. The change in the quantity demanded as price changes is a (*shift in/movement along*) the demand curve. Quantity demanded is also influenced by other factors, such as changes in consumer incomes and tastes, and changes in the prices of related goods. Changes in any of these factors will result in a (*shift in/movement along*) the demand curve. A demand curve is also defined for a particular period of time—a week, a month, or a year.

Economists use a *supply curve* as a useful summary of the factors influencing producers' decisions. Like the demand curve, the supply curve is a relationship between quantity and price. Supply curves usually

(2) have a (*negative/positive*) slope, indicating that at higher prices producers will be willing to supply (*more/less*) of the good in question. Like quantity demanded, quantity supplied is also influenced by factors other than price. Changes in the size of the industry, technological progress, changes in the prices of inputs or changes in the price of related outputs will all affect the quantity that producers are willing to supply. Changes in any of these factors will change the quantity supplied and can be represented by a (*shift in/movement along*) the supply curve.

Demand and supply curves are hypothetical constructs that answer what-if questions. For example, the supply curve answers the question "What quantity of milk would be supplied if its price were $2 a litre?" At this point it is not fair to ask whether anyone would buy milk at that price. Information about the quantity

(3) demanded is given by the _____ curve, which answers the question "What quantity would be demanded if its price were $2 a litre?" The viability of a price of $2 will be determined when we consider both curves simultaneously.

Figure 4-1 shows demand and supply curves for stereo sets. The market outcome will be a price of

(4) $ _____ and a quantity of _____ . If for some reason the price is $300, then the quantity demanded will be (*less/more*) than the quantity supplied. In particular, from Figure 4-1 we can see that at a price of $300 _____ sets will be supplied while consumers will demand only _____ sets. This imbalance is a (*shortage/surplus*) and will lead to a(n) (*increase/reduction*) in price as inventories start piling up and suppliers compete for sales. If, instead, the price of stereo sets is only $100, there will be a (*shortage/surplus*) as the quantity (*demanded/supplied*) exceeds the quantity _____. Price is apt to (*decrease/increase*) as consumers scramble for a limited number of stereos at what appear to be bargain prices.

These forces working to raise or lower prices will continue until price and quantity settle down at values

(5) given by the _____ of the demand and supply curves. At this point, barring any outside changes that would shift either curve, there will be no further tendency for change. Because there is no further tendency for change, the market-determined price and quantity are said to be in _____ . This price and quantity combination is the only one in which consumers demand exactly what suppliers produce. There are no frustrated consumers or producers. However, equilibrium price and quantity will change if anything happens to shift either the demand or supply curves. The Basic Exercise in this chapter asks you to examine a number of shifts in demand and supply curves.

Often one can identify factors that affect demand but not supply, and vice versa. For example,

(6) changes in consumer incomes and tastes will shift the (*demand/supply*) curve but will not shift the _____ curve. Following a shift in the demand curve, price must change to re-establish equilibrium. The change in price will lead to a (*shift in/movement along*) the supply curve until equilibrium is re-established at the intersection of the new demand curve and the original supply curve. Similarly, a change in

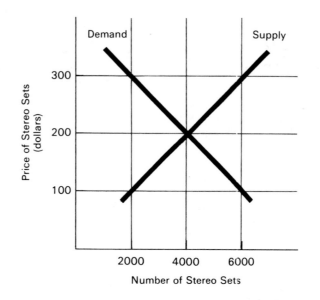

FIGURE 4-1

technology or the price of inputs will shift the _____ curve but will not shift the

_____ curve. Equilibrium will be re-established as the change in price induced by the

shift in the supply curve leads to a movement along the _____ curve to the new intersection.

In many cases the government has intervened in the market mechanism in an attempt to control prices. Some price controls dictate a particular price; other controls set maximum or minimum prices. A *price ceiling* is a maximum legal price, typically below the market-determined equilibrium price. Rent controls are an example of a price ceiling. A *price floor* sets a minimum legal price. To be effective, this price floor would have to be above the equilibrium price. Price floors are often used in various agricultural programs.

In general, economists argue that interferences with the market mechanism are likely to have a number

(7) of undesirable features. If there are a large number of suppliers, price controls will be (*hard/easy*) to monitor and evasion will be hard to police. In order to prevent the breakdown of price controls, governments are quite likely to

find it necessary to introduce a large number of _____ _____ . Firms are apt to try to get around effective price floors by offering non-price inducements for consumers to buy from them rather than from someone else. (Remember that effective price floors result in excess supply.) These non-price inducements are apt to be less preferred by consumers than would a general reduction in prices.

Price floors will result in inefficiencies because high-cost firms are protected from failing by artificially

(8) (*high/low*) prices. Price controls will also result in the misallocation of resources. One form of misallocation involves the use of time and resources to evade effective controls. Another form of misallocation arises when controlled prices do not reflect the social valuation of the underlying resources.

BASIC EXERCISES

These exercises ask you to analyse the impact of changes in factors that affect demand and supply.

1. **a.** Table 4-1 has data on the quantity of candy bars that would be demanded and supplied at various prices. Use the data to draw the demand curve and the supply curve for candy bars in Figure 4-2.

b. From the information given in Table 4-1 and represented in Figure 4-2, the equilibrium price is

_____ cents and the

equilibrium quantity is

_____ .

TABLE 4-1

DEMAND AND SUPPLY SCHEDULES
FOR CANDY BARS

Quantity Demanded (millions)	Price per Bar (cents)	Quantity Supplied (millions)
1200	25	1050
1100	30	1100
900	40	1200
800	45	1250
700	50	1300

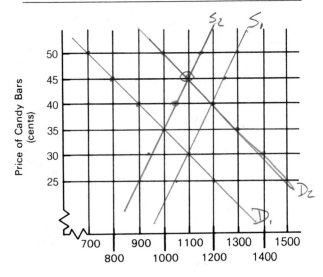

FIGURE 4-2

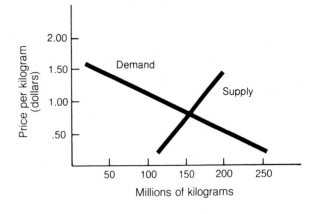

FIGURE 4-3

THE DEMAND AND SUPPLY OF CHICKEN

c. Now assume that increases in income and population mean that the demand curve has shifted. Assume that this shift is such that, at each price, the quantity demanded has increased by 300 candy bars. Draw the new demand curve. At the new equilibrium, price has (*increased/decreased*) to

_____ cents, and quantity has (*increased/decreased*) to

_____ .

d. Now assume that an increase in the price of sugar has caused a shift in the supply curve. Specifically, assume that, at each price, the quantity supplied has been reduced by 150 candy bars. Draw the new supply curve. The shift in the supply curve following the increase in the price of sugar will (*increase/decrease*) price

and _____ quantity. Using the demand curve you drew in part c, above, the new equilibrium price following the increase in the price of sugar will be

_____ cents and the equilibrium quantity will be

_____ .

2. Figure 4-3 shows the demand and supply of chicken. Fill in Table 4-2 to trace the effects of various events on the equilibrium price and quantity.

SELF-TESTS FOR UNDERSTANDING

Test A

Circle the correct answer.

1. A shift in the demand curve for sailboats that results from a general increase in incomes will lead to
   a. higher prices.
   b. lower prices.
   c. a shift in the supply curve.
   d. lower output.
2. A shift in the supply curve of bicycles that results from higher steel prices will lead to
   a. higher prices.
   b. lower prices.
   c. a shift in the demand curve.
   d. larger output.
3. Which of the following is likely to result in a shift in the supply curve for dresses?
   a. An increase in consumer incomes.

TABLE 4-2

Event	Which curve shifts?	Does the equilibrium price rise or fall?	Does the equilibrium quantity rise or fall?
a. Concerns about high cholesterol lead many consumers to switch from beef to chicken.			
b. A bumper grain crop cuts the cost of chicken feed in half.			
c. An extraordinary period of cold weather destroys a significant number of chickens			
d. A sudden interest in eastern religions converts many chicken eaters to vegetarians.			

    b. A reduction in tariffs that allows manufacturers to import cotton cloth at cheaper prices than before.
    c. An increase in dress prices.
    d. Higher prices for skirts, pants, and blouses.
4. Which of the following is likely to result in a shift in the demand curve for dresses?
    a. An increase in consumer incomes.
    b. A reduction in tariffs that allows dress manufacturers to import cotton cloth at cheaper prices than before.
    c. An increase in dress prices.
    d. The development of new machines that dramatically increase the productivity of dressmakers.
5. If for some reason the price of shoes is above its equilibrium value, which of the following is likely to occur?
    a. Shoe stores will find their inventories decreasing as consumers buy more shoes than shoe companies produce.
    b. Shoe stores and companies are likely to agree to reduce prices in order to increase sales, leading to a new lower equilibrium price.
    c. The demand curve for shoes will shift in response to higher prices.
    d. Equilibrium will be re-established at the original price as the supply curve shifts to the left.
6. From an initial equilibrium, which of the following changes will lead to a shift in the supply curve for Chevrolets?
    a. Import restrictions on Japanese cars.
    b. New environmental protection measures that raise the cost of producing steel.
    c. A decrease in the price of Fords.
    d. Increases in the cost of gasoline.

7. If the price of oil, a close substitute for coal, increases, then
    a. the supply curve for coal will shift to the right.
    b. the demand curve for coal will shift to the right.
    c. the equilibrium price and quantity of coal will not change.
    d. the quantity of coal demanded will decline.
8. Effective price ceilings are likely to
    a. result in the accumulation of surpluses.
    b. increase the volume of transactions as we move along the demand curve.
    c. increase production as producers respond to higher consumer demand at the low ceiling price.
    d. result in the development of black markets.
9. A surplus results when
    a. the quantity demanded exceeds the quantity supplied.
    b. the quantity supplied exceeds the quantity demanded.
    c. the demand curve shifts to the right.
    d. effective price ceilings are imposed.

Test B

Circle T or F for True or False as appropriate.

1. The Law of Supply and Demand is part of the BNA Act of 1867.   T F

2. The demand curve for hamburgers is a graph showing the quantity of hamburgers that would be demanded during a specified period of time at each possible price for hamburgers.   T F

3. The slope of the supply curve indicates the increase in price necessary to get producers to increase output. **T F**

4. An increase in consumer income will shift both the supply and demand curves. **T F**

5. Both demand and supply curves usually have positive slopes. **T F**

6. If at a particular price the quantity supplied exceeds the quantity demanded, then price is likely to fall as suppliers compete with one another. **T F**

7. Equilibrium price and quantity are determined by the intersection of the demand and supply curves. **T F**

8. Since equilibrium is defined as a situation with no inherent forces producing change, the equilibrium price and quantity will not change following an increase in consumer income. **T F**

9. A change in the price of important inputs will change the quantity supplied but will not shift the supply curve. **T F**

10. Price ceilings are likely to result in the development of black markets. **T F**

11. Price controls, whether floors or ceilings, are likely to increase the volume of transactions from what it would be without controls. **T F**

12. An effective price ceiling is normally accompanied by shortages. **T F**

13. An effective price floor is also normally accompanied by shortages. **T F**

14. An increase in both the market price and quantity of beef following an increase in consumer incomes proves that demand curves do not always have a negative slope. **T F**

SUPPLEMENTARY EXERCISES

1. Energy Policy—The Mix of Politics and Economics

The following quotation, written in the spring of 1977, is by two American economists, Robert E. Hall and Robert S. Pindyck. As you read it, try to understand Hall's and Pindyck's argument in terms of simple demand and supply analysis.

National energy policy faces a deep conflict in objectives, which has been a major reason for the failure to adopt rational measures: Consumers want cheap energy, but producers need high prices to justify expanded production. So far the goal of low prices has dominated.... the price of energy to consumers has been held far below the world level. Domestic producers have been prohibited from taking advantage of the higher world price, and in the case of oil, a heavy tax has been imposed on domestic production to finance the subsidization of imports. These steps have caused demand to increase more rapidly than production, and energy imports have risen to fill the gap. If recent policies are continued, imports will continue to grow....

The economics of the nation's energy problem involves little more than the principle that higher prices result in less demand and more supply. The exact size and timing of the effects of price on demand and supply are still open to debate, but a summary of recent evidence indicates that demand falls by about one per cent for each four-per-cent increase in price, and supply rises by about one

percent for each five-per-cent increase in price. Of course several years must pass before demand and supply fully respond to changes in price, and there is some uncertainty over the magnitude and speed of the supply response, but these numbers provide a reasonable basis for an initial description of the energy market in the United States. Policies in effect today [in the U.S.] have depressed the domestic price of energy, on the average, by about 30 per cent below the world price. Consumption, then, is about eight-per-cent higher than it would be otherwise, and supply is about six-per-cent lower. Stated in oil-equivalents, the total consumption of energy in the United States is about 38 million barrels per day: 31 million barrels are filled by domestically produced oil, natural gas, and coal, and the rest is imported. Eight per cent of consumption is just over three million barrels per day, and six per cent of domestic production is just under two million barrels, so the policy of depressing prices has the net effect of increasing imports by about five million barrels. But current imports are around seven million barrels per day, so a striking conclusion emerges from these simple calculations: *The problem of rising imports is largely of our own making.* Imports might well be much lower had our energy policy not been based on maintaining low prices.[1]

[1]Robert E. Hall and Robert S. Pindyck, "The Conflicting Goals of National Energy Policy." Reprinted with the permission of the authors from: *The Public Interest*, No. 47 (Spring 1977), pp. 3–4, © 1977 by National Affairs, Inc.

TABLE 4-3

Demand Quantity of Energy (millions of oil barrel equivalents)	Price per Barrel (dollars)	Domestic Supply Quantity of Energy (millions of oil barrel equivalents)
33.2	15	34.5
35.1	12	33.0
37.7	9	31.2
41.8	6	28.7

Table 4-3 presents data on U.S. demand for energy in oil equivalents and domestic U.S. supply, consistent with Hall's and Pindyck's argument.

a. From the data given in Table 4-3, plot the demand and domestic supply curves on a piece of graph paper. In 1977 the controlled U.S. price was $8.75 a barrel. What was the domestic demand for energy and what was the domestic supply? What was the demand for imports (the difference between demand and domestic supply)?

b. Hall and Pindyck indicate that the world price of energy in 1977 was $12.50 a barrel. What would have happened to demand, domestic supply, and imports if the price of energy in the United States had been permitted to rise to the world price?

c. What would have happened to energy prices and consumption if the U.S. had banned all imports and allowed domestic supply and demand to determine the equilibrium price and quantity?

d. Some people have argued that the demand and supply curves are actually much steeper. They contend that higher prices will not reduce demand by as much as Hall and Pindyck estimate and neither will higher prices increase supply by as much. Draw new, steeper demand and supply curves and examine the impacts of a market solution to the energy problem. (The new

curves should intersect the original curves at a price of $8.75.)

e. Why do you think it has taken so long for both Canada and the U.S. to develop national energy policies? The details of the Canadian energy policy are discussed in the text (pp. 692-94).

2. Imagine that the demand curve for tomatoes can be represented as

$$Q = 1000 - 250\ P.$$

The supply curve is a bit trickier. Farmers must make planting decisions on the basis of what they expect prices to be. Once they have made these decisions, there is little room for increases or decreases in the quantity supplied. Except for disastrously low prices, it will almost certainly pay a farmer to harvest and market his tomatoes. Assuming that farmers forecast price on the basis of the price last period, we can represent the supply curve for tomatoes as

$$Q = 200 + 150\ P_{-1},$$

where P_{-1} refers to price in the previous period. Initial equilibrium price and quantity of tomatoes are $2 and 500, respectively. Verify that at this price the quantity supplied is equal to the quantity demanded. (Remember that equilibrium implies the same price in each period.)

Now assume that an increase in income has shifted the demand curve to

$$Q = 1400 - 250\ P.$$

Starting with the initial equilibrium price, trace the evolution of price and quantity over time. Do prices and quantities seem to be approaching some sort of equilibrium? If so, what? Ask your instructor about cobweb models. Do you think that looking at last period's price is a good way to forecast future prices?

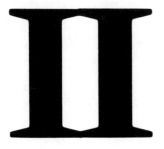

II

Essentials of Macroeconomics: Aggregate Supply and Aggregate Demand

Macroeconomics and Microeconomics

5

LEARNING OBJECTIVES

After completing the material in this chapter you should be able to:

- define, understand, and use correctly the terms and concepts listed below.
- explain the difference between microeconomics and macroeconomics.
- describe the role of economic aggregates in macroeconomics.
- explain how supply-demand analysis can be used to study inflation, recessions, and stabilization policy.
- distinguish between real and nominal GNP.
- characterize, in general terms, the movement in prices and output over the last 60 years.

IMPORTANT TERMS AND CONCEPTS

Microeconomics
Macroeconomics
National product
Aggregation
Aggregate-demand and aggregate-supply curves
Inflation
Deflation
Recession
Gross national product (GNP)
Nominal versus real GNP
Final goods and services
Intermediate goods
Stagflation
Disinflation
Stabilization policy

CHAPTER REVIEW

Economic theory is traditionally split into two parts, microeconomics and macroeconomics. If one studies

(1) the behaviour of individual decision-making units, one is studying _behaviour of the economy_. If one studies

the behaviour of entire economies, one is studying _individual decision-_
makers. This chapter is an introduction to macroeconomics.

The Canadian economy involves millions of firms, individuals, and different goods and services. Since it would be impossible to list each of these firms, individuals, and commodities, economists have found it useful to use certain overall averages or aggregates. The concept of *national output* is an example. If we concentrate on macroeconomic aggregates, we ignore much of the micro detail; whereas by concentrating on the micro detail, we may blind ourselves to the broad overall picture. The two forms of analysis are not substitutes; rather, they can be usefully employed together. (Remember the map example in Chapter 1 of the text.) It has been argued that only successful macroeconomic policy leads to a situation in which the study of microeconomics is important, and vice versa.

Supply and demand analysis is a fundamental tool of both micro and macro theory. In microeconomics one looks at the supply and demand for individual commodities, while in macroeconomics one studies aggregate supply and aggregate demand. The intersection of the demand and supply curves in microeconomics

(2) determines equilibrium _price_ and _quantity_. In macroeconomics the intersection of the aggregate demand and supply curves determines the cost of living, or the price level and aggregate output, or

the gross _national_ _product_.

(3) A sustained increase in the price level would be called _inflation_, whereas a

sustained decrease would be called _deflation_. National output in the Canadian economy usually increases every year for reasons that will be discussed in Chapter 40. Periods when national output declines

are referred to as _recession_. With an unchanged aggregate-supply curve, an outward (rightward) shift of the aggregate-demand curve would lead to (*higher*/lower) prices and (*higher*/lower) output, or (*inflation*/deflation) during a period of prosperity. Higher prices and inflation would also occur if the aggregate-supply curve shifted to the (*left*/right), but, this time, higher prices would be associated with a(n) (increase/*decrease*) in output. Such a combination of rising prices and declining output is called

stagflation. If both curves shift to the right at the same rate, then it is possible to have increased output with constant prices.

(4) The gross national product is defined as the sum of the _final_ values of all

finished goods and services produced by the economy during a specified period of time, usually one year. Economists and national income statisticians use prices to add up the millions of different kinds of output. If one uses today's prices, the result is (*nominal*/real) GNP. If one values output by prices from some base

period, one gets _real_ GNP. Which is the better measure of changes in output: (nominal/*real*) GNP? If all prices rise and all outputs are unchanged, (*nominal*/real) GNP will increase while

real _nominal_ GNP will not.

If you look at a long period of Canadian history, you will see that there have been periods when both

(5) output and prices have risen and fallen. The long-term trend for output is (*up*/down). While the trend for prices (*depends*/does not depend) upon the period you are looking at, since 1940 prices seem only to have

risen.

The government would like to keep output growing, thus avoiding recession; at the same time, it would

(6) like to keep prices from rising, thus avoiding (*inflation*/deflation). Attempts to do just this are called

stabilization policy. The Canadian government has been formally committed to such policies only since the end of World War II. A look at Figures 5-3 and 5-4 on text pages 78 and 79 suggests that since

1945 stabilization policy has been pretty good at avoiding _inflation_ but not so good at

avoiding _recessions_. Chapter 18 discusses why this result is not surprising; that is, why, if one concentrates on maintaining high levels of employment and output, the result is likely to be higher prices.

BASIC EXERCISES

These exercises use the aggregate-demand—aggregate-supply diagram to review a few basic concepts.

1. Figure 5-1 has four panels. The solid lines indicate the initial situation, and the dashed lines indicate a shift in one or both curves.
   a. Which diagram(s) suggests a period, or periods, of inflation? _c, d_

b. Which diagram(s) suggests a period, or periods of deflation? _____b_____ (Have prices in the Canadian economy ever declined in the twentieth century? _____yes_____ If so, when? _____before 1940_____)

c. Which diagram(s) illustrates growth in real output with stable prices?

_____a_____

d. Which diagram(s) illustrates stagflation?

_____c_____

2. Stabilization policy involves changes in government policies designed to shorten recessions and stabilize prices. For reasons explored in Chapters 7 through 19, stabilization policies have their primary effect on the aggregate-demand curve. For the cases of inflation and recession, explain how stabilization policy can re-establish the initial levels of output and prices. Do this by indicating the appropriate shift in the aggregate-demand curve. (The exact policies that will achieve these shifts will be described in detail in Chapters 7 through 19.)
   a. Inflation [diagram (d)]
   b. Recession [diagram (b)]

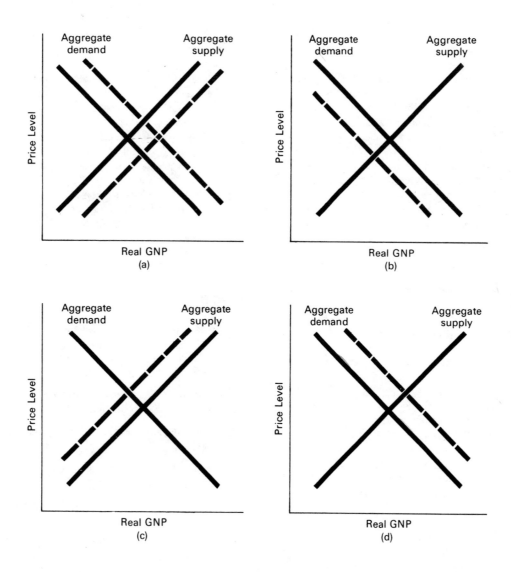

FIGURE 5-1

c. Consider diagram (c), the case of stagflation. If the government is restricted to policies that shift the aggregate-demand curve, what will happen to output if the government adopts policies to combat inflation and restore the original price level? What happens to prices if the government is committed to maintaining the original level of output?

SELF-TESTS FOR UNDERSTANDING

Test A

Circle the correct answer.

1. Which of the following is an example of a macroeconomic aggregate?
   a. The national output of Haiti.
   b. The total output of General Motors.
   c. Employment at Sears.
   d. The price Esso charges for unleaded gas.
2. Which of the following would not be included in GNP for 1985?
   a. The production of home computers in 1985.
   b. The government's purchase of paper clips in 1985.
   c. Consumer expenditures on haircuts in 1985.
   d. General Motors' expenditures on steel for producing Cadillacs in 1985.
3. Match up each of the following definitions with the appropriate concept.

_b_	A sustained decrease in price level.	a. Inflation
_d_	A decline in real GNP.	b. Deflation
_a_	A sustained increase in the price level.	c. Stagflation
_c_	Rising prices during a period of slow growth or actual declines in output.	d. Recession
_f_	Government management of the economy to achieve high employment and stable prices.	e. Real GNP
		f. Stabilization policy

4. Using today's prices to aggregate all final output in the economy will yield
   a. nominal GNP.
   b. real GNP.

c. the cost of living.
   d. GNP in constant dollars.
5. Real GNP is computed by valuing output by
   a. manufacturer's costs.
   b. current prices.
   c. some fixed set of prices.
   d. last year's rate of inflation.
6. Which of the following conditions will result in stagflation?
   a. The aggregate-demand curve shifts to the right.
   b. The aggregate-demand curve shifts to the left.
   c. The aggregate-supply curve shifts to the right.
   d. The aggregate-supply curve shifts to the left.
7. In the period following World War II, the historical record shows
   a. more frequent and more severe recessionary dips in real output than before World War II.
   b. an almost continuous increase in prices.
   c. little if any increase in real GNP
   d. relatively little inflation.
8. In 1981 nominal GNP was $339 million. In 1982 nominal GNP increased to $357 million. On the basis of just this information, which of the following statements is true?
   a. Total output of the Canadian economy was greater in 1982 than in 1981.
   b. The whole increase in nominal GNP was the result of inflation.
   c. Real GNP increased from $339 to $357 million.
   d. It is impossible to determine what happened to prices and output from data on nominal GNP alone.

Test B

Circle T or F for True or False as appropriate.

1. A study of the economy of Luxembourg would be an example of microeconomics.   T **F**
2. Gross national product is an example of a macroeconomic aggregate.   **T** F
3. A decrease in nominal GNP necessarily implies a recession.   T **F**
4. Real GNP is a better measure of national output than is nominal GNP.   **T** F
5. Deflation can occur only as a result of shifts in the aggregate-supply curve.   T **F**
6. Even during the Great Depression of the 1930s prices did not decline.   T **F**
7. Stagflation refers to the simultaneous occurrence of rising prices and large increases in output.   T **F**

8. Stabilization policy refers to attempts by the government to influence both prices and output by shifting the aggregate demand curve. (T) F

9. Stabilization policy to combat a recession would call for policies that shift the aggregate-demand curve to the left. T (F)

Unemployment and Inflation: The Twin Evils of Macroeconomics

6

LEARNING OBJECTIVES

After completing the material in this chapter you should be able to:

- define, understand, and use correctly the terms and concepts listed below.
- explain why unemployment insurance only spreads the *risk* of unemployment rather than eliminating the *cost* of unemployment.
- describe how Statistics Canada measures the number of unemployed and in what ways this number may be an overestimate or an underestimate of the unemployment level.
- summarize the debate over how much unemployment is consistent with full employment.
- distinguish between real and mythical costs of inflation.
- distinguish between real and nominal rates of interest.
- describe how the difference between real and nominal rates of interest is related to expectations about the rate of inflation.
- explain how the taxation of nominal interest income can mean that during a period of inflation savers will receive a reduced real, after-tax rate of return.

- distinguish between creeping and galloping inflation.

IMPORTANT TERMS AND CONCEPTS

Unemployment rate
Labour force
Discouraged workers
Frictional unemployment
Structural unemployment
Cyclical unemployment
Full employment
Unemployment insurance
Potential GNP
Purchasing power
Relative prices
Redistribution by inflation
Real rate of interest
Nominal rate of interest
Expected rate of inflation
Indexed taxes
Creeping inflation
Galloping inflation

CHAPTER REVIEW

Ever since the White Paper of 1945 committed the federal government to deliberate macroeconomic policy, policy-makers have been facing the choice between the twin evils of macroeconomics. Attempts to lower unemployment

(1) have usually meant (*more/less*) inflation and attempts to fight inflation have usually meant

_____ unemployment. How is one to make the choice? Economics cannot provide a definitive answer to this question, but the material in this chapter will help you understand the issues and enable you to make a more informed choice.

Unemployment has two sorts of costs. The personal costs include not only the lost income for individuals out of work, but also the loss of work experience and the psychic costs of undesired idleness. The economic costs for the nation as a whole can be measured by the output of goods and services that might have been produced by those who are unemployed.

Unemployment insurance can help ease the burden of unemployment for individual families, but it

(2) (*can/cannot*) protect society against the lost output that the unemployed might have produced. Employing these people in the future does not bring back the hours of employment that have already been missed. Unemployment compensation provides (*complete/partial*) protection for (*all/some*) unemployed workers.

Economists have attempted to measure part of the cost of unemployment by estimating how much output

(3) would have been produced at full employment. These figures are estimates of (*potential/actual*) GNP. The

economic cost of unemployment is the difference between potential GNP and _____.

(4) Full employment (*is/is not*) the same as zero unemployment. Some unemployment occurs naturally from the normal workings of labour markets, as people initially look for jobs, improve their own skills, look for better jobs,

move to new locations, and so forth. Such unemployment is called _____ unemployment and involves people who are temporarily without a job for more or less voluntary reasons. Full employment would not eliminate this kind of unemployment. Full employment would eliminate unemployment that is due to a decline in the economy's total production; that is, at full employment there would be no

_____ unemployment. Unemployment may also occur because people's skills are no longer in demand due to automation or massive changes in production. This type of unemployment is called

_____ unemployment.

Unemployment statistics come from a monthly survey by Statistics Canada. People are asked whether they have a job. If they answer no, they are asked if they are laid off from a job they expect to return to, are looking for work, or are not looking for work. From these answers government statisticians derive estimates of employment, unemployment, and the labour force. These numbers are not above criticism. When unemployment rates are high, some people give up looking for work because they believe that looking for work is not worth the effort. These

(5) people are called _____ workers. An increase in the number of people who have given up looking for work means a(n) (*increase/decrease*) in the amount of statistical unemployment and is an important reason why some observers feel that the official unemployment statistics (*understate/overstate*) the problem of unemployment.

Some argue that the increased importance of women and young workers in the labour force has increased the

(6) percentage of (*cyclical/frictional/structural*) unemployment. These groups have naturally high rates of unemployment because they more frequently enter and leave the labour force, and because they change jobs more often. Another factor may be that more liberal unemployment compensation induces people to call themselves unemployed even if they have no intention of looking for work.

There are important and valid reasons why people are concerned about continuing inflation. Nevertheless, quite a few popular arguments against inflation turn out to be based on misunderstandings. Many people worry that a

(7) high rate of inflation reduces their standard of living, or their (*real/nominal*) income. But the facts show that periods of high inflation are usually accompanied by equally large if not larger increases in wages. For most workers, the real standard of living, or the change in wages adjusted for the change in prices, continues to increase, even during periods of rapid inflation. A worker whose income doubles when prices double is able to consume (*more/less/the same*) goods and services (*than/as*) before the rise in prices and wages.

(8) During inflationary periods most prices increase at (*the same/different*) rates. As a result, goods and services with smaller than average price increases become relatively (*more/less*) expensive than they were before. Analogously, goods and services with larger than average price increases become relatively

_____ expensive. Relative prices change all the time, during both inflationary and non-inflationary periods. Change in relative prices usually reflect shifts in demand and/or supply curves or various forms of government interventions. It is inaccurate to blame inflation for an increase in relative prices.

(9)   But inflation does have real impacts. An important effect is the redistribution of wealth between borrowers and lenders in inflationary periods. If lenders expect higher prices in the future they will demand (*higher/lower*) interest rates to compensate them for the loss of purchasing power of the future dollars used to repay loans. Economists have thus found it useful to distinguish between nominal and real interest rates. If one looks at interest rates only in

terms of the dollars that borrowers must pay lenders, one is looking at _____ interest rates. If one looks at interest rates in terms of the expected purchasing power the borrower will pay the lender, one

is looking at _____ interest rates. The difference between these two measures of

interest rate is related to expectations of _____ .

(10)   If a change in the rate of inflation is accurately foreseen, and if nominal interest rates are correctly adjusted to reflect the change in expected inflation, then nominal interest rates (*will/will not*) change while real interest rates will (*also change/be unchanged*). More typically, expectations of inflation are incorrect, in which case inflation will result in a redistribution of wealth between borrowers and lenders. Who gains and who loses will depend on whether the adjustment of nominal interest rates is too large or too small. The tax treatment of interest payments can have a substantial impact on the real after-tax rate of return. Problems here reflect the fact that the tax system was originally designed for a world of no inflation.

Over the long run, small unexpected differences in the rate of inflation can compound into large differences in profits and losses. And since most business investments depend on long-term contracts, this area of economic activity may suffer during periods of high inflation.

Long-term inflation that proceeds at a fairly moderate and steady pace is referred to as

(11)   _____ inflation. Inflation that progresses at exceptionally high and often accelerating

rates, if only for brief periods of time, is called _____ inflation. There is no simple borderline between the two. In different countries or in different periods of time, the dividing line will vary considerably.

BASIC EXERCISE

1. **Unemployment and the Changing Composition of the Labour Force**

   This problem shows how a change in the composition of the labour force can affect the national unemployment rate. Table 6-1 shows data on the composition of the labour force, and the unemployment experience of three age-sex groups for 1955 and 1982.

   a. Fill in column 3 of Table 6-1 to compute the composition of the labour force in both years. Use these statistics to verify that in each year the overall unemployment rate represents a weighted average of the unemployment rates for each group, where the weights are the proportion of each group in total labour force.

   b. When you compare 1982 and 1955, which demographic group(s) has shown an increase in importance in the total labour force? Which group(s) has shown a decrease in importance?

   c. How important has this change in composition been for the overall unemployment rate? To answer this question compute a new total unemployment rate for 1982 that adjusts for the changing composition of the labour force by completing Table 6-2. After completing this table, you will have an estimate of what unemployment would have been in 1982 if the age–sex specific unemployment rates were unchanged from their actual 1982 values and if the composition of the labour force was unchanged from its 1955 value. What is the difference between the actual unemployment rate for 1982 and your adjusted unemployment rate? Which is higher? Why?

   d. Both unemployment rates for 1982 (i.e., the Statistics Canada figure of 9.2 percent and your adjusted estimate in Question c) are still above the rate for 1955. Can you explain why?

   e. (Optional) In 1955, the unemployment rate for females aged 25 and older was actually lower than the rate for men in this age group. Can you suggest a reason why this was so?

   f. (Optional) While most people do not change their sex, everyone ages. What is likely to happen to the age composition of the labour force over the next 15 years? What does this imply for the full-employment unemployment rate?

TABLE 6-1
LABOUR FORCE FACTS

Age–Sex Group	(1) Labour Force (thousands)	(2) Unemployment Rate (percent)	(3) Proportion of the Total Labour Force*
1955			
Both sexes, 14–24	1277	6.7	0. _____
Females, 25 and older	793	1.8	0. _____
Males, 25 and older	3539	4.0	0. _____
Total	5609	4.3	1.00 _____
1982			
Both sexes, 14–24	2410	11.8	0. _____
Females, 25 and older	3196	8.8	0. _____
Males, 25 and older	4968	8.1	0. _____
Total	10574	9.2	1.00

*For each year divide the number of labour force participants for each age-sex group by the total labour force.

Source: 1955: *Historical Statistics of Canada*, 2nd edition, F.H. Leacy (ed.). Ottawa: Statistics Canada and the Social Science Federation of Canada, 1983. 1982: Bank of Canada *Review*.

TABLE 6-2

	(1) 1955 Labour Force Proportions	(2) 1982 Unemployment Rates	(3) (1) × (2)
Both sexes, 14–24	_____	_____	_____
Females, 25 and older	_____	_____	_____
Males, 24 and older	_____	_____	_____
	Overall 1982 unemployment rate using 1955 age-sex composition _____		

Directions:
a. Fill in the first two columns from Table 6-1.
b. For each age-sex group multiply the entries in columns 1 and 2 and write the result in column 3.
c. Sum the entries in column 3.

2. Real and Nominal Interest Rates

This problem is designed to illustrate how the adjustment of nominal interest rates, when it is an accurate reflection of future inflation, can leave the real costs and returns to borrowers and lenders unchanged. For simplicity the exercise ignores taxes.

Frank Abbot has a manufacturing firm. After paying other costs he expects a cash flow of $10 million, out of which he must pay the principal and interest on a $5 million loan. If prices are unchanged and if the interest rate is 5 percent, Frank expects a nominal and real profit of $4,750,000. This result is shown in the first column of Table 6-3.

The next three columns reflect three possible alternatives. The second column shows the consequences of unexpected inflation of 10 percent. In the third column, nominal interest rates have adjusted in expectation of inflation of 10 percent, which actually occurs. And in the last column,

TABLE 6-3

	(1)	(2)	(3)	(4)
1. Price level	1.00	1.10	1.10	1.10
2. Sales revenue minus labour and materials costs*	10,000,000	11,000,000	11,000,000	11,000,000
3. Principal repayment	5,000,000	5,000,000	5,000,000	5,000,000
4. Interest rate	0.05	0.05	0.155	0.20
5. Interest payment [(4) × (3)]	250,000	_____	_____	_____
6. Total nominal payment to lender [(3) + (5)]	5,250,000	_____	_____	_____
7. Real payment to lender [(6) ÷ (1)]	5,250,000	_____	_____	_____
8. Nominal profits [(2) - (6)]	4,750,000	_____	_____	_____
9. Real profits [(8) ÷ (1)]	4,750,000	_____	_____	_____

*Inflation of 10 percent is assumed to increase sales revenue, labour costs, and materials costs by 10 percent each. As a result, the difference between sales revenue and labour and material costs also increased by 10 percent in column, 2, 3, and 4.

nominal interest rates reflect the consequences of expecting a higher rate of inflation than actually occurs.

a. Fill in the missing figures in the second column. Compare the real returns to both Frank and his lender with those of the non-inflationary situation in column 1. Who gains and who loses when there is unexpected inflation?

b. Fill in the missing figures in the third column. This is the case in which nominal interest rates have adjusted appropriately. (The approximation is to add the rate of inflation, 10 percent, to the rate of interest in the non-inflationary situation, 5 percent. The extra 0.5 percent comes from a more complex and complete adjustment.) Compare the real returns in rows 7 and 9 with the comparable figures in column 1. Who gains and who loses now?

c. Fill in the missing figures in column 4, where interest rates have adjusted in anticipation of an even higher rate of inflation than occurs. Who gains and who loses when inflation turns out to be less than expected?

SELF-TESTS FOR UNDERSTANDING

Test A

Circle the correct answer.

1. Which of the following factors imply that official statistics may overstate the magnitude of the problem of unemployment?

a. Discouraged workers.
b. The loss of expected overtime work.
c. Liberalized unemployment benefits.
d. Involuntary part-time work.

2. Which of the following are examples of frictional unemployment?

a. An older, unemployed telephone operator replaced by new, computerized switching machines.
b. An unemployed, final-year university student looking for her first job.
c. An ex-construction worker who has given up looking for work because of a belief that no one is hiring.
d. An unemployed retail clerk who is laid off because of declining sales associated with a general business recession.

3. Which of the following people are eligible for unemployment compensation?

a. A mechanic for Ford Motor Company laid off because of declining auto sales.
b. A housewife looking for work after six years spent at home with two small children.
c. A final-year university student looking for his first job.

4. A nominal interest rate of 10 percent and inflationary expectations of 4 percent imply a real interest rate of about _____ percent.

a. 4
b. 6
c. 10
d. 14

5. If suddenly everyone expects a higher rate of

inflation, economists would expect nominal interests rates to

a. rise.

b. fall.

c. stay unchanged.

6. The historical evidence suggests that in periods with high rates of inflation, nominal wages

a. increase at about the same rate as before.

b. increase at much lower rates than inflation.

c. also increase at high rates.

d. remain unchanged.

7. If prices rise less than expected, there is apt to be a redistribution of wealth from

a. borrowers to lenders.

b. lenders to borrowers

c. rich to poor.

d. poor to rich.

8. If your wages go up by 10 percent and prices go up by 7 percent, the increase in the purchasing power of your wages is about

_____ percent.

a. 3

b. 7

c. 10

d. 17

9. In a world with no inflation and no taxes, nominal interest rates of 5 percent offer a real return of 5 percent. If suddenly it is expected that prices will rise by 6 percent, what increase in nominal interest rates is necessary if the expected real interest rate is to remain unchanged at 5 percent?

a. 1 percent.

b. 5 percent.

c. 6 percent.

d. 11 percent.

10. Assume that taxes take 50 cents out of every dollar of interest income. In a world of no inflation, the after-tax real return from a nominal interest rate of 5 percent is 2.5 percent. If suddenly it is expected that prices will rise by 6 percent, what increase in nominal interest rates is necessary if the expected real after-tax rate of return is to remain unchanged at 2.5 percent?

a. 6 percent.

b. 8.5 percent.

c. 11 percent.

d. 12 percent.

Test B

Circle T or F for True or False as appropriate.

1. In periods of high unemployment the only people whose incomes are reduced are those who are out of work. **T F**

2. The official unemployment statistics are adjusted to reflect those people with part-time jobs who are looking for full-time work, but not those people who are between jobs. **T F**

3. All major social groupings, (for example, young-old, men-women), have essentially the same rate of unemployment. **T F**

4. Unemployment insurance protects society against lost output from unemployment. **T F**

5. Anyone who is officially counted as unemployed can collect unemployment benefits. **T F**

6. Potential GNP is an estimate of the maximum possible output our economy could produce under conditions similar to wartime. **T F**

7. The definition of full employment is an unemployment rate of zero. **T F**

8. Inflation does not redistribute wealth between borrowers and lenders because nominal interest rates are automatically adjusted to reflect actual inflation. **T F**

9. The historical record shows that creeping inflation will always lead to galloping inflation. **T F**

10. Predictable inflation is likely to impose less cost than unpredictable inflation. **T F**

Appendix: How Statisticians Measure Inflation

LEARNING OBJECTIVES

After completing the material in this appendix you should be able to:

● define, understand, and use correctly the terms and concepts listed below.

● construct a price index from data on prices and the composition of the market basket in the base year.

● use a price index to compute real measures of economic activity by deflating the corresponding nominal measures.

IMPORTANT TERMS AND CONCEPTS

Index number

Index number problem

Consumer Price Index (CPI)

Deflating by a price index

GNP deflator

BASIC EXERCISES

The following exercises should help you review the material on price indexes presented in the appendix to Chapter 6.

I. Table 6-4 presents data on expenditures and prices for a hypothetical family that buys only food and clothing. We see that in 1984 this family spent $5000 on food at $2 per unit of food, and $10,000 on clothing at $25 per unit. Note that between 1984 and 1985, dollar expenditures by this family increased by almost 16 percent, actually 15.7 percent, rising from $15,000 to $17,348. Is this family able to consume 16 percent more of everything? Clearly not, since prices have risen. How much inflation has there been on average? What is the increase in real income for this family? These are the sorts of questions that a good price index can help you answer.

1. Use the data in Table 6-4 to construct a family price index (FPI) using 1984 as the base year.
   a. Find the quantities of each good purchased in 1984. This is the base-period market basket.

      Quantity of food _____
      Quantity of clothing _____
   b. Use 1985 prices to find out how much the base-period market basket would cost at 1985 prices.
      1985 cost of 1984 market basket

      _____
   c. Divide the 1985 cost of the base-period market basket by the 1984 cost of the same market basket and multiply by 100 to compute the value of the FPI for 1985.

      FPI for 1985 _____
   d. Convince yourself that if you repeat steps b and c using 1984 prices you will get an answer of 100 for the value of the FPI for 1984.
   e. Measure the increase in the cost of living by computing the percentage change in your price index from 1984 to 1985.

Inflation between 1984 and 1985

_____

   f. Divide total dollar expenditures in 1985 by the 1985 FPI and multiply by 100 to get a measure of real expenditures for 1985.
      Real expenditures
      in 1985 _____
      Percentage change in
      real expenditures
      1984 to 1985 _____

Remember the following points about price indexes:

- Most price indexes, like the Consumer Price Index, are computed by pricing a standard market basket of goods in subsequent periods.
- A price index can be used to measure inflation and to deflate nominal values to adjust for inflation.
- Different price indexes, such as the Consumer Price Index and the GNP deflator, will show slightly different measures of inflation because they use different market baskets.

2. (Optional) Compute a new FPI using 1985 as the base period rather than 1984. Now the value of your price index for 1985 will be 100 and the price index for 1984 will be something less than 100. Does this index give the same measure of inflation as the index with 1984 as the base period? Do not be surprised if it does not. Can you explain why they differ?

II. Table 6-5 contains data on consumer prices for seven countries. Try to answer each of the following questions or explain why the information in Table 6-5 is insufficient to answer the question.
   1. In 1960 which country had the lowest prices?
   2. In 1982 which country had the highest prices?
   3. Over the period 1960-1982, which country experienced the most inflation as measured by the percentage change in the consumer price index? Which country experienced the least inflation?

TABLE 6-4
HYPOTHETICAL PRICES AND EXPENDITURES

Year	Food Price	Food Expenditures	Clothing Price	Clothing Expenditures	Total Expenditures
1984	$2.00	$5,000	$25.00	$10,000	$15,000
1985	2.36	5,900	26.50	11,448	17,348

TABLE 6-5
INDEX OF CONSUMER PRICES (1967 = 100)

	Canada	France	Italy	Japan	United Kingdom	United States	West Germany
1960	85.9	78.0	74.1	68.3	79.0	88.7	82.9
1965	93.1	94.8	94.2	91.6	93.9	94.5	95.0
1970	112.4	117.1	109.2	119.3	117.4	116.3	107.1
1975	160.1	178.9	186.8	205.8	216.5	161.2	144.2
1980	243.5	294.2	398.0	282.2	423.6	246.8	175.9
1982	303.5	373.1	549.4	304.1	514.7	289.1	196.2

Source: 1984 *Economic Report of the President*, Table B-108.

Income and Spending: The Powerful Consumer

7

LEARNING OBJECTIVES

After completing the material in this chapter you should be able to:

- define, understand, and use correctly the terms and concepts listed below.
- describe what spending categories make up aggregate demand.
- explain why, except for some technical complications, national product and national income are necessarily equal.
- explain why disposable income differs from national income.
- derive a consumption function given data on consumption and disposable income and compute the marginal propensity to consume at various levels of income.
- distinguish between factors that result in *movements along* the consumption function and factors that result in a *shift of* the function.
- explain why consumption spending is affected by a change in the level of prices even if real income is unchanged.
- describe why permanent and temporary changes in

taxes would be expected to have different impacts on consumption spending.

IMPORTANT TERMS AND CONCEPTS

Aggregate demand
Consumer expenditure (C)
Investment spending (I)
Government purchases (G)
Exports (X)
Imports (IM)
C + I + G + X - IM
National income (GNP)
Gross domestic product (GDP)
Disposable income (DI)
Circular flow diagram
Transfer payments
Scatter diagram
Consumption function
Marginal propensity to consume (MPC)
Movements along/shifts of the consumption function
Money fixed assets
Temporary/permanent changes in income taxes

CHAPTER REVIEW

This chapter introduces two key concepts that economists use when discussing the determination of an economy's output: *aggregate demand* and the *consumption function*. These basic concepts will be fundamental to the material in later chapters.

The total amount that all consumers, business firms, government units, and foreigners are willing to spend on

(1) goods and services is called aggregate _____. Economists typically divide this sum into four components: consumption expenditures, investment expenditures, government expenditures, and net exports. Food, clothing, movies, and hamburgers would be examples of (*consumption/investment/government/export*)

expenditures. Factories, office buildings, machinery, and houses would be examples of _____ expenditures. Red tape, bombers, filing cabinets, and the services of bureaucrats would be examples of

_____ purchases. Wheat, pulp and paper, and hydroelectric power are examples of

_____. Aggregate demand is a schedule. As we saw in Chapter 5, the exact amount of aggregate demand for any year will depend on a number of factors, including the price level.

Two other concepts that are closely related to aggregate demand are *national product* and *national income*.

(2) National product is simply the output of the economy. National income is the (*before/after*)-tax income of all the

individuals in the economy. Disposable income is the _____-tax income of individuals. The circular flow diagram shows that, as long as foreign-source incomes are ignored, national product and national income are two ways of measuring the same thing: Producing goods and selling them results in income for the owners and employees of firms.

Economists use the concept of a *consumption function* to organize the determinants of consumption expenditures. Specifically the consumption function is the relation between aggregate real consumption expenditures and aggregate real disposable income, if all other determinants of consumer spending are held constant. Higher

(3) disposable income leads to (*more/less*) consumption spending. A change in disposable income leads to a (*shift in/movement along*) the consumption function. A change in one of the other factors that affect consumer spending, such as inertia or habit, wealth, the level of prices, or the rate of inflation, leads to a

_____ _____ the consumption function. (Two, more technical, aspects of the consumption function, the *marginal propensity to consume* and the *average propensity to consume*, are considered more fully in the Basic Exercise section of this chapter.)

An increase in the price level affects consumption spending and is an important reason why aggregate

(4) demand, the sum of _____ + _____ + _____ +

_____, is a schedule. If prices are higher we expect (*more/less*) consumption spending. Consumption spending changes because the value of many consumer assets is fixed in money terms, and an increase in the price level will (*increase/decrease*) the purchasing power of these assets. It is important to remember that higher prices will lead to lower real consumption expenditures even if real disposable income is constant. A doubling of *all* prices will also double wages—the price for an hour of labour services. If wages and prices both double, there is no change in the purchasing power of labour income, but there is a loss of consumers from the decline in the purchasing power of their money fixed assets. It is this latter decline that leads to a shift in the consumption function in response to a change in the price level.

Separately from the level of prices, the rate of inflation may also affect consumption spending. On the one hand, the notion that one should buy now, before prices increase still further, suggests that inflation stimulates consumption spending. On the other hand, the notion that one may have to save more in order to meet higher prices tomorrow suggests that inflation depresses consumption spending. For rates of inflation experienced in Canada there is no clear evidence as to which tendency is greater.

A change in income taxes immediately changes disposable income. The consumption function, then, tells us how a change in disposable income will affect consumption spending. For example, a reduction in income taxes

(5) would (*increase/decrease*) disposable income. After computing the change in disposable income, one could estimate the initial impact on consumption spending by multiplying the change in disposable income by the (*marginal/average*) propensity to consume. A permanent increase in income taxes would be expected to have a (*larger/smaller*) effect on consumption expenditures than a temporary income-tax increase because the permanent increase changes consumers' long-run income prospects by (*more/less*) than the temporary increase. The same argument works in reverse and implies that temporary income-tax changes have a (*larger/smaller*) impact on consumption expenditures than do permanent income-tax changes. However, since temporary sales-tax changes affect the current versus the future price of goods (and not household income), they can have a significant impact.

BASIC EXERCISES

1. This exercise will give you practice using a consumption function. Table 7-1 reports some data on disposable income and consumption.
   a. For each change in income compute the marginal propensity to consume. (You will first have to compute the change in consumption.)
   b. The average propensity to consume is defined as the ratio of consumption expenditures to disposable income or APC = $C \div DI$. For the income of $12,000 the average propensity to consume is $11,000 \div \$12,000 = 0.92$. Use the data on income and consumption to fill in the column for the average propensity to consume.
   c. Are the average and marginal propensities equal? Do the differences surprise you? Can you explain them? Perhaps step f will help.
   d. Use the graph of Figure 7-1 to draw the consumption function consistent with the data in Table 7-1. (Locate each income-consumption data pair and then draw a line connecting the points.)
   e. The marginal propensity to consume is represented by what part of your graph?
   f. As step c indicated, the average propensity to consume depends upon the level of income. In Figure 7-1 it can be represented by the slope of a ray from the origin to a point on the consumption function. Remember the slope of any straight line, including a ray, is the vertical change over the horizontal change. When measured from the origin, the vertical change of a ray to a point on the consumption function is C and the horizontal change is DI. Thus the slope of the ray is ($C \div DI$) or the APC. Draw rays to represent the APC for incomes of $12,000 and $18,000. How does the slope of your rays change as income increases? Is this change consistent with changes in the APC you calculated in step c?

2. (Optional) Imagine an economy made up of 100 families each earning $12,000 and 100 families each earning $20,000. Each family consumes according to the consumption function described in Table 7-1.
   a. Fill in the following:
      Consumption of a family earning $12,000

      _____

      Consumption of a family earning $20,000

      _____

      Aggregate consumption of all 200 families

      _____
   b. What is the average propensity to consume of

      the richer families? _____
      What is the average propensity to consume of

      the poorer families? _____
   c. Randy argues that since the lower-income families are spending a greater proportion of their income than the higher-income families, a redistribution of income from high- to low-income families will increase total consumption expenditures. Test Randy's assertion by assuming that the government takes $2,000 from

TABLE 7-1
DATA ON DISPOSABLE INCOME AND CONSUMPTION

Average Propensity to Consume	Disposable Income (dollars)	Consumption (dollars)	Change in Disposable Income (dollars)	Change in Consumption (dollars)	Marginal Propensity to Consume
_____	12,000	11,000			
			2,000	_____	_____
_____	14,000	12,600			
			2,000		
_____	16,000	14,200			
			2,000	_____	_____
_____	18,000	15,800			
			2,000		
_____	20,000	17,400			

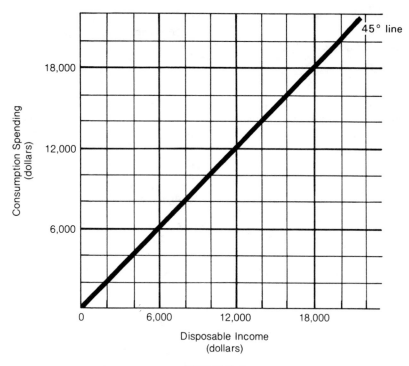

18,000

12,000

6,000

Consumption Spending
(dollars)

45° line

0   6,000   12,000   18,000

Disposable Income
(dollars)

FIGURE 7-1

each richer family and gives it to each poorer family, and that all families adjust their consumption in line with the consumption function described in Table 7-1. Then fill in the following:

Consumption of a family with $14,000 income

_____

Consumption of a family with $18,000 income

_____

Aggregate consumption of all 200 families

_____

   d. Explain why in this example aggregate consumption is unaffected by the redistribution of income.

3. (More difficult) Use the data in Table 7-1 to compute an algebraic expression for the consumption function.

   Consumption = _____ +

   0. _____ × (disposable income)

SELF-TESTS FOR UNDERSTANDING

Test A

Circle the correct answer.

1. Which of the following is not a part of aggregate demand?

   a. Consumption expenditures.

   b. National income.

   c. Government purchases of goods and services.

   d. Investment expenditures.

2. Which of the following would be an example of a government transfer payment?

   a. Wages paid to government bureaucrats.

   b. A tax refund for excess withholding.

   c. The purchase of paperclips by a government agency.

   d. Old age security payments.

3. In a circular flow diagram all but which one of the following would be depicted as an injection into the stream of spending?

   a. The purchase of a new submarine by the armed forces.

   b. The purchase of an existing house by Joyce and Jim.

   c. Alice's spending to rebuild her restaurant after the fire.

   d. The set of new micro-computers that Elaine's company bought for all its top management.

4. A graphical representation of how consumption spending varies with changes in disposable income is called the

   a. aggregate-demand curve.

   b. income-expenditure schedule.

   c. consumption function.

   d. Phillips curve.

5. Changes in which of the following would be

associated with a movement along the
consumption function?
a. Current disposable income.
b. Wealth.
c. The price level.
d. Expected future incomes.

6. If the marginal propensity to consume is 0.7, then a
$10 billion change in disposable income will be
associated with what change in consumption
spending?
a. $2 billion.
b. $3 billion.
c. $7 billion.
d. $10 billion.

7. If a $10 billion increase in disposable income
results in an $8 billion increase in consumption
spending, then the marginal propensity to consume
is
a. 0.2
b. 0.5
c. 0.8
d. 1.0

8. If the marginal propensity to consume is 0.75, what
decrease in taxes will initially increase
consumption spending by $15 billion?
a. $11.25 billion.
b. $15 billion.
c. $20 billion.
d. $60 billion.

9. If consumption spending declines by $45 billion
when disposable income declines by $50 billion,
what is the marginal propensity to consume?
a. 0.9
b. 0.1
c. –0.1
d. –0.9

10. If the marginal propensity to consume is 0.8, a $10
billion change in the wealth of consumers will lead
to
a. a $10 billion change in consumption spending.
b. an $8 billion change in consumption spending.
c. a movement along the consumption function.
d. a shift in the entire consumption function.

Test B

Circle T or F for True or False as appropriate.

1. Aggregate demand is the aggregate of individual
household consumption decisions.   T F

2. The consumption function reflects the close
relationship between consumption spending and
national output.   T F

3. A change in consumption divided by the change in
income that produced the change in consumption is
called the marginal propensity to consume.   T F

4. An increase in the level of prices is likely to reduce
consumption expenditures.   T F

5. The effect of a change in the level of prices on
consumption would be viewed graphically as a shift
in the consumption function.   T F

6. By increasing household wealth, a big increase in
the stock market is likely to lead to a movement
along the consumption function.   T F

7. The magnitude of the impact of a change in taxes
on consumption expenditures is likely to depend on
whether consumers view the change in taxes as
permanent or temporary.   T F

8. A temporary decrease in taxes is likely to have a
smaller impact on consumption than will a
permanent decrease.   T F

9. The initial impact of a change in income taxes on
consumption spending can be calculated by
multiplying the change in disposable income by the
marginal propensity to consume.   T F

Appendix A: The Saving Function and the Marginal Propensity to Save

LEARNING OBJECTIVES

Working through the exercise below should help you
understand the basic message of Appendix A to
Chapter 7; that is: *We could just as easily have used
the saving function instead of the consumption function.*

IMPORTANT TERMS AND CONCEPTS

Aggregate savings
Saving function
Marginal propensity to save (MPS)

BASIC EXERCISE

1. Table 7-2 reproduces the income and consumption
data from Table 7-1. Use the data in Table 7-2 to
compute the amount of saving at each level of
income. Remember that saving is just the difference
between disposable income and consumption, that
is $S = DI - C$.

TABLE 7-2
DATA ON INCOME, CONSUMPTION, AND SAVING

Average Propensity to Save	Saving (billions of dollars)	Consumption (billions of dollars)	Disposable Income (billions of dollars)	Change in Disposable Income (billions of dollars)	Change in Saving (billions of dollars)	Marginal Propensity to Save
————	————	11,000	12,000			
				2,000	————	————
————	————	12,600	14,000			
				2,000	————	————
————	————	14,200	16,000			
				2,000	————	————
————	————	15,800	18,000			
				2,000	————	————
————	————	17,400	20,000			

2. For each change in income, compute the marginal propensity to save. (You will first need to compute the change in savings.)
3. Using results from Tables 7-1 and 7-2, show that the sum of the marginal propensity to consume and the marginal propensity to save for each change in income is 1.0.
4. Use the data on income and saving to compute the average propensity to save.
5. Again, using results from Tables 7-1 and 7-2, show that the sum of the average propensity to consume and the average propensity to save at each level of income is 1.0.

It is because APC plus APS always equals 1.0 and MPC plus MPS always equals 1.0 that we can use the saving or consumption factor interchangeably.

Some simple algebra also gives the same result. Start with the identity.

$$DI = C + S$$

Now divide both sides of the equation by DI and interpret your results in terms of APC and APS.

We also know that since any change in income must be spent or saved

$$\Delta DI = \Delta C + \Delta S,$$

where Δ means change. Now divide both sides of the equation by ΔDI and interpret your results in terms of MPC and MPS.

Appendix B: National Income Accounting

LEARNING OBJECTIVES

After completing the material in this appendix you should be able to:

- define, understand, and use correctly the terms and concepts listed below.
- describe the three alternative ways of measuring GNP.
- explain in what ways GNP is an inadequate measure of total economic activity.
- explain in what ways GNP is an adequate measure of national well-being.
- explain the difference in theory and practice between the following macro measurements: GNP, NNP, national income, personal income, and disposable income.

IMPORTANT TERMS AND CONCEPTS

National income accounting
Gross national product (GNP)
Inventories

Gross private domestic investment
Government purchases
Transfer payments
Net exports
National income

Net national product (NNP)
Depreciation
Value added
Personal income
Disposable income

APPENDIX REVIEW

Although included in an appendix, this material on national income accounting deserves its own special treatment. When working through this material, do not lose sight of the forest for the trees. The forest has to do with broad income concepts, such as GNP, net national product, national income: what each of these concepts measures and how they relate to one another. This appendix is an introduction to the forest rather than to each individual tree.

The *national income accounts* measure economic activity: the production of goods and services and the incomes that are simultaneously generated. Accurate measurement of production and income is an important prerequisite to attempts to understand and control the economy. National income accounts are centred around measurement of the gross national product. Things like consumption (C) and investment (I) are parts of GNP. Other concepts, such as *net national product (NNP)* and *national income*, are alternative measures of total economic activity.

GNP is defined as the sum of the money values of all final goods and services that are produced during a specified period of time. Economists use money values or market prices to add up the very different types of output that make up GNP. Two of the three exceptions mentioned in Appendix B—government output and inventories—arise because some production is not sold on markets.

The emphasis on *final* goods and services is important, because it avoids double counting of intermediate goods. (The need to avoid double counting is also the key to why the three alternative ways of measuring GNP are conceptually equivalent.) The third part of the definition says that GNP is a statement of production, not sales. It is only production that creates new goods available for consumption or investment. Thus GNP, as a measure of production, is the appropriate measure of how much new consumption or investment our economy can enjoy.

There are three ways to measure GNP. Perhaps the simplest, most straightforward way to measure GNP is to add up the purchases of newly produced final goods and services by private individuals and firms—for consumption and investment—by the government, and by foreigners (net exports). For Canada in 1983, this sum of $C + I + G + X - IM$ was estimated to be 388.7 billion. We must add exports to $C + I + G$ because, even though bought by foreigners, exports are Canadian products and GNP is a measure of total Canadian production. We subtract imports because C and I and G are measures of total spending, including imports, and we want a measure that reflects only

(1) those goods and services (*purchased*/*produced*) in Canada.

All of a firm's sales receipts eventually end up as income for someone, directly in the case of workers, creditors, and firm owners, and indirectly in the case of payments to suppliers, who in turn use this money to pay their workers, creditors, and so forth. Thus, instead of measuring GNP as purchases of final goods and services, we could equivalently add up all incomes earned by all factors in the production of goods and services. This sum of

(2) factor incomes is also called national ＿＿＿＿＿＿＿＿＿＿＿ and is the second way to measure GNP. It is conceptually similar to GNP but differs for Canadian national income accounts because of several items. Indirect business taxes are included in market prices paid by consumers but (*do*/*do not*) result in income for any factor of production as they are immediately collected by the government. National income plus indirect business taxes is

equal to NNP or ＿＿＿＿＿＿＿＿＿＿＿ national product, which is almost, but not quite, equal to GNP.

The difference between NNP and GNP is ＿＿＿＿＿＿＿＿＿＿＿ and, conceptually, refers to the portion of current total production that is used to replace those parts of the capital stock that have deteriorated as a result of current production. If GNP were all one edible good, we could eat NNP while maintaining our productive capacity. Eating GNP would reduce our productive capacity as we would not be replacing worn-out plants and machines.

To measure GNP as the money value of final goods and services, one would start by collecting sales data for final goods. The second way of measuring GNP, total factor incomes, would start by collecting income data from firms and individuals. The third way of measuring GNP looks at the difference between a firm's sales receipts and

(3) its purchases from other firms. This difference, also called a firm's _____ _____, is the amount of money a firm has to pay the factors of production that it has employed. Thus, the sum of total value added in the economy is another equivalent way to measure GNP.

BASIC EXERCISE

Consider the following two-firm economy: Firm A is a mining company that does not make purchases from firm B. Firm A sells all its output to firm B, which in turn sells all its output to consumers.

	Firm A	Firm B
Total sales	$500	$1700
Wages	400	800
Profits	100	400
Purchases from other firms	0	500

1. What are the total sales for the economy?

   $_____

2. What is the total value of sales for final uses?

   $_____

3. What is the total of all factor incomes?

   $_____

4. What is value added for firm A?

   $_____

5. What is value added for firm B?

   $_____

6. What is the total value added of both firms?

   $_____

7. What is GNP? $_____

8. What is national income?

   $_____

SELF-TESTS FOR UNDERSTANDING

Test A

Circle the correct answers.

1. Which of the following would add to this year's GNP?
   a. Jim purchases a new copy of the textbook for this course.
   b. Jill purchases a used copy of the textbook for this course.
   c. Susan purchases 100 shares of GM stock.
   d. Steve sells last semester's textbooks.

2. Conceptually, GNP can be measured by all but which one of the following:
   a. Add up all factor payments by firms in the economy.
   b. Add up all purchases of final goods and services, $C + I + G + X - IM$.
   c. Add up total sales of all firms in the economy.
   d. Add up value added of all firms in the economy.

3. Which of the following events result in an addition to gross private domestic investment?
   a. Managers of the Good Earth, a newly formed food co-op, buy a used refrigerator case for their store.
   b. Roberta buys 100 shares of stock in Inco.
   c. The Canadian government purchases a new plane for the prime minister.
   d. Wardair purchases 20 new planes so it can expand its service.

4. Which of the following transactions represent the sale of a final good as opposed to sale of an intermediate good?
   a. Farmer Jones sells his peaches to the Good Food Packing and Canning Company.
   b. Good Food sells a load of canned peaches to Smith Brothers Distributors.
   c. Smith Brothers sells the load of canned peaches to Irving's Supermarket.
   d. You buy a can of peaches at Irving's.

5. An increase in government transfer payments to individuals will lead to an initial increase in which one of the following?
   a. GNP.
   b. NNP.
   c. Government purchases of goods and services.
   d. Disposable income.

6. In measuring GNP, government outputs are
   a. appropriately valued at zero.
   b. valued by estimates of their market prices.
   c. valued at the cost of inputs needed to produce them.

7. Net national product is
   a. always greater than GNP.
   b. considered by many economists to be a more meaningful measure of the nation's economic output than is GNP.

c. conceptually superior to GNP because it excludes the output of environmental "bads."

d. measured by subtracting indirect business taxes from GNP.

Test B

Circle T or F for True or False as appropriate.

1. GNP is designed to be a measure of economic well-being, not a measure of economic production. **T F**

2. If you measured GNP by adding up total sales in the economy, you would be double or triple counting many intermediate goods. **T F**

3. Production that is not sold but is instead added to inventories is not counted in GNP. **T F**

4. If GM started its own steel company rather than continuing to buy steel from independent steel companies, GNP would be lower because intrafirm transfers are not part of GNP but all interfirm sales are. **T F**

5. Since the output of government agencies is not sold on markets, it is not included in GNP. **T F**

6. Value added is the difference between what a firm sells its output for and the cost of its own purchase from other firms.. **T F**

7. The difference between GNP and NNP is net exports. **T F**

8. Disposable income is usually greater than net national product. **T F**

SUPPLEMENTARY EXERCISE

1. Consider the following non-linear consumption function.

$$C = 100 \sqrt{DI + 2500}$$

Restricting yourself to positive values for disposable income, graph this function. What happens to the marginal propensity to consume as income increases? Can you find an explicit expression for the marginal propensity to consume as a function of income? Use this new consumption function to re-answer Basic Exercise question 2 about income redistribution. Does your answer change? If so, why?

What is the savings function that goes with this consumption function? Does MPC + MPS = 1? Does APC + APS = 1?

Demand-Side Equilibrium: Unemployment or Inflation?

LEARNING OBJECTIVES

After you complete the material in this chapter you should be able to:

- define, understand, and use correctly the terms and concepts listed below.
- describe some of the major determinants of investment spending by firms and explain which of these determinants can be directly affected by government actions.
- draw an expenditure schedule, given information about investment and consumption spending.
- determine the equilibrium level of income and explain why the level of income tends toward its equilibrium value.
- describe how a change in the price level affects the expenditure schedule and the equilibrium level of income.
- describe how the impact of a change in prices on the expenditure schedule and the equilibrium level of

income can be used to derive the aggregate-demand curve.
- explain why equilibrium GNP can be above or below the full-employment level of GNP.

IMPORTANT TERMS AND CONCEPTS

Depreciation allowance
Equilibrium level of GNP
Expenditure schedule
Induced investment
$C + I = Y$
Income–expenditure (or 45° line) diagram
Aggregate-demand curve
Full-employment level of GNP (or potential GNP)
Recessionary gap
Inflationary gap
Co-ordination of S and I

CHAPTER REVIEW

This chapter is the introduction to explicit models of income determination. The model discussed in this chapter is relatively simple and is not meant to be taken literally. Do not be put off by the simplicity of the model or its lack of realism. Careful study now will pay future dividends in terms of easier understanding of later chapters, in which both the mechanics and policy implications of more complicated models are described.

The central concept in this chapter is the concept of the *equilibrium level of income and output*. (If necessary, review the material in Chapter 7 on the equality of national income and national output.) The models discussed in this chapter show us how the equilibrium level of GNP is determined.

When considering the determination of the equilibrium level of GNP, it is important to distinguish between output and income on the one hand and total spending on the other hand. If total spending exceeds current production,

(1) firms will find that their inventories are decreasing. They are then likely to take steps to (*decrease/increase*) production and output. Analogously, if spending is less than current output, firms are likely to find their inventories

_____ , and they are likely to take steps to _____ production.

The concept of equilibrium refers to a situation in which producers and consumers are satisfied with things the way they are and see no reason to change their behaviour. Thus the equilibrium level of GNP must be a level of GNP at which firms have no reason to increase or decrease output; that is, at the equilibrium level of GNP, total spending and output will be equal. The determination of the equilibrium level of output thus reduces to

1. describing how total spending changes as output (and income) changes, and

2. finding the one level of output (and income) at which total spending equals output.

In the simplified model discussed in this chapter there are only two components to total spending: consumption and investment. Chapter 7 discussed the important role that income plays as a determinant of consumption expenditures. There is no such central factor influencing investment expenditures. Instead, investment expenditures are influenced by a variety of factors, including business people's expectations about the future, interest rates, the level of capacity utilization, the rate of growth of demand, and various tax features. If any of these factors change, investment spending is likely to change.

The income-expenditure diagram is a useful tool for analysing the determination of the equilibrium level of output. As just mentioned, to find the equilibrium level of output and income we need to know how total spending changes as income and output change, and we need to know where total spending equals income. The relationship between total spending (here meaning consumption plus investment expenditures) and income is given by the *expenditure schedule*. The 45° line shows all combinations of spending and income that are equal. The one place

(2) where spending is equal to income is given by the _____ of the expenditure schedule and the 45° line. This is the equilibrium level of output because it is the only level of output where total spending is equal to output. At any other level of output, total spending will not be equal to output. (You should be sure that you understand why the economy tends to move to the equilibrium level of output rather than getting stuck at a level of income and output at which total spending is either larger or smaller than output. Do not get confused between this automatic tendency to move to the equilibrium level of output and the lack, sometimes, of an automatic mechanism to ensure full employment.)

Any particular expenditure schedule relates total spending to income for a given level of prices. As prices change, total spending will change, even for the same level of real income. In particular, a higher price level is apt

(3) to mean (*more/less*) consumption spending because of the decline in the purchasing power of the money assets of consumers. This effect of prices on consumption will lead to a (*downward/upward*) shift in the expenditure schedule and a new equilibrium of income that is (*higher/lower*) than before. In the opposite case, a lower price

level would mean _____ consumption spending and a new, (*higher/lower*) equilibrium level of income. The relationship between the price level and the equilibrium level of income is called the *aggregate-demand curve*. The aggregate-demand curve is derived from the income-expenditure diagram and, from the viewpoint of demand, shows the relationship between the level of prices and the equilibrium level of income. The qualifier "from the viewpoint of demand" is important. Complete determination of the equilibrium level of income/output and the equilibrium price level comes from the interaction of the aggregate-demand and aggregate-supply curves.

Nothing that has been said so far implies that the equilibrium level of output will equal the full-employment level of output. The equilibrium level of output will be determined in part by the strength of consumption and investment spending and may be greater or less than the full-employment level of output. If the equilibrium level of output

(4) exceeds the full-employment level of output, the difference is called the _____ gap. In a case where the equilibrium level of output is less than the full-employment level of output, the difference is called the _____ gap.

BASIC EXERCISES

These exercises are designed to give you practice with manipulations on the income-expenditure diagram. They are based on data for real income (output), real consumption spending, and real investment spending given in Table 8-1.

TABLE 8-1
(ALL FIGURES ARE IN BILLIONS OF CONSTANT DOLLARS; PRICE LEVEL = 100)

Income (Output)	Consumption Spending	Investment Spending	Total Spending
260	260	30	_____
280	270	30	_____
300	280	30	_____
320	290	30	_____
340	300	30	_____

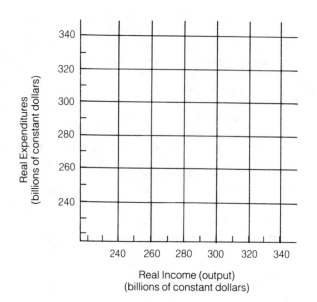

FIGURE 8-1

1. This exercise shows you how the expenditure schedule is derived and how it helps to determine the equilibrium level of income. For this exercise it is assumed that prices are constant with the consumer price index or price level having a value of 100.

   a. Use the data on consumption spending and income to draw the consumption function on the graph in Figure 8-1.

   b. Using the consumption function you have just drawn and the data on investment spending, now draw the expenditure schedule on the same graph. What is the difference between the expenditure schedule and the consumption function?

   c. Now draw a line representing all the points where total spending and income could be equal. (This is the 45° line. Do you know why?)

   d. The 45° line represents all the points that *could* be the equilibrium level of income. Now circle the one point that *is* the equilibrium level of income. What is the equilibrium level of income on your graph?

   e. Check your answer by filling in the Total Spending column in Table 8-1 to see where total spending equals income. You should get the same answer from Table 8-1 as you do from the graph.

   f. Why isn't the equilibrium level of output $280 billion? If for some reason national output and income started out at $280 billion, what forces would tend to move the economy toward the equilibrium you determined in Questions d and e?

   g. Using the data in Table 8-1 and assuming that the full-employment level of output income is $300 billion, is there an inflationary or recessionary gap? How large is the gap? If the full-employment level of income were $350 billion, how large would the inflationary or recessionary gap be?

   h. Assume now that an increase in business confidence leads to an increased level of investment spending. Specifically, assume that investment spending rises to $40 billion at all levels of national income. As a result of this shift, what happens to each of the following?

51

- The expenditure schedule.
- The equilibrium level of income.
- Consumption spending at the new equilibrium level of income.
- The aggregate-demand curve.

2. This exercise explores the implications of changes in the price level. It is designed to show how change in the price level implies a shift in the expenditure schedule and can be used to derive the aggregate-demand curve.

    a. The data in Table 8-1 assumed that prices were constant with the consumer price index, or the price level, at a value of 100. Mark the point in Figure 8-2 that shows the price level of 100 and the equilibrium level of income you found when answering Questions d and e of Exercise 1.

    b. Economic research has determined that if prices rose to 110, consumption spending would decline by $10 billion at every level of real income. Table

TABLE 8-2
(ALL FIGURES ARE IN
BILLIONS OF CONSTANT DOLLARS;
PRICE LEVEL = 110)

Income (Output)	Consumption Spending	Investment Spending	Total Spending
260	250	30	_____
280	260	30	_____
300	270	30	_____
320	280	30	_____
340	290	30	_____

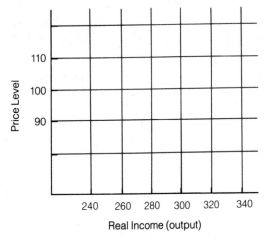

FIGURE 8-2

8-2 shows the relevant information. What is the new equilibrium level of income on the income-expenditure diagram with this higher price level? Mark the point in Figure 8-2 that shows the price level of 110 and this new equilibrium level of income.

    c. This same research determined that if prices fell to 90, real consumption spending would increase over amounts shown in Table 8-1 by $10 billion at every level of real income. What is the new equilibrium level of income on the income-expenditure diagram for this lower price level? Mark the point in Figure 8-2 that shows the price level of 90 and this new equilibrium level of income.

    d. The points you have marked in Figure 8-2 help to trace out what curve?

    e. Connect these points to verify that your curve has a (*negative/positive*) slope.

SELF-TESTS FOR UNDERSTANDING

Test A

Circle the correct answer.

1. The expenditure schedule is a relationship between
    a. the equilibrium level of income and prices.
    b. consumption spending and income.
    c. total spending and income
    d. consumption spending and prices.
2. When total spending is less than output
    a. inventories are likely to be increasing.
    b. inventories are likely to be decreasing.
    c. there will be a shift in the expenditure schedule.
    d. firms are likely to raise prices.
3. In the income-expenditure diagram, the equilibrium level of output is given by the intersection of the expenditure schedule and the
    a. consumption function.
    b. aggregate-demand curve.
    c. 45° line.
    d. level of full-employment output.
4. When total spending is equal to output.
    a. the resulting level of output is called the full-employment level of output.
    b. We know that consumers' savings plans and firms' investment plans are in balance.
    c. there is never an inflationary gap.
    d. the expenditure schedule and the aggregate-demand curve coincide.
5. Government policies can directly affect all but which one of the following determinants of investment spending?
    a. Interest rates.

b. The state of business confidence.

c. Tax incentives.

d. The overall state of aggregate demand.

6. If at the full-employment level of income, consumers' savings plans are equal to firms' investment plans, then

   a. the equilibrium level of income will be equal to the full-employment level of income.

   b. there will be an inflationary gap.

   c. firms will find their inventories increasing.

   d. the economy will be producing less than potential output.

7. The aggregate-demand curve is a relationship between the price level and

   a. consumption spending.

   b. the equilibrium level of income.

   c. full-employment GNP.

   d. the interest rate.

8. A lower price level will lead to a

   a. movement along the consumption function.

   b. shift in the consumption function.

   c. movement along the expenditure schedule.

   d. shift in the aggregate-demand curve.

9. A shift in the investment function will lead to all but which one of the following?

   a. A shift in the expenditure function.

   b. A new equilibrium level of income.

   c. A movement along the aggregate-demand curve.

   d. A shift in the aggregate-demand curve.

10. At the equilibrium level of income which one of the following is not necessarily true?

   a. The expenditure schedule will intersect the 45° line.

   b. The amount consumers want to save will equal the amount that businesses want to invest.

   c. There will be no unemployment.

   d. The equilibrium level of output and the price level will together determine one point on the aggregate-demand curve.

Test B

Circle T or F for True or False as appropriate.

1. It is an easy task for government policy-makers to influence the state of business confidence.   **T F**

2. The expenditure schedule refers to a relationship between total spending and the level of output (and income).   **T F**

3. The equilibrium level of GNP always equals the full-employment level of GNP.   **T F**

4. If total spending exceeds national output, the resulting decrease in inventories will lead firms to reduce the level of output and production.   **T F**

5. The intersection of the expenditure schedule and the 45° line help to determine one point on the aggregate-demand curve.   **T F**

6. The vertical difference between the 45° line and the aggregate-demand curve is called the inflationary gap.   **T F**

7. The term *recessionary gap* refers to a situation in which the equilibrium level of GNP is less than the full-employment level of GNP.   **T F**

8. Because consumers usually invest their savings at financial institutions, there can be no difference between desired savings and desired investment for the economy.   **T F**

9. An increase in the level of prices, through its impact on consumption spending, will lead to a movement along the expenditure schedule.   **T F**

10. The aggregate-demand curve refers to a relationship between the equilibrium level of income and the price level.   **T F**

Appendix A: The Saving and Investment Approach

LEARNING OBJECTIVE

The exercise below is intended to illustrate the basic content of Appendix A to Chapter 8, which is: *The condition for the equilibrium level of income can be stated as C + I = Y or it can be stated as S = I. Both statements lead to the same result.*

IMPORTANT TERMS AND CONCEPTS

S = I
Saving schedule
Investment schedule
Induced investment

BASIC EXERCISE

Table 8-3 reproduces the data in Table 8-1 on income, consumption spending, and investment spending.

1. Using the definition of saving, $S = Y - C$, determine the level of consumer saving at each level of income.

TABLE 8-3
(ALL FIGURES ARE IN
BILLIONS OF CONSTANT DOLLARS;
PRICE LEVEL = 100)

National Income	Consumer Spending	Investment Spending	Consumer Saving
260	260	30	_____
280	270	30	_____
300	280	30	_____
320	290	30	_____
340	300	30	_____

2. At what level of income is investment spending equal to consumer saving? How does this level of income compare with the equilibrium level of income you computed in Question d of the first Basic Exercise to this chapter?

3. If income is below the equilibrium level of income, which is greater, investment spending or consumer saving? Why is this not an equilibrium? What forces are set in motion to increase the level of income toward the equilibrium level of income? (You might answer this question in terms of changes in business inventories or by using the circular flow diagram.)

4. Change the fourth word in question 3 from "below" to "above" and give new answers to the questions. Why will the level of income fall?

5. Construct a new version of Table 8-3 in which investment spending is $40 billion. Find the new equilibrium level of income where saving equals investment. How does your answer compare with your answer to Question h of the first Basic Exercise to the chapter?

6. In addition to working the same numerical example in different ways, we can also show the equivalence of the two conditions for the equilibrium level of income by using a little high-school algebra. We know that in equilibrium

$$C + I = Y.$$

We also know that at each level of income consumers either spend or save their income; that is, $Y = C + S$ at every level of income. We can thus

substitute $C + S$ for Y in our equilibrium condition and get

$$C + I = C + S.$$

Subtracting C from both sides of this expression yields our alternative formulation of the equilibrium condition, or

$$\underline{\hspace{4cm}} = \underline{\hspace{4cm}}.$$

Appendix B:
The Simple Algebra
of Income Determination

BASIC EXERCISES

These exercises are meant to illustrate the material in Appendix B to Chapter 8. If we are willing to use algebra we can use equations rather than graphs or tables to determine the equilibrium level of output. If we have done all our work accurately, we should get the same answer regardless of whether we use graphs, tables, or algebra.

1. Determine the equilibrium level of income if the consumption function is given by

$$C = 130 + 0.5Y$$

and investment expenditures are $30 billion regardless of the level of income. Is your answer here the same as for Question d of the first Basic Exercise to this chapter? It should be.

2. Determine the equilibrium level of income, given the same consumption function as in Exercise 1 but the higher level of investment expenditure of $40 billion. Is your answer here the same as for Question h of the first Basic Exercise to this chapter? It should be.

3. The equilibrium level of income will be affected by shifts in the consumption function as well as by changes in investment spending. Determine the equilibrium level of income if, following a decrease in the level of prices, the consumption function is

$$C = 140 + 0.5Y$$

and investment spending is $30 billion.

Changes on the Demand Side: Multiplier Analysis

9

LEARNING OBJECTIVES

After completing the material in this chapter you should be able to:

- define, understand, and use correctly the terms and concepts listed below.
- explain why any autonomous increases in expenditures will have a multiplier effect on GNP.
- explain the difference between an autonomous and an induced increase in consumption expenditures.
- calculate the value of the multiplier in specific examples.
- explain how and why the value of the multiplier would change if the marginal propensity to consume changed.

- explain why the multiplier, as traditionally calculated, is oversimplified.
- explain why an increase in savings may be good for an individual but bad for the economy as a whole.
- describe how an autonomous increase in spending leads to a shift in the aggregate-demand curve.

IMPORTANT TERMS AND CONCEPTS

The multiplier
Induced increase in consumption
Autonomous increase in consumption
Paradox of thrift

CHAPTER REVIEW

The main topic of this chapter is the *multiplier*. It is a fundamental concept in economics, which is why a whole chapter is devoted to explaining how it works. The multiplier has already played an important but unheralded role in Chapter 8, so those of you who paid close attention to the subject matter of Chapter 8 should have an easier time grasping the concept of multiplier analysis presented here.

The basic idea of the multiplier is that an autonomous increase in spending by one sector of the economy will

(1) increase the equilibrium level of income by (*more than/the same as/less than*) the original increase in spending. The equilibrium level of GNP rises by a multiple of the original increase in spending, which is where the term "multiplier" comes from. The basic reason for this multiplier result is relatively simple: Increased spending by one sector of the economy means increased sales receipts for other sectors of the economy. Higher sales receipts will show up in bigger paycheques, or profits, or both; in short, higher income for some people. These higher incomes will then induce more consumer spending, which in turn will result in still higher incomes and more consumption spending by others, and so on and so on.

You may be wondering at this point whether the multiplier is finite or whether income will increase without limit. Another way of looking at this question is to ask what determines the value of the multiplier. There are several alternative, but equally good, ways of answering this question. The discussion in the text approaches the question by summing the increments to spending and income that follow from the original autonomous change in spending. When increments to spending depend upon the marginal propensity to consume the oversimplified multiplier

(2) expression is 1/(1 - _____).

Here is an alternative derivation of the same result. We know that in equilibrium, national output, or income, will equal total spending in symbols,

$$Y = C + I.$$

Now assume that there is an autonomous increase in investment spending that induces subsequent increases in consumption spending. At the new equilibrium we know that the change in the equilibrium level of national output will have to be equal to the change in total spending. The change in total spending has two parts: One is the autonomous change in investment spending and the other is the induced change in consumption spending. In words, we know that

(3)

Let us use some symbols to say the same things. Let ΔY represent the change in the equilibrium level of income and ΔI represent the autonomous change in investment spending. What about the induced change in consumption spending? The discussion in Chapter 7 told us that consumption spending will change as

(4) _____ changes. Further, with the use of the concept of the marginal propensity to consume, we can represent the change in consumption spending as the product of the change in income times the

_____ . In symbols we could represent the induced change in consumption spending as $\Delta Y \times$ MPC. If we substitute all these symbols for the words above, we see that

$$\Delta Y = \Delta I + (\Delta Y \times \text{MPC}).$$

We can now solve this equation for the change in income by moving all terms in ΔY to the left-hand side of the equation:

$$\Delta Y - (\Delta Y \times \text{MPC}) = \Delta I.$$

If we factor out the ΔY we can rewrite the expression as

$$\Delta Y (1 - \text{MPC}) = \Delta I.$$

We can now solve for ΔY by dividing both sides of the equation by (1 - MPC).

$$\Delta I = \left(\frac{1}{1 - \text{MPC}} \right)$$

Switching back to words, we find that

$$\begin{pmatrix} \text{Change in} \\ \text{equilibrium} \\ \text{level of} \\ \text{income} \end{pmatrix} = \text{Multiplier} \times \begin{pmatrix} \text{Autonomous} \\ \text{change in} \\ \text{investment} \\ \text{spending} \end{pmatrix}$$

(5)   The multiplier expression we just derived is the same as the one in Chapter 9 of the text and is subject to the same limitations. That is, this expression is oversimplified. There are five important reasons why an actual multiplier in the real world will be (*smaller/larger*) than our formula. These reasons are related to the effects of

_____ , _____ , _____ , _____ and

_____ .

(6)   The simplified multiplier expression we derived above comes from manipulating just the expenditure schedule in the 45° line diagram. As such, this expression assumes that prices (*do/do not*) change. In Chapter 8 we saw that the income-expenditure diagram is only a building block on the way to the aggregate-demand curve. (Remember from Chapter 5 that even the aggregate-demand curve is only part of the story. For a complete analysis we need

both the aggregate-demand and the aggregate-_____ curves.) Thus, to complete our analysis on the demand side, we need to see how our multiplier analysis affects the aggregate-demand curve. The multiplier analysis we have done by using the income-expenditure diagram shows us that if prices are constant, the equilibrium level of income will increase following an increase in (*autonomous/induced*) spending. This result is true for any price level and implies that an autonomous increase in spending leads to a shift in the aggregate-demand curve. In fact, it leads to a (*horizontal/vertical*) shift in the aggregate-demand curve. The magnitude of the shift can be computed with the help of the multiplier, as shown in Figure 9-4 of the text and Figure 10-4 of the study guide.

BASIC EXERCISES

These exercises are designed to illustrate the concepts of the multiplier and the paradox of thrift.

1. The Multiplier
a. Using the data in Table 9-1, fill in the values for total spending and then find the equilibrium level of income.
b. Table 9-2 has a similar set of data except that investment spending has risen by $10 billion. Find the equilibrium level of income after the rise in investment spending.
c. What is the change in the equilibrium level of income following the increase in investment

spending? _____
d. What is the value of the multiplier for this increase in autonomous investment spending?

Multiplier _____
(Remember that the multiplier is defined as the

ratio of the change in the _____

_____ of _____ divided

by the change in _____

_____ that produced the change in income.)
e. Now let us verify that the value of the multiplier that you found in Question d is the same as the simplified formula 1/(1 - MPC). To do this we will first need to calculate the MPC. Write the value of the MPC here:

_____ (If you do not remember how to calculate the MPC, review the material in Chapter 7 of the textbook and in this study guide.)
f. Now calculate the value of the multiplier from the oversimplified formula 1/(1 - MPC). Write your

answer here: _____ . (Check to see that it agrees with your answer to Question d.)

2. The Paradox of Thrift
Assume that in the aggregate all consumers suddenly decided to save $5 billion more than they have been saving at every level of income. If people want to save more it means they must consume

_____ . This change is an (*autonomous/induced*) change in savings and consumption. Table 9-3 shows the relevant numbers for consumption and investment following the increased desire to save. Notice that the numbers for consumption spending in Table 9-3 are all $5 billion less than the numbers in Table 9-2, while investment spending is the same.

a. Using the data in Table 9-3, find the new equilibrium level of income.

TABLE 9-1

National Income (billions of dollars)	Consumption Spending (billions of dollars)	Investment Spending (billions of dollars)	Total Spending $C + I$ (billions of dollars)
360	310	60	_____
380	325	60	_____
400	340	60	_____
420	355	60	_____
440	370	60	_____

TABLE 9-2

National Income (billions of dollars)	Consumption Spending (billions of dollars)	Investment Spending (billions of dollars)	Total Spending $C + I$ (billions of dollars)
360	310	70	_____
380	325	70	_____
400	340	70	_____
420	355	70	_____
440	370	70	_____

TABLE 9-3

National Income (billions of dollars)	Consumption Spending (billions of dollars)	Investment Spending (billions of dollars)	Total Spending $C + I$ (billions of dollars)
360	305	70	_____
380	320	70	_____
400	335	70	_____
420	350	70	_____
440	365	70	_____

b. What is the change in the equilibrium level of income compared with Table 9-2?

_____

c. At this point we can conclude that if consumer saving shows an autonomous increase and investment spending is unchanged, then the equilibrium level of income will (*rise/fall*).

d. By how much does income change in response to this autonomous change in saving and consumption? We can use our multiplier analysis to find the answer. The equilibrium level of

income changed by $ _____ billion in response to an autonomous decrease in consumption spending of $5 billion; thus the multiplier for this change is $_____.

e. How does this multiplier compare with the multiplier you computed for the increase in investment spending?

f. Why is the specific numerical value you have calculated likely to be an overstatement of multiplier response of a real economy to a change in either investment spending or saving?

SELF-TESTS FOR UNDERSTANDING

Test A

Circle the correct answer.

1. The multiplier is defined as the ratio of the change in
   a. autonomous spending divided by the change in consumption expenditures.
   b. the equilibrium level of income divided by the increase in consumption spending.
   c. the equilibrium level of income divided by the change in autonomous spending that produced the change in income.
   d. consumption spending divided by the change in autonomous spending.

2. Which of the following would not imply the beginning of the multiplier process?
   a. An autonomous increase in consumption spending.
   b. An induced increase in consumption spending.
   c. An autonomous increase in investment spending.

3. If the marginal propensity to consume were 0.6 and prices did not change, the multiplier would be

   a. $\dfrac{1}{0.6} = 1.67$.

   b. 0.6

   c. $\dfrac{1}{1 - 0.6} = 2.5$.

   d. $\dfrac{1}{1 + 0.6} = 0.63$

4. If the marginal propensity to consumer were 0.7 instead of 0.6, the textbook multiplier would be
   a. higher than in Question 3.
   b. lower than in Question 3.
   c. the same as in Question 3.

5. Real-world multipliers will be less than textbook multipliers because of effects related to all but which one of the following?
   a. Income taxation.
   b. Accounting practices.
   c. Inflation.
   d. Exchange rates.

6. The textbook multiplier would be largest if the marginal propensity to consume were
   a. 0.73
   b. 0.45
   c. 0.89
   d. 0.67

7. When compared with changes in investment spending, the multiplier associated with autonomous changes in consumption spending will be
   a. larger.
   b. smaller.
   c. about the same.

8. An autonomous increase in savings
   a. is necessarily accompanied by an increase in consumption spending.
   b. will shift the expenditure schedule down.
   c. will not affect the level of income as neither the aggregate-demand nor the aggregate-supply curve will shift.
   d. shifts the aggregate-demand curve up.

9. The multiplier is useful in calculating
   a. the slope of the consumption function.
   b. the horizontal shift in the aggregate-demand curve following an increase in autonomous spending.
   c. the slope of the expenditure curve.
   d. the shift of the consumption function following an increase in autonomous spending.

10. When compared with increases in autonomous spending, decreases in autonomous spending are likely to have
    a. greater effects on both prices and real output.
    b. greater effects on prices and smaller effects on real output.
    c. smaller effects on prices and greater effects on real output.
    d. smaller effects on both prices and real output.

Test B

Circle T or F for True or False as appropriate.

1. The multiplier is defined as the ratio of a change in autonomous spending divided by the resulting change in the equilibrium level of income.　　**T F**

2. Multiplier responses mean that the equilibrium level of national income is likely to change by less than any change in autonomous spending.　　**T F**

3. Multiplier increases illustrated on the income-expenditure diagram are based on the assumption that prices do not change.　　**T F**

4. In the actual world, multiplier responses to changes in autonomous spending are likely to be less than that suggested by the textbook formula $1/(1 - MPC)$.　　**T F**

5. If income increases because of an autonomous increase in investment spending, the resulting increase in consumption spending is called an autonomous increase.　　**T F**

6. An autonomous increase in savings by all

consumers will immediately lead to a higher level of real GNP, as resources are freed for higher levels of investment.   **T F**

7. The multiplier for autonomous increases in investment spending is always greater than the multiplier for autonomous increases in consumption spending.   **T F**

8. If the marginal propensity to consume suddenly became larger, the multiplier would become bigger.   **T F**

9. The multiplier works for increases in autonomous spending, but because of price and wage rigidities the multiplier is irrelevant when we examine decreases in autonomous spending.   **T F**

10. The impact of a shift in the aggregate-demand curve on prices and real output will depend upon the slope of the aggregate-supply curve.   **T F**

Supply-Side Equilibrium: Unemployment *and* Inflation?

10

LEARNING OBJECTIVES

After completing the material in this chapter you should be able to:

- define, understand, and use correctly the terms and concepts listed below.
- describe how the aggregate-supply curve is derived from an analysis of business costs and why it slopes upward.
- distinguish between factors that will lead to a movement along or a shift in the aggregate-supply curve.
- use a graph depicting both the aggregate-demand curve and the aggregate-supply curve to determine the price level and the final equilibrium level of real GNP.
- use the same graph as above to analyse how factors that shift either the aggregate-demand curve or the aggregate-supply curve will affect the equilibrium level of prices and output.

- use the same graph to explain what kinds of shifts in the aggregate-demand curve and the aggregate-supply curve can give rise to a period of stagflation.
- explain why an inflationary gap is apt to self-destruct.
- explain why a recessionary gap is not apt to self-destruct.

IMPORTANT TERMS AND CONCEPTS

Aggregate-supply curve
Productivity
Equilibrium of real GNP and the price level
Inflationary gap
Self-correcting mechanism
Stagflation
Recessionary gap
Inflation and the multiplier

CHAPTER REVIEW

In Chapter 4 we learned that for individual commodities equilibrium price and quantity are determined by the intersection of the relevant demand and supply curves. The same logic holds when analysing the economy as a whole. The level of prices and aggregate output is determined by the intersection of the aggregate-demand and aggregate-supply curves. In Chapter 8 we saw how the aggregate-demand curve could be derived from the spending decisions of consumers and businesses. In this chapter we will derive the aggregate-supply curve and use both curves to see how the price level and aggregate output are determined.

The aggregate-supply curve is a schedule showing for each possible price level the total quantity of goods and services that all businesses are willing to supply. While a full discussion of supply decisions of individual business firms can be found in Chapter 23, you should note that the same logic applies here and there: Businesses will adjust supply in pursuit of profits.

If prices rise while production costs per unit of output remain unchanged, we expect firms to

(1) (*increase/decrease*) the quantity of output supplied. In fact, if prices stayed higher and production costs did not increase at all, there would be no limit to the increase in profits firms could derive from increases in output. However, production costs will eventually rise as firms try to expand output, putting a limit on the profitable increase in output. This increase in output induced by an increase in prices is a (*movement along/shift in*) the aggregate-supply curve. Any change in production costs in the face of an unchanged price level—for example, an increase in energy prices imposed by a foreign supplier—will also affect profits and will lead to an adjustment in the quantity of goods and services that businesses are willing to supply. This time, however, the change in supply is a

_____ _____ the aggregate-supply curve.

The increase in production costs associated with higher levels of output, the very increases that put a limit on the profitable increase in supply and helped to define the aggregate-supply curve, are likely to be especially severe near full-employment levels of output and are an important reason why the slope of the aggregate-supply curve

(2) depends upon the level of resource utilization. Near full employment, the aggregate-supply curve is (*steeper/flatter*).

Now, having derived both the aggregate-demand curve and the aggregate-supply curve, we are in a position to use them to determine the final equilibrium level of prices and aggregate output, or GNP. See for example, Figure 10-1, where the equilibrium price level of 100 and the equilibrium level of GNP of $400 billion are given by the

(3) (*intersection/slope*) of the aggregate-demand and aggregate-supply curves. A higher price level, say, 110, implies (1) a lower quantity of aggregate demand as consumers respond to the loss of purchasing power of their money assets and (2) a larger quantity of aggregate supply as firms respond to higher prices. Clearly, more supply and less demand cannot be a point of equilibrium, since firms would experience continual (*increases/decreases*) in inventories. The result is likely to be price reductions to stimulate sales and a movement toward equilibrium. Similarly, a lower price level, such as 90, would induce analogous, although opposite, reactions.

Nothing in the analysis so far guarantees that the intersection of the aggregate-demand and aggregate-supply curves will be at the level of output corresponding to full employment of labour. If the final equilibrium level of output is different from the full-employment level of output, the result is either a recessionary gap or an inflationary gap.

(4) Consider Figure 10-2, which shows a(n) _____ gap. The gap (*is/is not*) likely to self-destruct as continuing increases in costs lead to shifts in the aggregate-supply curve. As unemployment falls below frictional levels and material inputs become scarce, increased production costs will shift the aggregate-supply curve (*up/down*) leading to a (*movement along/shift in*) the aggregate-demand curve, (*higher/lower*) prices, (*higher/lower*) output, and the elimination of the inflationary gap. Note that the simultaneous increase in prices and wages does not prove that increasing wages cause inflation. Both are best seen as a symptom of the inflationary gap.

The rigidity of wages and other input prices in the face of unemployment means that a recessionary gap is

(5) (*more/less*) likely to self-destruct than an inflationary gap.

Stagflation refers to the simultaneous occurrence of increasing prices and increasing unemployment. The previous analysis suggests that stagflation is a natural result of the self-destruction of a(n)

(6) (*inflationary/recessionary*) gap. Stagflation can also occur as a result of adverse shifts in the aggregate-

_____ curve.

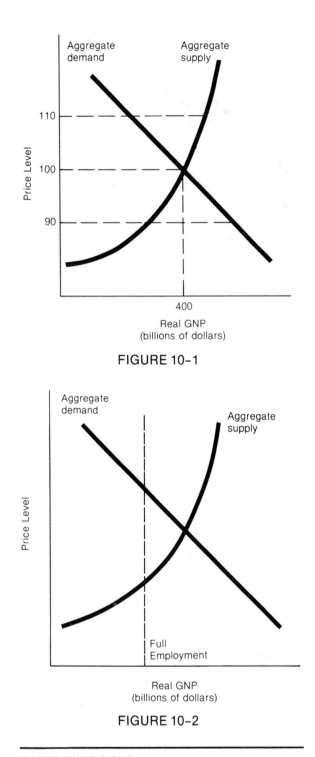

110

100

90

Price Level

Aggregate
demand

Aggregate
supply

400

Real GNP
(billions of dollars)

FIGURE 10-1

Aggregate
demand

Aggregate
supply

Price Level

Full
Employment

Real GNP
(billions of dollars)

FIGURE 10-2

BASIC EXERCISES

1. This exercise reviews the derivation of the aggregate-demand curve and then uses both the aggregate-demand and aggregate-supply curves to determine the equilibrium level of income. Figure 10-3 shows an income-expenditure diagram in the

top half of a price-level-aggregate-output diagram in the bottom half. The middle expenditure schedule in the top half duplicates the original situation described in Basic Exercise 1 of Chapter 9 and assumes that the price level associated with the expenditure schedule is 100. The dashed line extending into the bottom figure shows how this output level, together with its associated price level, can be plotted in the lower diagram. It is one point on the aggregate-demand curve.

a. A decrease in the price level to 90 would, because of its impact on the purchasing power of consumer money assets, increase real consumption expenditures. The shift in the consumption function shifts the expenditure schedule up. The new expenditure schedule, for a price level of 90, is shown in the top half of Figure 10-3. What is the equilibrium level of income in the income-expenditure diagram for a price level of 90?

b. Plot the combination of prices and output from question a in the lower diagram. This is a second point on the aggregate-demand curve.

c. A price level of 110 would depress consumer spending, shifting both the consumption function and the expenditure schedule. Use the expenditure schedule for a price level of 110 to plot a third point on the aggregate-demand curve.

d. Draw the aggregate-demand curve by connecting the three points now plotted in the lower diagram.

e. Using the aggregate-demand curve you have just derived and the aggregate-supply curve that is already drawn, what is the equilibrium level of prices and real GNP?

f. If the level of full-employment output were $400 billion, would there be an inflationary gap or recessionary gap? How, if at all, might such a gap self-destruct and where would the price level and real GNP end up?

g. If the level of full-employment output were $410 billion, would there be an inflationary gap or recessionary gap? How, if at all, might such a gap self-destruct and where would the price level and real GNP end up?

h. If the level of full-employment output were $420 billion, would there be an inflationary or recessionary gap? How, if at all, might such a gap self-destruct and where would the price level and real GNP end up?

2. This exercise reviews the impact of higher prices on the simple multiplier derived in Chapter 9. Consider Figure 10-4. The heavy lines show an initial expenditure schedule and the associated aggregate-demand curve. The initial equilibrium is at a level of income Y*, and price level P*. The dashed expenditure schedule follows an increase in

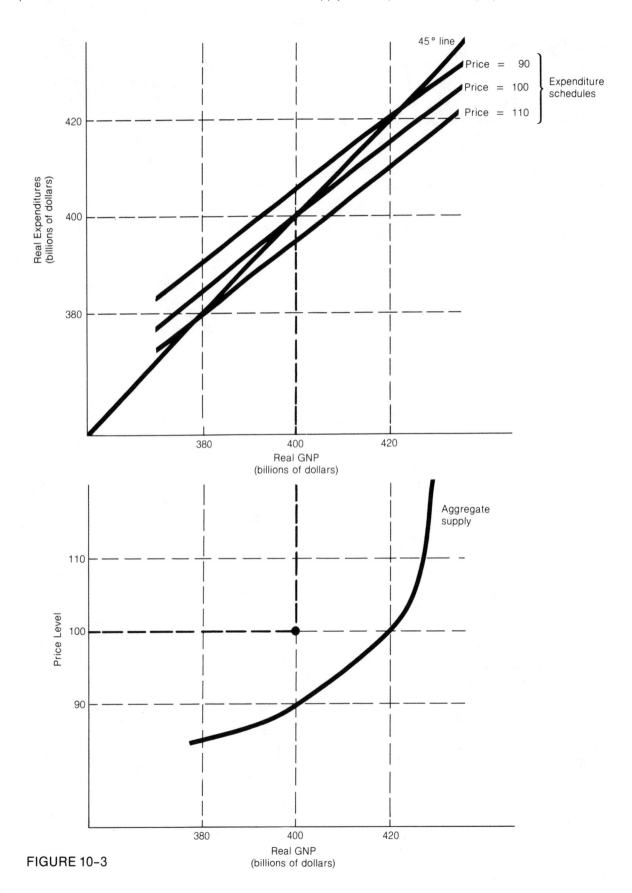

FIGURE 10-3

investment spending. Note that the shift in the expenditure schedule leads to a shift in the aggregate-demand curve. In fact, the initial new equilibrium on the income-expenditure diagram, Y_1, is equal to the (*horizontal*/*vertical*) shift of the aggregate-demand curve in the lower half of the diagram.

a. Is the combination Y_1, P^* the final equilibrium?

b. If Y_1, P^* is not the final equilibrium, describe what

will happen during the transition to the final equilibrium. If the aggregate-demand curve shifts, draw a new one. If the aggregate-supply curve shifts, draw a new one. If the expenditure schedule shifts, draw a new one.

3. In Table 10-1, fill in the blanks as indicated to analyse the response to each change. In the first two columns use S or M for "shift in" or "movement along." In the last two columns use + or −.

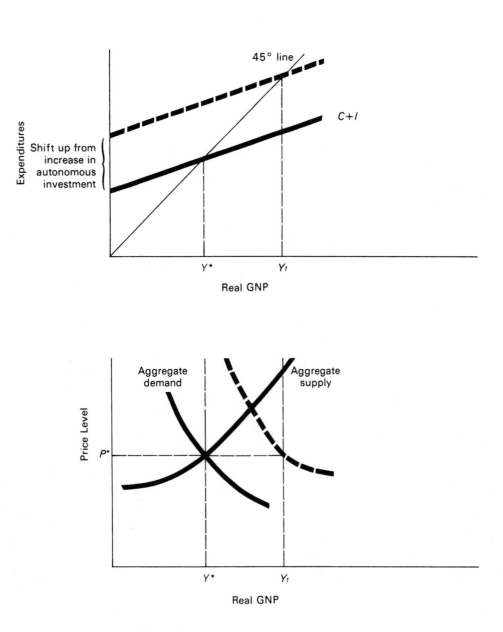

FIGURE 10-4

TABLE 10-1

	Aggegate-demand curve	Aggregate-supply curve	Equilibrium real GNP	Price level
A reduction in business investment spending				
An increase in the price of many basic commodities used as inputs in the production of final goods and services				
An increase in labour productivity due to a technological breakthrough				
An upward shift in the consumption function due to a stock-market boom				

SELF-TESTS FOR UNDERSTANDING

Test A

Circle the correct answer.

1. The aggregate-supply curve
   a. slopes down to the right.
   b. has a positive slope.
   c. slopes up to the left.
   d. has a negative slope.
2. The slope of the aggregate-supply curve reflects the fact that
   a. inflation increases the value of the oversimplified multiplier.
   b. the costs of important inputs, such as labour, are relatively fixed in the short run.
   c. the marginal propensity to consume is less than 1.0.
   d. recessionary gaps take a long time to self-destruct.
3. The aggregate-supply curve will shift following changes in all but which of the following?
   a. The price level.
   b. Wage rates.
   c. Technology and productivity.
   d. Available supplies of factories and machines.
4. The equilibrium price level and the equilibrium level of real GNP
   a. are determined by the intersection of the aggregate-demand and aggregate-supply curves.
   b. will always occur at full employment.
   c. can be found in the income–expenditure diagram.
   d. do not change unless the aggregate-demand curve shifts.
5. A change in the equilibrium price level
   a. will lead to a shift in the aggregate-supply curve.
   b. will lead to a shift in the aggregate-demand curve.
   c. reflects a shift in the aggregate-demand curve and/or aggregate supply curve.
   d. will always lead to stagflation.
6. Near full employment, the slope of the aggregate-supply curve is likely to
   a. become negative.
   b. drop to zero.
   c. decrease, but still remain positive.
   d. increase.
7. From an initial position of full employment, which one of the following will not lead to a recessionary gap?
   a. A shift in the aggregate-supply curve in response to an increase in energy prices.
   b. A reduction in investment spending due to an increase in business taxes.
   c. A reduction in consumer spending due to an adverse shift in consumer expectations.
   d. A shift in the aggregate-supply curve in response to a dramatic technological breakthrough that reduces production costs.
8. Which of the following is not associated with the elimination of an inflationary gap?

a. Rising prices.
b. Falling output.
c. Increased employment.
d. Increased unemployment.

9. The economy's self-correcting mechanisms are likely to work better when
   a. there is an inflationary gap.
   b. there is a recessionary gap.
   c. there is a federal government deficit.
   d. the multiplier is working.

10. Prices rise following an increase in autonomous spending whenever the
    a. aggregate-demand curve shifts.
    b. multiplier is greater than 1.0.
    c. aggregate-demand curve has a negative slope.
    d. aggregate-supply curve is not horizontal.

Test B

Circle T or F for True or False as appropriate.

1. The aggregate-supply curve shows for each possible price the total quantity of goods and services that the nation's businesses are willing to supply. **T F**

2. The aggregate-supply curve slopes upward because businesses will expand output as long as higher prices make expansion profitable. **T F**

3. The aggregate-supply curve is likely to be steeper at low levels of unemployment. **T F**

4. The impact of unemployment on wages and prices means that recessionary gaps are likely to quickly self-destruct. **T F**

5. If the aggregate-supply curve shifts to the right, the result will be stagflation. **T F**

6. A change in investment spending due to a shift in business confidence will lead to an immediate shift in the aggregate-supply curve. **T F**

7. The final equilibrium level of prices and aggregate output is determined by the slope of the aggregate-supply curve. **T F**

8. A period of excessive aggregate demand is likely to be followed by a period of stagflation as the inflationary gap self-destructs. **T F**

9. During the elimination of an inflationary gap, the real cause of inflation is excessive wage demands on the part of labour. **T F**

10. Analysis of the aggregate-supply curve shows that the multiplier derived from the income–expenditure diagram will understate the final change in output. **T F**

SUPPLEMENTARY EXERCISE

Given the following equations:

$C = 850 + .75Y - 5P$
$I = 650$
$C + I = Y$ (45° line)
$Y = 2200 + 20P$ (aggregate-supply curve)
C = real consumption expenditures
I = real investment
Y = real GNP
P = price level

1. Use the consumption function and the level of investment spending to determine an expression for the expenditure schedule. (Note that this expression will involve the variable P.)
2. Use the expenditure schedule and the equation for the 45° line to determine an expression for the aggregate-demand curve.
3. Now use both the aggregate-demand curve and the aggregate-supply curve to determine the equilibrium level of prices and GNP.
4. Resolve the system on the assumption that investment expenditures decrease to $600 billion.

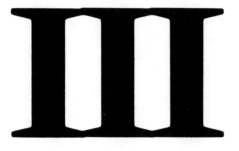

III

Fiscal, Monetary, and Exchange-Rate Policy

Fiscal Policy and Supply-Side Economics

LEARNING OBJECTIVES

After completing the material in this chapter you should be able to:

- define, understand, and use correctly the terms and concepts listed below.
- describe the process by which an increase in government or foreign purchases of goods and services will increase both prices and output.
- describe the process by which a reduction in income taxes will increase both prices and output.
- explain why taxes that depend upon income and why imports reduce the value of the multiplier below the oversimplified expression in Chapter 9.
- explain why the multiplier for a change in income taxes will be less than the multiplier for a change in government purchases of goods and services.
- explain why economists treat government transfer payments like taxes, not like government purchases of goods and services.
- explain why active stabilization policy need not imply that the size of government must get bigger and bigger.
- use the aggregate-demand and aggregate-supply diagram to show how supply-side tax cuts hope to reduce the impact on prices associated with the elimination of a recessionary gap.
- describe the kernel of truth in supply-side economics.
- discuss the reservations that most economists have in regard to supply-side economics.

IMPORTANT TERMS AND CONCEPTS

Fiscal policy
Government purchases of goods and services (G)
Effect of income taxes on the multiplier
Net exports (X — IM)
Tariffs
Government transfer payments
Effect of income taxes and imports on the multiplier
Supply-side tax cuts
Depreciation allowances
Capital gains and losses
Productivity of labour

CHAPTER REVIEW

This chapter reviews the models of income determination that were introduced in Chapters 8, 9, and 10, but this time for an economy that includes both a government that taxes and spends, and a foreign sector. With this expanded model we can then consider government fiscal policy and the impact of foreign tariffs. The only trick is to understand how government spending, taxes, exports and imports affect the curves we have already derived; that is, how they shift the expenditure schedule, the aggregate-demand curve, and the aggregate-supply curve. After this, the analysis proceeds exactly as before: For a given price level, the equilibrium level of income is determined by the

(1) intersection of the (*consumption/expenditure*) schedule and the 45° line. A change in prices will affect consumption spending and thus shift the expenditure schedule, resulting in a different equilibrium level of income. The different price levels and their associated equilibrium levels of income can be combined to form the aggregate-

_____ curve. This curve together with the aggregate- _____ curve will help determine both income and prices, just as before. A change in the government's fiscal policy will shift one or more of the curves and lead to new equilibrium values for income and prices.

There are three important ways government actions influence total spending in the economy:

1. The government *purchases goods and services.*
2. The government *collects taxes,* thereby reducing the spending power of households and firms.
3. The government gives *transfer payments* to some individuals, thereby increasing their purchasing power.

Government purchases of goods and services are a direct addition to total spending in the economy; that is,
(2) they shift the expenditure schedule (*up/down*) by the full amount of the purchases. Thus, if government spending

increased by $1, the expenditure schedule would shift up by $ _____ .
An increase in autonomous investment or export spending of $1 would also shift the expenditure schedule up by

$ _____ . Thus, we see that changes in government spending shift the expenditure schedule in exactly the same way as do autonomous changes in investment spending. Since the expenditure schedule shifts in an identical way, the oversimplified multiplier for a change in government spending is (*less than/equal to/greater than*) the oversimplified multiplier for a change in investment spending.

(3) Government taxes (*are/are not*) a direct component of spending on currently produced goods and services. Personal income taxes affect spending through their impact on disposable income. Following a decrease in personal income taxes, consumers' disposable income will be (*higher/lower*). The change in disposable income is likely to (*increase/decrease*) consumption expenditures. A reduction in personal income taxes of $1 will initially

(*increase/decrease*) disposable income by $ _____ , but consumption spending is likely to change by (*less/more*) than $1. The initial effect on consumption spending will be given by multiplying the change

in disposable income by the marginal _____ to consume, which is (*less/more*) than 1. Thus, changes in personal income taxes affect spending, but indirectly through their effect on consumption expenditures. A change in corporate income taxes will change corporate profits after taxes, and is likely to affect

_____ expenditures.

We saw earlier that a $1 increase in government purchases will shift the expenditure schedule up by $1. Now we see that a $1 reduction in personal income taxes will shift the expenditure schedule up, because of its effect on
(4) consumption; but the expenditure schedule will shift up by (*more/less*) than $1. Because the expenditure schedule shifts less in response to a change in personal income taxes as compared with an equal change in government purchases, the multiplier associated with changes in personal income taxes will be (*less/more*) than the multiplier associated with changes in government purchases.

The third important function of the government regarding total spending in the economy is the magnitude of government transfer payments. These payments, like taxes, are not a direct element of total spending on goods and services; and also like personal taxes, they affect total spending because they affect people's disposable

(5) _____ and thus their _____
expenditures.

An important feature of both taxes and transfer payments is that they vary with income. Typically taxes go

(6) (*up/down*) as aggregate income goes up, and transfer payments go _____ as aggregate income rises. These automatic, income-induced changes have an important implication for the value of our oversimplified multiplier. In Chapter 9 we saw that the multiplier process arises from the fact that any autonomous increase in spending means higher income for those who supply the newly demanded goods. These higher incomes will lead to more consumption spending, and so on, and so on. This process continues to take place, but now we see that each round of spending results in an increase in income *before* taxes. Because some of the increase in before-tax income goes to pay higher taxes, after-tax income (or disposable income) will increase by (*more/less*). Thus, each induced round of consumption spending, responding to the increase in disposable income, will be (*smaller/larger*) than before. Since imports vary directly with income, they have the same effect on the multiplier as income taxes.

(7) To summarize, in an economy with income taxes (and transfer payments and imports) that vary with income, each round in the multiplier process will be smaller than before, and thus the multiplier effect on income, from any increase in automatic spending, will also be (*smaller/larger*) than before. The impact of income taxes and imports on the multiplier are the second and third important reasons why Chapter 9's formula for the multiplier was oversimplified.

We have added government purchases of goods and services, taxes, and transfers to our model of income determination, as well as exports and imports. Taken together, these variables are an important determinant of the equilibrium level of income. Changes in these variables, just like the autonomous changes we considered in earlier chapters, will have multiplier effects on the equilibrium level of GNP. Thus deliberate manipulation of these variables may help the government achieve its desired objectives for the level of GNP. Manipulation of government fiscal policy variables for GNP objectives is an example of active *stabilization policy*. For example, if the government wants

(8) to increase GNP, it could decide to (*increase/decrease*) government purchases of goods and services,

_____ personal taxes, _____ corporate taxes, _____

transfer payments to individuals, or impose _____ on our imports.

One of the reasons it is so difficult to agree on fiscal policy is that there are so many choices, all of which could have the same impact on national income, but very different impacts on other issues, such as the size of the public versus private sector, the burden of taxes between individuals and corporations, the composition of output between consumption and investment spending, and the amount of income redistribution through transfers to low-income families.

One might believe that if we could decide upon the amounts of government purchases, taxes, and transfers, effective fiscal policy would be simply a technical matter of choosing the right numbers so that the expenditure schedule would intersect the 45° line, and the aggregate-demand curve would intersect the aggregate-supply curve at full employment. In actuality, uncertainties about (1) private components of aggregate demand, (2) the precise size of the multiplier, (3) exactly what level of GNP is associated with full employment, and (4) the slope of the aggregate-supply curve all mean that fiscal policy will continue to be subject to much political give and take. One hopes that appropriate economic analysis will contribute to a more informed level of debate.

Changes in government spending or tax rates shift the aggregate-demand curve directly, in the case of government purchases, and indirectly through impacts on private spending, in the case of taxes and transfer payments. Any shift in the aggregate-demand curve, including government shifts, affects both prices and

(9) output as we move along the aggregate- _____ curve. Thus, expansionary fiscal policy, designed to increase GNP, is also likely to (*increase/decrease*) prices. Supply-side policies attempt to minimize the impact on prices through changes in fiscal policy that shift the aggregate-supply curve at the same time that they shift the aggregate-demand curve. Recently there has been much attention given to supply-side tax cuts, including such measures as speeding up depreciation allowances, reducing taxes for increased research and development expenditures, reducing the corporate income tax, reducing taxes on income from savings, and reducing income taxes to encourage more work effort.

Most economists have a number of reservations about the exaggerated claims of ardent supporters of supply-side tax cuts: Specific effects will depend on exactly which taxes are reduced; increases in aggregate supply will take some time, while effects on aggregate demand will be much quicker; a realistic assessment suggests that by themselves supply-side tax cuts will have only a small effect on the rate of inflation; supply-side tax cuts are likely to lead to increased income inequality; and supply-side cuts are likely to lead to bigger, not smaller, government budget deficits. Do not let these serious objections to exaggerated claims blind you to the kernel of truth in supply-side economics: Marginal tax rates are important for decisions by individuals and firms. Reductions in marginal tax rates can improve economic incentives.

BASIC EXERCISE

This exercise is designed to show how changes in government purchases and taxes will have multiplier effects on the equilibrium level of income and how these multipliers can be used to help determine appropriate fiscal policy. To simplify the numerical calculations, the exercise focuses on the shift in the expenditure schedule holding prices constant. Table 11-1 shows data on national income, taxes, disposable income, consumption spending, investment spending, and government purchases of goods and services.

1. The equilibrium level of income is

   _____ . (To determine the equilibrium level of income you will first need to compute total spending at each level of income. Use column 7 to compute total spending.)

2. Assume now that government purchases decrease by $15 billion to $50 billion. Following the decrease in government purchases, the new equilibrium level

   of income is _____ . (Use column 8 to compute total spending after the decrease in government purchases.)

3. The multiplier for this decrease in government

   purchases is _____ . (This multiplier can be computed by dividing the change in the equilibrium level of income by the change in government purchases.)

4. Now consider a subsequent across-the-board reduction in income taxes of $25 billion. Table 11-2 shows the new relevant data for national income, taxes, disposable income, and consumption. The new equilibrium level of income

   after the reduction in taxes is

   _____ .

5. The multiplier for this change in taxes is

   _____ .

6. Why did it take a larger reduction in taxes to

restore GNP to its initial level following the reduction in government purchases?

7. Question 4 asked you to analyse the impact of a reduction in income taxes. Was this reduction in taxes self-financing? That is, was the increase in GNP stimulated by the reduction in taxes large enough so that on balance there was no decrease in government tax revenues? (Be sure to compare tax receipts at the equilibrium level of income in Table 11-2 with those at the equilibrium level in column 8 of Table 11-1).

8. Now let us use the multipliers computed in Question 3 and 5 to figure out what changes in government purchases or taxes would be necessary to raise the equilibrium level of income from its initial value given in Question 1 to its full-employment level of $375 billion. Assuming no change in tax rates, the necessary increase in government purchases is

   $ _____ billion. Assuming no change in government purchases, the necessary

   reduction in taxes is $ _____ billion. (You can answer this question by figuring out what appropriate change in government purchases or taxes, when multiplied by the relevant multiplier, will equal the desired change in income.)

9. What is the new equilibrium level of income if, from the initial equilibrium given in Question 1, investment expenditures rather than government purchases fall by $15 billion? (Now investment spending will be $55 billion while government purchases stay at $65 billion. Create a new version of Table 11-1 if necessary.) What can one say about multipliers for autonomous changes in public versus private purchases of goods and services?

10. (Optional) Use the data in Table 11-1 to compute the tax rate and the marginal propensity to consume. Use these numbers to calculate the multipliers for a change in government purchases and across-the-board taxes as described in the appendix to Chapter 11. Do these numbers agree

TABLE 11-1

(1) National Income (billions of dollars)	(2) Income Taxes (billions of dollars)	(3) Disposable Income (billions of dollars)	(4) Consumption Spending (billions of dollars)	(5) Investment Spending (billions of dollars)	(6) Government Purchases (billions of dollars)	(7) $C + I + G$	(8) $C + I + G$
300	50	250	195	70	65	_____	_____
330	55	275	210	70	65	_____	_____
360	60	300	225	70	65	_____	_____
390	65	325	240	70	65	_____	_____
420	70	350	255	70	65	_____	_____

TABLE 11–2

National Income (billions of dollars)	Income Taxes (billions of dollars)	Disposable Income (billions of dollars)	Consumption Spending (billions of dollars)	Investment Spending (billions of dollars)	Government Purchases (billions of dollars)	$C + I + G$
300	25	275	210	70	50	_____
330	30	300	225	70	50	_____
360	35	325	240	70	50	_____
390	40	350	255	70	50	_____
420	45	375	270	70	50	_____

with your answers to Questions 3 and 5?

11. (Optional) Construct a new version of Table 11–1 to analyse the effect on the multiplier of income taxes that do not vary with income. When constructing this table, assume that income taxes are $60 billion for all levels of income. (Note that this will mean different levels of disposable income and consumption spending. Use the data in the original Table 11–1 to figure out the consumption function; then use this function to compute the amount of consumption spending consistent with the new values for disposable income.) Now find the equilibrium level of income. Next assume that government purchases fall by $15 billion. Find the new equilibrium level of income and compute the multiplier for government purchases. How does this multiplier, computed for a case in which income taxes do not vary with income, compare with the multiplier you computed in Question 3? You might also use the data in the original Table 11–1 and from your new table to graph the two expenditure schedules for comparison.

SELF-TESTS FOR UNDERSTANDING

Test A

Circle the correct answer.

1. Fiscal policy involves decisions about all but which one of the following?
   a. Income tax rates.
   b. Eligibility rules for transfer payments.
   c. The money supply.
   d. Government purchases of goods and services.
2. A simultaneous reduction in income taxes and transfer payments of $15 billion will leave aggregate disposable income
   a. lower than before the change.
   b. unchanged.
   c. higher than before the change.

3. If the basic expenditure multiplier is 2.0 and if the government wishes to decrease the level of GNP by $8 billion, what decrease in government purchases of goods and services would do the job?
   a. $2 billion.
   b. $4 billion.
   c. $8 billion.
   d. $16 billion.
4. Instead of decreasing government expenditures, the same objectives, in terms of reducing GNP, could also be achieved by
   a. increasing both taxes and government transfer payments by equal amounts.
   b. reducing both taxes and government transfer payments by equal amounts.
   c. reducing taxes.
   d. reducing government transfer payments.
5. If the basic expenditure multiplier is 2.0, a reduction in personal income taxes of $25 billion is likely to
   a. increase GNP by $50 billion.
   b. increase GNP by more than $50 billion.
   c. increase GNP by less than $50 billion.
6. A 10 percent reduction in income tax rates would
   a. lower the value of the basic expenditure multiplier.
   b. raise the value of the basic expenditure multiplier.
   c. not affect the value of the basic expenditure multiplier.
7. An increase in tax rates will lead to all but which one of the following?
   a. A decrease in the multiplier.
   b. A movement along the aggregate-demand curve.
   c. A reduction in the equilibrium level of GNP.
   d. A shift of the expenditure schedule.
8. Assume that from a position of full employment the government wants to increase government purchases of goods and services by $15 billion for defense purposes. To avoid possible inflation, the government simultaneously decides to increase income taxes. In view of the different multipliers for changes in government purchases and taxes, the necessary change in taxes to keep the equilibrium level of income unchanged is

a. more than $15 billion.

b. less than $15 billion.

c. $15 billion.

9. Critics of supply-side tax cuts would agree with all but which one of the following?

a. Supply-side tax cuts are likely to increase inequality in the distribution of income.

b. Supply-side tax cuts will substantially reduce the rate of inflation.

c. Supply-side tax cuts are likely to mean bigger deficits for the federal government.

d. Supply-side tax cuts will have a larger initial impact on aggregate demand than on aggregate supply.

Test B

Circle T or F for True or False as appropriate.

1. An increase in income tax rates will increase the multiplier. **T F**

2. With income taxes, a $1 change in GNP will lead to a smaller change in consumption than would a $1 change in disposable income. **T F**

3. Income taxation reduces the value of the multiplier for changes in government purchases but does not affect the multiplier for changes in investment. **T F**

4. Since taxes are not a direct component of aggregate demand, changes in taxes do not have multiplier effects on income. **T F**

5. Changes in government purchases of goods and services and in government transfer payments to individuals are both changes in government spending and thus have the same multiplier effects on the equilibrium level of income. **T F**

6. Active stabilization policy implies that the government must get bigger and bigger. **T F**

7. Since income taxes and transfer payments to individuals have their first impact on the disposable income of consumers, they should have similar multipliers. **T F**

8. Only the aggregate-supply curve will shift following a supply-side tax cut that increases investment spending by firms. **T F**

9. There is general agreement among economists that supply-side tax cuts can increase output with little impact on prices. **T F**

10. The more a country is involved in foreign trade, the bigger is the multiplier. **T F**

SUPPLEMENTARY EXERCISE

1. The marginal propensity to consume is estimated to be 0.90. But the basic expenditure multiplier, applicable for any increase in autonomous spending, is estimated to be no more than 2, not 10 which comes from the oversimplified formula of Chapter 9, 1(1 − MPC). How can such a large marginal propensity to consume be consistent with such a small multiplier?

Appendix: Algebraic Treatment of Fiscal Policy and Aggregate Demand

BASIC EXERCISE

This exercise is meant to illustrate the material in the Appendix to Chapter 11. Just as in the Appendix to Chapter 8, we can use equations rather than graphs or tables to determine the equilibrium level of output and relevant multipliers. If we have done our work accurately, we should get the same answer regardless of whether we use graphs, tables, or algebra.

The following equations underlie the numerical example in the Basic Exercise:

$$C = 45 + 0.6DI$$
$$T = (1/6)Y$$
$$DI = Y - T$$
$$Y = C + I + G$$

1. What is the equilibrium level of income if investment spending is $75 billion and government purchases are $60 billion? Be sure that $C + I + G = Y$.

2. Assume that both across-the-board taxes and government purchases decline by $5 billion so that government purchases are $55 billion and the tax equation is

$$T = -5 + (1/6) \times Y.$$

(*I* is still $75.) Is the equilibrium level of income unchanged following this balanced reduction in the size of the government? Why?

Banking and the Creation of Money

12

CHAPTER REVIEW

Whether it is the root of all evil or not, there is no argument that money has an important influence on the way our economy operates. The right amount of money can help to keep employment up and prices stable. Too much money may lead to excessive inflation; too little money may lead to excessive unemployment. This chapter is an introduction to money. What is it? Where did it come from? What role do banks play in the creation of money? Chapter 13 discusses how the government now regulates the amount of money in the economy, and Chapters 14 and 15 discuss the influence of money on economic activity.

It is possible that a society could be organized without money. If everyone were self-sufficient there would, by definition, be no trading between individuals and no need for money. Even if people concentrated their productive activities on what they did best and traded among each other to get goods they did not produce themselves, they might still be able to get along without money. Direct trading of goods for goods, or goods for services, is called

(1) _____ . For it to be successful there must be a double coincidence of wants. As societies become more complicated and people become ever more specialized, it is clear that barter becomes increasingly (*harder/easier*).

When a society uses a standard object for exchanging goods and services, a seller will provide goods or services to a buyer and receive the standard object as payment. The efficiency of such a system should be obvious. You no longer have to find someone who not only has what you want but also wants what you have.

(2) Anyone who has what you want will now do. Economists would call the standard object _____ .
If the object serving as money has intrinsic value, such as gold or jewellery, it is called

(3) _____ money. Today money has little intrinsic value and is called _____ money. Such money has value because everyone believes that everyone else will exchange goods and services for it. The bedrock for this foundation of faith is that the government will stand behind the money and limit its production.

When it comes to measuring the quantity of money, exactly where one draws the line is a bit unclear. We have defined money as a standard object used for exchanging goods and services. On this count, the sum of all coins and currency outside of banks plus chequing accounts surely belongs in any measure of money. The measure

(4) that includes only these items is known as _____ . If one also includes savings accounts (because they can easily be transferred into chequing accounts), money-market deposit accounts, and money-

market mutual funds, one is measuring _____ .

Given the importance of bank deposits in all measures of money, it is important to understand *how the banking system can create money*. Banks subject to deposit reserve requirements must hold reserves that are at least as great as some stated percentage of their deposits. Reserves can be either money in a bank's vaults or money that the bank has on deposit at the Bank of Canada. We will learn more about the Bank of Canada in Chapter 13. The stated percentage is the required reserve fraction. Thus, only some of the money used to open or to add to a bank deposit must be kept by the bank to meet reserve requirements. The rest can be used to make loans in the search for more profits. This system is known as fractional reserve banking.

(5) The multiple creation of deposits is the counterpart to bank (*lending/borrowing*). Consider an individual bank that is subject to a 15 percent reserve requirement. Following a new deposit of $1 000, the maximum amount of the new deposit that this bank could lend out and still meet the reserve requirement is

$ _____ . As the proceeds of the loan are deposited in other banks, new deposits will be created. For the banking system as a whole, the maximum amount of loans it can make, and thus the maximum

amount of deposits it can create following an increase in bank reserves, is limited by the _____

_____ . The precise sequence of the multiple deposit creation is illustrated in the Basic Exercise for this chapter.

Mathematical formulas have been devised to determine the maximum increase in deposits that can be created by the banking system following an increase in bank reserves. In words,

(6)
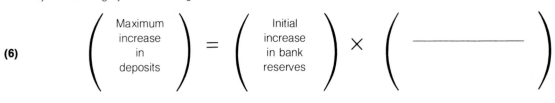

The increase in bank reserves may come from a deposit of cash. In this case, while deposits are up, cash outside banks is down, as some was deposited to start the process of multiple deposit creation. Thus, following a cash deposit, the maximum increase in the money supply will be (*more*/*less*) than the maximum increase in deposits.

The deposit-creation formula is oversimplified for two reasons:

1. The formula assumes that every bank makes as large a loan as possible; that is, each bank is assumed to hold

(7)   no _____ reserves. If banks do choose to hold such reserves, then the money-creation formula would be (*larger*/*smaller*).

2. The formula assumes that the proceeds of each loan will eventually be redeposited in the banking system. If some of the proceeds of a loan do not get redeposited, then the deposit-creation multiplier will be

_____ .

The discussion of the deposit-creation multiplier showed how deposits can be created following an increase in bank reserves. The emphasis was on how a change in reserves leads to a change in deposits. One should not be surprised to learn that *total* deposits in all banks are similarly limited by *total* reserves. The textbook discussion of a cash deposit at one bank implies an increase in total reserves of the banking system. Most increases in reserves at one bank are offset by a decrease in reserves at some other bank, with no increase in total reserves. Consider Fred, who takes money out of his account at Bank A. Fred uses the money to buy a home computer, and the dealer deposits this money in her bank, Bank B. At the same time reserves increase at Bank B, they decrease at Bank A. The process of multiple deposit creation initiated at Bank B is offset by a process of multiple deposit

(8)   _____ starting with Bank A, and the net effect is (*some*/*no*) increase in deposits. The important factor for total deposits is total reserves available to the banking system. We will learn in Chapter 13 how the Bank of Canada is able to influence total reserves available to the banking system.

BASIC EXERCISE

This exercise is designed to help you understand the multiple creation of bank deposits by working through a specific simplified example.

1. Column 1 of Table 12-1 is partly filled in for you to show the *changes* in the balance sheet of Bank A immediately following Janet's cash deposit of $1000. At this point, bank deposits have increased by

   _____ and the stock of money in the economy—that is, bank deposits plus currency outside banks—is (*higher*/*lower*/*unchanged*).

Assuming the required reserve fraction is 25 percent, fill in the last two rows of column 1, showing the initial increase in required and excess reserves.

2. Assume that Bank A responds to these changes by making as large a loan as it can to Earl, given the required reserve ratio. Now fill in column 2 to represent the changes in Bank A's balance sheet after the loan has been made and Earl has taken the proceeds of the loan in cash.

3. Earl uses the money from the loan to buy a used car and the used-car dealer deposits this cash in

TABLE 12-1

	(1) Bank A	(2) Bank A	(3) Bank B	(4) Bank B	(5) Bank C
Assets					
Reserves	$1000	_____	_____	_____	_____
Loans	0	_____	_____	_____	_____
Liabilities					
Deposits	1000	_____	_____	_____	_____
Addendum					
Required reserves	_____	_____	_____	_____	_____
Excess reserves	_____	_____	_____	_____	_____

Note: Required reserve fraction is 25 percent.

Bank B. Fill in column 3 to represent the changes in Bank B's balance sheet following this cash deposit. At this point, total bank deposits have increased by

$_____ and the stock of money in the

economy has increased by $_____ .

4. Assume now that Bank B also makes as large a loan as possible. Fill in column 4 to represent changes in Bank B's balance sheet after it makes the loan and this latest borrower takes the proceeds in cash.

5. Assume that the proceeds of this loan eventually get deposited in Bank C. Fill in column 5 to represent the changes in the balance sheet of Bank C following the increase in deposits. At this point total

bank deposits have increased by $_____ and the stock of money has increased by

$_____ .

6. Fill in the following sequence of increased deposits following the initial increase at Bank A assuming that each bank makes the largest possible loan.

Increased deposits at Bank A _____$1000_____

Increased deposits at Bank B _____

Increased deposits at Bank C _____

Increased deposits at Bank D _____

Increased deposits at Bank E _____

If you have not made any mistakes you will notice that each increase in deposit is less than the previous increase and can be expressed as

(1.0 - 0.25) × (the previous increase in deposits).

Mathematically this is an infinite geometric progression with decreasing increments. If we carried the sum out far enough it would approach a

limit given by $1000 ÷ _____ , or

$_____ . (If you have a suitable electronic calculator or computer you might try testing this result by actually calculating the sum for a very large number of terms.) This specific numerical example illustrates the more general principle that the multiplier for the maximum increase in deposits following an increase in bank

reserves is 1 ÷ _____ _____

_____ .

SELF-TESTS FOR UNDERSTANDING

Test A

Circle the correct answer.

1. Money serves all but which one of the following functions?
   a. Medium of exchange.
   b. Hedge against inflation.
   c. Unit of account.
   d. Store of value.

2. Which of the following is *not* an example of commodity money?
   a. Gold coins.
   b. Wampum.
   c. A $10 bill.
   d. Diamonds.

3. The most important government regulation of banks in terms of limiting the multiple creation of deposits is
   a. bank examinations and audits.
   b. limits on the kinds of assets that banks can buy.
   c. required reserve ratio.
   d. requirements to disclose the volume of loans to bank officials.

4. If the minimum reserve requirement for all bank deposits is 10 percent, then the maximum multiple creation of deposits by the banking system as a whole following a cash deposit of $1000 would be
   a. (0.1) × ($1000) = $100.
   b. (1 + 0.1) × ($1000) = $1100.
   c. ($1000) ÷ (1 - 0.1) = $1111.
   d. ($1000) ÷ (0.1) = $10 000.

5. The maximum increase in the money supply would be
   a. smaller than in Question 4.
   b. larger than in Question 4.
   c. the same as in Question 4.

   (In fact, it would be $_____ .)

6. If the reserve requirement is 15 percent instead of 10 percent, then the maximum multiple creation of deposits would be
   a. smaller than in Question 4.
   b. larger than in Question 4.
   c. the same as in Question 4.

7. If banks hold some of every increase in deposits in the form of excess reserves, then the amount of deposits actually created following a cash deposit would be
   a. less than that indicated in Question 4.
   b. the same as that indicated in Question 4.
   c. more than that indicated in Question 4.

8. If the required reserve ratio is 20 percent and Rachel deposits $100 in cash in the First National Bank, the maximum increase in deposits by the banking system as a whole is
   a. 0
   b. $20
   c. $100
   d. $500

9. If the required reserve ratio is 20 percent and Rachel deposits $100 in the First National Bank by depositing a cheque from her mother written on the Second National Bank, the maximum increase in deposits by the banking system as a whole is
   a. 0
   b. $20
   c. $100
   d. $500

10. If a bank's total reserve holdings are $35 million and it has $12 million of excess reserves, then its required reserves are
   a. $12 million.
   b. $23 million.
   c. $35 million.
   d. $47 million.

Test B

Circle T or F for True or False as appropriate.

1. A major advantage of the use of money rather than barter is that money avoids the problem of finding a "double coincidence of wants." **T F**

2. Chartered banks in Canada may redeem fiat money for gold from the Bank of Canada. **T F**

3. The use of gold as money is an example of fiat money. **T F**

4. Many assets serve as a store of value but only money is also a medium of exchange. **T F**

5. In periods with high rates of inflation, money is a good store of value. **T F**

6. Banks could increase their profitability by holding higher levels of cash reserves. **T F**

7. The existence of deposit insurance is an important reason why bank failures are so uncommon. **T F**

8. The oversimplified deposit-creation multiplier of 1 divided by the required reserve fraction is an underestimate of the more appropriate, but more complicated, multiplier. **T F**

9. Multiple deposit creation applies to increases in the money supply, but reductions in the money supply can come about only through government taxation. **T F**

10. Required reserves are part of a bank's liabilities, whereas excess reserves are part of a bank's assets. **T F**

11. If a bank's liabilities exceed its assets, the bank is said to have negative net worth. **T F**

SUPPLEMENTARY EXERCISES

1. If the required reserve ratio is 20 percent and banks want to hold 10 percent of any increase in deposits in the form of excess reserves and people want to hold $1 more in currency for every $10 increase in deposits, what is the eventual increase in deposits following a $1000 cash deposit in the First National Bank? What is the eventual increase in the money supply?

2. The central bank controls the monetary base, which is the sum of currency in public hands and both the required and excess reserves held by chartered banks. If M is the required reserve fraction, E is the ratio of excess reserves to deposits, and C is the ratio of currency to deposits, what is the formula that relates the change in deposits to a change in the monetary base?

Central Banking and Monetary Policy

13

LEARNING OBJECTIVES

After completing the material in this chapter you should be able to:

- define, understand, and use correctly the terms and concepts listed below.
- draw and explain the logic behind both the supply of money schedule and the demand for money schedule.
- analyse the impact of open-market operations in words, with T-accounts, and by using the demand for and supply of money schedules.
- explain why the Bank of Canada's control of the stock of money is not exact.
- explain how the Bank of Canada can peg the exchange rate.
- show on a supply-demand graph how fixed exchange rates lead to a balance of payments deficit or surplus.
- explain why the Bank of Canada cannot control both the exchange rate and the money supply.
- explain how interest rates are determined if foreign and domestic financial markets are independent.
- explain how either the money supply or the

exchange rate adjusts to maintain money-market equilibrium, when the interest rate is given from outside through an integration of domestic and foreign financial markets.

IMPORTANT TERMS AND CONCEPTS

Bank of Canada
Exchange rate
Appreciation
Depreciation
Devaluation
Revaluation
Supply and demand for foreign exchange
Floating, or flexible, exchange rates
Reserve requirements
Open-market operations
Contraction and expansion of the money supply
Bank Rate
Fixed exchange rates
Balance of payments deficit and surplus
Interest differential
Supply of money
Demand for money
Equilibrium in the money market

CHAPTER REVIEW

In Chapter 12 we learned how deposits are created by the actions of chartered banks. In this chapter we will see how actions taken by the Bank of Canada can influence the total amount of deposits that banks create. It is by influencing the creation of deposits by banks that the Bank of Canada works to control the stock of money. Reserve requirements and the total amount of bank reserves are important keys to the Bank of Canada's control of the stock of money.

(1) The Bank of Canada was established in _____ and is the nation's _____

bank. Policy actions by the Bank of Canada constitute the nation's _____ policy. The link between decisions of the Bank of Canada and GNP will be explored in Chapters 14 and 15.

We saw in Chapter 12 that the multiple creation of bank deposits is limited by the required reserve fraction and by the volume of bank reserves. The major monetary policy instrument—open-market operations—directly affects total bank reserves. We also saw in Chapter 12 that controlling the volume of bank reserves does not allow for the

(2) precise control of the stock of money because of possible changes in (*excess/required*) reserve holdings by banks and in currency holdings by the public. These slippages in the deposit-creation formula are an important reason why the Bank of Canada's control over the stock of money, while strong and important, is not complete.

(3) Open-market operations—the purchase and sale of government _____—represent the most important and most commonly used instrument of monetary policy. Open-market operations affect bank behaviour by adding to or subtracting from the amount of bank reserves. The essence of an open-market purchase is that the Bank of Canada uses cash to (*buy/sell*) a government security. This cash typically ends up as an increase in chartered bank reserves because the Bank of Canada either purchases the security directly from a bank or because the seller of the security deposits the cash in a bank account. In either case there is a(n) (*increase/decrease*) in noninterest-earning excess reserves, and the usual multiple deposit creation process is set in motion. An open-market sale has exactly opposite effects. The public, either a bank or an individual, uses cash to buy a government security from the Bank of Canada. The transaction results in a(n) (*reduction/increase*) in bank reserves and a process of multiple deposit (*creation/destruction*) is set in motion.

Banks can add to their reserve holdings by borrowing directly from the Bank of Canada. Such borrowings might facilitate a multiple expansion of deposits or, more frequently, might forestall a multiple destruction of deposits. The Bank of Canada controls the volume of borrowing by changing the interest rate it charges banks, which is called the

(4) _____.

Monetary policy decisions can be seen as putting an upper limit on the possible creation of bank deposits and hence on the stock of money. How much banks will want to exploit the potential to create deposits will be determined by the profitability of increased bank operations—more loans and more deposits. Higher interest rates on

(5) loans will induce banks to make (*more/fewer*) loans, and hold (*more/fewer*) non-earning excess reserves. These actions will expand the volume of deposits and hence the stock of money. In brief, considering just banks, higher interest rates will be associated with a (*larger/smaller*) stock of money.

This behaviour by banks is summarized in Figure 13-1, which shows an upward-sloping supply of money schedule. Movements along the schedule are predominantly related to the decisions of chartered banks. Shifts in the schedule come from changes in monetary policy. For example, an open-market purchase increases the

(6) amount of bank reserves and shifts the money-supply schedule to the (*left/right*). The actual stock of money and the interest rate will be determined by the intersection of the supply of money schedule and the

_____ for money schedule.

Figure 13-2 shows a demand schedule for money. The schedule has a negative slope, because as the

(7) interest rate rises, the demand for money (*increases/decreases*). The increase in interest rates means that the opportunity cost of holding money has (*increased/decreased*). If GNP increases, the demand schedule will shift to the (*right/left*) as more transactions associated with a higher GNP will lead to a(n) (*increased/decreased*) demand

for money at every interest rate. If GNP decreases, the demand schedule will shift to the _____ .

Equilibrium values for the stock of money and the rate of interest are determined by the forces of both supply and demand according to the process described in Chapter 4. Graphically, the equilibrium can be

(8) represented by the _____ of the demand and supply curves, as in Figure 13-3, as long as the domestic financial market is independent of the foreign financial market. Changes in monetary policy will change the equilibrium values for both the stock of money and the rate of interest. An expansionary change in

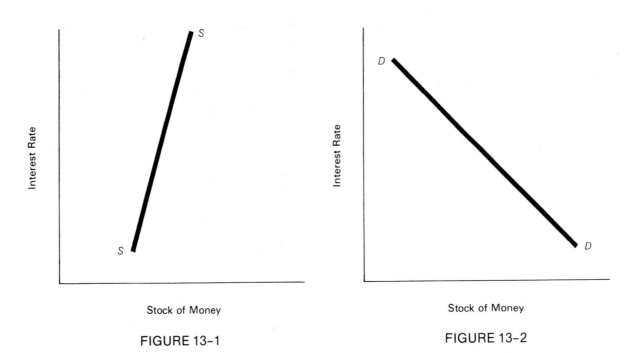

FIGURE 13-1   FIGURE 13-2

monetary policy would be represented by a shift of the (*demand/supply*) schedule to the (*left/right*), a(n) (*increase/decrease*) in the stock of money, and a(n) (*increase/decrease*) in the interest rate. A contractionary

change in monetary policy would be represented by a shift of the supply schedule to the _____,

a(n) _____ in the stock of money, and a(n) _____ in the interest rate.

    The analysis of equilibrium in the money market is somewhat more complicated if the domestic and foreign financial markets are integrated. This is particularly true for Canada, as investors transfer funds across the U.S. border to take advantage of even slight differentials in securities yields. This competitive pressure forces Canadian interest rates to stay closely in line with the level of U.S. interest rates. Before the implications of this for our money market can be fully appreciated, we must understand what exchange rates are and how they are determined.

    Find out how much it would cost, in dollars, to buy one German mark. This figure is the current dollar/

(9)   mark _____ rate, expressed in dollars. Many newspapers now publish exchange rates on a daily basis. A student in Germany could do the same thing and get a price for dollars in terms of marks. If you both call on the same day you should both get the same price (ignoring sales commissions.)[1] If the dollar price of

one mark increases, so that it takes more dollars to buy one mark, we say that the dollar has _____

relative to the mark. Alternatively, we could say that the mark has _____
relative to the dollar.

    Under a system of floating exchange rates, exchange rates will be determined by market forces of

(10)   _____ and _____ . Consider an example using two countries, Germany and the United States. The demand for German marks has three major sources: (1) the demand by Americans for German exports, such as cars, cameras, and clocks; and (2) the demand by Americans for German financial assets, such as stocks and bonds; and (3) the demand by Americans for German physical assets, such as factories and machines. The supply of German marks also has three sources: the demand by Germans for

American (*exports/imports*), American _____ assets, and American _____
assets. (Note that the demand and supply of marks has an interpretation in terms
of the demand and supply of dollars. The demand for marks by Americans is simultaneously a

---

[1]In Canada you might get a price like 50 cents for one mark. The German student would get a price like 2 marks for one dollar. If x is the dollar price of one mark, then 1/x is the mark price of one dollar.

_____ of dollars, while the supply of marks by Germans is simultaneously a

_____ for dollars.)

Under a system of floating rates, the equilibrium exchange rate will be at a level where demand equals supply. A change in any factor that affects demand or supply will change the exchange rate. For example a sudden

(11) demand for German wines on the part of Americans would shift the (*demand/supply*) curve for marks. The dollar price of marks will (*increase/decrease*), a result economists call a(n) (*appreciation/depreciation*) of the mark in terms of the dollar. Conversely, a sudden demand for California wines on the part of Germans would shift the

_____ curve of marks and would mean a(n) (*appreciation/depreciation*) of the mark in terms of the dollar. A simultaneous boom in the United States and recession in Germany are likely to lead to a(n)

_____ of the mark in terms of the dollar.

A floating exchange rate is a prerequisite for a country to have independent control of its money supply. Suppose the Bank of Canada pegs the Canadian dollar at too low a level, so that the supply of foreign exchange entering Canada exceeds the Canadian demand for foreign exchange. Canada will experience a balance of

(12) payments (*deficit/surplus*). The Bank of Canada would have to (*buy/sell*) the otherwise unwanted incoming foreign exchange, and to accomplish this purchase in the open market for foreign exchange, the Bank of Canada's liability (the quantity of Canadian currency issued or outstanding) would be increased. Thus, chartered bank

reserves will have _____ . Under fixed exchange rates, the private agents involved in the

_____ - _____ market dictate what open-market operation the Bank of Canada must do to peg the exchange rate. Both the magnitude and direction of this open-market operation are determined for the central bank, unless it avoids making any transactions in the foreign-exchange

market; that is, unless it allows a _____ exchange-rate policy.

Figure 13-4 shows how equilibrium in the money market is determined when the availability of foreign bonds pegs the domestic rate of interest. Under fixed exchange rates, the Bank of Canada must accept the otherwise unwanted Canadian currency (given by distance AB). This decreases the amount of money in circulation so the money-supply curve shifts left (to M_1S_1), and equilibrium obtains at point A. Under flexible exchange rates, the Canadian dollar depreciates (because of the excess supply, AB). This raises import costs and stimulates exports. The resulting increase in nominal GNP shifts the money-demand curve to the right (to M_1D_1), and equilibrium obtains at point B.

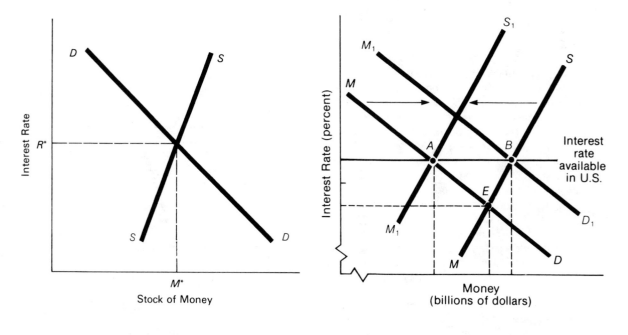

FIGURE 13-3   FIGURE 13-4

BASIC EXERCISE

This exercise is designed to review the impact of an open-market operation in various circumstances.

1. Use Figure 13-5 to analyse the impact of an open-market sale when the domestic financial market is independent from foreign financial markets. The sale of a government security by the Bank of Canada results in a(n) (*increase*/*decrease*) in total bank reserves. This change in bank reserves can be represented as a shift of the supply of money

   schedule to the _____ .
   (Be sure you can explain in words why the schedule shifts.) Draw a new supply of money schedule that represents the result of the open-market sale. As a result of this (*expansionary*/*restrictive*) change in monetary policy, the equilibrium stock of money will (*fall*/*rise*) and interest rates will

   _____ .

2. Use Figure 13-6 to analyse the impact of an open-market purchase of government bonds, when the domestic and foreign financial markets are integrated, and assuming that Canada is following a flexible exchange-rate policy. The purchase of securities by the Bank of Canada leads to a(n) (*increase*/*decrease*) in total chartered bank reserves, which can be represented as a shift of the

   supply of money schedule to the _____ .
   This creates an excess (*demand*/*supply*) of Canadian dollars, so that, given the flexible exchange-rate policy, the Canadian dollar must (*appreciate*/*depreciate*) in value. Given this change in the exchange rate, foreigners will find our products (*more*/*less*) expensive, and Canadians will find imports from other countries to be (*more*/*less*) expensive. As a result, net exports are (*increased*/*decreased*), so that aggregate demand in Canada increases. The resulting higher value of nominal GNP (*increases*/*decreases*) the demand for money so that the demand curve shifts to the (*left*/*right*), so that the new demand and supply for money schedules intersect on the line that indicates the level of foreign interest rates.

   If this same open-market purchase of government bonds is tried with a fixed exchange-rate policy, the bank of Canada will simply find that the initial excess supply of Canadian dollars is eliminated by the Bank's commitment to peg the exchange rate. As residual buyer for the otherwise unwanted (excess supply of) Canadian dollars, the Bank must issue (sell) the equivalent amount of foreign exchange. This open-market sale of foreign exchange just cancels off the original open-market

purchase of government bonds, leaving chartered bank reserves unaffected. Thus, the position of the money-supply schedule is given, if the central bank commits itself to eliminating any excess demand or supply in the money market (i.e., pegs the exchange rate).

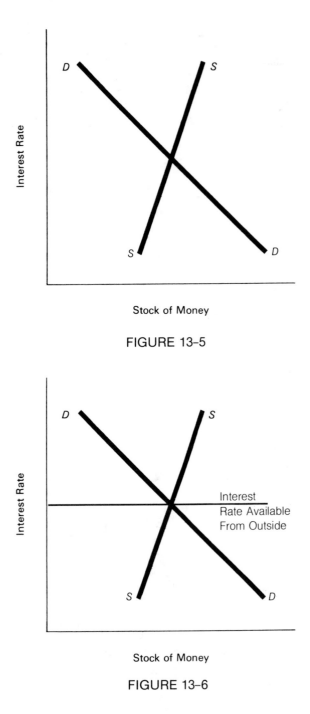

FIGURE 13-5

FIGURE 13-6

SELF-TESTS FOR UNDERSTANDING

Test A

Circle the correct answer.

1. Which of the following is *not* an instrument of monetary policy?
   a. Open-market operations.
   b. Lending to chartered banks.
   c. Legal actions to promote competition in banking.
2. Which of the following is *not* an example of expansionary monetary policy?
   a. An open-market purchase.
   b. A reduction in reserve requirements.
   c. An increase in the interest rate charged on loans by the Bank of Canada to chartered banks.
   d. A reduction in the Bank Rate.
3. Important determinants of the demand for money include all but which one of the following?
   a. The Bank Rate.
   b. The level of real output.
   c. Interest rates.
   d. The price level.
4. A change in which of the following would lead to a shift in the demand for money schedule?
   a. Market interest rates.
   b. Reserve requirements.
   c. GNP.
   d. The Bank Rate.
5. The positive slope of the supply of money schedule indicates that
   a. at higher interest rates people will demand more money.
   b. banks are likely to respond to higher interest rates by holding fewer excess reserves.
   c. minimum reserve requirements increase directly with interest rates.
   d. The Bank of Canada is likely to engage in expansionary monetary policy actions as interest rates increase.
6. If the domestic and foreign financial markets are independent, an open-market purchase of government securities by the Bank of Canada will result in a(n)
   a. increase in the stock of money and interest rates.
   b. increase in the stock of money and a decrease in interest rates.

   c. decrease in the stock of money and interest rates.
   d. decrease in the stock of money and an increase in interest rates.
7. If the domestic and foreign financial markets are integrated, and Canada is following a floating exchange-rate policy, an increase in reserve requirements would lead to all but which one of the following?
   a. A reduction in the stock of money.
   b. An initial increase in required reserves.
   c. A shift to the left of the demand for money schedule.
   d. A lasting increase in interest rates.

Test B

Circle T or F for True or False as appropriate.

1. Monetary policy decisions by the Bank of Canada are subject to review by the Prime Minister before being implemented.   T F

2. If the Bank of Canada wanted to lower interest rates directly without changing the stock of money, it could undertake an open-market purchase.   T F

3. A reduction in minimum reserve requirements would likely lead to an increase in both the stock of money and the interest rate.   T F

4. Changing the Bank Rate is the most effective instrument of monetary policy used today.   T F

5. Since many forms of money do not earn interest, people's demand for money is unaffected by changes in interest rates.   T F

6. Higher interest rates would normally lead banks to reduce the volume of deposits associated with a given amount of bank reserves.   T F

7. An open-market sale by the central bank is likely to lead to a reduction in the stock of money and an increase in interest rates.   T F

8. By simultaneously using open-market operations and making changes in minimum reserve requirements, the Bank of Canada would be able to achieve any desired combination of the money stock and the exchange rate.   T F

Stabilization Policy: Without International Capital Flows

14

LEARNING OBJECTIVES

After completing the material in this chapter you should be able to:

- define, understand, and use correctly the terms and concepts listed below.
- explain the conceptual difference between money and income.
- describe why the equation of exchange is not a theory of income determination and why monetarists' use of the same equation turns it into a theory of income determination.
- explain how investment spending and interest rates interact to help determine how monetary policy works in a Keynesian model of income determination.
- explain how expansionary fiscal policy, and related increases in the demand for money, interest rates, and velocity, interact to determine how fiscal policy works in a monetarist model.
- explain why the effect of higher prices on the demand for money for transaction purposes implies that the aggregate-demand curve slopes downward.
- distinguish between lags affecting fiscal policy and those affecting monetary policy.
- explain how and why the slope of the aggregate-supply curve helps to determine the effectiveness of stabilization policy.

IMPORTANT TERMS AND CONCEPTS

Why the aggregate-demand curve slopes downward
Quantity theory of money
Velocity
Equation of exchange
Effect of interest rate on velocity
Monetarism
Effect of monetary policy on inflation
Effect of fiscal policy on interest rates
Lags in stabilization policy
Shape of the aggregate-supply curve

CHAPTER REVIEW

This is one of the more important and difficult of the macroeconomic chapters. While not much new material is introduced, the chapter summarizes and synthesizes many of the concepts presented in preceding chapters concerning the theory of income determination. It is an important bridge between earlier chapters dealing with income determination, the price level, and fiscal and monetary policy. The analysis in this chapter rests on the unrealistic but simplifying assumption that Canada's financial markets operate independently of the American and other foreign financial markets. In fact, Canadian interest rates *are* closely tied to U.S. interest rates, but we have saved the complications that follow from this fact until the next chapter. A firm understanding of the material in this chapter will integrate your learning from earlier chapters and facilitate your understanding of the material to come.

Most macroeconomists are associated with viewpoints that are predominantly either Keynesian or monetarist. Earlier chapters presented an essentially Keynesian model of income determination. The monetarist viewpoint is a modern manifestation of an even older tradition known as the quantity theory of money. The concept of *velocity* is perhaps the most important tool associated with this theory. Velocity is the average number of times per year that a dollar changes hands to accomplish transactions associated with GNP. Velocity is measured as nominal

(1) _____ divided by the stock of _____ .

Related to the concept of velocity is something called the equation of exchange, which is simply another way of stating the definition of velocity. In words, the equation of exchange says:

(2) Money supply × velocity = _____ _____ . In symbols, it is:

_____ × _____ = _____ × _____ . Statisticians and national income accountants measure the stock of money and nominal GNP. Economists then calculate velocity by division. Different values of the stock of money could be consistent with the same level of nominal GNP if

_____ changes appropriately.

The quantity theory asserts that there is a close link between changes in nominal GNP and changes in

(3) the stock of _____ . This link comes about because the quantity theory assumes that velocity (*does/does not*) change very much. If velocity is constant, then a change in the money stock translates

directly into a change in _____ _____ . If velocity is 5 and the

money stock increases by \$2 billion, then nominal GNP will rise by \$_____ billion.

Measures of velocity, as well as an analysis of the determinants of velocity, suggest that one

(4) (*should/should not*) expect velocity to be constant. Velocity reflects how much money people hold to make transactions, which in turn reflects such institutional factors as the frequency of paycheques and the efficiency of moving money between chequing accounts and other assets, such as savings accounts. In Chapter 13 we saw that the amount of money people want to hold, and hence velocity, is also affected by the interest rate as a measure of

the _____ _____ of holding money.

Monetarism, like the quantity theory, starts with the equation of exchange. But rather than assuming that velocity does not change, monetarists try to predict *how* velocity will change. From a monetarist perspective, determinants of nominal GNP are broken down into implications for the stock of money and implications for

(5) _____ . After accounting for appropriate changes, simple multiplication can be used to predict what the nominal GNP will be.

At first glance it appears that a Keynesian approach to income determination cannot analyse changes in monetary policy, whereas a monetarist approach ignores fiscal policy. Such a conclusion would be oversimplified and misleading. In formal theory the two viewpoints are closer than is commonly recognized. Keynesian theory implies that monetary policy can have important impacts on aggregate demand through its impact on interest rates and investment spending. In Chapter 13 we saw that expansionary monetary policy will lead to

(6) a(n) (*decline/increase*) in interest rates. In Chapter 8 we saw that as a result of lower interest rates investment spending will (*increase/decrease*). In Chapter 8 we also saw that an increase in investment spending shifts both the expenditure schedule and the aggregate-demand curve. Putting all the pieces together we can see that expansionary monetary policy will tend to (*increase/decrease*) GNP. Restrictive monetary policy would work in exactly the opposite way.

We are now in a position to consider another important reason why the aggregate-demand curve slopes downward—that is, why, if prices are higher, the demand for real output will fall. In addition to impacts on the purchasing power of consumers' money assets, higher prices and the same real output would mean an

(7) (*increased/decreased*) demand for money for transaction purposes. In other words, the demand for money schedule in Chapter 13 would shift to the right and interest rates would (*rise/fall*) as we move along an unchanged supply of money schedule. (If you are a bit unsure about this point, look back at Figure 13-3 in this study guide and trace the implications of a shift in the demand schedule to the right.) Higher interest rates, we know, will lead to a(n) (*decline/increase*) in investment spending, which in turn means that demand for real output and the equilibrium level of income will decline.

At this point we should stop, take a deep breath, and review the implications of what we have just discussed. Although we have not done anything new, it may not be easy to grasp immediately how all the parts go together.

Implication 1:

Higher prices will increase the transaction demand for money, leading to higher interest rates, less investment spending, and a lower equilibrium level of output. *This is an important reason why the aggregate-demand curve slopes downward.*

Implication 2:

Whether or not prices rise, higher nominal GNP, say as the result of expansionary fiscal policy, will still increase the demand for money for transaction purposes. Interest rates will rise as we move along an unchanged supply of money schedule. The reduction in investment spending induced by the rise in interest rates *is the third important reason why the multiplier formulas of Chapter 9 were oversimplified*; they ignored the increase in interest rates that accompanies any increase in autonomous spending.

One more implication of what we have just discussed allows us to see how monetarists are able to analyse the impact of changes in fiscal policy. Implication 2 tells us that expansionary fiscal policy will be associated with

(8) higher interest rates. As a result of higher interest rates, velocity will (*increase/decrease*) and the monetarist

forecast for nominal GNP will _____ .

The choice between monetary and fiscal policy is also influenced by how quickly changes in policy can occur and how long it takes for changes, once made, to affect the behaviour of firms and consumers. In

(9) general, lags in formulating policy are shorter for (*fiscal/monetary*) policy, whereas spending responses of firms

and households are typically shorter for _____ policy.

Stabilization policy, whether from a Keynesian or monetarist perspective, affects the economy primarily by shifting the aggregate-demand curve. The final result, however, in terms of changes in output and prices, also depends upon the slope of the aggregate-supply curve. A flat aggregate-supply curve means that shifts

(10) in the aggregate-demand curve will have large effects on (*output/prices*) with only a small change in

_____ . On the other hand, shifts of the aggregate-demand curve will have big effects on

prices without much change in output if the aggregate supply is (*steep/flat*). Keynesians tend to believe that the

aggregate-supply curve is relatively _____ while monetarists believe that it is relatively

_____ . When the economy is operating close to full employment, the

_____ viewpoint is apt to be correct. When there is a large amount of slack in the

economy, the _____ viewpoint is likely to be more relevant.

BASIC EXERCISE

This exercise is designed to give you practice computing and using velocity.

Table 14-1 contains historical data for nominal GNP, M1 and M2
1. Use this data to compute V_1, velocity based on M1, and V_2, velocity based on M2.

2. Assume you are a monetarist working for the Bank of Canada and are supposed to estimate nominal GNP. Even if you knew the money supply, *M*, you would still need an estimate of *V*. One way to estimate velocity is to use data from the previous year. The idea is that, since you can't know velocity for, say, 1978 until you know nominal GNP and M1 or M2 for 1978, you might use velocity for 1977 to predict GNP for 1978. Table 14-2 assumes that the

Bank of Canada can control the money supply exactly. Use your numbers for velocity to fill in the blank columns in Table 14-2 to predict income.

3. Did predictions based on M1 or M2 do better? Why?
4. The predictions in Question 2 assumed you knew the actual changes in the money supply. In reality, one never knows M until the end of the year, and by that time no one is interested in forecasts of what has already happened. How might you forecast M? How might you forecast V?

SELF-TESTS FOR UNDERSTANDING

Test A

Circle the correct answer.

1. The equation of exchange says that
   a. for every buyer there is a seller.
   b. $M \times V$ = Nominal GNP.
   c. demand equals supply.
   d. P.T. Barnum was right when he said, "There is a sucker born every minute."
2. Velocity is measured by
   a. dividing the money stock by nominal GNP.
   b. computing the percentage change in nominal GNP from year to year.
   c. dividing nominal GNP by the stock of money.
   d. subtracting the rate of inflation from nominal interest rates.
3. During 1981, M1 was constant and yet nominal GNP rose by about 9 percent. It must be that
   a. velocity increased.
   b. velocity decreased.
   c. velocity was unchanged.
4. If velocity is constant at 5 and the stock of money increased by 5 percent, then nominal GNP will increase by
   a. 0 percent.
   b. 5 percent.
   c. 10 percent.
   d. 25 percent.

TABLE 14-1

	Nominal GNP ($ billion)	M1 ($ billion)	M2 ($ billion)	V_1	V_2
		average through the year			
1978	232.2	21.5	73.6	_____	_____
1979	264.3	23.0	85.1	_____	_____
1980	296.6	24.5	101.3	_____	_____
1981	339.1	25.4	116.6	_____	_____
1982	356.6	25.6	127.5	_____	_____
1983	388.7	28.2	134.8	_____	_____

Source: Department of Finance, *Economic Review*.

TABLE 14-2

	(1) Actual M1 ($ billion)	(2) V_1, from Previous Year	(3) Estimated Income ($ billion)	(4) Actual Income ($ billion)	(5) Estimate Income ($ billion)	(6) V_2 from Previous Year	(7) Actual M2 ($ billion)
1979	23.0	_____	_____	264.3	_____	_____	85.1
1980	24.5	_____	_____	296.6	_____	_____	101.3
1981	25.4	_____	_____	339.1	_____	_____	116.6
1982	25.6	_____	_____	356.6	_____	_____	127.5
1983	28.2	_____	_____	388.7	_____	_____	134.8

Source: Department of Finance. *Economic Review*.

5. Initially the stock of money is $60 billion and velocity is 5. If one can be sure that velocity will not change, what increase in *M* will be required to increase real GNP by $2.5 billion?
   a. $0.5 billion.
   b. $1.0 billion.
   c. $2.5 billion.
   d. Insufficient information

6. Which of the following developments is *not* likely to lead to an increase in velocity?
   a. An increase in the expected rate of inflation.
   b. A reduction in the required reserve ratio for banks.
   c. An increase in interest rates as a result of an expansionary change in fiscal policy.
   d. A widespread trend toward more frequent pay periods.

7. Which of the following is *not* likely to increase nominal GNP according to a monetarist analysis of income determination?
   a. An open-market purchase that increases the stock of money.
   b. An increase in government spending.
   c. A technological change in banking practices that increases velocity.
   d. An increase in income taxes.

8. Which of the following is an example of a lag in policy-making as opposed to a lag in spending by firms and households?
   a. The construction of a new plant, induced by lower interest rates, cannot start for nine months, because it takes that long to prepare architectural drawings and contractors' bids.
   b. Parliament takes five months to consider a tax proposal.
   c. Through multiplier impacts, a $3 billion increase in government spending eventually raises GNP by $5 billion.
   d. Refrigerator sales rise in the month following a $300 tax rebate.

9. Increases in the money supply are likely to lead to some increase in prices
   a. only when the GNP exceeds potential output.
   b. only if velocity also increases.
   c. whenever the aggregate-supply curve has a positive slope.
   d. whenever the percentage increase in the money supply is greater than the growth in potential output.

10. If the aggregate-supply curve is relatively flat, then
    a. velocity will be constant.
    b. both monetary and fiscal policy will have relatively large effects on output without much effect on prices.
    c. a change in interest rates will have little impact on investment.

d. monetary policy will be effective while fiscal policy will not.

Test B

Circle T or F for True or False as appropriate.

1. If the stock of money is $60 billion and nominal GNP is $360 billion, the velocity is 6.   **T F**

2. Historically, velocity has been constant.   **T F**

3. The quantity theory is not really a theory because velocity, by definition, is equal to the ratio of nominal GNP divided by the money stock.   **T F**

4. Monetarist and Keynesian theories are both incomplete in that they concentrate on demand and ignore the supply side of the economy.   **T F**

5. Monetarist analysis, because it concentrates on the stock of money and velocity, cannot analyse changes in fiscal policy.   **T F**

6. Keynesian models of income determination show that only fiscal policy can affect the level of output; monetary policy has no effect on real output.   **T F**

7. Both monetarist and Keynesian analyses agree that expansionary monetary policy that increases the stock of money will only increase prices with no impact on real output.   **T F**

8. The lag between change in fiscal policy and its effects on aggregate demand is probably shorter than the lag between a change in monetary policy and its effects on aggregate demand.   **T F**

9. The lag in adopting an appropriate policy is probably shorter for fiscal policy than for monetary policy.   **T F**

10. The shape of the aggregate-supply curve is likely to be relatively steep when the economy is operating near full employment and relatively flat during periods of high unemployment and low rates of capacity utilization.   **T F**

SUPPLEMENTARY EXERCISE

Consider an economy where consumption and investment spending are given by

$$C = 425 + 0.6 \, DI$$
$$I = 470 - 10r$$

where *r* is the interest rate. In this economy, taxes are one-sixth of income.

1. If government purchases are 425 and r is 12 (that is, 12 percent), what is the equilibrium level of income?
2. If the central bank lowers the interest rate to 8, what happens to the equilibrium level of income?
3. The central bank can lower the interest rate by an appropriate increase in bank reserves; that is, an appropriate shift in the money-supply schedule. But what is appropriate? Assume the demand for money is

$$M^D = 0.25\ Y - 10r$$

and the supply of money is

$$M^S = 5\ BR + 2.5r$$

where BR is the amount of bank reserves. If BR = 90, what is the equilibrium level of income? r? and

M? _____

4. What increase in BR will reduce the interest rate to 8 and produce the increase in Y you found in Question 2? What happens to M? (You might start by trying an increase in BR of 10 and figuring out what happens to Y and r. Then use these results to figure out how to get r to drop to 8.)

Stabilization Policy: With International Capital Flows

15

LEARNING OBJECTIVES

After completing the material in this chapter you should be able to:

- define, understand, and use correctly the terms and concepts listed below.
- explain why a significant differential between Canadian and American interest rates cannot persist.
- explain why fiscal policy has a lasting effect on aggregate demand under fixed exchange rates, but not under flexible exchange rates.
- explain why monetary policy has a lasting effect on aggregate demand under floating exchange rates, but not under fixed exchange rates.
- explain why a lower value of the Canadian dollar increases the costs of domestic producers.

IMPORTANT TERMS AND CONCEPTS

Interest-rate differential
Foreign exchange market intervention
Floating, or flexible, exchange rates

CHAPTER REVIEW

Like Chapter 14, this chapter is important because it synthesizes much of the material that has been presented in previous chapters. Chapter 14 presented an integrated analysis of fiscal *and* monetary policy for an economy whose financial market is independent from foreign financial markets. One of the results of that analysis was that both fiscal and monetary policies cause changes in the level of interest rates. But in Canada, our financial market is so integrated with (and so small in comparison to) the U.S. financial market that competitive pressure precludes any lasting significant differential between Canadian and U.S. interest rates. Thus, we must regard the predictions derived in Chapter 14 as representing only the "initial" effects of fiscal and monetary policy. The "lasting" effects can only be derived once we trace through how the "temporary" interest rate-differential is eliminated.

As in Chapter 14, this chapter's analysis revolves around a two-part diagram: one part depicting the

(1) aggregate supply and demand for _____ , and the other depicting the supply and demand

for _____ . Initially, expansionary fiscal and monetary policies shift the demand for goods

to the (*right*/*left*). In the money market, expansionary fiscal policy shifts the demand curve to the

_____ , while expansionary monetary policy shifts the _____

_____ curve to the right.

    The only difference from Chapter 14 is that the foreign interest rate line is added to the money market diagram. All lasting equilibrium points in the money market must occur on this line, because foreign investors stand ready to move large quantities of funds across the border in search of the higher yield. This competitive pressure forces the

(2) level of Canadian interest rates to depart from the level of _____ interest rates for only short intervals. This fact implies that we should regard the predictions of Chapter 14 as providing just the "initial" effects of macroeconomic policies. The "final" effects stem from what happens as a result of the temporary

interest-rate _____ .

    The large flows of funds across the border that follow a temporary interest rate differential cause one of two

(3) things: either a movement of the exchange rate (if it is allowed to _____), or a change in

the domestic _____ _____ (if we are on a _____

exchange-rate policy). As a result, there are further shifts in demand and/or supply in the goods and money market. We now consider each case in turn.

    Fiscal policy has no lasting effect on aggregate demand under a floating exchange rate. Any initial expansion of

(4) demand just causes temporarily _____ interest rates in Canada, which attract foreign

funds. The Canadian dollar _____ , forcing a(n) (*expansion*/*contraction*) in net export

demands. Increased government expenditure "crowds out" pre-existing _____ demand

for Canadian products.

(5)   Fiscal policy has a lasting effect on aggregate demand under _____ exchange

rates. The temporary rise in interest rates following an increase in government expenditure attracts foreign funds,

which the _____ _____ _____ must absorb to

peg the exchange rate. The increase in the domestic _____

_____ that the Bank must allow to buy the incoming foreign exchanges (*counteracts*/*reinforces*) the initial fiscal expansion.

    Monetary policy cannot be used as an independent instrument in a fixed exchange-rate regime. Any initial

(6) expansion of the money supply involves temporarily _____ domestic interest rates, which

cause foreign funds to leave the country. The Bank of Canada must accept the _____

_____ that is relinquished as foreign exchange is purchased to buy foreign bonds. The resulting decrease in domestic money circulating (*conteracts*/*reinforces*) the original monetary policy.

(7)   Monetary policy has a lasting effect on aggregate demand under a _____ exchange rate. As before, an increase in the money supply by the Bank of Canada initially involves lower interest rates. As foreign funds leave the country, and the Bank of Canada does not react, the Canadian dollar

_____ . The resulting (*stimulation*/*contraction*) of net exports (*counteracts*/*reinforces*) the initial expansionary monetary policy.

    Thus far, we have considered only the aggregate-*demand* effects (or the lack of them) of fiscal and monetary

(8) policies. But both these tools can have aggregate-supply effects under a _____ exchange-rate regime. Since the exchange rate affects the cost of imported intermediate products, it affects

business _____ and shifts the position of the aggregate supply curve for goods.

BASIC EXERCISE

This brief exercise is designed to help you understand the relationship between interest rates and the exchange rate in an integrated financial market.

You are a Canadian considering the purchase of one of two bonds: a domestic one-year bond that currently yields 12 percent, and an American one-year bond that currently yields 10 percent. The Canadian bond costs 100 Canadian dollars today, and returns 112 Canadian dollars in one year. The American bond costs 100 U.S. dollars today, and returns 110 U.S. dollars in one year.

a. If the current exchange rate is one Canadian dollar equals one U.S. dollar, which bond will you buy today?

b. If the Canadian dollar is 95 cents U.S. today, and is expected to stay at this level indefinitely, which bond will you buy today?

c. If the Canadian dollar is equal to one U.S. dollar today, but is expected to drop sometime during the year to 95 cents U.S., which bond will you buy today?

Your answers to these questions should convince you of the following. For a country to maintain lower interest rates than those available elsewhere in an integrated financial market, that country must allow a *continual* appreciation of its currency, for *each* year into the future. For this appreciation to take place and not force a profit squeeze on the country's exporting firms, the value of the country's currency must fall now to "make room" for this continual appreciation. The more investors expect the country to attempt the lower interest rate policy, the bigger is the fall in the country's currency that is required in the first instance.

SELF-TESTS FOR UNDERSTANDING

Test A

Circle the correct answer.

1. Following an increase in government spending in a small open economy with a floating exchange rate, there will be
   a. a lasting increase in the price level and a lasting depreciation of the domestic currency.
   b. a lasting increase in the price level and a lasting appreciation of the domestic currency.
   c. a lasting decrease in the price level and a lasting depreciation of the domestic currency.
   d. a lasting decrease in the price level and a lasting appreciation of the domestic currency.
   e. none of the above

2. An increase in U.S. GNP will cause
   a. a lasting increase in Canadian GNP, but only if we have a pegged exchange rate.
   b. a lasting increase in Canadian GNP, but only if we have a floating exchange rate.
   c. a lasting increase in Canadian GNP, under either exchange-rate regime.
   d. have no lasting effect on Canadian GNP, under either exchange-rate regime.

3. The value of the American dollar in terms of Canadian dollars was highest in which of the following years?
   a. 1954
   b. 1964
   c. 1974
   d. 1984

4. For a small open economy on a floating exchange rate, a depreciation of the domestic currency can be caused by all but which one of the following events?
   a. An increase in the money supply.
   b. An increase in the reserve requirement ratio for chartered banks.
   c. An increase in income tax rates.
   d. A decrease in exports.

5. If there is an increase in government spending and Canada is on a fixed exchange rate, the Bank of Canada must
   a. keep the money supply constant.
   b. increase the money supply.
   c. decrease the money supply.
   d. increase the interest rate.
   e. decrease the interest rate.

6. A depreciation of the Canadian dollar can be caused by either
   a. an increase in the money supply or an increase in government spending.
   b. a decrease in the money supply or an increase in government spending.
   c. an increase in the money supply or a decrease in government spending.

7. If Canada is on a fixed exchange rate, a lasting increase in real GNP can be caused by either
   a. an increase in exports or a decrease in income-tax rates.
   b. an increase in the money supply or a decrease in exports.
   c. a decrease in the money supply or an increase in exports.
   d. an increase in the money supply or an increase in income-tax rates.
   e. a decrease in the money supply or a decrease in income-tax rates.

8. An increase in foreign interest rates
   a. must cause a recession in Canada, no matter what the exchange-rate regime.

b. must cause a recession in Canada under a floating exchange-rate regime.

c. must cause a recession in Canada under a fixed exchange-rate regime.

d. may cause an increase in Canadian real GNP under fixed exchange rates.

e. may cause an increase in Canadian real GNP under either exchange-rate regime.

Test B

Circle T or F for True or False as appropriate.

1. An increase in income-tax rates has a strong and lasting effect on aggregate demand, under a fixed exchange-rate regime. **T F**

2. An increase in foreign tariffs has no lasting effect on aggregate demand, as long as we have a fixed exchange rate. **T F**

3. An increase in tariffs levied by the federal government on Canadian imports will have a lasting effect on aggregate demand, as long as we have a floating exchange rate. **T F**

4. The Bank of Canada has no choice but to increase the money supply following an increase in government expenditure, if the Bank is pegging the exchange rate. **T F**

5. Canada had a floating exchange rate in 1960. **T F**

6. The experience of 1969-70 showed that it is not technically possible for Canada to have a monetary policy that is independent from that of the United States, even if we allow the exchange rate to float. **T F**

7. An increase in foreign interest rates will cause an increase in Canadian interest rates, no matter what Canada's exchange-rate policy is. **T F**

8. As long as Canada follows a floating exchange-rate policy, the Canadian dollar will depreciate following a contractionary monetary policy. **T F**

The International Monetary System

16

LEARNING OBJECTIVES

After completing the material in this chapter you should be able to:

- define, understand, and use correctly the terms and concepts listed below.
- identify the factors that help determine a country's exchange rate under a system of floating exchange rates.
- distinguish between long-, medium-, and short-run factors that help determine the demand and supply of currencies.
- use a demand-and-supply diagram to show how changes in GNP, inflation, or interest rates can lead to an appreciation or depreciation of the dollar under a system of floating exchange rates.
- show, on a supply-demand graph, how fixed exchange rates can lead to a balance of payments deficit or surplus.
- describe the options, other than changing the exchange rate, that were available under the Bretton Woods system to a country wanting to eliminate a balance of payments deficit or surplus.
- explain why, under a system of fixed exchange

rates, there was very little risk in speculating against an overvalued currency.

- explain why, under the gold standard, countries lost control of their domestic money stock.
- discuss the declining role of gold in determination of exchange rates.
- explain what exporters and importers can do to reduce the uncertainty they face under a system of floating exchange rates.

IMPORTANT TERMS AND CONCEPTS

Purchasing-power parity
Current account
Capital account
Balance of payments
Gold standard
Gold-exchange system (Bretton Woods system)
International Monetary Fund (IMF)
Exchange controls
"Dirty" or "managed" floating
The LDC debt problem
The European Monetary System (EMS)

CHAPTER REVIEW

This chapter discusses the determination of exchange rates, that is, the price of one currency in terms of another. The discussion in the text covers the economic factors that determine exchange rates, the implications of attempts by governments to fix exchange rates, and a review of recent history focusing on the evolution of the world's current mixed international monetary system.

Discussions of international monetary arrangements usually involve a whole new vocabulary of fixed and floating exchange rates, current and capital accounts, appreciating and depreciating currencies and devaluations and revaluations. It may help you to keep the vocabulary straight if you remember that a large part of the analysis of international monetary arrangements is merely an application of the supply-demand analysis originally introduced in Chapter 4.

If you are not familiar with our earlier brief treatment of these issues in the chapter on central banking (Chapter 13, pages 248-54), you are strongly encouraged to review this material before reading this chapter. Once you have reviewed this initial use of supply-demand analysis applied to foreign-exchange markets, you will be able to appreciate this chapter's discussion of the major factors that shift the demand and supply curves for foreign exchange.

In the long run, the exchange rate will be dominated by the relative movement of domestic prices

(1) according to the theory of _____ _____ _____ . In order that its goods remain competitive on world markets, a country with a very high rate of inflation will see its exchange rate (*appreciate/depreciate*). In the medium run, a country that experiences an economic boom will find its imports

rising and its exchange rate _____ . In the short run, exchange rates will be affected by the movement of large pools of investment funds that are sensitive to differences in interest rates. Restrictive monetary policy that increases interest rates will attract funds, (*appreciating/depreciating*) the exchange rate.

Governments may try to peg the exchange rate. In fact from the end of World War II until 1973, the world

(2) operated on a system of fixed exchange rates, established at the _____ Woods conference. At the time, it was thought that fixed exchange rates were necessary to stimulate the growth of international trade, so countries could reap the benefits of specialization according to the law of comparative advantage. Pegging an exchange rate is very similar to any other sort of price control and is subject to similar problems.

If, say, the Japanese government pegs the exchange rate at too high a level, the supply of Japanese yen

(3) will exceed the demand for yen, and Japan will experience a balance of payments (*deficit/surplus*). If the

government pegs the rate too low, then (*demand/supply*) will exceed _____ and the

result will be a balance of payments _____ .

A government pegging its exchange rate and faced with a deficit will need to use its holdings of reserves,

(4) that is, gold or foreign currencies, in order to (*buy/sell*) its own currency. A country faced with a surplus will need to supply its own currency. As a result it will find its reserves (*increasing/decreasing*).

Under fixed exchange rates, most of the pressure for adjustment is placed on countries experiencing a

(5) balance of payments (*deficits/surplus*). If nothing else, such a country will eventually run out of international reserves. If a country refuses to change its exchange rate, other adjustment options include monetary and fiscal policies that (*increase/decrease*) interest rates, (*increase/decrease*) the rate of inflation, or induce a general (*contraction/expansion*) in the level of economic activity.

A major weakness of the Bretton Woods system of fixed exchange rates was that deficit countries

(6) (*liked/disliked*) adjusting their domestic economies for balance of payments reasons rather than for domestic political and economic reasons. Another weakness was the special role accorded the U.S. dollar.

In recent years the world's major industrialized countries have operated under a mixed system of floating rates. Exchange rates are allowed to change on a daily basis in response to market forces. At the same time, many governments intervene by buying or selling currencies, hoping to influence the exchange rate to their advantage. Some have worried that floating exchange rates would be so volatile as to destroy world trade. However, market-determined prices need not be volatile, and importers and exporters can often relieve the business risk of

(7) changes in exchange rate by dealing with _____ .

Since 1980 there has been a great deal of concern about the substantial appreciation of the U.S. dollar and the international debts of many developing countries. An appreciation of the U.S. dollar makes foreign goods

(8) (*less*/*more*) expensive for Americans and American goods _____ expensive for foreigners. The result is likely to be a(n) (*decrease*/*increase*) in American imports and a(n) _____ in American exports. A number of developing countries borrowed extensively from European and American banks during the 1970s. These countries need to earn marks, pounds, and dollars to repay these loans. The sluggish growth of the industrialized economies and high real interest rates have created major problems for both debtor and creditor countries.

BASIC EXERCISE

1. This exercise is designed to illustrate the theory of purchasing power parity. This theory has important policy implications. Put most simply, if countries have fixed exchange rates, they must have similar inflation rates.

    Assume that the United States and France are the only suppliers of wine on the world market. Consumers of wine are indifferent between French and California wines and buy whichever is cheaper. Initially, the dollar–franc exchange rate is assumed to be 12 cents to the franc. California wine sells for $3.60 a bottle.

    Ignoring transportation costs, the initial dollar price of French wines must be $3.60. Accordingly, we know that the initial franc price of French wine is

    _____ francs.

    Assume now that inflation in the United States has raised the price of California wine to $6.00 a bottle, while inflation in France has raised the price of French wine to 40 francs. Based on this data, answer each of the following:
    a. If the exchange rate is fixed at 12 cents to the franc, what is the new dollar price of French

    wine? $ _____ What would happen to the sales of French and California wines? What happens to the American balance of payments?
    b. If the dollar–franc exchange rate is free to adjust, what is the new exchange rate; that is, what dollar price of a franc is necessary to equalize the dollar (or franc) price of both wines?

    _____

    c. Assuming that the change in the price of wine is typical of the change in other prices, which country had the higher rate of inflation?

    _____

    d. From Questions a and c, it is seen that the purchasing-power parity theory implies that under fixed exchange rates, a country with more inflation will experience a balance of payments (*deficit*/*surplus*).
    e. From Questions b and c, it is seen that the purchasing-power parity theory implies that under

floating exchange rates a country with more inflation will have a(n) (*appreciating*/ *depreciating*) currency.

SELF-TESTS FOR UNDERSTANDING

Test A

Circle the correct answer.

1. If a Mexican peso used to cost 2 cents and now costs less than a penny, one would say that the
    a. peso has appreciated relative to the dollar.
    b. peso has depreciated relative to the dollar.
    c. Mexico has a balance of payments deficit.
    d. Mexico has a balance of payments surplus.
2. If the German mark appreciates relative to the British pound, then it takes
    a. more marks to buy a pound than before.
    b. fewer marks to buy a pound than before.
    c. the same number of marks to buy a pound.
3. Under a system of floating exchange rates, which one of the following conditions will tend to depreciate the French franc relative to the German mark?
    a. An economic boom in Germany.
    b. A higher level of inflation in France than in Germany.
    c. An increase in interest rates in France.
    d. A sudden increase in German demand for imports from France.
4. Consider a country that is attempting to peg its currency at an unrealistically high exchange rate under a system of fixed exchange rates. Which one of the following is *not* true?
    a. The exchange rate will be said to be overvalued.
    b. The country will have a balance of payments deficit.
    c. The country will have a balance of payments surplus.
    d. The country will be forced to use foreign exchange reserves—gold and holdings of other currencies—in order to buy its own currency.
5. Purchasing-power parity theory says that
    a. only the volume of exports and imports

determines exchange rates; interest rates have nothing to do with exchange rates.

b. all countries are better off with a system of fixed exchange rates.

c. adjustment of fixed exchange rates should be symmetrical as between deficit and surplus countries.

d. in the long run, exchange rates adjust to reflect differences in price levels between countries.

6. If inflation in Germany is at an annual rate of 2 percent and inflation in the United States is at 8 percent, then the purchasing-power parity theory suggests that in the long run the dollar price of one mark will
   a. increase at an annual rate of 8 percent.
   b. decrease at an annual rate of 6 percent.
   c. increase at an annual rate of 6 percent.
   d. increase at an annual rate of 2 percent.

7. In Question 6 above, one would say that the higher rate of inflation in the United States results in a(n)
   a. depreciation of the mark relative to the dollar.
   b. appreciation of the dollar relative to the mark.
   c. depreciation of the dollar relative to the mark.

8. Assume that the mark-dollar exchange rate is fixed and that Germany and the United States are the only two countries in the world and that inflation rates differ as described in Question 6. Which country will have a balance of payments surplus?
   a. The United States.
   b. Germany.

9. If it takes 12 cents to buy one Swedish krona and 36 cents to buy one German mark, then how many kronor will it take to buy one mark?
   a. .33 (12 ÷ 36).
   b. 3 (36 ÷ 12).
   c. 8.33 (1.0 ÷ 0.12).
   d. 2.78 (1.0 ÷ 0.36).

Test B

Circle T or F for True or False as appropriate.

1. If one mark used to cost 50 cents and now costs 40 cents, the dollar has appreciated relative to the mark. **T F**

2. A pure system of floating exchange rates requires government intervention—purchases and sales of its own currency—in order to maintain fixed parities between currencies. **T F**

3. Under a system of floating exchange rates a sudden increase in the demand for Canadian exports will lead to appreciation of the Canadian dollar relative to other currencies. **T F**

4. Under a system of fixed exchange rates a sudden increase in Canadian imports would increase the Canadian balance of payments deficit (or reduce the size of the surplus). **T F**

5. Purchasing-power parity is a theory of the short-run determination of exchange rates. **T F**

6. Under a system of fixed exchange rates, a country that attempts to peg its exchange rate at an artificially low level will end up with a balance of payments deficit. **T F**

7. Today, world international monetary relations are based on the gold standard. **T F**

8. A major advantage of the gold standard was that countries could control their own domestic money stock. **T F**

9. The Bretton Woods gold-exchange system established a system of fixed exchange rates based on the convertibility of dollars into gold. **T F**

10. Under the Bretton Woods system of fixed exchange rates, both surplus and deficit countries felt the same pressure to correct any imbalance in their balance of payments. **T F**

SUPPLEMENTARY EXERCISES

1. **The Risks of Speculation Against Fixed Exchange Rates**
   Assume that in the mid-1960s you are treasurer for a large multinational corporation with 5 million British pounds to invest. The fixed official exchange rate vis-a-vis the U.S. dollar has been $2.80. At this exchange rate Britain has been experiencing large and growing deficits in its balance of payments and has been financing this deficit by buying pounds with foreign currencies. Britain's holdings of foreign currencies are running low, and there is a general feeling that Britain will have to devalue the pound. Exactly how large the devaluation will be and exactly when it will occur are uncertain, but there is absolutely no chance that the pound will be revalued.

   Fill in Table 16-1 to measure the risks of speculating against the pound. (Changing from pounds to dollars and back again will involve transactions costs. Table 16-1 abstracts from these costs, which are apt to be small.)

   What is the worst outcome?

   As the talk of devaluation heats up, what are you apt to do? How will your actions affect the British deficit and the pressures for devaluation?

2. **World Trade Under Fixed and Flexible Exchange Rates**
   Some observers worried that the introduction of a

TABLE 16-1

	(1)	(2)	(3)
Initial holdings of pounds	5,000,000	5,000,000	5,000,000
Current exchange rate	$2.80	$2.80	$2.80
Number of dollars if you sell pounds for dollars	_____	_____	_____
Possible new exchange rate	$2.80*	$2.60	$2.40
Number of pounds following reconversion to pounds after devaluation	_____	_____	_____

*This exchange rate assumes Britain takes other steps and does not devalue the pound.

system of floating exchange rates would have adverse effects on the volume of world trade, as exporters and importers would have trouble coping with short-run fluctuations in exchange rates. Go to the library and look up data on the volume of international trade. (You might try data from one of a variety of international organizations, including the United Nations, the International Monetary Fund, or the World Bank.) What is the percentage change in the annual physical volume of trade since the establishment of the current mixed system of floating exchange rates in 1973? How does the growth in trade compare with the growth in world output, that is, the sum of all countries' GNP?

Budget Deficits and the National Debt: Fact and Fiction

17

LEARNING OBJECTIVES

After completing the material in this chapter you should be able to:

- define, understand, and use correctly the terms and concepts listed below.
- explain the difference between the government's budget deficit and the national debt.
- discuss some facts about budget deficits and the national debt: When have budget deficits been largest? When has the national debt grown fastest? What has happened to the national debt as a proportion of GNP?
- explain how appropriate fiscal policy depends on the strength of private demand and the conduct of monetary policy.
- explain how measures to balance the budget may unbalance the economy.
- compare and contrast the high-employment budget with the government's actual budget.
- describe how traditional accounting procedures will overstate the interest component of government

expenditures during a period of inflation.
- describe the inflationary consequences of a budget deficit and explain why deficits will be more inflationary if they are monetarized.
- distinguish between real and bogus arguments about the burden of the national debt.
- explain how interest-rate-induced crowding out of investment can occur.
- explain how exchange-rate-induced crowding out of export sales can occur.

IMPORTANT TERMS AND CONCEPTS

Budget deficit
National debt
Real versus nominal interest rates
Inflation accounting
High-employment budget
Monetization of deficits
Interest-rate crowding out
Exchange-rate crowding out
Burden of the national debt

CHAPTER REVIEW

The large federal budget deficit is viewed as a fundamental constraint which limits the government's ability to use expansionary policies to stimulate employment. It is, therefore, important for everyone to appreciate to what extent this constraint is real or imaginary.

(1)   The government runs a deficit when its (*spending/revenue*) exceeds its _____ .

There is a surplus when _____ is greater than _____ . The national debt measures the government's total indebtedness. The national debt will increase if the government budget shows a (*deficit/surplus*). The national debt will decrease if the government budget shows a

_____ .

What is appropriate deficit policy? Earlier chapters discussed the use of fiscal and monetary policy to strike an appropriate balance between aggregate demand and aggregate supply in order to choose between inflation and unemployment. Considerations of balanced budgets, per se, were absent from that discussion. The conclusion that budget policy should adapt to the requirements of the economy is widely shared by most economists. At the same time, it is recognized that government deficits do affect employment, inflation, and interest rates.

Some have advocated a policy of strict budget balance. There is good reason to expect that such a policy would balance the budget at the cost of unbalancing the economy. Consider an economy in an initial equilibrium at full employment with a balanced budget. An autonomous decline in consumption spending would shift the

(2)   expenditure schedule (*down/up*), resulting in a shift of the aggregate (*demand/supply*) schedule to the (*right/left*). In the absence of any further policy action the result would be a (*decline/increase*) in income and output. Since income taxes are a major component of government revenues, the change in income will also mean a(n)

_____ in government tax revenues. The government's budget will move from its initial position of balance to one of (*deficit/surplus*). At this point, deliberate policy actions to re-establish budget balance would call for either a(n) (*decrease/increase*) in taxes or a(n) (*decrease/increase*) in government expenditures. In either case the result would be an additional shift in the expenditure schedule and aggregate-demand curve that would (*accentuate/counteract*) the original shift that was due to the autonomous decline in consumption expenditures.

The fact that tax revenues depend on the state of the economy is important to understanding many complicated issues about the impact of deficits. As seen above, it helps to explain why a policy of budget balancing can unbalance the economy in the face of declines in private spending. It helps to explain why deficits can sometimes be associated with a booming economy and at other times with a sagging economy. It also helps to explain interest in alternative measures of the deficit. The high-employment budget is an attempt to separate out the impact of the economy on the deficit. It does so by looking at spending and revenues at a fixed level of income,

(3)   the full-employment level of income. Changes in tax revenues due to changes in income (*will/will not*) affect the actual deficit but (*will/will not*) affect the high-employment deficit. For this reason many analysts prefer to use the high-employment deficit as a measure of the stance of fiscal policy.

Inflation and, especially, the impact of inflation on interest rates raise complicated measurement problems. As we learned in Chapter 6, during periods of inflation, increases in nominal interest rates that reflect expectations of future inflation may not imply any change in real interest rates. To the extent that nominal interest rates include such inflationary premiums, a proportion of interest payments is not interest in the sense of payment for the use of the purchasing power embodied in the original loan; rather it is a repayment of the purchasing power embodied in the loan.

Are deficits inflationary? The short answer is yes and the more complete answer asks for more details. If the alternative to any deficit is more taxation or less spending, then any deficit, whether the result of deliberate policy or a reduction in autonomous spending, will mean a higher price level, a higher level of output, less unemployment, and more inflation than the alternative of a balanced budget, because the deficit would keep the aggregate-demand curve farther to the right than it would be with either a decrease in spending or an increase in taxes. The exact inflationary consequences of a budget deficit depend on where along the aggregate-supply curve the economy finds itself and what monetary policy is doing. A government deficit during a period of recession may find the economy operating on a relatively flat portion of the aggregate-supply curve. If so, any reduction in the deficit will

(4)   will likely have a (*large/small*) impact on the price level. On the other hand, substantial budget deficits at a time of full employment will find the economy on a relatively steep portion of the aggregate-supply curve. In this case, a

reduction in the deficit is likely to have a (*large/small*) impact on output and a _____ impact on the price level.

A deficit that is associated with a deliberate reduction in taxes will increase output, prices, and interest rates as it shifts the aggregate-demand curve to the right. Concerns about the impact of the deficit on interest rates may lead the Bank of Canada to increase the money supply. If the Bank of Canada increases the money supply by

(5) buying government securities, one says it has _____ the deficit. As we learned in Chapter 13, the deficit-related expansion of the money supply will imply a further expansionary shift in the aggregate-demand curve and will mean even higher prices.

Many feelings about the burden of the national debt may be as deeply ingrained and just as irrational as a Victorian's ideas about sex or a football coach's ideas about winning. Many bogus arguments about the burden of the debt do, however, contain some elements of truth. Arguments about the burden of future interest payments or the cost of repaying the national debt are not relevant when considering debts held by domestic citizens but are

(6) relevant when considering debts held by _____. To the extent that debt is held by domestic citizens, interest payments and debt repayments impose little burden on the nation as a whole, because they are only transfers from taxpayers to bondholders, who may even be the same individuals. But this cancelling out cannot occur when the national debt is foreign-owned.

A second real burden of the debt arises from a deficit in a high-employment economy that crowds out

(7) private (*consumption/investment*) spending and leaves a smaller capital stock to future generations. There will continue to be arguments as to whether Canadian deficits have entailed such a burden. Major concerns about deficits projected for the mid 1980s are that they are projected to occur even if we return to reasonably high levels

of employment so that they are thus likely to lead to crowding _____, and to an increased ownership of our national debt.

BASIC EXERCISE

This exercise is designed to show how a rigid policy of balanced budgets may unbalance the economy. To simplify the calculations, the exercise assumes that exports and imports do not exist and that prices do not change and thus focuses on the horizontal shift in the aggregate-demand curve.

1. Complete column 7 of Table 17-1 to determine the initial equilibrium level of income. The equilibrium

   level of income is _____ .
2. What is the deficit at the initial equilibrium level of

   income? _____
3. The full-employment level of income is $420. Is the high-employment budget in surplus or deficit?

   _____

What is the magnitude of the high-employment surplus or deficit?

_____

4. Investment spending now declines by $8 billion. Use Table 17-2 to compute the new equilibrium level of income. What is the new equilibrium level of

   income? _____ How

   has the deficit changed, if at all? _____
   How has the high-employment (*deficit/surplus*)

   changed, if at all? _____

   _____
5. If the government is committed to a balanced budget, would it raise or lower taxes to restore a

TABLE 17-1

(ALL FIGURES ARE IN BILLIONS OF REAL DOLLARS)

(1) National Income	(2) Taxes	(3) Disposable Income	(4) Consumption Spending	(5) Investment Spending	(6) Government Spending	(7) C + I + G
340	85	255	214	50	100	_____
360	90	270	226	50	100	_____
380	95	285	238	50	100	_____
400	100	300	250	50	100	_____
420	105	315	262	50	100	_____

TABLE 17-2

(ALL FIGURES ARE IN BILLIONS OF REAL DOLLARS)

National Income	Taxes	Disposable Income	Consumption Spending	Investment Spending	Government Spending	$C + I + G$
340	85	255	214	42	100	_____
360	90	270	226	42	100	_____
380	95	285	238	42	100	_____
400	100	300	250	42	100	_____
420	105	315	262	42	100	_____

balanced budget? _____ What would this change in taxes do to national income?

_____

_____

6. If the government decides to change government purchases to eliminate the deficit, would it raise or lower spending? _____ What would this change do to the equilibrium level of national income? _____

_____

7. (Optional) How large a lump-sum change in taxes, that is, the same change at every level of income, would balance the budget? $ _____ billion. The new equilibrium level of income would be $_____ billion.

8. (Optional) How large a change in government spending would balance the budget? $_____ billion. The new equilibrium level of income would be $_____ billion.

SELF-TESTS FOR UNDERSTANDING

Test A

Circle the correct answer.

1. The ratio of the national debt to GNP
   a. has declined continuously since WWII.
   b. has increased continuously since WWII.
   c. is about 3 to 1.
   d. has risen somewhat in recent years from its low point in the mid-1970s.
2. A comparison of the federal government's actual deficit and the high-employment deficit for recent years would show that the actual deficit has been

a. smaller than the high-employment deficit.
b. about the same size as the high-employment deficit.
c. larger than the high-employment deficit.
3. Rigid adherence to budget balancing will
   a. help the economy adjust to shifts in private spending.
   b. have little impact on business cycles.
   c. accentuate swings in GNP from autonomous changes in private spending.
   d. help maintain full employment.
4. A decline in private investment spending will lead to all but which one of the following?
   a. A downward shift in the expenditure schedule.
   b. A decline in the equilibrium level of GNP.
   c. An increase in the government deficit or a reduction in the surplus.
   d. A decline in the high-employment budget surplus.
5. If the Bank of Canada monetizes a budget deficit, there will be a(n)
   a. smaller inflationary impact.
   b. unchanged inflationary impact.
   c. larger inflationary impact.
6. The inflationary consequences of a budget deficit are likely to be greatest when
   a. the deficit is the result of a decline in private spending.
   b. the deficit is the result of a deliberate decision to raise taxes and monetize the resulting deficit.
   c. the deficit is the result of a deliberate decision to increase government spending and to monetize the resulting deficit.
   d. the rate of unemployment is high.
7. Using real interest rates when measuring the deficit during a period of inflation would have what impact?
   a. It would make the deficit smaller.
   b. It would leave the deficit unchanged.
   c. It would make the deficit larger.
8. Which of the following is a valid argument about the burden of the national debt for an economy whose debt is held entirely by its own citizens?
   a. Future generations will find interest payments a heavy burden.

b. When the debt is due, future generations will be burdened with an enormous repayment.

c. The debt will bankrupt future generations.

d. If the deficits causing the debt crowded out private investment spending, then future generations would be left with a smaller capital stock.

9. "Crowding out" refers to

a. increased population pressures and arguments for zero population growth.

b. the effects of government deficits on private investment spending.

c. what happens at the start of the New York City marathon.

d. the impact of higher prices on the multiplier.

Test B

Circle T or F for True or False as appropriate.

1. A policy of continuous balanced budget will help offset shifts in autonomous private demand. **T F**

2. Inflation accounting would increase the interest portion of government expenditures because real interest rates have typically exceeded nominal interest rates. **T F**

3. Increases in the government's deficit are always associated with increases in interest rates. **T F**

4. The inflationary impact of any budget deficit depends on the conduct of monetary policy. **T F**

5. Recent government deficits have meant that the ratio of national debt to GNP has never been higher than it is today. **T F**

6. Interest payments on the national debt, whether to domestic citizens or foreigners, are not really a burden on future generations. **T F**

7. A major limitation of the simple crowding-out argument is the assumption that the economy's total pool of savings is fixed. **T F**

8. Large budget deficits can crowd out export sales, if foreign funds enter the country to buy the bonds the government sells to cover the deficit. **T F**

9. Government deficits may impose a real burden on future generations if, as a result of crowding out, there is less private investment and a smaller capital stock in the future. **T F**

SUPPLEMENTARY EXERCISES

1. Consider the Following Argument:

If the national debt is so onerous, we could solve the problem by simply repudiating the debt; that is, we would make no more interest or principal payments on the outstanding debt.

Imagine that in keeping with democratic principles such a proposition were put to Canadian voters. Who do you think would vote pro and who would vote con? Which side would win? Would the outcome of the vote be different if the debt were held entirely by foreigners? By banks and other financial institutions? (You might want to consider what would happen to depositors, shareholders, and pensioners, both current and prospective, if the national debt held by banks, corporations, and pension funds was suddenly worthless.)

Repudiating the national debt might well limit future budget flexibility. What are the likely consequences during periods of recession? Inflation? War?

2. What are the long-run consequences of continual budget deficits? If you have access to a programmable hand calculator or to a micro-computer, experiment with the following simulation model to discover how results depend on particular coefficients.

a. Assume that nominal GNP grows at a constant rate, λ:

$$GNP_t = (1 + \lambda) \, GNP_{t-1}$$

b. Assume that tax receipts are proportional to nominal GNP.

$$T_t = \tau \, GNP_t$$

c. Assume that government purchases of goods and services plus all transfer payments except for interest on the national debt are also some constant percentage of nominal GNP:

$$G_t = g \, GNP_t; \, g > \tau$$

(This specification means that, not counting interest payments, the government deficit will always be a constant proportion $[g - \tau]$ of nominal GNP.)

d. Assume that the government must pay interest on the national debt at a rate of interest R:

$$\text{Interest Payments} = IP_t = R \, (\text{Debt}_{t-1})$$

e. The government's total deficit is:

$$\text{Deficit}_t = G_t + IP_t - T_t$$

f. The government debt grows as follows:

$$\text{Debt}_t = \text{Debt}_{t-1} + \text{Deficit}_t$$

g. Use these relationships to simulate your model economy and investigate what happens to the ratio of debt to GNP. To start your simulations you will need values for the four parameters, λ, τ, g, and R, and initial values for GNP and the national debt.

Try starting with the following:

$$\lambda = 0.10$$
$$\tau = 0.25$$
$$g = 0.27$$
$$R = 0.07$$
$$\text{GNP} = 3300$$
$$\text{Debt} = 1000$$

What happens to the ratio of debt to GNP as your model economy evolves?

h. Try experimenting with some alternative parameters and initial values.

    (i) Change the initial value of GNP, then change the initial value of the national debt.

Do these changes affect what happens over time?

(ii) Now change τ and g. What happens? Do these changes affect the eventual ratio of debt to GNP? If so, how?

(iii) Finally, change λ and R, individually and then together. Remember that λ is the growth rate of nominal GNP and R is nominal interest rates. Higher inflation would be expected to change both λ and R, whereas a change in real growth or real interest rates would change them individually. Do these changes affect the eventual ratio of debt to GNP? If so, how?

The Trade-Off Between Inflation and Unemployment

18

LEARNING OBJECTIVES

After completing the material in this chapter you should be able to:

- define, understand, and use correctly the terms and concepts listed below.
- explain how prices can rise following either the rapid growth of aggregate demand or the sluggish growth of aggregate supply.
- explain what the Phillips curve is.
- explain how the source of fluctuations in economic activity—whether predominantly from shifts of the aggregate-demand curve or from shifts of the aggregate-supply curve—will affect the slope of the Phillips curve.
- explain how the accuracy of expectations about inflation can affect the slope of both the aggregate-supply curve and the Phillips curve.
- use the long-run Phillips curve to show how the temporary impact of aggregate-demand policy on unemployment can have a permanent impact on the rate of inflation.
- explain why the economy's self-correcting mechanism, especially in the case of an inflationary

gap, means that the economy's true long-run choices lie along a vertical Phillips curve.
- explain how and why one's views on appropriate aggregate-demand policy are likely to depend upon one's views on
  —the social costs of inflation vs. unemployment.
  —the efficiency of the economy's self-correcting mechanism.
  —the current level of output vis-a-vis full-employment output.

IMPORTANT TERMS AND CONCEPTS

Demand-side inflation
Supply-side inflation
Phillips curve
Self-correcting mechanism
Natural rate of unemployment
Vertical (long-run) Phillips curve
Trade-off between inflation and unemployment in the short run and in the long run
Inflationary expectations
Rational expectations
Stagflation caused by supply-side shocks

CHAPTER REVIEW

This chapter discusses the hard choices that policy-makers must make when deciding how to respond to inflation or unemployment. Chapters 11 through 17 discussed how changes in various tools of fiscal, monetary, and exchange-rate policy can be used to influence aggregate demand. Chapter 18 integrates this material on aggregate demand with the aggregate-supply curve to study the implications for both unemployment and inflation. Here, as in many other areas of life, one cannot have one's cake and eat it too. Actions taken to reduce unemployment will often lead to higher rates of inflation, while actions to reduce inflation will often lead to higher rates of unemployment. Economists can help to define the nature of this trade-off, examine the factors that are responsible for it, and clarify the implications of different choices; but they cannot tell anyone which choice to make. In a democratic society, this decision is left to the political process.

Any shift in the aggregate-demand or aggregate-supply curve, whether induced by policy or not, is likely to affect both prices and output. The nature of the association between changes in prices and changes in output will depend upon which curve shifts. If fluctuations in economic activity are predominantly the result of shifts in the

(1) aggregate-demand curve, higher prices will be associated with (*higher/lower*) levels of output. The transition to higher prices is a period of inflation. The associated higher level of output will require more employment, leading to a lower level of unemployment. Hence, shifts in the aggregate-demand curve imply that inflation and unemployment are (*negatively/positively*) correlated. That is, if you plotted the rate of unemployment on the horizontal axis and

the rate of inflation on the vertical axis, the resulting curve, called the _____ curve, would have a (*positive/negative*) slope.

Data available through the end of the 1960s was consistent with the view sketched above and seemed to imply that policy-makers could choose between inflation and unemployment. In particular, it used to be thought that the Phillips curve implied that policy-makers could permanently increase output beyond the level of potential output at the cost of only a small increase in the rate of inflation. Subsequent experience and thought have shown that this

(2) view is (*correct/incorrect*). We saw earlier that output beyond the level of potential output results in a(n) (*inflationary/recessionary*) gap. The economy's self-correcting mechanism will shift the aggregate-supply curve to

re-establish long-run equilibrium at the _____ rate of unemployment. Only continual shifts of the aggregate-demand curve will consistently maintain the lower rates of unemployment. These continual shifts of the aggregate-demand curve will imply an ever-increasing rate of inflation. The only true long-run choices lie along

a _____ Phillips curve.

In the short run, shifts in the aggregate-demand curve will move the economy up or down the short-run Phillips curve; but the economy's self-correcting mechanism implies that this trade-off is only temporary. How temporary depends upon the speed of the economy's self-correcting mechanism. Differing views about the speed of the mechanism are part of the explanation of differences in Keynesian and monetarist policy prescriptions.

Autonomous changes in wages are an important determinant of shifts in the aggregate-supply curve that lead an inflationary gap to self-destruct. It is the original increase in prices above wages that induces firms to expand output. As workers recognize that the purchasing power of their money wages has declined, the subsequent increases in wages to restore real wages will lead to shifts in the aggregate-supply curve. Rather than always being a step behind, workers can try to protect their real wages by anticipating the increase in prices. The expectation of higher prices will lead to higher wages and a shift in the aggregate-supply curve in anticipation of inflation. Compared with cases where the aggregate-supply curve did not shift, a shift in the aggregate-demand curve

(3) accompanied by an expectations-induced shift in the aggregate-supply curve will have a (*larger/smaller*) impact

on output and a _____ impact on prices. The result will be a (*higher/lower*) rate of inflation and the slope of the short-run Phillips curve will be (*steeper/flatter*).

Economists associated with the doctrine of rational expectations have focused attention on the formation of expectations. While much remains to be learned, these economists argue that errors in predicting inflation cannot be systematic. An implication of this view is that except for random elements, the short-run Phillips curve is vertical. Not only is there no long-run trade-off between inflation and unemployment, but, according to this view, there is also no exploitable short-run trade-off.

Others are less convinced that expectations are rational in the sense of no systematic errors. These economists believe that people tend to underpredict inflation when it is rising and overpredict it when it is falling. Long-term contracts also make it difficult to adjust to changing expectations of inflation. These economists argue that policy measures to shift the aggregate-demand curve do affect output and employment in the short run. But remember that these short-run impacts are constrained by the true long-run menu of choices which lie along a

(4) _____ Phillips curve.

Most economists believe that aggregate-demand policy will affect employment in the short run and may also affect the place at which the economy ends up on the long-run Phillips curve. Thus, a policy to fight a recession rather than to wait for the economy's self-correcting mechanism will mean more employment in the short run and is likely to mean more inflation in the long run. Whether one wants to use aggregate-demand policy or wait for natural processes depends, in part, on one's assessment of the costs of inflation and unemployment, the efficiency of the economy's self-correcting mechanisms, and the current level of output vis-a-vis full employment, especially as it has implications for the slope of the aggregate-supply curve. Deliberate policy measures can speed up the transition to a sustainable long-run equilibrium, given either a recessionary or inflationary gap. By speeding up the process, policy can affect where the economy ends up on the long-run Phillips curve. Thus, policy will have temporary impacts on the rate of employment and permanent impacts on the rate of inflation.

Keynesians tend to believe that below full employment the Phillips curve is relatively flat and the economy's self-correcting mechanism is relatively slow. Thus, in the absence of activist policy, there is likely to be a long period of high unemployment with little reduction in the rate of inflation. In this case expansionary policy offers a quick reduction in unemployment with little impact on the rate of inflation. Monetarists and rational expectationists, on the

(5) other hand, tend to believe that the short-run Phillips curve is (*flat/steep*) and that the economy's self-correcting mechanism is (*slow/fast*). Thus, it is not surprising that their policy recommendations (*coincide/conflict*) with Keynesian recommendations.

Inflation can also come from shifts in the aggregate-supply curve. In the case of an adverse shift in the

(6) aggregate-supply curve—a shift to the left—higher prices will be associated with (*higher/lower*) output. If fluctuations in economic activity are predominantly the result of shifts in aggregate supply, then the plot of inflation and unemployment is likely to have a (*positive/negative*) slope. Many economists feel that adverse supply shocks are an important part of the explanation of inflation in Canada and other Western countries during the 1970s.

BASIC EXERCISE

This exercise is designed to illustrate the nature of the inflation–unemployment trade-off that policy-makers must face when planning aggregate-demand policy.

1. Figure 18-1 shows an economy with a recessionary gap. Which of the following monetary and fiscal policies could be used to help eliminate this gap?
   - open market (*purchase/sale*).
   - (*increase/decrease*) in taxes.
   - (*increase/decrease*) in government transfer payments to individuals.
   - (*increase/decrease*) in government purchases of goods and services.

2. Assume the full-employment level of income is $380 billion. Draw a new aggregate-demand curve, representing one or more of the appropriate policies you identified in Question 1, that will restore full employment for this economy. Following a shift in the aggregate-demand curve, prices will rise to

   _____ .

3. Consider the following statement: "The increase in prices that resulted when we restored full employment was a small price to pay for the increased output. Why not try moving even farther along the aggregate-supply curve? If we further stimulate the economy to lower unemployment we can increase output to, say $390 billion and prices will only rise to 109. We can thus have a permanent increase in output of $10 billion every year in return for a one-time increase in prices of about 6 percent. That's a pretty favourable trade-off." What is wrong

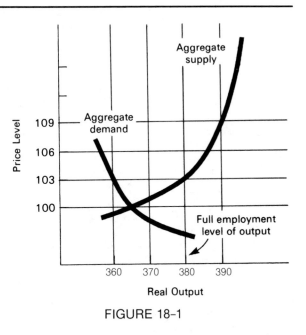

FIGURE 18-1

with the reasoning of this argument?

Is the output–price combination of $390 billion and 109 a viable long-run equilibrium position? (Figure 18-2 illustrates such a combination. What is apt to happen to the aggregate-supply curve? Draw in the new aggregate-supply curve that restores full employment.) What would happen if government policy-makers tried to keep output at $390 billion on a permanent basis? (That is, what would happen if

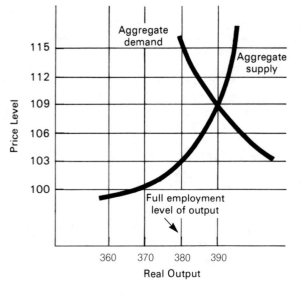

FIGURE 18-2

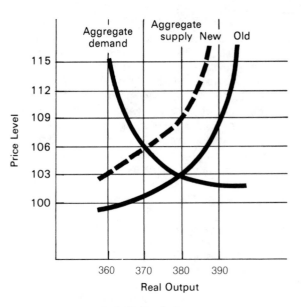

FIGURE 18-3

every time the aggregate-supply curve shifted, policy-makers undertook appropriate expansionary fiscal or monetary policy to shift the aggregate-demand curve in an effort to avoid any reduction in output?) What does this imply about the slope of the long-run Phillips curve?

4. Figure 18-3 shows an economy following an adverse shift in the aggregate-supply curve. Equilibrium used to be at an output of $380 billion and a price level of 103.
   a. What is the new equilibrium immediately following the adverse shift in the supply curve?

      Output_____

      Prices _____

   b. If there is to be no decline in employment, the government must undertake (*expansionary/restrictive*) policies to shift the aggregate-demand curve. The government could maintain employment but at the cost of an increase in

      prices to _____ .

   c. Alternatively, the government could avoid any increase in prices. Such a decision would require (*expansionary/restrictive*) policies and would result in a new equilibrium level of output of

      _____

SELF-TESTS FOR UNDERSTANDING

Test A

Circle the correct answer.

1. If prices are expected to rise by 8 percent, what increase in money wages is necessary to offer the prospect of a 3 percent increase in real wages?
   a. 3 percent.
   b. 5 percent.
   c. 8 percent.
   d. 11 percent.
2. If prices increase by more than expected, then real wages will likely turn out to be
   a. lower than expected.
   b. higher than expected.
   c. unchanged from initial expectations.
3. The Phillips curve refers to
   a. the relation between tax revenues and tax rates.
   b. the pitch that won the World Series for the Dodgers in 1955.
   c. the correlation between the rate of unemployment and the percentage change in wages or prices.
   d. the correlation between the rate of growth of money and the rate of inflation.
4. In the long run, the Phillips curve is likely to
   a. have a negative slope.
   b. have a positive slope.
   c. be horizontal.
   d. be vertical.

5. If fluctuations in economic activity are caused by shifts in the aggregate-demand curve, then
   a. prices and output will be negatively correlated.
   b. the short-run Phillips curve will be vertical.
   c. the long-run Phillips curve will have a negative slope.
   d. the rates of inflation and unemployment will tend to be negatively correlated.

6. If fluctuations in economic activity are caused by shifts in the aggregate-supply curve, then
   a. prices and output will be negatively correlated.
   b. the short-run Phillips curve will have a negative slope.
   c. the long-run Phillips curve will be horizontal.
   d. the rates of inflation and unemployment will tend to be negatively correlated.

7. An adherent to the doctrine of rational expectations would be surprised by which one of the following occurrences?
   a. An announcement by the Bank of Canada that it will increase the rate of growth of the money supply leads to expectations of higher inflation.
   b. Plans to lower taxes give rise to expectations of higher prices.
   c. Plans to fight inflation by restrictive policy succeed in reducing the rate of inflation with no increase in unemployment.
   d. An examination of the record shows that people consistently underestimate the rate of inflation during periods when it is increasing.

8. The doctrine of rational expectations implies that increases in output beyond the level of potential output can be produced by
   a. expected increases in prices.
   b. unexpected increases in prices.
   c. any increase in prices whether expected or not.
   d. pre-announced increases in the money supply.

9. Using deliberate stabilization policy to cure a recession rather than waiting for the economy's self-correcting mechanism
   a. means that we will end up with the same output and price level, only sooner.
   b. means that we will end up with a permanently higher level of output.
   c. will give us a temporary period of higher employment at the cost of more inflation.
   d. means that the price level will be permanently lower.

10. Which of the following is *not* a feasible alternative for aggregate-demand policy following an adverse shift of the supply curve to the left?
    a. Do nothing and initially experience both higher prices and lower output.
    b. Avoid the reduction in output at the cost of even higher prices.
    c. Avoid the increase in prices at the cost of an even greater decline in output.
    d. Avoid both the reduction in output and increase in prices by appropriate policies to shift the aggregate-demand curve.

Test B

Circle T or F for True or False as appropriate.

1. Inflation occurs only as a result of shifts in the aggregate-demand curve.　　　　　　　　T F

2. In contrast to expansionary monetary or fiscal policy, an autonomous increase in private spending will increase output without increasing prices.　T F

3. If fluctuations in economic activity are predominantly the result of shifts in the aggregate-supply curve, the rate of unemployment and the rate of inflation will tend to be positively correlated.　　　　　　　　　　　T F

4. The economy's self-correcting mechanism implies that the only long-run policy choices for the economy lie along a vertical Phillips curve.　T F

5. The natural rate of unemployment is given by the position of the long-run Phillips curve.　　T F

6. A belief that the economy's self-correcting mechanism works quickly is an argument in favour of activist demand-management policy.　　T F

7. Expectations of inflation that lead to higher wages will be somewhat self-fulfilling as the increase in wages shifts the aggregate-supply curve.　T F

8. One can minimize the inflationary effects of fighting a recession by using fiscal policy rather than monetary policy.　　　　　　　　　　　T F

9. Following an adverse shift in the aggregate-supply curve, aggregate-demand policies can stop the rise in prices with no increase in unemployment.　T F

10. The economy's self-correcting mechanism means that, in the face of an inflationary gap, output and prices will eventually be the same with or without restrictive stabilization policy.　　　T F

Further Controversies Over Stabilization Policy

19

LEARNING OBJECTIVES

After completing the material in this chapter you should be able to:

- define, understand, and use correctly the terms and concepts listed below.
- discuss measures that have been advocated to reduce the natural rate of unemployment.
- describe the various kinds of incomes policies and other plans that have been tried in Canada and elsewhere in an effort to improve the inflation-unemployment trade-off.
- calculate how indexing would be applied to wages and interest rates, given the appropriate data on prices.
- discuss the advantages and disadvantages of universal indexing.
- explain how long lags might mean that efforts to stabilize the economy could end up destabilizing it.
- summarize monetarist objections to activist stabilization policy.

- summarize Keynesian objections to non-activist stabilization policy.
- explain how automatic stabilizers help to reduce fluctuations in GNP.

IMPORTANT TERMS AND CONCEPTS

Incomes policy
Jawboning
Wage-price guidelines
Wage-price controls
Anti-Inflation Board (AIB)
Inflationary expectations
Wage-price freezes
Tax-based incomes policy (TIP)
Indexing (escalator clauses)
Real versus nominal interest rates
Rules versus discretionary policy
Automatic stabilizers

CHAPTER REVIEW

This chapter first considers a number of policies that are advocated in the hope that they will improve the inflation–unemployment trade-off. It then considers whether or not the government should engage in any stabilization policy.

(1) Many economists, politicians, and government officials have advocated what are called incomes policies; that is, policies designed to reduce inflation without reducing aggregate (*demand/supply*). These policies run the gamut from a prime minister's exhortations to elaborate wage-price monitoring bureaucracies to the use of the tax system as either a carrot or a stick.

Verbal intimidation, threats, and cajoling to induce businesses to hold the line on prices are a form of

(2) _____ . *Voluntary wage-price guidelines* call for business and labour to set wages and prices in line with standards determined, in part, by increases in labour productivity. The logic of these guidelines is that competitive markets can allow wage increases in line with increases in productivity without inflation. Thus, if labour productivity is increasing at 2 percent a year and the government is aiming to hold inflation to 3 percent a

year, the guideline standard for wage increases would be _____ percent.

More drastic forms of incomes policies include wage-price controls or even a wage-price freeze. Neither policy is a desirable long-run option. If adhered to for a long time, either policy undermines the allocative role of prices and results in inefficient alternatives. A wage-price freeze or a set of controls might work if it resulted in a significant

(3) lowering of inflationary _____ . However, if there is no change in the underlying forces of aggregate demand and supply, there (*is/is not*) likely to be much change in expectations. Luckily these underlying forces were consistent with the controls schemes tried in Canada in recent years (the

_____ - _____ _____ during 1975-78, and the "6 and 5" public sector wage controls in 1983-84.)

A number of individuals have argued that rather than trying to reduce the rate of inflation we should simply learn to live with it and rely on automatic adjustments of monetary payments to reflect changes in prices, also called indexing. The automatic adjustment of Canada Pension Plan benefits and the exemption and tax-bracket levels in

(4) the personal income tax system, and escalator clauses in wage contracts are examples of _____ . A number of observers also advocate this mechanism for interest rates.

Indexing does seem to offer some relief from many of the social costs of inflation discussed in Chapter 6. As workers, firms, and lenders scramble to protect themselves against anticipated future increases in prices, current

(5) prices and interest rates will (*increase/decrease*) to reflect the expectation of inflation. If actual inflation turns out to be greater or less than expected, there will be a redistribution of wealth that many feel is essentially arbitrary. Uncertainty over future prices may make individuals and businesses extremely reluctant to enter into long-term contracts.

Indexing offers relief from all these problems. Contracts and other agreements could be written in real rather than nominal terms, and arbitrary redistributions would be avoided because money payments would reflect actual, not expected, inflation. At the same time there is concern that learning to live with inflation may make the economy

(6) (*more/less*) inflation prone.

(7) *Stabilization policy* involves manipulation of the tools of monetary and fiscal policy to stabilize the economy at full employment with minimal inflation. Keynesians tend to be (*more/less*) activist-oriented and to support (*more/less*) discretionary stabilization policy than do monetarists, who tend to be in favour of

_____ activism, with more reliance on _____ stabilizers. These differences reflect differing political philosophies as well as different judgments of the importance of such factors as the economy's self-correcting mechanisms, the length of various policy lags, the stability of the multiplier and velocity, and the accuracy of economic forecasting.

It takes time before someone notices that the economy is not operating as hoped for and before the appropriate part of the government can decide on what policy measures should be adopted. Even once a particular policy is decided upon, there will not be much effect on output and prices until the buying habits of households and firms adjust to new policy. Because of lags, it is not enough to design policies just for today's problems. Economists must also try to predict the future. One way they attempt to do this is through the use of mathematical formulas called econometric models. Another method concentrates on historical timing relationships of some economic variables, called leading indicators.

In addition, the Canadian government and several private organizations periodically ask people and firms about their spending plans for the future. This survey data can also be a useful tool in forecasting. The more accurate the economic forecasts, the more demanding the standards we can set for stabilization policy. At the present time

(8)   economic forecasts (*are/are not*) good enough for fine-tuning the economy.

Active use of fiscal policy to correct persistent and sustained deviation from potential output calls for changes in government spending or taxes. The fact that spending or taxes can be changed means that active stabilization policy need not imply that government spending takes an ever larger proportion of the economic pie.

BASIC EXERCISES

1. *Wages, prices, and productivity.* If all prices remain stable, all hourly labour costs may increase as fast as economy-wide productivity without, for that reason alone, changing the relative share of labour and non-labour incomes in total output. At the same time, each kind of income increases steadily in absolute amount. If hourly labour costs increase at a slower rate than productivity, the share of non-labour incomes will grow or prices will fall, or both. Conversely, if hourly labour costs increase more rapidly than productivity, the share of labour incomes in total product will increase or prices will rise, or both. It is this relationship among long-run economy-wide productivity, wages, and prices that makes the rate of productivity change an important benchmark for non-inflationary wage and price behaviour.

This exercise is designed to illustrate some of the ideas associated with wage-price guidelines based on increases in labour productivity. In particular, we will see that even if firms do not increase prices there can be *increases in both wages and profits* when wages increase in step with increases in labour productivity.

Column 1 of Table 19-1 illustrates the initial position of the Acme Manufacturing Company, a firm that produces gizmos. In all the remaining columns it is assumed that labour productivity has increased by 10 percent. (In reality, 10 percent would be a most unusually large increase; we use it here to simplify the calculations. The same principle would apply even if the increase in labour productivity were smaller.)

a. Column 2 assumes that hourly wages increase in step with labour productivity. Fill in the appropriate spaces for total output, total revenue, and profits plus overhead. What is the percentage increase in total wages and in profits plus overhead? Are they equal?

b. Column 3 assumes that hourly wages increase by less than the increase in labour productivity. Fill in the appropriate spaces for total output, total revenue, and profits and overhead. What is the percentage increase in total wages and in profits plus overhead? Are they equal? Are your answers to this and the preceding question

consistent with the summary presented at the start of this exercise?

c. Column 4 is meant to illustrate a situation of general inflation. As discussed in Chapter 19 of your textbook, the claim of wage-price guidelines is that wage increases equal to the increase in labour productivity plus the target rate of inflation will, in combination with price increases equal to the target rate, allow equal percentage increases in both wages and profits plus overhead. Prices and wages in column 4 are based on a target rate of inflation of 5 percent. Fill in the appropriate spaces for total output, total revenue, and profits plus overhead to see if the inflation plus productivity standard favours workers or capitalists.

d. If things work so simply, why can't we eliminate inflation overnight by adopting an inflation target of zero?

2. This exercise is designed to illustrate the mechanics of indexing interest rates. Table 19-2 has data showing the market yield on one-year Government bonds as of December in each of five recent years. For example, if in December 1979 you spent $10,000 for a one-year Government security, in December 1980 you would have received $11,224 ($10,000 × 1.1224). This is a nominal return; that is, the interest rate reflects the number of dollars you will receive in one year, not how much purchasing power you will have.

Imagine that instead of purchasing these government securities you had the option of purchasing an indexed security that offered you a 2 percent real return, regardless of the rate of inflation. That is, in December of the following year you would receive interest dollars equal to 2 percent plus the percentage increase in the CPI, December to December. Which security would you prefer: the Government security offering you a known number of dollars of unknown purchasing power or the hypothetical indexed security offering you an unknown number of dollars of known purchasing power?

To help you choose, Table 19-2 also has data on consumer prices over this period. Follow the instructions in Table 19-2 to compare the dollar yield of the indexed security with the dollar yield of the Government securities.

What interest rate could you get today if you invested your money for one year? What could you earn at a bank or trust company? Would you prefer an indexed security offering a real return of 2 percent? 1 percent? 0 percent (that is, just enough interest to match inflation)?

TABLE 19-1

ACME MANUFACTURING COMPANY

	(1)	(2)	(3)	(4)
1. Employment (people)	100	100	100	100
2. Labour productivity (gizmos per employee)	4,000	4,400	4,400	4,400
3. Total output [(1) × (2)]	400,000	_____	_____	_____
4. Price per gizmo	$ 5.00	$ 5.00	$ 5.00	$ 5.25
5. Total revenue [(4) × (3)]	$2,000,000	_____	_____	_____
6. Hourly wage	$ 8.00	$ 8.80	$ 8.60	$ 9.24*
7. Total wages [(6) × 2000 × (1)]	$1,600,000	$1,760,000	$1,720,000	$1,848,000
8. Profits plus overhead [(5) - (7)]	400,000	_____	_____	_____

*If x is the percentage increase in labour productivity and y is the rate of inflation, the correct adjustment of wages is $(1 + x)(1 + y) - 1 = x + y + xy$. In our case, this formula works out to 15.5 percent, slightly greater than the 15 percent implied by looking just at $x + y$.

TABLE 19-2

	(1) Nominal Yield One-Year Government of Canada Bonds (percent)	(2) Consumer Price Index (1981 = 100)	(3) Percentage Change CPI	(4) 2 Percent Real Return	(5) Nominal Return on Indexed Security (percent)
December 1979	12.24	84.0		2.0	
December 1980	12.95	93.4	_____	2.0	_____
December 1981	15.22	104.7	_____	2.0	_____
December 1982	10.24	114.4	_____	2.0	_____
December 1983	10.39	119.6	_____	2.0	_____
December 1984	10.44	124.1	_____	2.0	_____

Directions:
a. Fill in column 3 by figuring the percentage change in the CPI from one December to the next. For December 1980 the appropriate entry is (93.4 - 84.0)/84.0 = 11.19 percent.
b. Fill in column 5 by adding columns 3 and 4.
c. Remember that to compare the nominal yield on the Government security with the hypothetical indexed security you must compare the December entry for the Government security with the succeeding December entry for the indexed security. Why? The Government security, as well as savings deposits and corporate bonds, offers you a nominal yield that is determined at the beginning of the period. The nominal yield of an indexed security for the same period cannot be determined until the end of the period, until you know how much inflation has actually occurred.

Source: Bank of Canada *Review*.

SELF-TESTS FOR UNDERSTANDING

Test A

Circle the correct answer.

1. Which of the following policies is aimed at reducing the natural rate of unemployment?
   a. A constant growth-rate rule for the money supply.
   b. Vocational retraining for unemployed auto workers.
   c. The distribution of surplus cheese to low-income families.
   d. Indexing income taxes.
2. Which of the following is *not* an example of an incomes policy?
   a. A wage–price freeze designed to break inflationary expectations.
   b. Open market sales to slow down the increase in the stock of money.
   c. Tax incentives to firms and workers who agree to wage increases below some national standard.
   d. The Anti-Inflation Board.
3. Wage-price controls
   a. may be effective if they succeed in changing expectations of inflation.
   b. have been used with great success in Great Britain.
   c. have little long-run impact on economic efficiency.
   d. can be imposed on some parts of the economy without affecting the rest of the economy.
4. A general policy of indexing.
   a. is an attempt to shift the aggregate-supply curve downward and to the right.
   b. is an attempt to ease the social cost of inflation, not an attempt to improve the terms of the inflation–unemployment trade-off.
   c. runs little risk of accelerating the rate of inflation.
   d. would help to balance the federal government's budget.
5. If a $100 one-year indexed security offers you a real return of 3 percent, and if during the year inflation occurs at a rate of 7 percent, then at the end of the year you will receive about
   a. $103
   b. $107
   c. $110
   d. $121
6. Which of the following is an example of indexing?
   a. Tax penalties on firms that grant excessive wage increases.
   b. The adjustment of nominal interest rates in response to expectations of inflation.
   c. The average change in prices on the Toronto Stock Exchange.
   d. Increases in Canada Pension cheques computed on the basis of changes in the consumer price index.
7. Which one of the following is *not* a valid reason to oppose activist stabilization policy?
   a. Doubts about the accuracy of economic forecasting.
   b. Uncertainties about the response of the private economy to any change in policy.
   c. A concern that activist policy necessarily means a growing public sector.
   d. A strong belief that, if left alone, the economy is apt to correct quickly most problems by itself.
8. Which of the following is *not* an example of an automatic stabilizer?
   a. Unemployment Insurance.
   b. The corporate income tax.
   c. Increased highway building enacted during a recession.
   d. Personal income taxes.

Test B

Circle T or F for True or False as appropriate.

1. Evidence to date suggests that expanded job retraining programs are an especially effective anti-inflationary policy.   T F

2. A period of wage–price controls might actually increase the variability of inflation if, following the control period, prices rebound to where they would have been in the absence of the controls.   T F

3. A government agency to admonish firms to reduce prices is an example of jawboning.   T F

4. Indexing interest rates could make real rates more certain and nominal rates less certain.   T F

5. Long lags will help make for better stabilization policy because there is more time for a complete analysis of possible actions.   T F

6. Automatic stabilizers reduce the sensitivity of the economy to shifts in aggregate demand.   T F

7. A temporary income-tax rebate is an example of an automatic stabilizer.   T F

8. Lags can mean that policies adopted to stabilize the economy might end up destabilizing it instead.   T F

IV

Essentials of Microeconomics: Consumers and Firms

The Common Sense of Consumer Choice

20

LEARNING OBJECTIVES

After completing the material in this chapter you should be able to:

- define, understand, and use correctly the terms and concepts listed below.
- distinguish between total and marginal utility.
- explain the role of marginal utility as a guide to the maximization of total utility.
- explain how the law of diminishing marginal utility can be used to derive an optimal purchase rule.
- explain how the optimal purchase rule can be used to derive a demand curve.
- explain what economists mean by inferior goods and why inferior goods may have demand curves that slope upward.

- distinguish between the income and substitution effects of a price change.

IMPORTANT TERMS AND CONCEPTS

Diamond-water paradox
Marginal analysis
Total utility
Marginal utility
Diminishing marginal utility
Optimal purchase rule (P = MU)
Scarcity and marginal utility
Inferior goods
Income effect
Substitution effect

CHAPTER REVIEW

This chapter discusses economic models of consumer choice. These models are what lie behind negatively sloped demand curves. The appendix to the chapter discusses indifference curve analysis, which is a more sophisticated treatment of the same material.

Economists derive implications for individual demand curves by starting with some assumptions about individual behaviour. One relatively innocent assumption should be sufficient. This assumption concerns consumer preferences and is called the "law" of diminishing marginal utility. Perhaps we should first start with utility.

Economists use the term *utility* to refer to the benefits people derive from consuming goods and services. The actual utility, or benefit, that individuals derive from consuming commodities is unique to each one of us and thus incapable of being measured. To get around the measurement problems associated with personal satisfaction, we will use the term *total utility* to refer to the maximum amount of money that a consumer will pay for a given quantity of the commodity. (It should be obvious that this amount of money will be influenced by a person's income and preferences.) Rather than focusing on total utility, however, economists have found it useful to pay attention to the additional amount of money that a consumer would pay for one more unit of the commodity, or

(1) _____ utility, measured in money terms. (Marginal utility (*will*/*will not*) also be influenced by a person's income and preferences.) The "law" of diminishing marginal utility is a hypothesis about consumer preferences. It says that additional units of any commodity normally provide less and less satisfaction. As a result, the additional amount a consumer will pay for an additional unit of some commodity will (*increase*/*decrease*) the more units he or she is already consuming.

The law of diminishing marginal utility can be used as a guide to optimal commodity purchases. Optimal purchases are ones that maximize the difference between total utility and total expenditures on a commodity. Our optimal purchase rule says that an individual consumer should buy additional units of a commodity as

(2) long as the marginal utility of the additional units exceeds the _____ of the commodity. If marginal utility exceeds price, the addition to total utility from consuming one more unit will be (*greater*/*less*) than the addition to total spending, and the difference between total utility and expenditures will (*increase*/*decrease*).

Now, with our optimal purchase rule it is easy to derive an *individual-demand curve*. A demand curve shows the quantity demanded at different possible prices. To derive an *individual-demand* curve we simply confront our consumer with different prices and see how the quantity demanded changes. Our optimal purchase rule tells us that

(3) she will purchase more units as long as the marginal utility of the unit being considered is (*greater*/*less*) than the price of the unit. She will stop when the two are equal. If we now lower the price, we know that she will again try to equate _____ and _____ utility, which she does by purchasing (*more*/*less*). Thus, as price goes down, the quantity demanded goes (*down*/*up*), and this individual-demand curve has a (*positive*/*negative*) slope.

Price is not the only variable that affects an individual's demand for various commodities. Income is also

(4) an important variable. We saw in Chapter 4 that a change in income will shift the (*demand*/*supply*) curve. In terms of the concepts of this chapter, a change in income will influence how much a person would be willing to spend to buy various commodities; that is, a change in income will influence total and marginal

_____ . Following a change in income we could again conduct our demand curve experiment of the last paragraph, and it would not be surprising if the resulting demand curve had shifted. An increase in income will typically mean an increase in the demand for most commodities, but occasionally one will find that the demand for some commodity decreases following an increase in income. Commodities whose

consumption decreases as a consumer's income increases are called _____ goods.

We can now use the possibility of inferior goods to see why the quantity demanded might decrease following a reduction in price. We start by noting that the impact of a price change can be divided into an *income effect* and a *substitution effect*. Consider a price reduction on some good, say potatoes. The fact that potatoes are now cheaper relative to other goods implies an increase in demand for potatoes. This relative price effect is also called the

(5) _____ effect. But that is not the whole story. Following the price decline, a consumer could buy exactly the same amount of all commodities, including potatoes, as she did before and still have money left over. This leftover money comes from the decline in the price of potatoes, and it is similar to an increase in income, which will, as noted above, affect her demand for all goods. This leftover money effect is also called the

_____ effect of a price change. If potatoes were an inferior good, increased income would lead our consumer to demand (*fewer*/*more*) potatoes. The final change in demand for potatoes, or any other

commodity following a price change, will be determined by the net effect of the _____

and _____ effects of a price change. These two effects work for price increases as well as declines.

BASIC EXERCISE

This exercise reviews how one can use the law of diminishing marginal utility to derive a negatively sloped demand curve. Table 20-1 presents data on Dolores's evaluation of different quantities of dresses.

1. Use these data to compute the marginal utility of each dress.
2. The optimal purchase rule says to buy more dresses as long as the marginal utility of the next dress exceeds the price of the dress. According to this rule, how many dresses should Dolores buy if they cost

   $45 each? _____ ;

   $30 each? _____ ;

   $20 each? _____ .

3. Now, fill in columns 3, 5, and 7 of Table 20-2 to compute the difference between total utility and total expenditures for each different price. At what quantity is the surplus of total utility over total expenditures maximized if prices equal

   $45? _____ ;

   $30? _____ ;

   $20? _____ . How do these quantities compare with the quantities given by the optimal purchase rule in Question 2?
4. Use the information in Table 20-1 to plot Dolores's demand curve for dresses in Figure 20-1. Is your demand curve consistent with your answer to Question 2? (It should be.)

SELF-TESTS FOR UNDERSTANDING

Test A

Circle the correct answer.

1. The total utility of any commodity bundle
   a. should be the same for all individuals.
   b. is defined as the maximum amount of money that a consumer will spend for the bundle.
   c. will be equal to expenditures on the commodity in question.
   d. is not likely to change even if a consumer's income changes.
2. Rick is willing to spend up to $200 for one ski trip this winter and up to $250, in total, for two trips. The marginal utility of the second trip to Rick is
   a. $50.   b. $75.   c. $100.   d. $150.

3. The law of diminishing marginal utility
   a. implies that total utility declines as a consumer buys more of any good.
   b. is an important psychological premise that helps to explain why all demand curves have a negative slope.
   c. must hold for every commodity and every individual.
   d. says that increments to total utility will decrease as an individual consumes more of the commodity in question.

TABLE 20-1

Dresses	Total Utility (measured in dollars)	Marginal Utility (measured in dollars)
1	55	55
2	105	50
3	145	40
4	180	35
5	205	25
6	220	15
7	230	10

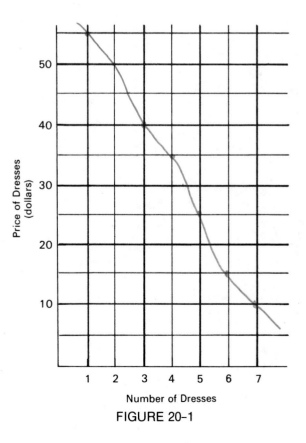

FIGURE 20-1

TABLE 20-2

	Price = $45			Price = $30			Price = $20	
Dresses	Total Expenditure	Difference*		Total Expenditure	Difference*		Total Expenditure	Difference*
1	$ 45	10		$ 30	25		$ 20	35
2	90	15		60	45		40	65
3	135	10		90	55		60	85
4	180	0		120	60		80	100
5	225	-20		150	55		100	105
6	270	-50		180	40		120	100
7	315	-85		210	20		140	90

*Differences between total utility and total expenditure.

4. The optimal purchase rule says that to maximize the difference between total utility, measured in money terms, and total expenditures, a consumer should purchase additional units
   a. as long as total utility is increasing.
   b. until marginal utility equals zero.
   c. as long as marginal utility exceeds price.
   d. until marginal utility equals total utility.

5. The diamond-water paradox indicates that
   a. contrary to economists' assumptions, consumers are really irrational.
   b. price is more closely related to marginal utility than to total utility.
   c. water is an inferior good.
   d. the demand for diamonds is very elastic.

6. When economists say that some commodity is an inferior or a normal good, they are referring to the impact of
   a. a change in price on the quantity demanded.
   b. an increase in the quantity consumed on total utility.
   c. an increase in the quantity consumed on marginal utility.
   d. a change in income on the quantity demanded.

7. For an inferior good, the demand curve
   a. must have a negative slope.
   b. is likely to be horizontal.
   c. must have a positive slope.
   d. may have a positive slope.

8. The impact of a change in the price of cheese on the demand for cheese can be decomposed into
   a. micro and macro effects.
   b. inflation and price-level effects.
   c. income and substitution effects.
   d. general and partial effects.

9. If cheap hamburger meat with a high fat content is an inferior good, then we know that
   a. the demand curve for this good must slope upward.
   b. consumer demand may increase following an increase in price.

   c. the income effect of a price reduction works in the same direction as the substitution effect.
   d. the income effect of a price increase works in the same direction as the substitution effect.

10. If restaurant meals are not inferior goods, then the income effect of a price change
   a. will work in the same direction as the substitution effect.
   b. will work in the opposite direction from the substitution effect.
   c. implies, on balance, that people will demand fewer restaurant meals following a price reduction.
   d. means that at higher prices people may demand more, not fewer, restaurant meals.

Test B

Circle T or F for True or False as appropriate.

1. The diamond-water paradox can be resolved by realizing that scarcity reduces total utility and simultaneously increases marginal utility.   T F

2. The term *marginal utility* refers to the total amount of dollars that consumers would pay for a particular commodity bundle.   T F

3. The term *inferior good* refers to those commodities that economists do not like.   T F

4. If the law of diminishing marginal utility holds for pizza, and if pizzas are not an inferior good, then the demand curve for pizza will have a negative slope.   T F

5. If, following a reduction in price, the quantity of hamburgers demanded declines, we can conclude that hamburgers are an inferior good.   T F

6. If a consumer is interested in maximizing the difference between total utility and expenditures, it is optimal to consume more of a commodity as

long as the marginal utility of additional units exceeds the market price. T F

7. The income and substitution effects of a change in price will always work in the same direction, implying that a reduction in price must increase the quantity demanded. T F

8. Part of the impact of an increase in the price of any good can be analysed as a reduction in money income. T F

9. A consumer who is rational will never buy an inferior good. T F

10. If potatoes are an inferior good, then an increase in the price of potatoes might lead to an increase in the quantity demanded. T F

Appendix: Indifference Curve Analysis

LEARNING OBJECTIVES

After completing the material in this appendix you should be able to:

- define, understand, and use correctly the terms and concepts listed below.
- draw a budget line, given data on prices and money income.
- explain why economists usually assume that indifference curves (1) have a negative slope and (2) are bowed in toward the origin.
- determine optimal commodity bundle(s) for a consumer, given a budget line and a set of indifference curves.
- explain why, if indifference curves are smooth and bowed in to the origin, the optimal commodity bundle is the one for which the marginal rate of substitution equals the ratio of commodity prices.
- use indifference curve analysis to derive a demand curve; that is, show the change in the quantity demanded of a good as its price changes.
- use indifference analysis to analyse the impact on commodity demands of a change in income.

IMPORTANT TERMS AND CONCEPTS

Budget line
Indifference curves
Marginal rate of substitution
Slope of an indifference curve
Slope of a budget line

APPENDIX REVIEW

Indifference curve analysis is a more rigorous treatment of the material covered in Chapter 20. As the appendix shows, we can study consumer choices by confronting a consumer's desires or preferences, indicated by indifference curves, with a consumer's opportunities, indicated by a budget line.

(1)   The *budget line* represents all possible combinations of commodities that a consumer can buy, given her money income. The arithmetic of a budget line for two commodities shows that it is a (*straight/curved*) line with a (*positive/negative*) slope. An increase in money income will produce a change in the (*intercept/slope*) of the budget line. A change in the price of either commodity will mean a change in the _____ of the budget line. The slope of the budget line is equal to the ratio of the prices of the two commodities. (The price of the commodity measured along the horizontal axis goes on top.)

The budget line indicates only all the different ways a consumer could spend her money income. In order to figure out what consumption bundle is best for her, we must examine her own personal preferences.

(2)   Economists use the concept of _____ curves to summarize an individual's preferences. These curves are derived from a person's ranking of alternative commodity bundles. For two commodities, a single indifference curve is a line connecting all possible combinations (bundles) of the two commodities between which our consumer is _____ . From the assumption that more is better, we can deduce (1) that higher indifference curves (*are/are not*) preferred to lower indifference curves, and (2) that indifference curves will have a (*positive/negative*) slope. (Another property of indifference curves is that they do not intersect. Can you explain why?)

(3)   Indifference curves are usually assumed to be curved lines that are bowed (*in/out*). The slope of an indifference curve indicates the terms of trade between commodities that our consumer is indifferent about. For a given reduction in one commodity the slope tells us how much (*more/less*) of the other commodity is necessary to keep our consumer as well off as before. The slope of the indifference curve is also known as the marginal rate of

_____ . If indifference curves are bowed in, or convex to the origin, it means that the marginal rate of substitution (*increases/decreases*) as we move from left to right along a given indifference curve. This change in the marginal rate of substitution is a psychological premise that is similar to our earlier assumption about declining marginal utility, and it is what makes the indifference curves convex to the origin.

We are now in a position to determine optimal consumer choices. The optimal choice is the commodity bundle that makes our consumer as well off as possible, given her opportunities. In this case opportunities

(4)   are represented by the _____ line and the evaluation of alternative commodity bundles

is given by the _____ curves. The best choice is a commodity bundle that puts our consumer on her (*highest/lowest*) possible indifference curve. This consumption bundle is indicated by the

indifference curve that is just tangent to the _____ .

From the definition of the slope of a *curved line* (review the material in Chapter 2 if necessary) we know that at the point of tangency the slope of the associated indifference curve will just equal the slope of the budget line. Since the slope of the budget line is given by the ratio of the prices of the two goods, we know that at the optimal decision the slope of the indifference curve, or the marginal rate of substitution, will just equal the ratio of prices.

The marginal rate of substitution tells how our consumer is *willing* to trade goods and the price ratio tells us how she can trade goods in the market by buying more of one good and less of the other. If these two trading ratios are different, our consumer can make herself better off by changing her purchases. It is only when the two trading ratios are equal that her opportunities for gain have been eliminated.

Once you master the logic and mechanics of indifference curve analysis you can use it to investigate the impact on demand of changes in price or incomes. A change in either income or prices will shift the

(5)   _____ _____ . It is the resulting change in the optimal commodity bundle that helps trace out a movement along the demand curve in the case of a change in prices, and the shift in the demand curve, in the case of a change in income. (It is possible to draw a picture of both the income and substitution effects. If interested, ask your instructor.)

BASIC EXERCISE

This problem is designed to review the logic of the optimal decision rule using indifference curve analysis, which says that a consumer should choose the commodity bundle associated with the point of tangency between the budget line and the highest indifference curve.

Figure 20-2 shows a set of indifference curves for Gloria between books and hamburgers.
1. Gloria has an income of $60 that she will spend on books and hamburgers. Hamburgers cost $1.50 each and paperback books cost $3 each. Draw the budget line in Figure 20-2 that constrains Gloria's choices. (You might first compute the maximum number of hamburgers Gloria can buy; then determine the maximum number of books; and then connect these two points with a straight line.)
2. How many hamburgers will Gloria buy?

_____ . How many books will she

buy? _____ . In Figure 20-2, label

this combination B for best choice. (If you drew the budget line correctly this point should lie on indifference curve I_3.)
3. The combination of 30 hamburgers and 5 books, point Z, is obviously not a better choice as it lies on a lower indifference curve. Assume for the moment that Gloria tentatively chooses point Z and is considering whether this choice is best. If you put a ruler along indifference curve I_2 and look very carefully you should be able to verify that at point Z the marginal rate of substitution of hamburgers for books is 3. This means that Gloria would be willing

to give up _____ hamburgers in order to be able to buy one more book. (You can check this by noting that the combination of 27 hamburgers and 6 books is on the same indifference curve.[1] However, since books cost only

---

[1]Most indifference curves that economists draw do not have straight-line segments. The straight-line segment is used for convenience, the general argument is still correct.

$3 while hamburgers cost $1.50 Gloria has only to give up _____ hamburgers in order to buy 1 book. This is clearly a good deal for Gloria, and she will reduce her consumption of hamburgers in order to buy more books; that is, she will move down the budget line away from point Z.

4. Consider point W, on indifference curve I_1. Tell a similar story that convinces both yourself and someone to whom you explain this analysis, that Gloria will be better off moving along the budget line away from point W.

5. Arguments similar to those in 3 and 4 above indicated that for smooth indifference curves as in Figure 20-2, the optimal consumer choice cannot involve a commodity bundle for which the marginal rate of substitution differs from the ratio of market prices. The conclusion is that the optimal decision must be the commodity bundle for which the marginal rate of substitution

_____.

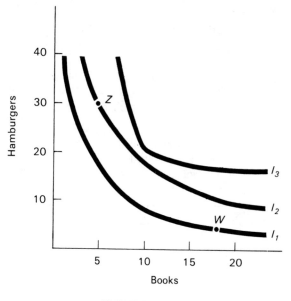

FIGURE 20-2

GLORIA'S INDIFFERENCE CURVES

SELF-TESTS FOR UNDERSTANDING

Test A

Circle the correct answer.

1. The budget line
   a. determines an individual's optimal consumption bundle.
   b. will not shift at all if prices of both commodities increase and money income is unchanged.
   c. determines an individual's possible consumption bundles.
   d. is a straight line whose slope is given by the rate of inflation.
2. Following an increase in income
   a. a consumer's indifference curves will shift.
   b. the slope of the budget line will increase.
   c. individual commodity demand curves will not shift.
   d. the budget line will shift in a parallel fashion.
3. A set of indifference curves is
   a. usually assumed to have a positive slope.
   b. used by economists to to represent a person's preferences among different commodity bundles.
   c. the same for everyone.
4. The slope of an indifference curve.
   a. is constant if the indifference curve is convex to the origin.
   b. is always equal to the slope of the budget line.
   c. indicates what commodity trades an individual would be indifferent about.

5. Indifference curve analysis of the choice between two commodities shows that an increase in the price of one commodity will
   a. change the slope of the budget line.
   b. lead a consumer to choose a new commodity bundle, but one that is on the same indifference curve.
   c. shift consumer preferences.
   d. necessarily lead to a reduction in the demand for both commodities.

Test B

Circle T or F for True or False as appropriate.

1. The budget line is a curved line, convex to the origin.   T F

2. An increase in income will change the slope of the budget line.   T F

3. A change in the price of one commodity will result in a parallel shift of the budget line. T F

4. The assumption that consumers prefer more to less is sufficient to establish that indifference curves will be convex to the origin.   T F

5. The slope of indifference curves at any point is given by the ratio of prices.   T F

6. The slope of an indifference curve is also called the marginal rate of substitution.   T F

7. Optimal decision-making implies that a consumer should never choose a commodity bundle for which the marginal rate of substitution equals the ratio of market prices.   **T F**

8. Indifference curve analysis shows us that the demand for all goods is interrelated in the sense that changes in the price of one good can affect the demand for other goods.   **T F**

9. Indifference curve analysis suggests that a doubling of all prices and of money income will not change optimal consumption bundles.   **T F**

SUPPLEMENTARY EXERCISE

Consider a consumer whose total utility can be represented as

$$U = (F + 12)(C + 20)$$

where F = quantity of food, C = quantity of clothing, and U = the arbitrary level of utility associated with a particular indifference curve. (A different value for U will imply a different indifference curve.)

1. On a piece of graph paper draw a typical indifference curve.
2. If the price of food is $1.50, the price of clothing is $3, and total money income is $300, what combination of food and clothing will maximize utility?
3. Assume the price of food rises to $2. Now what combination of food and clothing maximizes utility?
4. Assume income increases to $330 while prices are as given in Question 2. What happens to the demand for food and clothing? Is either good an inferior good?
5. Can you derive an expression for the demand for food? For clothing? (Can you use the equation for the indifference curves and what you know about optimal consumer choice to derive an equation that expresses F or C as a function of prices and income? The particular form of these demand curves comes from the mathematical specification of the indifference curves. A different specification of the indifference curves would lead to a different demand function.)

Consumer Demand and Elasticity

LEARNING OBJECTIVES

After completing the material in this chapter you should be able to:

- define, understand, and use correctly the terms and concepts listed below.
- explain how to derive a market-demand curve from individual-demand curves.
- define the "law" of demand and discuss why there may be exceptions to it.
- compute the elasticity of demand, given appropriate data from a specific demand curve.
- describe how the elasticity of demand is affected by various factors.
- explain how the impact of a change in price on consumer expenditures depends on the price elasticity of demand.
- explain how the concept of cross elasticity of demand relates to the concepts of substitutes and complements.

- explain how factors other than price can affect the quantity demanded.
- distinguish between changes in the quantity demanded that come from a shift in the demand curve from those that come from a movement along the demand curve.
- describe the pitfalls of using historical data on actual prices and quantities in order to estimate a demand curve.

IMPORTANT TERMS AND CONCEPTS

Market-demand curve
Excise tax
"Law" of demand
(Price) elasticity of demand
Elastic, inelastic, and unit-elastic demand curves
Complements
Substitutes
Cross elasticity of demand
Shift in demand curves

CHAPTER REVIEW

The material in this chapter offers a more intensive look at demand curves. In effect, it is an extension of the material presented in Chapters 4 and 20. Demand curves provide important information for analysing business decisions, market structures, and public policies.

In Chapter 20 we saw how the logic of consumer choice leads to individual-demand curves. Business firms are usually less interested in individual-demand curves than they are in market-demand curves. It is the market-demand curve that tells a firm how much of its product it can sell, in total, at different prices. Given individual-demand curves, and assuming that the one person's demand does not depend upon the actions of

(1) another, we can derive the market-demand curve by (*horizontal/vertical*) summation of all individual-demand curves.

(2) In Chapter 20 we saw that individual-demand curves will usually have a (*positive/negative*) slope. If all individual-demand curves have a negative slope, the market-demand curve will necessarily have a

_____ slope. Even if some or many individual-demand curves are vertical—that is, if they show no change in the quantity demanded to a change in price—the market-demand curve can still have a negative slope if a reduction in prices induces new customers to enter the market. The result that market-demand

curves usually have a negative slope is called the "_____" of demand and is an important reason why demand is not a fixed amount, but rather should be thought of as a schedule that depends upon many factors, including price. It may be easy to think of exceptions to the "law"; snob appeal and a tendency to judge quality by price are two examples. However, there is overwhelming evidence that the "law" is valid for most goods and services.

The price of a commodity is not the only variable influencing demand for it. Changes in other factors,
(3) say, consumers' income, tastes, or the price of a close substitute, will mean a (*shift in/movement along*) a demand curve drawn against price. Finally, remember that a demand curve refers to a particular period of time.

An important property of demand curves is the responsiveness of demand to a change in price. If a firm raises its price, how big a drop in sales is likely to occur? Or if a firm lowers its price, how large an increase in sales will there be?

To avoid problems with changing units, economists have found it useful to measure these changes as percentages. If, for a given change in price, one divides the percentage change in the quantity demanded by the percentage change in the price producing the change in quantity and ignores the negative sign, one has

(4) just computed the price _____ of _____ . Remember, this calculation ignores minus signs and uses the average price and quantity to compute percentage changes.

It is useful to know the elasticity properties of certain, special types of demand curves. If the demand curve is truly a vertical line, then there is no change in the quantity demanded following any change in price and the

(5) elasticity of demand is _____ . (No demand curve is likely to be vertical for all prices, but it may be for some.) The other extreme is a perfectly horizontal demand curve where a small change in price produces a very large change in the quantity demanded. Such a demand curve implies that if price declines, even just a little, the quantity demanded will be infinite while if the price rises, even a little, the quantity demanded will fall to zero. In this case, a very small percentage change in price produces a very large percentage change in the

quantity demanded, and the price elasticity of demand is said to be _____ . The price elasticity of demand along a negatively sloped straight-line demand curve (*is constant/changes*). One of the basic exercises illustrates just this point.

(6) A demand curve with a price elasticity of demand greater than 1.0 is commonly called _____

while demand curves with a price elasticity of demand less than 1.0 are called _____ . If the price

elasticity of demand is exactly 1.0 the demand curve is said to be a _____ _____ demand curve.

Some simple arithmetic, not economics, can show that there is a connection between the price elasticity of demand and the change in total consumer expenditure (or, equivalently, the change in sales revenue) following a change in price. We know that total expenditures or revenues are simply price times quantity, or

$$\text{Total expenditures} = \text{Total revenues} = p \times q.$$

A decrease in price will increase quantity as we move along a given demand curve. Whether total revenue increases clearly depends on whether the increase in quantity is big enough to outweigh the decline in price. (Remember the old saying: "We lose a little on each sale but make it up on volume.")

Again, it is mathematics, not economics, that tells us that the percentage change in total expenditures or revenue is equal to the *sum* of the percentage change in price and the percentage change in quantity.[1] Remember that as we move along a given demand curve, a positive change in price will lead to a negative change in quantity, and vice versa.

If the absolute value of the percentage change in quantity is equal to the absolute value of the per-

(7) centage change in price, then total revenue (*will/will not*) change following a change in price. In this case, the

price elasticity of demand is equal to _____ .

If the price elasticity of demand is greater than 1.0, and if we ignore any negative signs, a given percentage

(8) change in prices will result in a (*greater/smaller*) percentage change in quantity demanded. From the equation above we can also see that if the price elasticity of demand is greater than 1.0, a reduction in price will

(*increase/decrease*) total revenue and an increase in price will _____ total revenue. Exactly opposite conclusions apply when the price elasticity of demand is less than 1.0.

The price elasticity of demand refers to the impact on the quantity demanded of a change in a commodity's price. There is a related elasticity concept that compares the change in the quantity demanded of one good with a

(9) change in the price of another good. This quotient is called the _____ elasticity of demand. In this case we must keep track of any negative signs.

Some goods, such as tables and chairs, hot dogs and buns, are usually demanded together. Such pairs

(10) are called _____ and are likely to have a (*positive/negative*) cross elasticity of

demand. Other goods, such as different brands of toothpaste, are probably close _____ and are

likely to have a _____ cross elasticity of demand. (Would you expect the price elasticity of demand for Crest toothpaste, given that the prices of Colgate and other toothpastes are unchanged, to be high or low? Why?)

BASIC EXERCISES

1. The Price Elasticity of Demand

These exercises are designed to give you some practice in the calculation and interpretation of price elasticities of demand.

a. Table 21-1 has some data on possible prices and the associated demand for both schmoos and gizmos. Use these data to plot the demand curves in Figure 21-1 and 21-2. Looking at these demand curves, which curve looks more elastic? More inelastic?

b. Now use the data in Table 21-1 to calculate the elasticity of demand for schmoos for a change in price from $60 to $50.[2] It is

_____ .

c. Use the same data to calculate the elasticity of demand for gizmos for a change in price from $1 to 50 cents. It is

_____ .

d. For these changes, which demand curve is more elastic? In fact, if you look more closely at the underlying data for both curves—for example, by computing the total revenue—you will see that for both curves the elasticity of demand is

_____ .

[1]This result is strictly true only for very small changes in *p* and *q*. Total revenue always equals *p* × *q*, but this simple way of calculating the percentage change in total revenue is only true for small changes.

[2]When computing the percentage change in both price and quantity, remember to use the average of the two prices or quantities when computing each percentage change. For example, compute the price change from $60 to $50 as

$$\left[\frac{40}{220} \right] \div \left[\frac{10}{55} \right].$$

TABLE 21-1

The Demand for Schmoos		The Demand for Gizmos	
Price (dollars)	Quantity	Price (dollars)	Quantity
60	200	2.00	2000
50	240	1.25	3200
48	250	1.00	4000
40	300	0.50	8000

2. Table 21-2 contains data on possible prices and the associated quantity of demand for jeans in Collegetown, Ontario. Plot this demand curve in

Figure 21-3. It is a _____ line.
 a. Using the data in Table 21-2, compute the elasticity of demand for each change in price.[3] What general conclusion can you draw about the elasticity of demand along a straight-line demand curve? The elasticity of demand (*increases*/*decreases*) as one moves down and to the right along a straight-line demand curve.
 b. Use the same data to compute total revenue for each price-quantity pair in Table 21-2. Compare the change in total revenue to the elasticity of demand. What conclusion can you draw about this relationship?

[3]Again, remember to use the average of the two prices and quantities. For a change in price from $18 to $15 compute the elasticity of demand as

$$\frac{9000}{31,500} - \frac{3}{16.50}$$

TABLE 21-2
THE DEMAND FOR JEANS

Price (dollars)	Quantity	Elasticity of Demand	Total Revenue
18	27 000		486,000
		1.57	
15	36 000		540,000
		1.0	
12	45 000		540,000
		0.64	
9	54 000		486,000

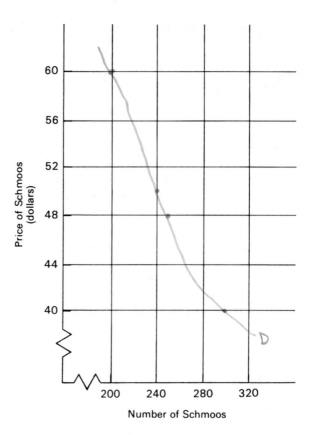

FIGURE 21-1

THE DEMAND FOR SCHMOOS

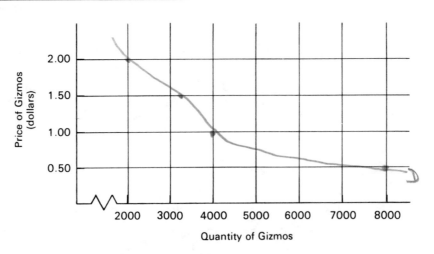

FIGURE 21-2

THE DEMAND FOR GIZMOS

SELF-TESTS FOR UNDERSTANDING

Test A

Circle the correct answer.

1. Which of the following would be an exception to the "law" of demand?
   a. Increased advertising expenditures for Fords result in increased sales.
   b. An increase in the price of a particular 35 mm camera, with no change in the camera itself, results in increased sales.
   c. Sales of CGE refrigerators decline when Hotpoint reduces the price on its refrigerators.
   d. While plotting historical data on price and sales, Rhoda notices that the sales of French bicycles rose at the time prices were also rising.

2. Which of the following will *not* lead to a shift in the demand curve for Chevrolets?
   a. A limit on the number of Japanese cars that can be imported into Canada.
   b. A reduction in the price of Fords.
   c. An increase in the price of Chevrolets.
   d. A dramatic decline in the price of gasoline.

3. Which of the following will lead to a movement along the demand curve for Fords?
   a. A limit on the number of Japanese cars that can be imported into Canada.
   b. A reduction in the price of Fords.
   c. An increase in the price of Chevrolets.
   d. A dramatic decline in the price of gasoline.

4. If a 20 percent decrease in the price of long distance phone calls lead to a 35 percent increase in the quantity of calls demanded, we can conclude that the demand for phone calls is
   a. elastic.
   b. inelastic.
   c. unit elastic.

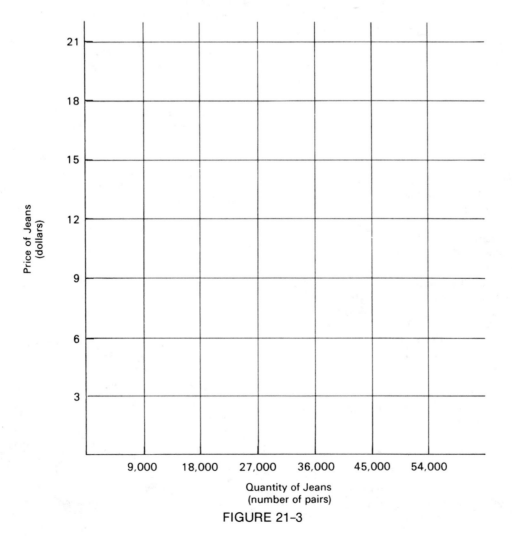

FIGURE 21-3

5. From the data given above what would happen to total revenue following a 20 percent decrease in the price of long distance phone calls? It would
   a. increase.
   b. decrease
   c. remain the same.
6. If a 10 percent increase in price leads to a 12 percent decline in the quantity demanded, the price elasticity of demand is
   a. .83 (10 ÷ 12).
   b. 1.2 (12 ÷ 10).
   c. 2 (12 − 10).
   d. 22 (12 + 10).
7. Which one of the following pairs is *not* a likely example of substitutes?
   a. A flight from Toronto to Calgary on Air Canada and the same flight on CP Air.
   b. Stereo tuner-amplifiers and pairs of speakers.
   c. Calculators made by Texas Instruments and calculators made by Commodore.
   d. Gasoline from the Texaco station and gasoline from the Petro-Canada station across the street.
8. If the cross elasticity of demand between two goods is positive, we would conclude that the two goods are
   a. substitutes.
   b. complements.
   c. both likely to be viewed as necessities.
   d. both likely to have inelastic demand curves.
9. If following an increase in the price of schmoos, the quantity demanded of gizmos declined, we would conclude that
   a. the demand for gizmos is inelastic.
   b. gizmos and schmoos are substitutes.
   c. gizmos and schmoos are complements.
   d. schmoos are likely to be a luxury good.
10. If skis and boots are complements, then which one of the following statements is false?
   a. A reduction in the price of skis is likely to increase the sales of boots.
   b. Sales revenue of ski manufacturers will increase following a reduction in the price of ski boots.
   c. An increase in the price of boots is likely to reduce the sales of skis.
   d. The cross elasticity of demand between skis and boots is likely to be positive.

Test B

Circle T or F for True or False as appropriate.

1. The "law" of demand states that for most commodities people will buy more at a lower price.   T F

2. If each individual's demand for a particular commodity is independent of the actions of others, then an aggregate-demand curve for all individuals can be derived by horizontal summation of individual demand curves.   T F

3. The price elasticity of demand is defined as the change in quantity divided by the change in price.   T F

4. The elasticity of demand will be constant at all points along a straight-line demand curve.   T F

5. A vertical demand curve would have a price elasticity of zero.   T F

6. A demand curve is elastic if, following a decrease in price, the quantity demanded increases.   T F

7. If the demand for airplane travel is elastic, then a reduction in the price of airline tickets will increase total expenditures on airplane trips.   T F

8. If two goods are substitutes, then an increase in the price of one good is likely to reduce the demand for the other good.   T F

9. The cross elasticity of demand between complements is normally negative.   T F

10. If sales of Whoppers at Burger King increase following an increase in the price of Big Macs at McDonald's, we can conclude that Whoppers and Big Macs are complements.   T F

SUPPLEMENTARY EXERCISES

1. Consider the data on cheese consumption and prices in Table 21-3. Use a piece of graph paper to plot these data. What does this tell you about the demand for cheese? Why?
2. Angela's annual demand for apples is given by

$$Q = 300 - 10P$$

where Q = quantity of apples, and P = price of apples (20 cents = 20). Dan's demand curve is also given by

$$Q = 300 - 10P$$

   a. Write down an expression for the market-demand curve on the assumption that Angela and Dan constitute the total market.
   b. How does the slope of the market-demand curve compare with the slope of the individual-demand curves? Is it flatter, steeper, or the same?
   c. Calculate the price elasticity of demand for the individual-demand and market-demand curves when the price of apples changes from 20 to 25 cents. How does the price elasticity of demand of the market-demand curve compare with the price elasticity of the individual-demand curves? Is it larger, smaller, or equal?

d. Let Dan's demand be given by: $Q = 300 - 8P$.
   Re-answer a, b, and c.

TABLE 21-3

Year	Quantity (millions of kilograms)	Price (dollars per kilogram)
1970	2356	0.65
1971	2490	0.67
1972	2757	0.71
1973	2891	0.84
1974	3077	0.97
1975	3017	1.04
1976	3423	1.16
1977	3577	1.19
1978	3794	1.30
1979	3888	1.41
1980	4149	1.56
1981	4346	1.68
1982	4555	1.68
1983	4817	1.68

Source: Adopted from *Survey of Current Business*, various issues.

The Common Sense of Business Decisions: Inputs and Costs

LEARNING OBJECTIVES

After completing the material in this chapter you should be able to:

- define, understand, and use correctly the terms and concepts listed below.
- compute the average and marginal physical product for a single input given information on total output at different input levels.
- explain the "law" of diminishing marginal returns.
- compute the marginal revenue product for additional units of some input given information on the marginal physical product and on the price of the output.
- explain why a profit-maximizing firm will expand the use of each input until the marginal revenue product equals the price of the input.
- explain the difference between fixed and variable costs and how these concepts relate to average and marginal cost.
- explain why the law of diminishing returns implies that a profit-maximizing firm will use less of an input following an increase in price.
- explain how total costs—and hence average costs—

can be computed given information on the production function and input prices.

- explain why fixed costs and administrative problems of large organizations imply that the short-run average-cost curve is usually U-shaped.
- explain how to determine the long-run average-cost curve from a set of short-run average-cost curves.
- determine whether a particular production function shows increasing, decreasing, or constant returns to scale, given data on the output and on various input combinations.
- explain the relationship between returns to scale and the long-run average-cost curve.
- explain the difference between analytical and historical cost curves.

IMPORTANT TERMS AND CONCEPTS

Total physical product
Average physical product (APP)
Marginal physical product (MPP)
"Law" of diminishing marginal returns
Total-cost curve

Average-cost curve
Marginal-cost curve
Fixed costs
Variable costs
Short runs and long runs
Substitutability of inputs
Cost minimization
Marginal revenue product (MRP)

Rule for optimal input use
  (MRP = *P* of input)
Production function
Economies of scale
  (Increasing returns to scale)
Constant returns to scale
Decreasing returns to scale
Historical versus analytical cost relationships

CHAPTER REVIEW

We will again make extensive use of the concept of *marginal analysis* as a guide to optimal decision-making. In Chapter 20 we saw that the optimal purchase rule for a consumer implied that he or she should purchase additional units of a commodity until marginal utility equals the price of the commodity. In this chapter we will see how marginal analysis can help a firm make optimal decisions about the use of productive inputs and how these decisions in turn can be used to derive cost curves.

This chapter introduces a potentially bewildering array of curves and concepts, for example, marginal physical product, marginal revenue product, fixed costs, variable costs, long run, and short run. All these curves and concepts relate to each other and underlie optimal firm decisions. Spending time now to get these relationships clear will save you time in later chapters and the night before the exam.

In deciding whether to use an additional unit of some input, say, hiring more workers, a firm should look at the contribution of the additional workers to both total revenue and total cost. If the increase in revenue is

(1)   greater than the increase in cost, then profits will (*increase/decrease*). The increase in revenue comes from producing and selling additional units of output. Economists call the amount of additional output from the use of one more unit of input the marginal (*physical/revenue*) product of the input. For a firm selling its output at a constant price, the increase in revenue comes from multiplying the additional output by the price at which it can be sold.

Economists call this the marginal _____ product.

Common sense tells us that a profit-maximizing firm should use additional units of any input if the addition to total revenue exceeds the addition to total cost. Another way of saying the same thing is that the firm should

(2)   consider using more of an input as long as the _____ _____

product exceeds the _____ of the input. One has clearly gone too far if additions to revenue are less than additions to cost. Thus a profit-maximizing firm should expand the use of any factor until the marginal revenue product equals the price of the input. (This condition is completely analogous to the marginal rule given in Chapter 20.

If the price of an input is constant, firms will use more and more units of this input until the marginal revenue product falls to a point where it is equal to the input price. As a result, firms will usually expand the use of any input past any region of increasing marginal returns and into the region of decreasing returns to the one input.

We have talked about the optimal use of one input. Our rule still holds for the simultaneous consideration of more than one input. The appendix to this chapter uses geometry to consider two inputs simultaneously.

If the price of an input changes, it is natural to expect the firm's optimal input combination to change.

(3)   Specifically, it is natural to expect that a profit-maximizing firm will (*reduce/increase*) the use of any factor whose price has risen. Changing the quantity of one input will typically affect the marginal physical product of other inputs. As a result, a firm will want to rethink its use of all inputs following a change in price of any one input. It is quite likely that following an increase in the price of one input, a profit-maximizing firm will decide to use relatively

(*less/more*) of the more expensive input and relatively _____ of the inputs with unchanged prices.

The relationship between inputs and outputs has been formalized by economists into something that measures the maximum amount of output that can be produced from any specified combination of inputs given current

(4)   technology, or, for short, the _____ function. Information about the marginal physical product for a single factor comes from the production function. (The appendix to this chapter discusses one geometrical representation of such a function through the use of a contour-line diagram.) The concept of a production function is also useful in separating what happens if one increases the use of all factors or of just one factor. If all inputs are increased by the same percentage amount, then the percentage increase in output is used to indicate the degree of *economies of scale*. If output increases by more than the common percentage increase in all inputs, the production function exhibits _____ returns to scale. If output increases by

less, there are _____ returns to scale, and if output increases by the same percentage,

we would say that returns to scale are _____ .

Information from the production function can be used to construct *cost curves* for a firm. When talking about costs economists find it important to make a distinction between various periods of time. Over a very short time horizon, previous commitments may limit a firm's ability to adjust all inputs. These commitments often imply that the magnitude of one input is predetermined and cannot be adjusted immediately. Imagine a farmer with a five-year lease on a particular parcel of land and unable to rent additional land. The interval of of time over which none of

(5)   can be adjusted is called the _____ _____ .

The total cost of producing any given level of output in the short run can be computed with the help of the production function and input prices. We will be interested only in minimum total costs for any level of output. We can use what we know about optimal factor use to figure out minimum total cost. As an example, assume that production requires two inputs, one of which is fixed in the short run. To compute total cost, the firm must first use the production function to see what amount of the variable input is optimal to produce different levels of output. Then it can compute total cost by multiplying the quantity of the fixed input and the optimal quantity of the variable input by their prices and adding the results. After computing total cost for each level of output, the firm can

(6)   compute average cost by dividing total cost by the level of _____ . The firm can also compute marginal cost by examining the way (*average/total*) cost changes when output changes. We will make extensive use of the marginal-cost curve in Chapter 23 when we examine supply curves.

(7)   The period of time over which a firm can adjust all its fixed commitments is called the _____

_____ . Long-run cost curves can be derived by either of two equivalent methods. One procedure would first derive short-run cost curves for each possible amount of the fixed input. One would then

determine the long-run cost curve by joining the _____ segments of the short-run cost curves. An alternative and equivalent method would treat both factors as variable. One would first use the production function and input prices to determine the *optimal level of both* inputs to produce any given level of output. (The material in the appendix describes how to do this.) Total cost for each level of output is computed from input prices and from optimal input levels by multiplication and addition. Average and marginal cost are then easily computed.

Since in the long run all factors can be changed, the shape of the long-run average-cost curve is related to economies of scale. Constant returns to scale imply that a doubling of output requires twice as much of all

(8)   inputs. In this case, total costs also double and average cost (*falls/is unchanged/rises*). Increasing returns to scale mean that twice the output can be produced with (*more/less*) than twice the inputs and average cost will

(*fall/rise*). With decreasing returns to scale, twice the output requires _____ than twice

the inputs and average cost _____ .

We've covered a lot of ground and a lot of curves. You may want to take a deep breath before a quick review. The production function contains the basic technical information about inputs and output. From this information one can derive total physical product and marginal physical product for a single input. Knowing the price of output will let us compute marginal revenue product. Comparing marginal revenue product with input prices will determine the optimal input quantities. Optimal input quantities, in turn, determine (minimum) total cost for alternative levels of output. Once we know total cost, we can easily compute average and marginal cost. In the short run there may be fixed costs. In the long run all inputs, and hence all costs, are variable. In either run the same optimizing principles apply.

BASIC EXERCISE

These questions review the concept of a production function and optimal input decisions.

Megan and Jamie have invested in Greenacre Farms to grow cornbeans. Since they both work in the city, they will need to hire workers for the farm. Table 22-1

has data on various input combinations and the resulting output of cornbeans.

1. Use the data in Table 22-1 to draw, on Figure 20-1, the relationship between total output and labour input for 100 hectares of land. What is the region of increasing marginal returns?

_____

TABLE 22-1
TOTAL OUTPUT OF CORNBEANS
(thousands of tonnes)

Number of Workers

		1	2	3	4	5	6
Hectares	100	1	4	6	7	6	4
of	200	2	6	9.5	12	13	12
Land	300	3	7.5	11	14	16	17

Marginal Physical Product of Labour

		1	2	3	4	5	6
Hectares	100	__	__	__	__	__	__
of	200	__	__	__	__	__	__
Land	300	__	__	__	__	__	__

Marginal Revenue Product of Labour

		1	2	3	4	5	6
Hectares of Land	200	__	__	__	__	__	__

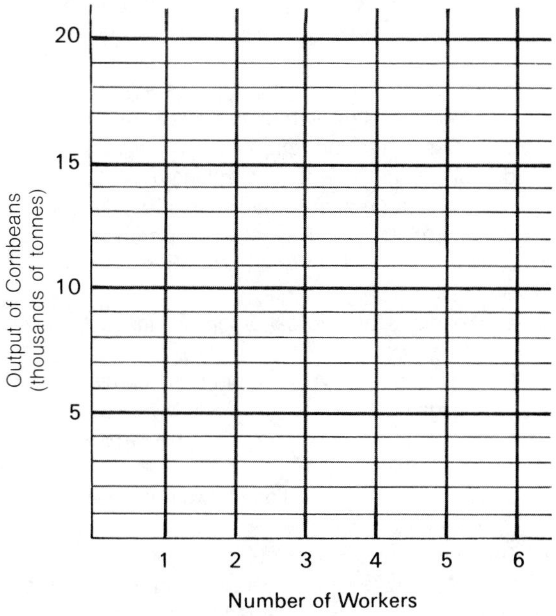

FIGURE 22-1

TOTAL OUTPUT OF CORNBEANS

What is the region of decreasing marginal returns?

_____

What is the region of negative marginal returns?

_____

2. Use Figure 22-1 to draw the relationship between total output and labour input, assuming the use of 200 hectares of land. Identify the regions of increasing, decreasing, and negative returns. Do the same assuming the use of 300 hectares of land. How does the output-labour curve shift when more land is used?

3. Fill in the middle part of Table 22-1 by computing the marginal physical product of each worker. Check to see that the regions of increasing, diminishing, and negative returns that you identified above correspond to information about the marginal physical product of labour. (You might also check to see that your entries in the middle of Table 22-1 equal the slopes of the total product curves you drew in Figure 22-1.)

4. Your answers to Questions 1, 2, and 3 should confirm that the production function for cornbeans eventually shows decreasing returns to labour for all three potential farm sizes. (What about returns to the increased use of land for a fixed amount of labour?)

5. Now consider the following pairs of inputs (hectares, workers) and indicate for each whether economies of scale are increasing, decreasing, or constant.

ECONOMIES OF SCALE

(100, 2) to (200, 4) _____

(100, 3) to (200, 6) _____

(200, 2) to (300, 3) _____

(200, 4) to (300, 6) _____

6. Assume that cornbeans can be sold for $5 a tonne. Greenacre Farms has 200 hectares of land. Calculate the marginal revenue product of labour for 200 hectares of land in the bottom part of Table 22-1. Plot the marginal revenue product in Figure 22-2. Hired help costs $8000. Draw a horizontal line in Figure 22-2 at $8000 to indicate the price of labour. How many workers should Megan and Jamie hire? _____ . At the level of labour input you just determined, what is the difference between the proceeds from selling cornbeans (output) and labour costs? _____ . (Check to see that your labour input choice maximizes this difference by considering the use of one more or one less worker.)

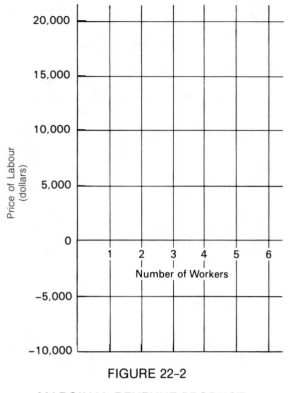

FIGURE 22-2

MARGINAL REVENUE PRODUCT

SELF-TESTS FOR UNDERSTANDING

Test A

Circle the correct answer.

1. The "law" of diminishing marginal returns
   a. says that eventually the marginal physical product of any input must become negative.
   b. applies to only a simultaneous increase in all inputs.
   c. can only be true for a production function with decreasing returns to scale.
   d. refers to what happens to output as only one factor is increased, all other inputs being held constant.

2. Consider the following data on workers and output.

Workers	1	2	3	4	5
Output	10	25	35	42	40

   Where do diminishing marginal returns to workers begin to set in?
   a. After the first worker.
   b. After the second worker.
   c. After the third worker.

d. After the fourth worker.

3. For a firm that sells output at a fixed price, the marginal revenue product of additional units of some input is found by
   a. dividing the marginal physical product by the input price.
   b. multiplying the marginal physical product by the sales price of the output.
   c. multiplying the marginal physical product by the input price.
   d. dividing the price of the output by the price of the input

4. The rule for optimal input use implies that a firm should use additional units of an input until
   a. average cost equals the price of the input.
   b. marginal physical product is maximized.
   c. marginal revenue product equals the price of the input.
   d. increasing returns to scale are exhausted.

5. The term *economies of scale*
   a. refers to the change over time in average cost as firms grow larger.
   b. is measured by dividing the percentage change in the marginal revenue product by the percentage change of the associated input.
   c. refers to the increase in output when only one input is increased.
   d. refers to what happens to total output following a simultaneous and equal percentage increase in all inputs.

6. If all inputs are doubled and output more than doubles, one would say that the production relationship
   a. shows decreasing returns to scale.
   b. shows constant returns to scale.
   c. shows increasing returns to scale.
   d. violates the "law" of diminishing returns.

7. Assume that on a small farm with 10 workers, the hiring of an 11th worker actually lowers total output. Which of the following statements is not necessarily true?
   a. The marginal physical product of the last worker is negative.
   b. The marginal revenue product of the last worker is negative.
   c. A profit-maximizing firm would never hire the 11th worker.
   d. The production function shows decreasing returns to scale.

8. The optimal choice of input combinations
   a. is a purely technological decision, unaffected by input prices, and better left to engineers than economists.
   b. can be determined by looking at information on the marginal revenue product and the prices of various inputs.

c. will always be the same in both the short and long run.

d. is likely to include more of an input if its price rises and if other input prices are unchanged.

9. A change in which of the following will *not* shift the short-run average cost curve?
   a. The price of output.
   b. The price of inputs.
   c. The quantity of fixed factors.
   d. The marginal physical product of variable inputs.

10. In the long run,
    a. inputs are likely to be less substitutable than in the short run.
    b. all production functions will exhibit constant returns to scale.
    c. a firm is assumed to be able to make adjustments in all its fixed commitments.
    d. average cost must decline.

Test B

Circle T or F for True or False as appropriate.

1. The "law" of diminishing returns says that economies of scale can never be increasing. **T F**

2. The marginal physical product of an input refers to the increase in output associated with an additional unit of that input when all other inputs are held constant. **T F**

3. The marginal revenue product measures the total revenue that a firm will have at different use levels of a particular input. **T F**

4. If a production function shows increasing returns to scale from the additional use of all inputs, it violates the "law" of diminishing returns. **T F**

5. If a production function shows decreasing returns to scale, long-run average costs will be increasing. **T F**

6. The short run is defined as a period so short that only a few of a firm's fixed commitments will lapse and need to be renegotiated. **T F**

7. Cost curves derived for a given set of fixed commitments are called short-run cost curves. **T F**

8. Long-run cost curves will always lie above short-run cost curves. **T F**

9. Inputs are likely to be more substitutable in the long run than in the short run. **T F**

10. Historical data on costs and output is a good guide to the relevant cost curves for a firm's current decisions. **T F**

Appendix: Production-Indifference Curves

LEARNING OBJECTIVES

After completing the material in this appendix you should be able to:

• define, understand, and use correctly the terms and concepts listed below.

• determine what input combination will minimize costs for a given level of output given information about production indifference curves and input prices.

• explain how a firm's expansion path helps determine (minimum) total cost for every possible level of output.

IMPORTANT TERMS AND CONCEPTS

Production-indifference curve (isoquant)
Budget line
Expansion path
Point of tangency between the budget line and the corresponding production-indifference curve

APPENDIX REVIEW

A set of *production-indifference curves* is a geometrical device that can be used to represent a production function involving two inputs and one output. The horizontal and vertical axes are used to measure quantities of each input. A line connecting all input combinations capable of producing the same amount of output is called the

(1) _____ - _____ curve. Each separate curve represents a particular level of output. Higher curves will mean (*more/less*) output.

(2)   Production-indifference curves will usually have a (*negative/positive*) slope and (*will/will not*) be convex to

the origin. This last property follows from the "law" of _____ _____ returns.
       Production-indifference curves will tell a firm what alternative combinations of inputs can be used to produce
the same amount of output. However, an optimizing firm should not be indifferent between these alternatives. In
order to make an optimal decision, the firm will need to know the price of each input. From this information the firm
can construct a budget line showing various combinations of inputs that can be purchased for the same total cost.
(This budget line plays the same role as the consumer's budget line of Chapter 20.) The budget line is a

(3)   (*curved/straight*) line. The slope of the budget line is given by the ratio of factor prices. The price of the factor
measured on the (*horizontal/vertical*) axis is on the top of the ratio. The intercept on each axis comes from
dividing the total budget by the price of the factor measured on that axis.
       To minimize cost for a given level of output, the firm chooses that combination of inputs lying on the

(4)   (*highest/lowest*) budget line consistent with the given level of output. For smooth and convex production-
indifference curves, one chooses an input combination such that a budget line is just tangent to the relevant
production-indifference curve. A change in the price of either input will shift the budget line and result in a new
optimal input combination.
       The procedure we have just described will determine the optimal input combination to minimize cost for a given
output target. Using the same procedure to find the lowest cost input combination for different levels of output

(5)   defines the firm's _____ path. It also allows us to compute total cost for any level of
output. At this point, division and subtraction will allow us to compute average and marginal cost. Which level of
output maximizes profits is another question, one that will be addressed in Chapter 23.
       Is the solution to the question of optimal input in this appendix consistent with our earlier rule that MRP = *P*?
Yes. Although it may not be immediately obvious, the slope of the production-indifference curve is equal to the ratio
of marginal physical products. If we choose an input combination such that the slope of the production-indifference
curve equals the slope of the budget line, we will set the ratio of marginal products equal to the ratio of input prices.
If you look at footnote 6 on page 438 in the text, you will see that this result is consistent with our earlier rule.

BASIC EXERCISE

Figure 22-3 shows a production-indifference curve for
producing 6000 tonnes of cornbeans. This curve is
derived from data given in Table 22-1.

1. (Read all of this question before answering.) If land
   can be rented at $65 per hectare a year and if
   labour costs work out to $8000 a worker, what is the
   least cost combination for producing 6000 tonnes of
   cornbeans? Restrict your answer to the dots in
   Figure 22-3 that correspond to data from Table

   22-1. _____ hectares and

   _____ workers.
      If land rents for $125 a year and labour costs
   $8000 a worker, what is the least cost input
   combination for producing 6000 tonnes of

   cornbeans? _____ hectares and

   _____ workers.
      In this example it is perhaps easiest to answer
   both questions by direct computation of total cost at
   each of the three input combinations. The following
   procedure, using budget lines, is potentially more
   versatile: You should first realize that for any given
   budget line, total cost can be computed from the

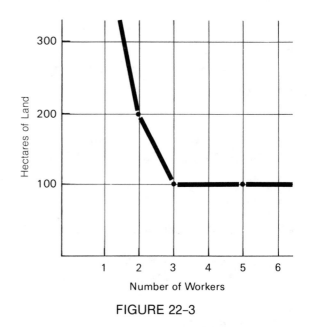

FIGURE 22-3

PRODUCTION–INDIFFERENCE CURVE

horizontal or vertical axis intercept. Either intercept is simply the total cost divided by the relevant input price. Remember that the ratio of input prices determines the slope of the budget line. For a given set of input prices draw the budget lines that pass through each of the three input combinations. Remember that these lines should be parallel. For a given set of input prices, the least cost combination is given by the lowest budget line. Can you explain why?

2. From your answer to the previous question you know that if the cost of using land is relatively low, the least cost input combination will use more land with a smaller number of workers. You also know that if the cost of using land rises enough, an optimizing farmer would be induced to use less land and more workers. What is the rental price of land that just tips the balance away from the input combination of 200 hectares and 2 workers to the combination of 100 hectares and 3 workers?
$ _____ .

You should be able to answer this question by "rotating" a budget line around the outside of the production-indifference curve. For given input prices, find the one budget line that just touches, or is tangent to, the production-indifference curve. This point will show the lowest cost-input combination. As one input price changes, the slope of the budget line will change and the tangency point will move as the lowest cost-budget line rotates around the outside of the production-indifference curve. If the price of land is low, the input combination of 200 hectares and 2 workers will be on the lowest budget line. As the price of land rises, the slope of the budget line becomes flatter, and there will come a point where suddenly the input combination of 100 hectares and 3 workers is on the lowest budget line.

SELF-TESTS FOR UNDERSTANDING

Test A

Circle the correct answer.

1. Which of the following properties is *not* true of production-indifference curves?
   a. They have a negative slope.
   b. Their slope is always equal to the ratio of input prices.
   c. They are convex to the origin because of the "law" of diminishing returns.

   d. Each curve shows different input levels consistent with the same output.
2. The budget line relevant for choosing the optimal amount of two inputs
   a. has a positive slope, unlike the budget line for the problem of consumer choice.
   b. will shift in a parallel fashion in response to an increase in the price of one input.
   c. is a straight line with a negative slope reflecting relative input prices.
   d. will have a different slope following an equal percentage change in the price of all inputs.
3. Which one of the following will not occur after a reduction in the price of one input?
   a. The budget line will shift in such a way that a fixed production budget can now buy more of the cheaper input.
   b. The optimal input combination for a given level of output is likely to involve the use of more of the cheaper input.
   c. The minimum total cost for producing a given level of output will fall.
   d. Each production-indifference curve will show a parallel shift.

Test B

Circle T or F for True or False as appropriate.

1. Production-indifference curves have a positive slope because higher output usually requires more of both inputs. T F
2. Typically a production-indifference curve will bow in at the middle because of the "law" of diminishing returns. T F
3. A firm minimizes cost for any level of output by choosing the input combination given by the tangency of the budget line to the production-indifference curve. T F
4. An increase in the price of either input will make the budget line steeper. T F
5. If production requires the use of two inputs, x_1 and x_2, a change in the price of input x_1 will never affect the optimal use of input x_2. T F
6. A change in the price of output will change the cost-minimizing input combination for a given level of output. T F
7. For given input prices, the tangencies of production-indifference curves with alternative budget lines trace out a firm's expansion path. T F

SUPPLEMENTARY EXERCISE*

Assume that the production of widgets (W) requires labour (L) and machines (M) and can be represented by the production function

$$W = L^{\frac{1}{2}} M^{\frac{1}{2}}$$

1. Draw a production-indifference curve for the production of 500,000 widgets.

2. L measures labour hours and M measures machine hours. In the long run, both machines and labour hours are variable. If machine hours cost $48 and labour hours cost $12, what is the cost-minimizing

*This particular mathematical representation of a production function is called the Cobb-Douglas production function. Cobb was a mathematician. Douglas was President of the American Economic Association and a United States Senator from Illinois from 1948 to 1966. You might enjoy reading the comments by Albert Rees and Paul Samuelson about Douglas and his work in the *Journal of Political Economy*, October 1979, Part 1.

number of labour and machine hours to produce 500,000 widgets? (Whether it is profitable to produce 500,000 widgets depends upon the price of widgets.)

3. Assume now that the firm has 125 machines capable of supplying 250,000 machine hours.
   a. Draw a picture of total output as a function of the number of labour hours.
   b. Use the production function to derive an expression for the marginal physical product of labour conditional on the 250,000 machine hours. Draw a picture of this function. What, if any, is the connection between your picture of total output and the marginal physical product?
   c. Divide your picture of the marginal physical product into regions of increasing, decreasing, and negative marginal returns to labour. (Note: Not all areas need exist.)
   d. If the price of widgets is $50 and the price of labour is $12 per hour, what is the optimal number of labour hours that the firm should use? How many widgets will the firm produce?

The Common Sense of Business Decisions: Outputs and Prices

LEARNING OBJECTIVES

After completing the material in this chapter you should be able to:

- define, understand, and use correctly the terms and concepts listed below.
- explain why a firm can make a decision on output *or* price, but not usually on both.
- calculate average and marginal cost from data on total cost.
- explain why the demand curve is the curve of average revenue.
- calculate total and marginal revenue from data on the demand curve.
- use data on costs and revenues to compute the level of output that maximizes profits.
- explain why the point of maximum profit cannot be associated with a positive or negative marginal profit.

- explain how and why an economist's definition of profit differs from that of an accountant.
- explain why a change in fixed costs will not affect marginal cost.

IMPORTANT TERMS AND CONCEPTS

Profit maximization
Satisficing
Total profit
Economic profit
Total revenue and cost
Average revenue and cost
Fixed cost
Marginal revenue and cost
Marginal analysis
Marginal profit

CHAPTER REVIEW

This is the second consecutive chapter to make extensive use of *marginal analysis*, one of the most important tools an economist has. You have already used marginal analysis in deriving a consumer's optimal purchase rule and a firm's optimal use of inputs. In this chapter the concept is used to help decide how much output a firm should produce in order to maximize its profits.

While marginal analysis is a powerful tool for business decision-making, it is applicable in many non-business situations as well. For example, how much should the government spend to clean up the environment? Or a related question: To clean up our lakes and rivers, should the government require all industries and towns to reduce their discharges by an equal percentage or is there a more efficient alternative? As discussed in Chapter 34 marginal analysis can help answer these and similar questions.

You may already have had more experience with the concept of marginal analysis than you realize. Have you ever had to pay federal income taxes? If so, you might dig out your records and make two calculations. Your

(1) total taxes divided by your total income would be your (*average/marginal*) tax rate. Now assume that you had $100 more income. Figure out how much more taxes you would have owed. This increase in taxes divided by the $100 additional income would be your (*average/marginal*) tax rate.

Your average exam grade is another example of the distinction between marginal and average. If you want to raise your overall average, what sorts of grades do you need this term? The grades you earn this term are the marginal contribution to your overall average grade. Similarly, a baseball player's daily batting record is a marginal measure when compared with his season's batting average.

In whatever context, marginal analysis focuses attention on the effect of changes. For business output decisions, marginal analysis looks at the effect on costs, revenues, and profits as output changes. The change

(2) in total cost from changing output by one unit is called _____ cost. The change in total

revenue from producing and selling one more unit is _____ revenue. Marginal profit is

the change in total _____ as output expands by one unit. Because profits equal

revenue minus costs, marginal profit equals marginal _____ minus marginal

_____ .

(3) Economists usually assume that business firms are interested in *maximizing* (*average/marginal/total*) profit. This assumption need not be true for all firms, but economists have found that models based on this assumption provide useful insights into actual events. (You might want to refer back to the discussion in Chapter 1 about the role of abstraction in theory.) Economists are interested in marginal profit not as an end in itself, but because marginal profit is an extremely useful guide to the maximizing of total profit.

It should be common sense that any firm that is interested in maximizing profit will want to expand output as long as the increase in total revenue is greater than the increase in total costs. Rather than looking at total revenue and total cost, one could just as easily look at the changes in revenue and cost as output changes. An increase in output will add to profits if the change in revenue is greater than the change in costs. An economist might make the

(4) same point by saying that an increase in output will add to total profits if (*marginal/average*) revenue exceeds (*marginal/average*) cost. We could also say that an increase in output will add to total profits as long as marginal profits are (*positive/zero/negative*). Total profits will stop rising when marginal profits fall to zero; that is, when

marginal revenue _____ marginal costs.

As discussed in Chapter 22, it is often convenient to divide a firm's costs into two categories: *fixed* and *variable*

(5) costs. Even if output is zero a firm may have to meet certain costs. These are _____ costs. Other costs will vary directly with the level of output, usually rising as output increases. These are

_____ costs. Total cost is the sum of fixed and variable costs. Average cost reflects both fixed and variable costs because it is the average of total costs. Marginal cost measures the change in total

costs and thus reflects only _____ costs. If fixed costs increase and variable costs are unchanged, then total and average costs for each level of output will increase and marginal cost (*will/will not*) change.

BASIC EXERCISES

1. This exercise is designed to review the use of marginal revenue and marginal cost as a guide to the maximization of profits.
   a. Table 23-1 below has data on demand for

widgets from Wanda's Widget Company as well as data on the costs of production. Use these data to compute marginal cost, total revenue, and marginal revenue. Ignore the columns on total profits and average cost for now.

   b. From the data on marginal cost and revenue that

you just calculated, marginal revenue exceeds marginal cost up to what level of output?

_____ 7 _____

c. Restricting yourself to levels of output listed in Table 23-1, what is the profit-maximizing level of output? _____ 7 _____ Why?

d. At the level of output determined in Question c, total profits are ___7700___ (Check to be sure you have maximized total profits by computing total profits at different output levels.)

e. Use the data from the third and fourth columns of Table 23-1 to plot the demand curve for widgets in Figure 23-1. Now compute average cost from the data in Table 23-1 and plot that in Figure 23-1.

   Still using Figure 23-1, plot the data on marginal revenue and marginal cost from Table 23-1. Where do these two curves intersect? It should be just beyond, but less than 1 unit beyond, the profit-maximizing output level previously identified.

f. Identify the profit-maximizing level of output on your graph. Draw the rectangle for total revenue and shade it lightly with positively sloped lines. Draw the rectangle for total cost and shade it

lightly with negatively sloped lines. This rectangle should overlap part of the rectangle of total revenue. The non-overlapped portion of the total-revenue rectangle is a picture of total

_____ . Maximizing total-profit maximizes this total-profit rectangle. It (*does/does not*) minimize average cost.

g. Assume now that the fixed costs Wanda must pay have increased by $1000; that is, every entry for total cost in Table 23-1 is $1000 higher. Compute marginal cost, now that fixed costs have increased. How does your answer compare with your entries for marginal cost in Table 23-1? (What about average cost?) What is the new profit-maximizing level of output? What are total profits?

2. The geometry of marginal revenue
a. Figure 23-2 shows the demand curve for Medalist bicycles. Draw a rectangle for total revenue on the assumption that 100,000 bicycles are sold. Lightly shade this rectangle with horizontal lines.

b. Assume now that 120,000 bicycles are sold rather than 100,000. Draw a rectangle for total revenue at this higher level of sales. Lightly shade this rectangle with vertical lines.

TABLE 23-1

WANDA'S WIDGET COMPANY

| Marginal Revenue | Total Revenue | Demand | | Total Cost (dollars) | Marginal Cost | Average Cost | Total Profits |
		Price (dollars)	Output				
	3500	3,500	1	2,000		2000	1500
3300					1900		
	6800	3,400	2	3,900		1950	2900
3100					1800		
	9900	3,300	3	5,700		1900	4200
2900					1700		
	12,800	3,200	4	7,400		1850	5400
2700					1600		
	15,500	3,100	5	9,000		1800	6500
2500					1500		
	18,000	3,000	6	10,500		1750	7500
2300					2100		
	20,300	2,900	7	12,600		1800	7700
2100					2600		
	22400	2,800	8	15,200		1900	7200
1900					2800		
	24300	2,700	9	18,000		2000	6300
1700					3000		
	26000	2,600	10	21,000		2100	5000

147

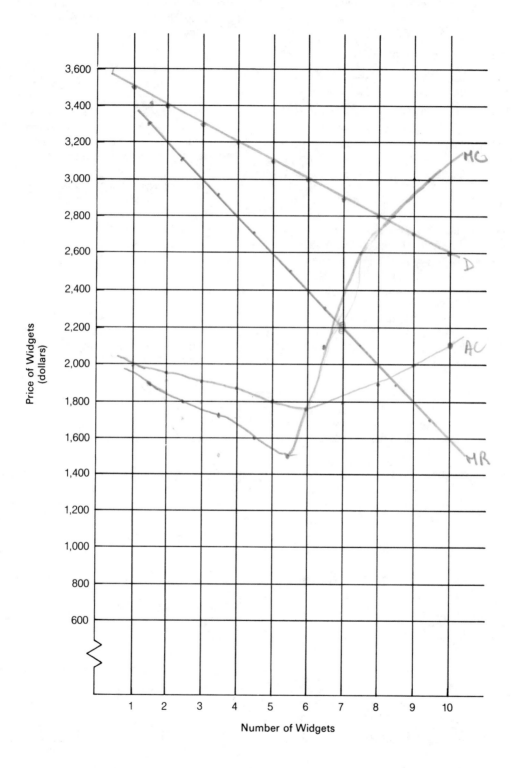

FIGURE 23-1

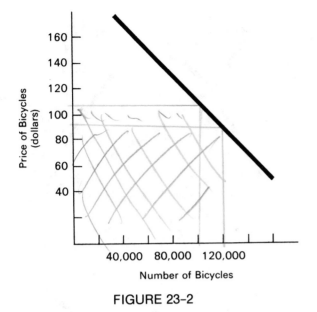

FIGURE 23-2

THE DEMAND FOR MEDALIST BICYCLES

If you have drawn and shaded the rectangles correctly you should have a large cross-hatched rectangle and two smaller rectangles; one long, horizontal rectangle on the top of the cross-hatched rectangle and one thin, vertical rectangle. The thin vertical rectangle represents revenue from additional sales at the new lower price. This rectangle (*is/is not*) a complete measure of marginal revenue. It measures the receipts of additional sales but neglects the drop in revenue from the reduction in price that helped to expand the sales in the first place. This reduction in revenue on previous units is

represented by the _____ rectangle. The geometric representation of marginal revenue is the (*vertical/horizontal*) rectangle minus the

_____ rectangle.

SELF-TESTS FOR UNDERSTANDING

Test A

Circle the correct answer.

1. Marginal cost equals
   a. total cost divided by total output.
   b. the change in total cost associated with an additional unit of output.
   c. the change in average cost.

d. the slope of the average-cost curve.
2. The demand curve is the curve of
   a. total revenue.
   b. average revenue.
   c. marginal revenue.
   d. variable revenue.
3. Marginal revenue to a firm is
   a. the same as the demand curve for the firm's output.
   b. found by dividing price by output.
   c. found by dividing output by price.
   d. the change in revenue for an additional unit of output.
4. When output increases by one unit, marginal revenue will typically be
   a. less than the new lower price.
   b. equal to the new lower price.
   c. greater than the new lower price.
5. Marginal profit equals the difference between
   a. total revenue and total cost.
   b. average revenue and average cost.
   c. marginal revenue and marginal cost.
   d. the demand curve and the marginal-cost curve.
6. If a firm has chosen a level of output that maximizes profits, then at the chosen level of output
   a. marginal profits are also maximized.
   b. average cost is minimized.
   c. an increase in output will involve negative marginal profits.
   d. the difference between average revenue and average cost is maximized.
7. Which of the following is consistent with profit maximization?
   a. Produce where marginal cost is minimized.
   b. Produce where average cost is minimized.
   c. Produce where marginal revenue equals marginal cost.
   d. Produce where marginal revenue is maximized.
8. An economist's definition of profit differs from that of an accountant because
   a. the economist is only interested in marginal cost and marginal revenue.
   b. the economist includes the opportunity cost of owner-supplied inputs in total cost.
   c. accountants cannot maximize.
   d. economists cannot add or subtract correctly.
9. An increase in fixed costs will affect which one of the following?
   a. Marginal cost.
   b. Average variable cost.
   c. Average total cost.
   d. Marginal revenue.
10. A decrease in fixed cost will affect which one of the following?
    a. Total profits.
    b. Marginal profits.

c. The profit-maximizing level of output.
d. Total revenue at the profit-maximizing level of output.

Test B

Circle T or F for True or False as appropriate.

1. Business firms can decide both the price and quantity of their output.   T F

2. Firms always make optimal decisions.   T F

3. The demand curve for a firm's product is also the firm's marginal revenue curve.   T F

4. Marginal cost is computed by dividing total cost by the quantity of output.   T F

5. Marginal revenue is simply the price of the last unit sold.   T F

6. An output decision will generally not be optimal unless it corresponds to a zero marginal profit. T F

7. Marginal profit will be zero when marginal revenue equals marginal cost.   T F

8. Marginal cost will decline as output increases because fixed costs are being spread over a larger number of units.   T F

9. As long as average revenue exceeds average cost, a firm is making profits and should increase output.   T F

10. It never pays to sell below average cost.   T F

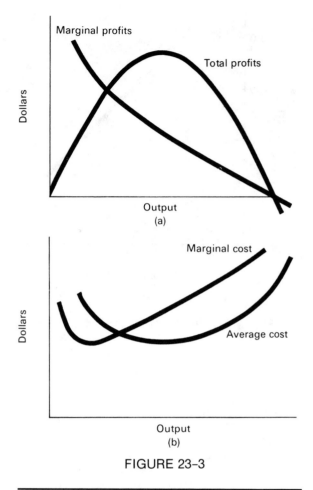

FIGURE 23–3

Appendix: The Relationships Among Total, Average, and Marginal Data

BASIC EXERCISE

This exercise is designed to help you review the relationships between total, average, and marginal measures described in the appendix to Chapter 23.

1. Explain what is wrong with both of the illustrations below.

2. For part (a) of Figure 23–3, assume that the total-profit curve is correct and draw an appropriate marginal-profit curve.

3. For part (b) of Figure 23–3, assume that the average-cost curve is correct and draw an appropriate marginal-cost curve.

SUPPLEMENTARY EXERCISES

1. A Mathematical Example of Profit Maximization
   The demand for Acme stereos is

$$Q = 1200 - 4P,$$

where Q represents output measured in thousands of sets and P represents price. The total cost of producing stereos is given by

$$TC = 16,000 + 120Q - 0.4Q^2 + 0.002Q^3.$$

a. What are Acme's fixed costs?
b. What mathematical expression describes average costs? Marginal costs?
c. On a piece of graph paper plot average cost and marginal cost. Does your marginal-cost curve go through the minimum point of your average-cost curve?
d. Use the information from the demand curve to derive a mathematical expression for marginal revenue.
e. On the same graph as in c draw the demand curve (the average-revenue curve) and the marginal-revenue curve.

f. What does your graph suggest about the profit-maximizing level of output?

g. Does your answer in f coincide with a direct mathematical solution for Q, where MR = MC? It should. (To answer this question you will need to use the expressions you derived for marginal revenue and marginal cost.)

h. What is Acme's maximum profit?

i. Shade in the portion of your graph that represents maximum profit.

j. What if fixed cost were $20,000? How, if at all, do your answers to b, c, d, g, and h change?

2. **Profit Maximization and the Elasticity of Demand**
A profit-maximizing firm will not try to produce so much output that it is operating in the inelastic portion of its demand curve. Why not? In Chapter 21 we saw that if demand is inelastic, total revenue will increase following a reduction in output. (The higher price more than compensates for the reduction in output.) Total costs will decline if output is reduced. Thus, profits—revenue minus costs—must increase following a decline in output if a firm is originally operating in the inelastic portion of its demand curve. What are the elastic and inelastic portions of the demand for Acme stereos? (Check to be sure that the profit-maximizing output you determined in Question 1 is not in the inelastic region.)

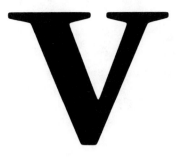

V

The Market System:
Virtues and Vices

Firms in Reality: The Corporation and the Stock Market

24

LEARNING OBJECTIVES

After completing the material in this chapter you should be able to:

- define, understand, and use correctly the terms and concepts listed below.
- explain the major advantages and disadvantages of alternative forms of business organization.
- explain the advantages of ploughback as a source of funds to both a corporation and its shareholders.
- describe the advantages and disadvantages of investing in stocks or bonds.
- discuss the role of speculation both in the economy in general and in the securities markets in particular.
- explain why bond prices fall when interest rates go up and vice versa.
- explain how the use of stocks or bonds shifts risk between a corporation and financial investors.
- explain why the stock market is of critical importance to the financing of corporations, even though new stock issues account for only a very small proportion of new funds raised by corporations.
- describe how portfolio diversification can reduce the risk faced by a financial investor.

IMPORTANT TERMS AND CONCEPTS

Proprietorship
Unlimited liability
Partnership
Corporation
Limited liability
Ploughback or retained earnings
Common stock
Bond
Portfolio diversification
Stock exchanges
Speculation
Random walk

CHAPTER REVIEW

The purpose of this chapter is to explore the advantages and disadvantages of alternative legal forms of business organization. Special attention is given to the different ways in which corporations can raise funds and to the markets on which corporate securities are traded.

(1)   A business that is owned and operated by a single individual is called a _____ . This is by far the most common form of business organization in Canada. When instead a firm's ownership and decision-making

are shared by a fixed number of individuals, the business is called a _____ . Another form of business organization is one in which the firm has the legal status of a fictional individual and is owned by a large number of shareholders and run by an elected board of directors and officers. This form of organization is

called a _____ . A major advantage of the latter form of organization is that shareholders, the legal owners of the business, are not liable for the firm's debts. The fact that corporations have

_____ liability has made it possible for corporations to raise very large sums of money in the pursuit of profits.

   Corporations raise funds by one of four means. A corporation that raises funds by selling shares of
(2)   ownership and offering a stake in future profits is issuing (*stock/bonds*). If a corporation issues securities that

promise to pay a fixed sum of money as interest and principal, it is issuing _____ . Borrowing directly from large financial institutions, such as banks or insurance companies, is a third source of funds. The most common way of raising funds is to directly reinvest part of a corporation's profits. This method of raising

funds is called _____ .

   Assuming a firm does not become bankrupt, a bond that is held to maturity offers the bondholder a fixed and known stream of payments. Investing in stock promises future dividend payments and stock prices that
(3)   (*are/are not*) known at the time of purchase. The greater uncertainty of future dividends and stock prices as compared to bond payments lead economists to conclude that from the viewpoint of individual investors, stocks are (*more/less*) risky than bonds. From the viewpoint of a firm (*bonds/stocks*) are more risky, because a failure to (*meet bond payments/pay dividends*) can force a firm into bankruptcy.

   However, this comparison understates the riskiness to individual investors of investing in bonds. If a bond must be sold before maturity, and interest rates have changed, the market price of the bond will also change. If interest
(4)   rates have risen, existing bonds with low coupon payments will look less attractive unless their price (*rises/falls*). Holders of these bonds will suffer a capital (*gain/loss*). Conversely, if interest rates have fallen, competition for existing bonds with high coupon payments will (*increase/decrease*) the price of existing bonds, giving holders of

these a capital _____ .

   Stocks and bonds are traded in markets that sometimes have a specific location, such as the Toronto Stock Exchange, but are often just handled by dealers and brokers who keep track, by telephone or computer, of the latest price changes. Two important functions served by established exchanges include (1) reducing the

(5)   _____ of stock ownership by providing a secondary market in existing shares and (2) determining the current price of a company's stock. In the latter role, established exchanges help to allocate the economy's resources to those firms that, in the market's judgment, are expected to make the most profitable use of those resources.

   Anyone who buys a share of stock is buying a risky asset in the hopes of substantial gain. In this sense, anyone who buys stock is behaving much like a speculator, who hopes to profit from changes in prices. From a general perspective, speculation serves two important functions. First, it can help to decrease price fluctuations. Buying now at low prices in anticipation of being able to sell next year at high prices will, in fact, make prices today

(6)   (*higher/lower*) than they would otherwise be and will also make prices next year _____ than they otherwise would be. The second function of speculation is that it can work to provide

_____ for those who want to avoid taking risks. Commodity speculators will agree now on a price to be paid for buying crops next year, thus insuring a farmer against the adverse effects of a decrease in price. Other speculators may agree now on a price at which to sell crops next year to a milling company, thus insuring the miller against the adverse effects of an increase in price.

   The behaviour of individual stock prices has long fascinated many investors. Much time and effort is spent trying to forecast the movement of stock prices. Some investors look at things like a firm's earnings and its current stock price; others plot recent stock prices and try to discover laws of motion in their graphs. Economists have also studied the changes in individual stock prices. Much of this research supports the conclusion that changes in stock

(7) prices are essentially unpredictable, that is they look like a _____ _____ .
Such a result could arise because of essentially random waves of buying and selling as investors try to outguess each other. It could also arise from investors' careful study and analysis of individual companies, study that is so complete that all anticipated future events are fully reflected in current stock prices. The expectation today of higher profits tomorrow raises stock prices (*today*/*tomorrow*). In this view, changes in stock prices can only reflect currently unanticipated events, events that will likely look like random events. This viewpoint has been formalized in the hypothesis of "efficient markets." Much advanced research in financial economics is concerned with testing this hypothesis.

BASIC EXERCISE

This exercise is designed to illustrate how the prices of stocks are adjusted by market forces to reflect alternative yields that are available to investors.

The XYZ corporation earns $9.123 million in profits a year and pays $3.923 million in profits tax to the government, leaving $5.2 million that is paid out as a $4 dividend on each of 1.3 million shares. (XYZ does not plough back any of its after-tax profits.) Investors in XYZ stock have the option of investing in corporate bonds and earning a return of 10 percent on which they will have to pay income taxes, just as they must pay taxes on dividend income. (Assume for this exercise that dividends and bond interest are taxable at the same rate.)

Stock Price	Dividend Before Taxes	Dividend Yield (col. 2 ÷ col. 1)
$ 25	$4	_____
40	4	_____
64	4	_____
100	4	_____

a. Fill in the blank column to compute the dividend yield on a share of XYZ stock at various prices.
b. Assume that the XYZ dividend has always been $4 and is expected to remain $4 in the future. Further, since XYZ does not plough back any of its after-tax profits, the price of XYZ stock is not expected to change. If investors require the same return on shares of XYZ stock as they do on corporate bonds, what will be the price of XYZ stock?

_____

c. What is likely to happen to the price of XYZ stock if the interest rate of government bonds rises to 16 percent? Falls to 6.25 percent?
d. Suddenly and unexpectedly, the president of XYZ announces that oil has been discovered on company property. The revenues from this discovery will double profits for the foreseeable future. Furthermore, XYZ announces that starting next year and continuing into the future, the dividend per share will also be doubled to $8. Why will the price

of XYZ stock rise immediately rather than waiting until next year when higher dividend payments start?
e. If everyone believes that dividends on XYZ stock will double next year, never changing again, and if alternative investments continue to yield 10 percent, what is the likely new stock price? Why?

SELF-TESTS FOR UNDERSTANDING

Test A

Circle the correct answer.

1. Which one of the following is *not* true of proprietorships?
   a. The proprietor has complete and full personal control of the business.
   b. Limited liability on the part of the proprietor for the debts of the business.
   c. The proprietor will have comparative difficulty raising funds.
   d. Few legal complications.
2. Ways in which corporations can raise money include all but which one of the following?
   a. Issuing shares of stock.
   b. Borrowing money in the form of bonds.
   c. The reinvestment, or ploughback, of profits.
   d. Paying dividends.
3. Which of the following is the most important source of new funds for corporations?
   a. New stock issues.
   b. Corporate bonds.
   c. Retained earnings.
   d. Bank loans.
4. A decrease in the general level of interest rates will tend to
   a. increase bond prices.
   b. lower bond prices.
   c. have no effect on bond prices.
5. Emerson purchased a newly issued Canadian General Electric bond last year with coupon payments offering an interest rate of 10 percent. Since then, market interest rates on similar bonds have risen to 12 percent. Which of the following is true?

a. The market value of the bonds that Emerson bought will have increased from the price he paid.

b. If held to maturity, and CGE does not default, Emerson will earn 12 percent on his original investment.

c. Anyone purchasing such bonds today, at their current market price and holding them to maturity, can expect to earn only 10 percent on the investment.

d. If Emerson sold his bonds today, at their current market price, he would have a capital loss.

6. There are 5 million outstanding shares of stock in the XYZ corporation. If the price of XYZ stock rises by $1, then

a. the XYZ corporation will have $5 million more to invest or use to pay higher dividends.

b. existing shareholders will have a capital gain of $1 a share.

c. investors who hold XYZ bonds will have suffered a capital loss.

7. Which of the following $100,000 investments offers the most diversification?

a. $100,000 of Bell Canada stock.

b. $100,000 of Province of Quebec bonds.

c. $100,000 of gold.

d. $25,000 invested in each of the following: Falconbridge, Bell, Bank of Nova Scotia, Dome Petroleum.

8. The important economic functions of organized stock exchanges include all but which one of the following?

a. Offering investors insurance against the risk of changes in stock prices.

b. Reducing the risk of purchasing stock by offering investors a place to sell their shares should they need the funds for some other purpose.

c. Helping to allocate the economy's resources, since companies with high current stock prices will find it easier to raise additional funds to pursue investment opportunities.

9. If Maxine is to be a successful speculator she must

a. buy during a period of excess supply and sell during a period of excess supply.

b. buy during a period of excess supply and sell during a period of excess demand.

c. buy during a period of excess demand and sell during a period of excess demand.

d. buy during a period of excess demand and sell during a period of excess supply.

Test B

Circle T or F for True or False as appropriate.

1. Corporations, while constituting a minority of the *number* of business organizations, are the most

important form of organization when measured by total *sales*.   T F

2. When measured by the number of firms, partnerships are the most common form of business organization in Canada.   T F

3. Assuming no bankruptcy, a corporate bond is a riskless investment even if the bond must be sold before maturity.   T F

4. Any individual who wants to buy or sell shares of stock can do so by walking onto the floor of the Toronto Stock Exchange and announcing his or her intentions.   T F

6. Whenever a share of Bell Canada stock is sold on the Toronto Stock Exchange, Bell Canada gets the proceeds.   T F

7. Established stock exchanges, such as the Toronto Stock Exchange, are really just a form of legalized gambling and serve no useful social function. T F

8. The finding that stock prices follow a random walk implies that investing in stocks is essentially a pure gamble.   T F

9. Profitable speculation involves buying high and selling low.   T F

SUPPLEMENTARY EXERCISES

1. Get a copy of any newspaper that lists bonds. Find the listing for several regular bonds of different corporations with a similar maturity date that is sometime past 1995. Write down their coupon rate, current yield, and market price. Also note stock prices for the same companies. After three months, look up the stock prices and the current yield and price of the bonds again. Check to see that any increase (or decrease) in the current yield is matched by an opposite movement in the bond price. Had you actually bought these bonds, would you now have a capital gain or loss? What if you had bought shares of stock? Have all or most of the bond prices moved together? Have all the stock prices moved together? (It would not be surprising if the prices of bonds of different corporations rose or fell together. Stock prices are much less likely to change together. Can you explain why?)

2. Assume you have $10,000 to invest in the stock market. Choose 10 companies listed on the Toronto Stock Exchange. Write down each company and the price of its stock on Table 24-1. Three months later look up the stock prices and complete Table 24-1.

The sum of the entries in column (6) will show you the return on your diversified portfolio. Column (7) will show you possible gains and losses had you put all your eggs in one basket. It is easy to pick the winners after the fact, but in reality you have to choose without knowing the future stock prices. How do your results illustrate the link between portfolio diversification and risk?

TABLE 24-1

(1) Company	(2) Initial Stock Price	(3) Number of Shares if Investing $1000[a]	(4) Number of Shares if investing $10,000[b]	(5) Stock Price in 3 Months	(6) Value of $1000 Investment[c]	(7) Value of $10,000 Investment[d]
1						
2						
3						
4						
5						
6						
7						
8						
9						
10						

Value of portfolio[e] _____

[a](3) = $1000 ÷ price in (2). [b](4) = $10,000 ÷ price in (2). [c](6) = (3) × (5). [d](7) = (4) × (5). [e]Sum the 10 entries in (6).

The Firm in the Marketplace: Perfect Competition

LEARNING OBJECTIVES

After completing the material in this chapter you should be able to:

- define, understand, and use correctly the terms and concepts listed below.
- describe the conditions that distinguish perfect competition from other market structures.
- explain why under perfect competition the firm faces a horizontal demand curve while the industry faces a downward-sloping demand curve.
- explain why a perfectly competitive firm's short-run supply curve is the portion of its marginal cost curve that is above average variable costs.
- derive an industry's short-run supply curve given information on the supply curves for individual firms.
- use the concept of opportunity cost to reconcile economic and accounting profits.
- explain how freedom of entry and exit imply that in the long run firms operating under perfect competition will earn zero economic profit.

- explain how perfect competition implies the efficient production of goods and services.

IMPORTANT TERMS AND CONCEPTS

Market
Perfect competition
Pure monopoly
Monopolistic competition
Oligopoly
Price taker
Horizontal demand curve
Short-run equilibrium
Average variable cost
Total variable cost
Supply curve of the firm
Supply curve of the industry
Long-run equilibrium
Opportunity cost
Economic profit

CHAPTER REVIEW

This chapter uses the concepts developed in earlier chapters to study in more detail the supply decisions of firms. While this discussion makes use of these concepts it also adds important material about *market structures*. The decisions of individual firms depend not only upon their production functions and cost curves, but also upon the type of market structure the firm faces. This chapter focuses on the abstraction of the market structure of perfect competition. Later chapters will investigate other market structures—monopolistic competition, oligopoly, and pure monopoly.

Perfect competition is distinguished from other market structures by four conditions

(1)
1. (*Few/Many*) buyers and sellers.
2. (*Differentiated/Identical*) product.
3. (*Easy/Difficult*) entry and exit.
4. (*Perfect/Imperfect*) information.

Conditions 1, 2, and 4 imply that the actions of individual buyers and sellers (*do/do not*) affect the market price for the one identical product. Condition 3 implies that the number of firms can easily expand or contract and leads to the condition that long-run equilibrium will be characterized by (*positive/zero/negative*) economic profits.

An important first step to analysing the firm's decisions in a particular market structure is to be careful about what the market structure implies for variables such as marginal revenue. Let us first consider the short-run supply decision of an individual firm under perfect competition. Since the actions of this firm will not affect the market price, the firm can sell as much or as little as it wants at the prevailing market price. Alternatively, we may say that the **(2)** firm faces a (*horizontal/vertical*) demand curve. In Chapter 23 we saw that the demand curve is also the curve of average revenue. If the demand curve is horizontal, then besides being the curve of average revenue it is also the

curve of _____ revenue. (Remember the picture of marginal revenue in the Basic Exercise to Chapter 23 of this study guide. If the demand curve is horizontal, there is no horizontal rectangle to subtract.) As we saw in Chapter 23, the firm maximizes profits by producing where MC = MR. Under perfect competition, MR = P, thus under perfect competition the firm should produce where MC = MR = P.

We can now derive the short-run supply curve for the firm by imagining that the firm faces a variety of possible prices and considering what output the firm would supply at each price. These price-output pairs will define the firm's short-run supply curve. For many possible prices short-run supply will be given by the intersection of price **(3)** and the (*average/marginal*) cost curve. If price drops below the minimum of the average total cost curve, the MC =

P rule maximizes profits by minimizing _____ . Even if price is less than average total

cost, the firm should continue to produce as long as price is above average _____ cost. If the firm decides to produce nothing it still must cover its (*variable/fixed*) costs. As long as price exceeds average variable cost, there will be something left over to help cover fixed costs.

(4) The industry short-run supply curve is given by the (*horizontal/vertical*) summation of individual firms' supply curves. Market price, the variable so crucial to individual firms' decisions, will be given by the intersection of the

market _____ and _____ curves. In the short run, the number of firms in the industry is fixed; and the short-run industry supply curve will come from the supply decisions of existing firms.

In the long run, there will be more (fewer) firms if the short-run equilibrium involves economic profits (losses). For example, if general market returns are around 15 percent and accounting profits show a return of 12 percent to **(5)** investments in the firm, an economist would conclude that the firm has an economic (*loss/profit*) of

_____ percent. In this case, by investing elsewhere and earning 15 percent, the firm's

owners would be (*better/worse*) off. The 15 percent is the _____ cost of capital to the firm and it is an important part of costs as counted by the economist. Thus, economists focus on economic profits as the indicator of entry or exit rather than on accounting profits.

As firms enter or leave, the short-run supply curve will shift appropriately, price will adjust as we move along the industry demand curve, and industry long-run equilibrium will be achieved when there are no further incentives for entry or exit. Figure 25-1(a) illustrates a firm in a perfectly competitive industry. Figure 25-1(b) shows the **(6)** industry demand and supply. The illustrated firm will be making economic (*profits/losses*). Shade in the appropriate rectangle showing economic profits or losses. There will be an incentive for some firms to (*enter/leave*) the industry. As the number of firms in the industry changes, the supply curve in Figure 25-1(b) will shift to the *(right/left)* and price will _____ . If the cost curves in Figure 25-1(a) are representative of the costs for all current and potential firms in the industry, long-run equilibrium will involve a price of

$ _____ . Note that at all times our representative firm is producing where MC = *P*. But

in long-run equilibrium, MC = *P* = minimum _____ cost. It is this last condition that explains the efficiency of perfectly competitive markets.

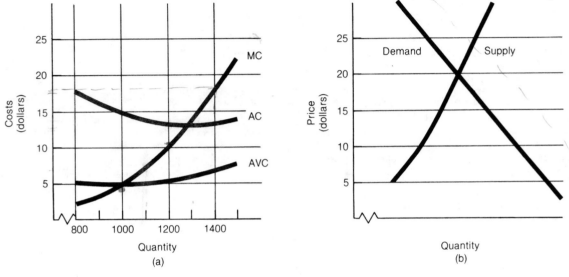

FIGURE 25-1

BASIC EXERCISE

This exercise is designed to explore the short-run supply curve for a firm under perfect competition.

Assume that widgets are produced by perfectly competitive firms. The data in Table 25-1 are consistent with Figure 25-1 and are for a representative widget firm. Although not listed in Table 25-1, the production of widgets involves fixed costs of $10,140.

1. If the price of widgets is $17.80, what is the profit-maximizing level of output?

   ____1400____ .

   What are economic profits at this level of output?

   $ ___5544___ . Check to be sure that this level of output maximizes profits by calculating profits for output levels 1000 units higher and lower.

   Economic profits at higher output = $ __5310__

   Economic profits at lower output = $ __5330__

2. If the price of widgets is $10.20, what is the profit-maximizing level of output?

   ____1200____

   What are economic profits at this level of output?

   $ __-4380__ . Check to be sure that this

TABLE 25-1

COSTS OF PRODUCING WIDGETS

Quantity	Average Cost (dollars)	Average Variable Cost (dollars)	Marginal Cost (dollars)
900	16.37	5.10	3.30
1000	15.14	5.00	5.00
1100	14.32	5.10	7.30
1200	13.85	5.40	10.20
1300	13.70	5.90	13.70
1400	13.84	6.60	17.80
1500	14.26	7.50	22.50

level of output maximizes profits or minimizes losses by considering output levels 1000 units higher, 1000 units lower, and no production.

Economic losses at higher output = $ __4550__

Economic losses at lower output = $ __4532__

Economic losses at zero output = $ __10,140__

3. If the price of widgets is $4.90, what is the profit-maximizing level of output?

_O_ ~~1000~~ . Why isn't it higher? _because_ _any lower + the firm could shutdown_

4. If many firms can produce with the same cost functions, what is the long-run equilibrium price of widgets? $____ 13.70 ____. What is the associated level of production for the representative firm? ____ 1300 ____.

SELF-TESTS FOR UNDERSTANDING

Test A

Circle the correct answer.

1. Which of the following is not a condition for perfect competition?
   a. Perfect information about products.
   b. One firm producing many products.
   c. Freedom of entry.
   d. Freedom of exit.

2. If production is limited to a few large firms, the resulting market structure is called
   a. perfect competition.
   b. monopolistic competition.
   c. oligopoly.
   d. pure monopoly.

3. Which one of the following is not true under perfect competition?
   a. The firm's demand curve is horizontal.
   b. The firm's demand curve is also the curve of average revenue.
   c. The firm's demand curve is also the curve of marginal revenue.
   d. The firm's demand curve is inelastic.

4. The short-run supply curve for a firm under perfect competition is the portion of the firm's marginal-cost curve that is above the
   a. average total cost curve.
   b. average fixed cost curve.
   c. average variable cost curve.
   d. minimum of the marginal-cost curve.

5. Which of the following is not a characteristic of long-run equilibrium under perfect competition?
   a. Production where P = MC.
   b. Zero accounting profits.
   c. Zero economic profits.
   d. Production where P = minimum average cost.

6. Under perfect competition, price will equal minimum average cost
   a. in the short run.
   b. in the long run.
   c. always.
   d. never.

7. Under perfect competition, firms will produce where P = MC
   a. in the short run.
   b. in the long run.
   c. always.
   d. never.

8. Under perfect competition, price is determined by the intersection of the industry supply and demand curves
   a. in the short run.
   b. in the long run.
   c. always.
   d. never.

9. Imagine that pencils are produced by firms with U-shaped average costs under conditions of perfect competition. A large expansion of federal government aid to education has disturbed the original long-run equilibrium by shifting the demand curve for pencils to the right. Which one of the following is not a likely response?
   a. Pencil prices rise initially in response to the increase in demand.
   b. Existing firms are likely to earn positive economic profits in the short run.
   c. Existing firms in the industry initially expand output to the point where average cost equals the new, higher price.
   d. New firms are likely to enter the industry in response to earnings above the opportunity cost of capital.

10. Widgets are produced by perfectly competitive firms. The demand curve for widgets has a negative slope. A technological innovation dramatically reduces average and marginal costs for current and potential widget manufacturers. All but which one of the following will occur?
    a. The quantity supplied increases in the short run.
    b. The price of widgets declines in the short run.
    c. Economic profits increase in the short run.
    d. Economic profits will be positive in the long run.

Test B

Circle T or F for True or False as appropriate.

1. Perfect competition is characterized by many firms producing similar but not ~~identical~~ products.   T **F**

2. Under perfect competition, firms will maximize profits by always producing at the minimum of their average cost.   **T** F

3. Freedom of entry and exit are really unnecessary for the existence of perfect competition.   T **F**

4. Under perfect competition a firm is always guaranteed to earn positive economic profits if it produces where MC = P.   T **F**

5. Under perfect competition, the demand curve facing the industry is horizontal.   T (F)

6. A competitive firm should always expand output as long as price exceeds average cost.   T (F)

7. The firm's short-run supply curve is given by the portion of its marginal-cost curve with a positive slope.   T (F)

8. In long-run equilibrium, perfectly competitive firms will show positive accounting profits but zero economic profits.   (T) F

9. If price is less than average total cost, a firm is always better off shutting down.   T (F)

10. Perfect competition is studied because a very large proportion of markets satisfy the conditions for perfect competition.   T (F)

SUPPLEMENTARY EXERCISE

Consider a firm with the following total cost curve:

$$TC = 10{,}140 + 0.00001\,Q^3 - 0.02\,Q^2 + 15\,Q,$$

where Q is output. (This cost curve is consistent with the Basic Exercise.)

1. Derive equations for the firm's
   a. average cost.
   b. average variable cost.
   c. marginal cost.
2. Draw a picture showing these various measures of cost as a function of output.
3. Verify that the marginal-cost curve goes through the bottom of the average-cost curve and the average variable cost curve.
4. Assume this firm operates in a perfectly competitive market. Derive a mathematical expression for the firm's supply curve.

The Price System and the Case for Laissez Faire

26

After completing the material in this chapter you should be able to:

- define, understand, and use correctly the terms and concepts listed below.
- list three questions that must be answered by any system of resource allocation.
- explain the difference between efficient and inefficient allocation of resources.
- explain how competitive markets, in which all producers and consumers respond to market prices, can achieve an efficient allocation of resources.
- describe the conditions under which an inefficient

allocation of resources might be preferred to an efficient allocation.

IMPORTANT TERMS AND CONCEPTS

Efficient allocation of resources
Co-ordination tasks: output selection, production planning, distribution of goods
Laissez faire
Input–output analysis
MC = P requirement of perfect competition
MC = MU efficiency requirement

CHAPTER REVIEW

This chapter discusses the role of prices in the economy; specifically, how prices work to allocate resources and how they affect the efficiency of the economy. In particular, it is shown that in a competitive economy, the self-serving actions of utility-maximizing individuals and profit-maximizing firms can lead to an efficient allocation of the economy's resources. The complete, rigorous proof of this proposition is usually discussed only in graduate courses in economic theory and involves the use of some fairly advanced mathematics. The discussion in this chapter is a simpler introduction to this material.

The efficiency implications of a laissez-faire, competitive economy are important reasons why economists have a great deal of respect for the workings of the price system. But the proof of this abstract proposition is not a proof that we should dismantle the federal government and that all markets should be unregulated. The proposition refers to the efficiency of a perfectly competitive economy. There are many aspects of the Canadian economy that

(1) (*are/are not*) consistent with the requirements for a competitive economy. The implications of these real-world imperfections are the subject of Chapters 27–31 and 33–34. Also, efficiency is not the only way to judge the workings of an economy. Notions of fairness, or equity, are also important and may at times lead one to prefer less efficient, but fairer, non-market procedures.

(2)   All economies must somehow answer three questions. First there is the question of output _____ : How much of each type of good and service should be produced in the aggregate? Next, there is the

question of production _____ : How should various productive inputs be allocated among the millions of firms and plants in order to meet the original output decisions? Finally, there is the question of the

_____ of products: How are the available goods and services to be divided among consumers? How does one evaluate the job that an economy does in answering these questions? Economists typically use two yardsticks: efficiency and equity. The discussion in this chapter concentrates on efficiency.

Economic efficiency is a very important but relatively abstract concept. If by redistributing the commodities that are produced we can make everyone better off in his or her own estimation, we would say that the initial allocation

(3) of commodities (*was/was not*) efficient. It is only when there are no more opportunities to make some individuals better off while not worsening the situation of others that economists would characterize the operation of the

economy as _____ .

You should realize that for any economy there are many possible efficient allocations of resources. Each

(4) point on an economy's production possibilities frontier is (*efficient/inefficient*) in terms of the production of output. If an economy is operating on this frontier, it is impossible to increase the output of one good without

_____ the output of one or more other goods. Whether the economy is efficient or fair in terms of distributing this output is another question.

Let us consider in more detail how a competitive economy achieves efficiency in the selection of output. (The appendix to this chapter discusses efficiency in production planning and output distribution.) Efficiency in the

(5) selection of output requires that, for the quantity produced, the marginal _____ of the last

unit to consumers must equal the marginal _____ of producers.

Why is this condition necessary for an efficient output selection? Remember that the definition of efficiency refers to consumers' evaluations of their own well-being, an evaluation that economists assume consumers are making when they maximize the difference between total utility and spending. If the marginal utility of some good exceeds the marginal cost of producing more units, then the production of at least one more unit of output will

(6) result in a net (*increase/decrease*) in consumer well-being. Consumers benefit by the increase in their utility while

the cost to society of additional production is given by the marginal _____ . If marginal utility exceeds marginal cost, the benefit to consumers from increased production will be (*greater/less*) than the cost to society and the initial output selection (*is/is not*) efficient. It is only when marginal utility (*exceeds/equals/is less than*) marginal cost that there are no more opportunities for net gains.

It is one of the beauties of a competitive economy that utility-maximizing individuals and profit-maximizing firms will, while pursuing their own self-interests, make decisions that result in marginal utility being equal to marginal cost. Our optimal purchase rule of Chapter 20 showed that a utility-maximizing consumer will purchase additional units

(7) until the marginal utility of the last unit consumed equals the _____ of the commodity. The discussion in Chapter 23 showed that a profit-maximizing firm will equate marginal revenue and

_____ _____ . The discussion in Chapter 25 showed that for a firm under perfect

competition, marginal revenue is equal to _____ . Thus a profit-maximizing firm under perfect competition, producing where marginal cost equals marginal revenue, will be producing where the marginal

cost of the last unit produced equals the _____ of the commodity.

(8)   To summarize, utility-maximizing consumers set marginal _____ equal to price and

profit-maximizing competitive firms set marginal _____ equal to price. The result is that marginal utility (*exceeds/equals/is less than*) marginal cost, our condition for efficiency in the selection of output.

A centrally planned economy attempts to answer the three basic questions of output selection, production planning, and product distribution by direct decree, without the use of prices. Often in these economies decisions about output selection are made with little attention to individual consumer preferences. More weight is given to the planners' preferences for such things as increased production of steel and electricity, although periodic newspaper accounts of a readjustment of production goals in response to consumer unrest indicate that even planners cannot forget entirely about consumers.

Once decisions about output levels have been made, a central planner must be sure that productive inputs are allocated to ensure that the production goals can in fact be achieved. One type of analysis that takes account of

(9) the interindustry flows of inputs necessary for the production of goods for final use is _____ -

_____ analysis. A major limitation of this analysis is the enormity and complexity of the sets of equations. It is a major conceptual advantage that the price system in a competitive economy does not require that this information be centralized.

BASIC EXERCISE

This problem is designed to illustrate the logic of the rule for efficiency in output selection. The discussion in the chapter indicated that efficiency in the selection of output requires that marginal utility equals marginal cost for all commodities. If not, it is possible, by changing the selection of output, to improve consumers' well-being.

Consider an economy that produces records, among other things. At the current level of record output, the marginal utility of records is $7 and the marginal cost is only $5.

1. The production of one more record will increase

    total utility by $ _____ . The production of one more record will cost society

    $ _____ .

2. In Chapter 20 we assumed that utility-maximizing consumers will maximize the difference between total utility and total spending. It is this difference that is the money value of their well-being. For the economy as a whole, the relevant measure of consumer well-being is the difference between total utility and total social costs. Looking at the change in both utility and cost, we can see that the production of one more record will increase

    consumer well-being by $_____ . Efficiency in the production of records requires (*more*/*less*) records.

3. What if the marginal utility of an additional record was $3 and the marginal cost was $5? Then the production of an additional record will *increase*/*decrease*) consumer well-being by

    $_____ , and efficiency in the production of records will call for (*more*/*fewer*) records.

4. If the marginal cost of additional records is constant at $5, then in order that there be no opportunity for a change in the production of records to increase consumer well-being, enough records should be produced so that the marginal

utility of an additional record is

$_____ .

SELF-TESTS FOR UNDERSTANDING

Test A

Circle the correct answer.

1. For any economy that uses the price system, which of the following is not necessarily true?
    a. Prices play an important role in shaping the allocation of resources.
    b. Prices play an important role in shaping the distribution of income and wealth.
    c. Prices will reflect the preference and incomes of consumers.
    d. Prices of necessities will be low and prices of luxuries will be high.
2. The price system distributes goods and services on the basis of income and
    a. scarcity.
    b. consumer preferences.
    c. education.
    d. planner preferences.
3. The condition for optimal output selection is
    a. $MC = P$.
    b. $MC = MU$.
    c. $MRP = P$.
    d. $MU = P$.
4. If the marginal utility of colour television sets is $400 and the marginal cost is $300, then efficiency in output selection requires that the production of colour television sets
    a. be increased.
    b. be decreased.
    c. should be neither increased nor decreased.
5. The change in the production of colour television sets from Question 4 will likely
    a. increase marginal cost and marginal utility.
    b. increase marginal cost and decrease marginal utility.

c. decrease marginal cost and marginal utility.
d. decrease marginal cost and increase marginal utility.

6. An efficient allocation of resources
   a. will always be fair.
   b. is the best allocation possible.
   c. would mean the economy is operating somewhere on its production opportunity frontier.
   d. is always better than an inefficient allocation.

7. Leon does not now own a motorcycle. He would be willing to pay up to $120 for one. Motorcycles produced by competitive firms in long-run equilibrium earning zero economic profit, cost $600 to produce. Which of the following is false?
   a. Leon is not likely to buy a motorcycle.
   b. Since Leon's marginal utility is less than the marginal cost of production, there would be a social gain if direct government controls reduced the production of motorcycles.
   c. The marginal utility of a motorcycle to someone must be at least $600.

8. If resources have been allocated in a way that meets the requirements of economic efficiency, then we know that
   a. output is being produced in accordance with the preferences of the Economic Council of Canada.
   b. production occurs at a point inside the economy's production possibilities frontier.
   c. there is no reallocation of resources that can make some individuals better off without making others worse off.
   d. the marginal cost of producing every commodity has been minimized.

9. Efficiency in the distribution of output among consumers requires that
   a. all consumers must have the same marginal utility for any single commodity.
   b. the price of all goods must be the same.
   c. marginal cost equal marginal revenue.
   d. income be equally distributed among all consumers.

10. Efficiency in the allocation of productive inputs requires that
   a. the marginal revenue product of any input be the same in all industries.
   b. marginal cost equal marginal utility.
   c. price equal marginal utility.
   d. marginal cost be minimized.

Test B

Circle T or F for True or False as appropriate.

1. The term *laissez faire* refers to an economy that is essentially free of all government regulations.   T F

2. If resources are being allocated efficiently, we know that there is no better allocation possible.   T F

3. Efficient resource allocation always requires the intervention of a central planner to set prices correctly.   T F

4. Efficiency in the selection of output requires that the marginal utility of every commodity be equal to its marginal cost.   T F

5. An unregulated competitive economy is simply incapable of seeing that appropriate efficiency conditions are achieved for all commodities.   T F

6. Input-output analysis is a mathematical tool to aid in the distribution of output among consumers without using the price system.   T F

7. Charging lower prices on public transportation during non-rush hours is an example of off-peak pricing.   T F

8. Considerations of fairness may sometimes lead a society to prefer an inefficient allocation to an efficient one.   T F

9. Efficiency in the distribution of goods implies that everyone will get an equal share of all goods.   T F

10. Competitive markets promote efficiency in output selection because both firms and consumers respond to the same price.   T F

Appendix: The Invisible Hand in the Distribution of Goods and in Production Planning

BASIC EXERCISES

These exercises are designed to illustrate and help you review the implications of the rules for efficiency in the allocation of productive inputs and in the allocation of output between consumers, as discussed in the appendix to Chapter 26.

1. Efficiency in the Distribution of Output Among Consumers
   The rule for efficiency in the distribution of output among consumers is that _____

   _____

   _____

   _____

Imagine that Todd and Nicole both consume steaks and pizzas. The initial allocation of steak and pizza has resulted in the following marginal utilities:

MARGINAL UTILITY

	Todd	Nicole
Steaks	$9.00	$6.00
Pizzas	4.00	4.00

a. Is the condition for efficiency in the distribution of output satisfied? _____ . If not there should be some, possibly many, reallocations of output that will increase either (or both) Todd's or Nicole's total utility without reducing total utility for the other.

b. Imagine that Nicole gives Todd one steak in exchange for two pizzas. On net, considering the full effects of the trade, what is the change in

Todd's utility? (*increase/decrease*) $ _____

Nicole's utility? (*increase/decrease*) $ _____
An implication of the utility changes of the reallocation is that the initial allocation was (*efficient/inefficient*).

c. How do competitive markets work to ensure that unco-ordinated individual demands will satisfy the condition for efficiency in the distribution of output among consumers?

2. **Efficiency in the Allocation of Productive Inputs**
Our rule for efficiency says that if two inputs, labour and land, are both used to produce corn and tomatoes, then inputs should be assigned to each output until the _____

_____

_____

_____

a. We know from Chapter 22 that this condition will be automatically satisfied under perfect competition for profit-maximizing firms that can buy inputs at given prices. What is perhaps less clear is that if this condition is not satisfied, then it would be possible to reallocate inputs among firms and produce more total output—with the same amount of inputs. Consider the following table showing the initial marginal revenue products of land and labour in the production of corn and tomatoes.

MARGINAL REVENUE PRODUCT OF LABOUR AND LAND IN THE PRODUCTION OF CORN AND TOMATOES

	Corn (dozens)	Tomatoes (kilograms)
Labour (person)	$300	$600
Land (hectare)	100	100

Let the price of tomatoes be 50 cents a kilogram and the price of corn be $2.50 a dozen. Consider the reallocation of one worker from corn production to tomato production. As a result of this reallocation of labour, the production of corn

will fall by _____ dozen and the production of tomatoes will rise by

_____ kilograms. (Remember,

marginal revenue product equals _____

_____ _____ times

_____ . If necessary, review material in Chapter 22 on marginal revenue product.) Now consider moving 3 hectares of land from tomato production to corn production. As a result of the reallocation of land,

the production of corn will rise by _____ dozen and the production of tomatoes will fall by

_____ kilograms. In total, counting the reallocations of both land and labour, the production of corn changes by

_____ dozen and the production

of tomatoes changes by _____ kilograms.

In competitive markets, tomato growers will be able to outbid corn growers for labour. The influx of labourers into tomato growing will tend to lower the marginal physical product of labour in tomato raising while the marginal physical product of labour in corn growing will increase. Market pressures for the reallocation of labour will cease when the marginal revenue product of labour in both activities equals the price of labour or the market wage rate.

b. Efficiency in the selection of inputs helps to achieve efficiency in the choice of outputs. We have seen that efficiency in the selection of outputs requires that MU = MC. In competitive markets, MU = MC because utility-maximizing individuals see to it that MU = P, and profit-maximizing firms see to it that MC = P. In fact, the optimal input rule, that the marginal revenue product equals the input price, helps to ensure that MC = P. Using symbols, our optimal input rule says

$$P_Q \, \text{MPP}_X = P_X,$$

where P_Q is the product price, P_X is the input price, and MPP_X is the marginal physical product of input X in the production of Q. If we divide both sides of the equation by MPP_X we get

$$P_Q = \frac{P_X}{\text{MPP}_X}$$

A little thought should suggest that P_X/MPP_X is the marginal cost of producing more output by using more of input X. Note that a profit-maximizing firm will use the optimal input rule for all its inputs. Thus, the marginal cost of an output expansion by the use of any single input, of the many that a firm may use, will be equal to the marginal cost from the additional use of any other input.

SUPPLEMENTARY EXERCISE

Go to the library and look up the most recent input-output table for the Canadian economy. (At this writing, the most recent input-output data can be found in the

August, 1984, Statistics Canadian publication *The Input-Output Structure of the Canadian Economy, 1971–1980*, which reports data on 43 industries and 100 commodities and primary inputs.)

There are three types of input-output tables or matrices. A make (or output) matrix shows how much of each 100 commodities is produced by each of the 43 industries. A use (input) matrix shows how much of each commodity is used by each industry. A final demand matrix shows the value of commodity inputs to thirty final demand categories, such as fixed capital formation, personal expenditures, inventory, and exports.

1. How many separate pieces of information does it take to prepare these matrices? How long do you think it would take to construct the three matrices for the Canadian economy for one year? (The most recent table in the 1984 Statscan publication is for 1980. Why did it take four years to publish this table?) How long do you think it would take you to solve all the interrelationships and produce a table of final demands?

2. *The Input-Output Structure* contains data for the 1971 input-output matrices. Compare these data to the 1980 tables. Pick one or two favourite industries and see how input and output have changed over time. If you were a planner concerned with 1990, what input and output estimates might you use?

Pure Monopoly and the Market Mechanism

LEARNING OBJECTIVES

After completing the material in this chapter you should be able to:

- define, understand, and use correctly the terms and concepts listed below.
- calculate a monopolist's profit-maximizing price and output, given information on costs and the demand for his output.
- explain why for a monopolist marginal revenue is less than price.
- describe what factors allow a particular monopoly to persist.
- explain why, unlike the case of a competitive firm, there is no supply curve for a monopolist.
- explain why a monopolist will receive positive economic profits in both the short and long runs.

- describe why a monopolist's demand and cost curves may differ from those of a comparable competitive industry.
- explain how a monopoly can give rise to an inefficient allocation of resources.
- explain why a monopolist cannot pass on all of any pollution charge or other increase in cost.

IMPORTANT TERMS AND CONCEPTS

Pure monopoly
Barriers to entry
Patents
Natural monopoly
Monopoly profits
Inefficiency of monopoly
Shifting of pollution charges

CHAPTER REVIEW

In Chapter 25 we studied the decisions of firms operating in markets characterized as pure competition; that is, markets with lots of firms competing to produce and sell one good. Chapter 23 considered optimal firm decisions and Chapter 26 considered the implications of these decisions for the efficiency of resource allocation. In this

(1)   chapter we will consider a *pure monopoly*, a market with (*one/many*) firm(s) producing a single good with (*no/lots*

of) close substitutes. The essence of a pure monopoly is one producer without effective competition.

A pure monopoly could arise for one of two reasons. If the technology of large-scale production implies that one firm can produce enough to satisfy the whole market at lower average costs than a number of firms,

(2)   we say that the result is a _____ monopoly. Legal restrictions, such as exclusive licensing or patents, or advantages that the monopolist acquires for himself, such as control of a vital input or technical superiority, could also create a pure monopoly. All of these factors would deter potential competitors and

are called _____ to _____ .

The study of pure monopoly often starts by assuming that some enterprising entrepreneur is able to monopolize a previously competitive industry. It is also traditional to assume that the monopolist initially faces the previous industry demand curve and operates with the same cost curves.

Under pure competition, individual firms face demand curves that are horizontal; that is, the firm can sell as much as it wants to at the market price. A monopolist will face the industry demand curve with a

(3)   (*positive/negative/zero*) slope. If the monopolist wants to sell more she must (*raise/lower*) her price.

The monopolist maximizes profit just like any other profit-maximizing firm; that is, the monopolist

(4)   chooses the level of output at which (*marginal/average*) cost equals (*marginal/average*) _____ . Now the only trick is to figure out what the relevant cost and revenue curves look like. Marginal cost comes from the monopolist's total costs in exactly the same way that it does for anyone else. The tricky part is marginal revenue. Marginal revenue is the addition to total revenue from producing and selling one more unit of output. Under pure competition, the actions of an individual firm have no effect on the market price and marginal revenue equals

_____ . But in the case of a monopolist, quantity decisions do affect price and marginal revenue (*is/is not*) equal to price.

(5)   Remember from Chapter 23 that the demand curve is the curve of (*average/total*) revenue. From Rule 4 in the appendix to Chapter 23, we know that when average revenue is declining, marginal revenue will be (*less/more*) than average revenue. In other words, for the monopolist with a downward-sloping demand curve, the curve of marginal revenue will lie (*above/below*) the curve of average revenue. (Remember the geometry of marginal revenue in the exercise to Chapter 23 in the Study Guide or in Figure 27–3 in the text.) (A similar use of Rule 4

indicates that when average cost is rising, the marginal cost curve will lie _____ the average cost curve.)

Once we have used the marginal cost and marginal revenue curves to compute the monopolist's profit-

(6)   maximizing level of output we can use the (*demand/supply*) curve to figure out what price she should charge. We know that since the curve of marginal revenue lies below the demand curve the monopolist's market price will be (*greater/less*) than both marginal revenue and marginal cost. We also know that if average cost is rising, average

cost will be (*greater/less*) than marginal cost and hence also _____ than the market price given by the demand curve. Thus, for a profit-maximizing monopolist, operating at a level where average cost is rising, price will be greater than average cost and the monopolist will receive positive economic profits. Since, by definition, the monopolist is the only supplier, there (*will/will not*) be entry of new firms to compete away these profits. Compared with results under pure competition, the monopolist's profit-maximizing behaviour will result in a (*higher/lower*) price and a (*higher/lower*) level of output in both the short and long run.

In Chapter 26 we saw that pure competition leads to an efficient allocation of resources. Efficient resource allocation requires that the marginal utility (MU) of each commodity be equal to its marginal cost (MC). Optimal

(7)   consumer decisions lead to the result that MU equals _____ .

Under pure competition, optimal firm decisions imply that MC equals _____ . The upshot is clearly that under pure competition MU equals MC. With a pure monopoly, as outlined above—that is, with the same demand and cost curves—we know that while consumers will continue to equate MU and *P*, the

monopolist will equate MC to _____ _____ , which is (*greater/less*) than *P*. The result is that with a pure monopoly, MU is (*greater/less*) than MC. Increased quantity of the monopolized commodity would yield marginal benefits, measured by MU, that are (*greater/less*) than marginal costs as measured by MC. In this sense the monopoly leads to an inefficient allocation of resources.

An important part of the comparison above is that the monopolist faces demand and cost curves that are the same as those of the previously competitive industry. There are, however, several factors that would tend to shift

(8)   these curves following a change in market structure. Advertising might shift both curves (*up/down*). Savings from centralizing various operations and avoiding duplication might shift the cost curves

_____ . Greater inefficiencies from greater size would have the opposite effect. Particular results will depend upon particular circumstances.

Why do we say there is no supply curve for a monopolist? Remember that the supply curve shows the relationship between each possible market price and the quantity supplied. Under pure competition a firm takes price as given and then decides how much to produce, knowing that its individual quantity decision

(9) (*will/will not*) affect the market price. The firm's supply curve comes from considering its reaction to different possible prices. But the monopolist (*does/does not*) take price as given. The monopolist is interested in trading off the revenue implications of different price-quantity combinations, as given by the demand curve, against the cost implications of producing those different amounts. The monopolist chooses the *one* quantity that maximizes profits and receives the price given by the point on the demand curve consistent with the quantity. The monopolist is a price (*maker/taker*).

BASIC EXERCISE

This exercise is designed to give you practice computing the profit-maximizing quantity and price for a monopolist. Mario has a monopoly in the production of widgets. Table 27–1 contains some relevant data on the demand for widgets and the cost of producing widgets.

1. You will use this data to computer Mario's profit-maximizing quantity and the associated price. There are essentially two ways to do this.

   a. One way is to fill in columns 2 and 5 of Table 27–2 by computing total revenue and total cost. Next, choose the level of output that maximizes the difference. That level of output is

   _____ 14 _____ widgets.

   b. The second way is to fill in columns 3 and 4 of Table 27–2 by computing marginal revenue and marginal cost. Mario could maximize profits by increasing production as long as marginal

   _____*revenue*_____ exceeds marginal

   _____*costs*_____ . In this case, Mario maximizes profits by producing

_____ 1–4 _____ widgets.

c. To maximize profits Mario should charge a price

   of $ _____ 9100 _____ .

d. His profits are $ _____ 30884 _____ .

2. Unfortunately, the production of widgets involves significant pollution, and the government has decided to fight pollution by imposing pollution charges. In Mario's case, this means a pollution charge of $1,000 a widget. Table 27–3 contains the original data on demand along with the new average cost data that reflect the $1,000 a widget pollution charge.

TABLE 27–1

Quantity	Average Revenue (Price)	Average Cost
12	9,500	$7,068.00
13	9,300	6,957.00
14	9,100	6,894.00
15	8,900	6,869.40
16	8,700	6,876.00

TABLE 27–2

(1) Quantity	(2) Total Revenue	(3) Marginal Revenue	(4) Marginal Cost	(5) Total Cost
12	114000			84816
		6900	5625	
13	120900			90441
		6500	6075	
14	127400	✗ = ✗		96516
		6100	6519	
15	133500			103035
		5700	6981	
16	139200			110016

a. Use Table 27-4 to compute the new profit-maximizing level of output. Mario's new profit-maximizing level of output is ___13___ and the associated price is

$ ___9 300___ . How much pollution tax in total does Mario pay?

___200___ . Note that while the pollution charge is $1,000 a widget, Mario's profit-maximizing price increases by

only $ ___~~1751~~___ . Why doesn't Mario simply raise his price by the full $1,000?

b. What is the new level of profits?

$ ___17459___

3. (Optional) Your answer to Question 2 should indicate that the pollution tax has reduced both the output of widgets and the associated volume of pollution. What would have happened if, instead of a per-unit tax, the government had simply fined Mario $13,000 for polluting and imposed no further charges? Compared with the initial situation in Question 1, what happens to Mario's profit-maximizing level of output, the associated level of pollution output, and actual profits with this lump-sum pollution charge? (When answering this question be sure you are working with the correct cost curves. Adjust Table 27-2, remembering that at each level of output, total costs will now be $13,000 higher than the entries in column 5.)

SELF-TESTS FOR UNDERSTANDING

Test A

Circle the correct answer.

1. Pure monopoly is characterized by
   a. many firms producing a homogeneous product.
   b. many firms producing slightly different products that are close substitutes.
   c. such a small number of firms that each must figure out how the others will respond to its own actions.
   d. one firm, with no competitors, producing a product with no close substitutes.
2. Which one of the following is *not* likely to lead to a monopoly?
   a. Patents.
   b. Control of the sole source of an important commodity.
   c. A commodity with many close substitutes.
   d. Significant increasing returns to scale.
3. A natural monopoly arises when
   a. natural resources are an important input.
   b. there are significant cost advantages to large-scale production.
   c. the government prohibits entry.
   d. patents protect a firm's technology.
4. If in order to sell more, a firm must reduce the price on all units sold, we can conclude that marginal revenue will
   a. exceed average revenue.

TABLE 27-3

Quantity	Average Revenue (Price)	Average Cost
12	9,500	$8,068.00
13	9,300	7,957.00
14	9,100	7,894.00
15	8,900	7,869.40
16	8,700	7,876.00

TABLE 27-4

(1) Quantity	(2) Total Revenue	(3) Marginal Revenue	(4) Marginal Cost	(5) Total Cost
12	114000			96816
		6900	6625	
13	120900			103441
		6500	7075	
14	127400			116516
		6100	7525	
15	133500			118041
		5700	7975	
16	139200			126016

b. equal average revenue.

c. be less than average revenue.

5. A monopolist maximizes profit by producing where

a. marginal cost equals marginal revenue.

b. marginal cost equals marginal utility.

c. average cost equals average revenue.

d. the difference between average cost and average revenue is greatest.

6. A monopolist's economic profits will

a. be competed away in the long run.

b. be driven to the opportunity cost of capital.

c. persist in the short run and the long run.

d. be limited by usury laws.

7. An entrepreneur who monopolizes a previously competitive industry and now faces the same demand curve and produces with the same cost function will typically maximize profits by

a. forcing consumers to buy more at a higher price.

b. producing less but charging a higher price.

c. increasing volume.

d. lowering both output and price.

8. An increase in a monopolist's average cost will lead to a(n)

a. increase in price by the same amount, as the monopolist simply passes on the price increase.

b. increase in price if marginal cost also increases.

c. decrease in price as the monopolist needs to sell more in order to cover increased costs.

d. increase in price only if the elasticity of demand is less than 1.0.

9. An increase in a monopolist's fixed cost will

a. reduce the profit-maximizing level of output.

b. not affect the profit-maximizing level of output.

c. increase the profit-maximizing level of output as the monopolist needs to sell more to cover costs.

10. If marginal cost is greater than zero, we know that a monopolist will produce where the elasticity of demand is

a. greater than unity.

b. equal to unity.

c. less than unity.

Test B

Circle T or F for True or False as appropriate.

1. A pure monopoly results when there are only a few firms supplying a particular commodity for which there are no close substitutes.　　T F

2. Significant increasing returns to scale, which reduce average costs as output expands, may result in a natural monopoly.　　T F

3. A pure monopolist can earn positive economic profits only in the short run.　　T F

4. An entrepreneur who successfully monopolizes a competitive industry will face a horizontal demand curve just like each of the previous competitive firms.　　T F

5. A monopolist maximizes profits by producing at the point at which marginal cost equals marginal revenue.　　T F

6. If, in a monopolistic industry, demand and cost curves are identical to a comparable competitive industry, and the demand curve slopes downward while the average-cost curve slopes upward, then the monopolist's price will always exceed the competitive industry's price but the monopolist's output will be larger.　　T F

7. A monopolist has a greater incentive to advertise than does an individual firm under pure competition.　　T F

8. If current market price is greater than average cost, a monopolist can always increase profits by producing more.　　T F

9. A monopolist will increase price by the full amount of any per-unit tax, such as a per-unit pollution charge.　　T F

10. A firm operating under conditions of pure competition will not be able to pass on any of a per-unit excise tax and must therefore pay the whole tax out of reduced profits.　　T F

SUPPLEMENTARY EXERCISE

The demand curve for the problem in the Basic Exercise is

$$Q = 59.5 - 0.005P.$$

In Question 1 of the Basic Exercise, the total cost curve is

$$TC = 52,416 + 225Q^2.$$

a. Derive mathematical expressions for total revenue, marginal revenue, average cost, and marginal cost.

b. Use a piece of graph paper to plot the demand, marginal-revenue, and marginal-cost curves.

c. Use your expressions for marginal revenue and marginal cost to solve for the profit-maximizing level of output. Is your answer consistent with your graph in part b and your answer to the Basic Exercise?

d. What is the impact of the per-unit pollution tax and the fixed-charge pollution tax on your expressions for total, average, and marginal cost? Do differences here help explain the impact of these taxes on the profit-maximizing level of output?

Between Competition and Monopoly

28

LEARNING OBJECTIVES

After completing the material in this chapter you should be able to:

- define, understand, and use correctly the terms and concepts listed below.
- explain why and how the long-run equilibrium of a firm under monopolistic competition differs from that of a firm under pure competition.
- explain why it is so difficult to make a formal analysis of an oligopolistic market structure.
- describe briefly the alternative approaches to modelling oligopolistic behaviour.
- use marginal-cost and marginal-revenue curves to derive the implications for price and quantity of sales maximization as opposed to profit maximization.
- use the maximin criterion to determine the final outcome in a game-theory setting.
- use marginal-cost and marginal-revenue curves to explain how a kinked demand curve could imply sticky prices.

- explain how the concept of contestable markets means that even in an industry with few firms, no firm will earn long-run profits in excess of the opportunity cost of capital and inefficient firms will not survive.

IMPORTANT TERMS AND CONCEPTS

Monopolistic competition
Excess-capacity theorem
Oligopoly
Oligopolistic interdependence
Cartel
Price leadership
Sales maximization
Game theory
Maximin criterion
Sticky price
Kinked demand curve
Perfectly contestable markets

CHAPTER REVIEW

Pure competition and pure monopoly are the polar examples of market structure most easily analysed in textbooks. Actual markets tend more toward what economists call *monopolistic competition* and *oligopoly*, which are the subjects of this chapter. It is harder to model firm behaviour in these market structures, especially in the case of oligopoly. However, you should not lose sight of the notion that profit maximization is still a dominant characteristic of most firms and that marginal-cost and marginal-revenue curves remain the important tools to help determine which decisions will maximize profits.

A market structure in which there are numerous participants, freedom of entry and exit, perfect information

(1) and product heterogeneity is referred to as a situation of _____ competition. Because each seller is able to partially differentiate his product, individual firms will face a demand curve with a (*negative/positive/zero*) slope. At each point in time, profit-maximizing firms will try to produce at the level of output where _____ _____ equals _____ _____ . The assumption of freedom of entry and exit implies that in the long run under monopolistic competition, firms will earn (*negative/positive/zero*) economic profit. If an individual firm is earning positive economic profits, the (*entry/exit*) of new firms will shift the demand curve down (and may raise costs) until the demand curve is just _____ to the (*average/marginal*)-cost curve.

A market structure with only a few firms producing a similar or identical product, and in which some

(2) firms are very large, is called a(n) _____ . Formal analysis of such market structures is difficult because when considering the decisions of one firm, one must take into account the possible reactions of competitors. No single model describes all the possible outcomes under oligopoly, and economists have found it useful to consider a number of possible models and outcomes. If firms in an oligopolistic market band together and act like a single profit-maximizing monopolist, the resulting group is called a _____ . If most firms look to pricing decisions made by a dominant firm, economists refer to the outcome as one of

_____ _____ .

Oligopolistic firms tend to be large corporations with professional managers. Some argue that managers are likely to be more interested in maximizing total revenue than in maximizing profits. This outcome is more likely if the salary of managers depends more upon the size of the firm than upon its profitability. A firm interested in maximizing

(3) sales revenue will increase output until marginal revenue equals _____ . Compared with profit maximization, sales maximization will mean a (*higher/lower*) price and a _____ quantity.

Game theory has been fruitfully used in the study of oligopolistic behaviour by a number of economists. Game theory involves listing the possible outcomes of your moves and your opponents' countermoves in a(n)

(4) _____ matrix and then choosing an appropriate _____ . If the size of the pie for which you and your competitors are competing is fixed, so that your gains are his losses and vice versa, the result is called a(n) _____ _____ game.

Another traditional element of the analysis of oligopoly is the concept of a *kinked demand curve*. Such a

(5) demand curve comes from assuming that your competitors (*will/will not*) match any decrease in your price but (*will/will not*) match any increase in your price. As a result, there is a gap in the marginal- (*cost/revenue*) curve and profit-maximizing prices may not change unless there is significant shift in the marginal- _____ curve.

The concept of perfectly contestable markets suggests that even oligopolists may be limited in their ability

(6) to earn monopolistic profits. The crucial condition for perfect contestability is that _____ and _____ are costless and unimpeded. In such a case, competitors could and would get into and out of the market whenever profits exceeded the _____ _____ of _____ . While no market may be perfectly contestable, the notion of contestability clearly can limit the ability of firms to charge monopolistic prices.

BASIC EXERCISES

1. Our discussion of monopolistic competition argued that long-run equilibrium implies that the firm's demand curve will be tangent to its average-cost curve. We have also argued that profit maximization requires that marginal revenue equal marginal cost (or, alternatively, that firms should expand output as long as marginal revenue exceeds marginal cost). How do we know that marginal revenue equals marginal cost at the quantity given by the tangency between the demand curve and the average-cost curve?

   a. Table 28-1 contains data on weekly costs and revenue for Gretchen's restaurant. This data is plotted in Figure 28-1. Note that the demand curve is tangent to the average-cost curve. Complete Table 28-1 to compute total profit. Plot total profits in the left half of Figure 28-1. What output level maximizes profits?

   b. Use your results in Table 28-1 to compute marginal revenue and marginal cost in Table 28-2. According to Table 28-2, what level of output maximizes profits? Why?

2. The following example illustrates how the analysis of a game-theory situation can become quite complicated. Table 28-3 is based on Table 28-1 in the text but contains some important differences.

   a. What is our maximin strategy?

   b. What is our rival's maximin strategy?

   c. If each company chooses its maximin strategy, what is the actual outcome?

   d. Assume now that we believe that the rival firm will stick to the maximin strategy. Which strategy maximizes our market share?

   e. If the rival firm assumes that we will now stick to our new strategy, what strategy will it choose to maximize its market share?

   f. What happens as you extend this series of alternative adjustments?

   g. Now answer questions d, e, and f in terms of the payoff matrix given in Table 28-1 in the text. Are your answers different? Can you explain why?

SELF-TESTS FOR UNDERSTANDING

Test A

Circle the correct answer.

1. Which of the following is the important difference between pure and monopolistic competition?
   a. Few sellers rather than many.
   b. Heterogeneous rather than homogeneous product.
   c. Barriers to rather than freedom of entry.

TABLE 28-1

Quantity	Average Revenue	Average Cost	Total Revenue	Total Cost	Total Profit
600	$19	$21.67	_____	_____	_____
800	17	17.50	_____	_____	_____
1000	15	15.00	_____	_____	_____
1200	13	13.33	_____	_____	_____
1400	11	12.14	_____	_____	_____

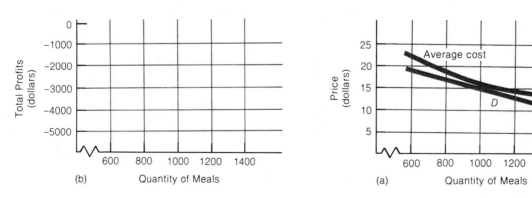

FIGURE 28-1

TABLE 28-2

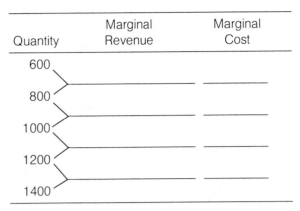

Quantity	Marginal Revenue	Marginal Cost
600		
800		
1000		
1200		
1400		

TABLE 28-3
A PAYOFF MATRIX

	Rival's Strategy		
	U: Set price at $6000	V: Offer 5-year warranty	W: Offer diesel engine
A: Install TV set	80	35	30
B: Cut price to $5500	28	70	45
C: Offer three-year loan	45	50	90

Our Strategy

The entries represent the share of market our firm will receive under any combination of strategies offered by itself and our competitor.

    d. Long-run positive economic profits rather than zero economic profits.

2. Which of the following characterizes a firm's long-run equilibrium position under monopolistic competition?
    a. Marginal cost equals price.
    b. Production at minimum average cost.
    c. A horizontal demand curve.
    d. Zero economic profits.

3. Under monopolistic competition the heterogeneity of output implies that
    a. individual firms face downward-sloping demand curves.
    b. both marginal cost and marginal revenue will increase with additional units of output.
    c. individual firms can make positive economic profits even in the long run.
    d. in the long run, individual firms will produce at minimum average cost.

4. Oligopoly may be associated with all but which one of the following?
    a. Price leadership.
    b. Collusive behaviour.
    c. Advertising.
    d. Lots of firms.

5. If oligopolistic firms get together to carve up the market and act like a monopolist, the result is called a
    a. cabal.
    b. contestable market.
    c. cartel.
    d. natural monopoly.

6. A firm interested in maximizing sales revenue will produce at a point where
    a. marginal revenue equals marginal cost.
    b. average cost is minimized.
    c. the elasticity of demand is unity.
    d. average revenue equals average cost.

7. A firm that maximizes sales revenues instead of profits will charge
    a. a higher price.
    b. a lower price.
    c. the same price but will advertise more.

8. Game theory may be especially useful in analysing a firm's behaviour under conditions of
    a. pure competition.
    b. monopolistic competition.
    c. oligopoly.
    d. pure monopoly.

9. The term *kinked demand curve* refers to
    a. economists' inability to draw straight lines.
    b. the demand for X-rated movies.
    c. a situation where competitors match price decreases but not price increases.
    d. industries with substantial economies of scale.

10. Markets can be perfectly contestable if
    a. products are identical
    b. entry and exit is free and easy.
    c. only two firms are bidding against each other.
    d. long-run economic profits are zero.

Test B

Circle T or F for True or False as appropriate.

1. Firms that operate under conditions of monopolistic competition are likely to engage in lots of advertising.   T F

2. Heterogeneity of output is an important feature of monopolistic competition.   T F

3. Under monopolistic competition, freedom of entry and exit will guarantee that a firm always earns a zero economic profit, in both the short run and the long run.   T F

4. Under monopolistic competition, marginal revenue equals marginal cost in the short run but not in the long run.　　T　F

5. There would be an unambiguous social gain if some firms in a market with monopolistic competition were forced by regulation to stop producing.　　T　F

6. Oligopoly is characterized by a small number of firms, some very large, producing an identical or similar product.　　T　F

7. Arrangements, such as price leadership and geographical market sharing, are not uncommon in oligopolistic markets.　　T　F

8. A firm that maximizes sales revenue will typically charge a higher price than a firm that maximizes profits.　　T　F

9. An oligopolist facing a kinked demand curve will see a more elastic demand curve for price increases than for price decreases.　　T　F

10. The term *payoff matrix* refers to the details of how a cartel will divide up output and profits.　　T　F

SUPPLEMENTARY EXERCISE

The equations below for demand and total cost underlie the first problem in the Basic Exercises. Use these equations to derive explicit expressions for marginal cost, marginal revenue, and average cost. Now solve for the level of output that maximizes profits. Compare your answer with the results you obtained in the Basic Exercises.

$$Q = 2500 - 100\,P$$
(demand curve)
$$TC = 10{,}000 + 5\,Q$$
(total-cost curve)

where Q = total quantity, P = price, and TC = total cost.

Shortcomings of the Market Mechanism and Government Attempts to Remedy Them

29

LEARNING OBJECTIVES

After completing the material in this chapter you should be able to:

- define, understand, and use correctly the terms and concepts listed below.
- list the seven major shortcomings of free markets.
- explain why the existence of externalities, whether beneficial or detrimental, will result in an inefficient allocation of resources.
- explain why detrimental externalities mean that marginal private costs will understate marginal social costs.
- describe the important characteristics of public goods.
- explain why these characteristics mean that private profit-maximizing firms will not supply public goods.
- explain how uneven productivity growth results in the cost disease of personal services.
- explain why some people believe that free markets

are unlikely to result in an appropriate allocation of resources between the present and the future.

IMPORTANT TERMS AND CONCEPTS

Opportunity cost
Resource misallocation
Production possibilities frontier
Prices above and below marginal cost
Externalities (detrimental and beneficial)
Marginal social cost and marginal private cost
Public goods
Private goods
Depletability
Excludability
Cost disease of personal services
Irreversible decisions
Rent seeking
Moral hazard

CHAPTER REVIEW

This chapter lists seven major shortcomings of unregulated markets. Some of these shortcomings have been discussed in previous chapters, and several others will receive a more complete treatment in later chapters. The discussion here focuses on four of the seven: externalities, public goods, the cost disease of personal services, and the trade-off between present and future consumption.

The material in Chapter 3 introduced the concept of an economy's *production possibilities frontier*. At that time we saw that the slope of the frontier measured how much of the output of one commodity must be decreased in order to increase the production of another commodity. In other words, the slope of the production possibilities

(1) frontier measures the _____ cost of increasing the output of any one commodity.

Chapter 26 explained how a market economy can lead to an *efficient allocation of resources*; that is, one where marginal utilities and marginal costs are equal. If the utility of an increase in the output of some good is less than the marginal cost of producing that output, the result is a *misallocation of resources*. The virtue of competitive

(2) markets is that firms maximize profits by producing where price equals _____

_____ and individuals maximize by consuming where price equals

_____ _____ . Thus, our condition for an efficient allocation is automatically satisfied. An economy that satisfies all the assumptions necessary for pure competition will result in an efficient allocation of resources. The economy will operate (*on/inside*) the production possibilities frontier, and the ratio of product prices will equal the ratio of marginal costs, which is also the opportunity cost of changing the composition of output. That is, the ratio of product prices and the ratio of marginal costs will both equal the slope of the production possibilities frontier.

Many of the reasons mentioned at the beginning of the chapter may imply that an economy does not satisfy the conditions for perfect competition. In this case the wrong prices may get established, leading to an inefficient

(3) allocation of resources. If price is greater than marginal cost, the economy will tend to produce too (*much/little*) of a good to maximize consumer benefits. There may be a case for government intervention to allocate resources directly or, preferably, to help establish prices that will lead to an efficient allocation.

Externalities

Many economic activities impose incidental burdens or benefits on other individuals for which there is no

(4) compensation. These sorts of activities are said to involve _____ . If an activity, such as

pollution, harms others and there is no compensation, one says that there are _____ externalities. If an activity benefits others who do not pay for the benefits they receive, one says that there are

_____ _____ .

Externalities are important for questions of resource allocation because they imply that many activities are likely to have private benefits and costs that are different from social benefits and costs. In the case of detrimental

(5) externalities, social costs will be (*higher/lower*) than private costs, while in the case of beneficial externalities,

social benefits will be _____ than private benefits.

(6) Private profit-maximizing firms will base their production decisions on (*private/social*) benefits and costs. If there are detrimental externalities, the result will be an (*efficient/inefficient*) use of resources. From a social viewpoint, too (*much/little*) of the commodity in question will be produced. In the case of beneficial externalities, unregulated markets are likely to produce (*less/more*) output than is socially desirable. Schemes for taxes and subsidies are, in principle, capable of adjusting costs and benefits to more adequately reflect social costs and benefits.

Public Goods

Most goods provided by private profit-maximizing firms have two primary characteristics. The first is that you

(7) must pay for them to be able to use them. This characteristic is called _____ . The second is that the more of a good you use, the less there is for someone else. This characteristic is called

_____. Goods that have neither of these characteristics are called

_____ goods. Things like national defence, police protection, beautiful parks, and clean streets are examples of such goods.

(8)   Once public goods are provided to one individual, their benefits cannot easily be restricted to just a few people. It is (*difficult/easy*) to exclude non-payers. As a result it may be difficult to get individuals to make voluntary contributions to pay for the goods they can enjoy by reason of someone else's paying for them. This is sometimes

referred to as the free-_____ problem.

    Besides the problem of lack of excludability, one person's use of public goods, such as enjoying a beautiful park, does not usually deplete the supply for others. In technical language, the marginal cost of

(9)   serving additional users is _____ . This is to be contrasted to the case of private goods, where providing additional units of output does require additional resources and does entail a positive marginal cost. An efficient allocation of resources requires that price equal marginal social cost. The clear implication is that from

an efficiency standpoint, the use of public goods should be priced at _____ and one should not be surprised if profit-maximizing firms fail to provide public goods.

Cost Disease of Personal Services

Many services—doctor visits, education, police protection—require mainly labour input and offer

(10) (*limited/substantial*) opportunities for increases in labour productivity. By contrast, increasing mechanization and technological innovations have resulted in substantial increases in labour productivity in the production of many commodities. Increased labour productivity has led to higher wages for workers in these industries. Since workers can move between occupations, the wages of teachers and police, for example, have had to increase to remain competitive with opportunities in other jobs. In manufacturing industries, increased labour productivity helps to offset the cost pressures from higher wages. (Remember the Basic Exercise in Chapter 19.) In service industries there are little or no increases in labour productivity to help contain cost pressures. The result is that many personal services have become more expensive over time because of the uneven pattern of increases in labour productivity. Increases in productivity always make an economy better off in the sense that the economy can now produce more of all goods, including personal services. But at the same time, society will find that lagging productivity in service industries means that the cost of many services has also increased.

Present and Future Consumption

The productive use of resources is time-specific. Loafing today will not make tomorrow twice as long. A machine that is idle one day does not mean that there will be twice as many machine hours available the next day. While the use of resources is time-specific, the consumption of output is not. Output can be saved, either directly by adding to inventories in warehouses or indirectly by building plants and machines. Thus, an economy does have the ability to transfer consumption through time by acts of saving and investment.

    The rate of interest is an important determinant of how much investment will actually take place. A number of observers have questioned whether the private economy will result in interest rates and investment spending that are socially optimal. Monetary and fiscal policies (especially those undertaken in the United States) can manipulate Canadian interest rates and hence to influence investment for many different purposes. Some, such as the English economist A. G. Pigou, have argued that people are simply shortsighted when it comes to saving for the future.

    Individual investment projects often entail great risk for the individual investors, but little risk for society.

(11) Bankruptcy may wipe out an investor's financial investment, but it (*does/does not*) destroy buildings and machines. These capital goods will still be around for others to use. It has been argued that the high individual risk will result in a level of investment that is (*less/more*) than socially optimal.

(12)   Many decisions, such as damming a river for hydroelectric power, are essentially _____ , and some people are concerned that unregulated market decisions in these cases do not adequately represent the interests of future generations. All these arguments suggest that even competitive markets are likely to result in inappropriate decisions about saving and investments.

BASIC EXERCISE

This exercise is designed to illustrate the cost disease of personal services.

Table 29-1 has spaces to compute the costs of producing both widgets and police services; both are assumed to be produced with only labour input. (Wages for police officers and for workers in the widget factory are assumed to be equal, as individuals can choose between these occupations.)
1. Fill in the missing spaces in the first column to determine the cost per widget of producing 240,000 widgets and the cost per hour of 200,000 hours of police services.
2. The first entry in the second column assumes that labour productivity in the production of widgets has risen. The increase in average labour productivity is

_____ percent. The earnings of both widget workers and police officers are assumed to increase by the same percentage as productivity. Now fill in the rest of the second column. What has happened to the average cost, and hence price, of producing one hour of police services?
3. The first entry in column 3 assumes that the growth in average labour productivity has continued for 11 years. Again, the growth in earnings is assumed to match the growth in productivity. Fill in the rest of column 3. What is the increase in the cost of producing one widget?

_____

What about the cost of one hour of police services?

_____

4. One way to hold the line on police costs is to refuse to increase salaries for police officers. Another way is to reduce the number of police officers. What are the long-run implications of both these policies?

If you want to read more about the cost disease of personal services, see "The Cost Disease of the Personal Services and the Quality of Life," by William Baumol and Wallace Oates, in *The Urban Economy*, a book of readings edited by Harold M. Hochman (W. W. Norton and Company, 1976).

SELF-TESTS FOR UNDERSTANDING

Test A

Circle the correct answer.

1. Which of the following is a clear indicator of a misallocation of resources?
   a. Dave and Ellen, who subscribe to *Gourmet* magazine, despair over the increasing number of fast-food outlets.
   b. In the long run, Farmer Fran makes zero economic profit.
   c. After careful study, economists have concluded that the economy of Arcadia is operating at a point inside its production possibilities frontier.
   d. The latest census survey indicates that the top 10 percent of the income distribution has an

TABLE 29-1

COSTS OF PRODUCING 240,000 WIDGETS

	(1)	(2)	(3)
Widgets per worker	1920	2000	3000
Number of workers[a]			
Annual earnings per worker	$21,120	$22,000	$33,000
Total labour costs (total cost)			
Cost per widget			
COSTS OF PRODUCING 200,000 HOURS OF POLICE SERVICES			
Hours per police officer	2000	2000	2000
Number of police officers[b]			
Annual earnings per police officer	$21,120	$22,000	$33,000
Total labour cost (total cost)			
Cost per hour of police services			

[a]240,000 ÷ widgets per worker
[b]200,000 ÷ hours per police officer

average income that is over 12 times that of the bottom 10 percent.

2. Which of the following is an externality?
   a. Imperfect information.
   b. Your pride in the new stereo system you just purchased at a bargain price.
   c. Natural monopolies, such as the local electric utility.
   d. The new road that was built for the new airport that has substantially reduced transportation costs for local farmers.

3. Detrimental externalities imply all but which one of the following?
   a. The marginal social cost of an increase in output will exceed marginal private cost.
   b. A misallocation of resources will result from the private market supplying less output than is socially desirable.
   c. Private firms will concentrate on private costs, ignoring the cost burden they are imposing on others.
   d. Taxes that impose additional private costs on those causing the externalities are, in principle, capable of correcting the misallocation.

4. If the production of gizmos involves beneficial externalities, then it is likely that
   a. marginal private benefits are less than marginal social benefits.
   b. a free market will produce too many gizmos.
   c. a tax on the production of gizmos will lead to a more efficient allocation.
   d. the use of gizmos does not involve depletion.

5. Which of the following is not true?
   a. Public goods are all things the government spends money on.
   b. Public goods are unlikely to be supplied by profit-maximizing firms.
   c. Public goods are defined as goods and services that many people can enjoy at the same time and from which it is difficult to exclude potential customers who do not want to pay.
   d. Public goods have a zero marginal cost of serving additional users.

6. Which of the following does not have the characteristics of a public good?
   a. Clean rivers.
   b. Gasoline.
   c. Police and fire protection.
   d. Radio and television signals.

7. The "free-rider" problem refers to
   a. the difficulty of stopping kids from sneaking onto the local merry-go-round.
   b. the difficulty of getting people to voluntarily contribute to pay for public goods.
   c. the use of subsidies to encourage the production of goods with beneficial externalities.

d. increasing problems with hitchhikers on highways.

8. Which of the following is *not* an argument that free markets will result in an inappropriate amount of saving and investment?
   a. Investment projects are often riskier to individuals than to the community.
   b. During periods of inflation, nominal interest rates will rise to incorporate expectations of continuing inflations.
   c. Due to "defective telescopic faculties," people do not give enough consideration to the future.
   d. Many decisions concerning natural resources are made without enough consideration given to their irreversible consequences.

9. Which of the following explains the cost disease of personal services?
   a. The supply effects of price controls, such as rent control.
   b. The existence of monopoly elements in the economy.
   c. Detrimental externalities.
   d. The uneven prospects for improved labour productivity in different sectors of the economy.

10. Which of the following is *not* likely to suffer from the cost disease of personal services?
    a. Individual piano lessons.
    b. The production of television sets.
    c. Small liberal arts colleges that maintain an unchanged student-faculty ratio.
    d. Orchestras and symphonies.

Test B

Circle T or F for True or False as appropriate.

1. An unregulated market economy would never have business cycles. **T F**

2. Externalities, whether beneficial or detrimental, imply that marginal social cost is always less than marginal private cost. **T F**

3. An activity that causes damage to someone else and for which there is no compensation is said to involve a detrimental externality. **T F**

4. A beneficial externality is likely to result in marginal social cost exceeding marginal private cost. **T F**

5. Economists define public goods as anything for which the government spends money. **T F**

6. The fact that it is difficult to restrict the use of public goods to those who are willing to pay is the problem of depletability. **T F**

7. The provision of public goods is complicated by the "free-rider" problem. **T F**

8. The fact that public goods are not depleted by use implies that the marginal cost of providing the goods to one more consumer is zero.   **T F**

9. The rate of interest plays an important role in the allocation of resources between the present and the future, because it affects the profitability of investment projects.   **T F**

10. Many investment projects will entail less risk for the individual investor than for the community as a whole   **T F**

SUPPLEMENTARY EXERCISES

1. Consider the economy of Beethovia, which produces two goods: widgets and music recitals. Widgets are manufactured with capital and labour according to the following production function:

$$W = 60\, L^{\frac{1}{2}}\, K^{\frac{1}{2}},$$

where L = number of workers producing widgets and K = number of machines.
Music recitals are labour intensive and produced according to the following production function:

$$M = 50 \times L.$$

Initially there are 10,000 workers in Beethovia, meaning that the sum of labour allocated to the production of widgets or recitals cannot exceed 10,000. Initially, there are also 10,000 machines, or $K = 10,000$.

a. Draw the production possibilities frontier for Beethovia showing the trade-off between the production of widgets and recitals. (It is probably easiest to arbitrarily fix the number of recitals and then calculate the maximum production of widgets with the remaining labour and all the machines.)

b. Competitive markets have resulted in 8100 widget workers and 1900 musicians. At this allocation, what is the marginal product and average product of labour in the production of widgets? In the production of recitals?

c. With the passage of time, saving and investment by the people of Beethovia have increased the number of machines to 12,100. At the initial allocation of labour, but with the new number of machines, what is the marginal and average product of labour in the production of widgets? What has happened to the productivity of workers in the production of recitals?

d. What has happened to the opportunity cost of music recitals; that is, what is the new slope of the production possibilities frontier at the allocation specified in Question b? To answer this question either draw a new production possibilities frontier or derive a mathematical expression for the slope of the frontier.

e. If you have answered Question d correctly you should have determined that the cost of recitals has increased. Recitals suffer from the cost disease of personal services. At the same time, how can you show that the increase in productivity has made Beethovia unambiguously richer?

2. Go to the library or bookstore and get a copy of *Encounters with the Archdruid* by John McPhee. The book reports on three encounters between David Brower, who was president of the Sierra Club, and other individuals who want to dam the Colorado River, build a copper mine in the Cascades, and develop Hilton Head Island. Many think that McPhee's description of the raft trip down the Colorado River with Brower and Floyd Dominy, who was head of the U.S. Bureau of Reclamation, is especially good.

   Whose position do you favour?
   Is Brower always right? Is he ever right?

VI

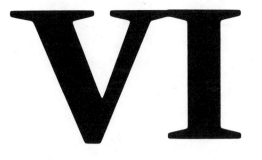

The Government
and the Economy

Limiting Market Power: Regulation of Industry

30

LEARNING OBJECTIVES

After completing the material in this chapter you should be able to:

- define, understand, and use correctly the terms and concepts listed below.
- identify the major regulatory agencies and their client industries.
- critically evaluate each of the arguments given in favour of regulation.
- explain why regulators often raise prices.
- discuss the implications of "fully distributed costs" as a basis for price floors.
- explain why marginal cost pricing may be infeasible in an industry with significant economies of scale.
- explain why allowing a firm to earn profits equal to the opportunity cost of its capital provides no incentive for increased efficiency.

- evaluate the alternatives suggested for present regulatory practices.

IMPORTANT TERMS AND CONCEPTS

Nationalization
Price floor
Price ceiling
Natural monopoly
Economies of scale
Economies of scope
Cross subsidy
Self-destructive competition
Fully distributed cost
Short-run and long-run marginal cost
Marginal cost pricing
Ramsey Pricing Rule
Regulatory lag

CHAPTER REVIEW

(1) By and large Canada has chosen to (*regulate/nationalize*) rather than to _____ industries where there is concern about the exploitation of excessive market power. This chapter discusses a number of the controversies about current regulatory practices and the roles played by the regulatory agencies.

Regulatory procedures have been adopted basically for five reasons:

(2)   1. To regulate the actions of natural monopolies in industries where economies of _____ and

economies of _____ mean that the free competition between a large number of

suppliers (*is/is not*) sustainable.

2. To ensure service at reasonable prices to isolated areas of the country. It is argued that regulation is necessary in this case so that suppliers can offset (*above/below*)-cost prices in isolated areas with (*above/below*)-cost prices elsewhere and thus be protected from competitors who concentrate only on the profitable markets.

3. To avoid self-destructive competition among firms in industries with high (*fixed/variable*) costs and low short-run

_____ costs.

4. To ration fairly a limited public resource, such as radio and television airspace.

5. To protect consumers from unscrupulous business practices.

The first three justifications for regulation often lead to direct regulation of prices and/or earnings. There is no limit on the earnings of TV or radio stations; and the last reason, concerning consumer protection, usually does not involve the direct regulation of prices, although compliance often imposes substantial costs on firms.

Regulation of prices has turned out to be a very complicated undertaking. Established to prevent abuses of monopoly power such as charging prices that are "too-high," the regulatory agencies have, in many cases, actually
(3)   raised prices. In these cases, regulation preserves the shadow of competition only by protecting (*high/low*)-cost, inefficient firms.

Several criteria have been proposed to evaluate whether prices are "fair". One method looks at all costs related to a given line of business as well as some portion of shared overhead costs. This method leads to what is called

(4)   _____ _____ costs.

(5)   Economists typically argue for the use of long-run _____ cost as a more appropriate basis for price floors. One can conceive of cases, often in connection with regulated earnings where any price above long-run marginal cost yet below fully distributed costs will allow (*higher/lower*) prices for all of a firm's customers. The application of marginal cost pricing is difficult in an industry with significant economies of scale. In this case, average cost will be declining as output increases. When average cost declines, marginal cost is (*greater/less*) than average cost. Economists and some regulators have urged the use of the Ramsey Pricing Rule,

under which the excess of price over marginal cost depends upon the elasticity of _____ .

Has regulation made a difference? Are prices in regulated industries lower than they would be in the absence of regulation? It is very difficult to answer this question because we really do not know what would have happened in the absence of regulation. Different studies have reached different conclusions.

A number of alternatives to the present system of regulation have been considered. In some markets it
(6)   appears that viable competition is now possible. In these cases, many observers have argued for (*more/less*) regulation. Recently there has been significant deregulation of airlines, trucking, railways, telecommunications, and banking in the United States and similar moves are being actively promoted in Canada. In other cases, the problem

of incentives for efficiency might be addressed by the use of explicit _____ criteria, which would reward firms for increased efficiency.

(7)   The term _____ lag has been coined to describe the long and drawn-out regulatory process. Some suggest that this process itself offers one of the few incentives for efficiency and innovation, since it

actually builds in some penalty for _____ and some reward for

_____ .

BASIC EXERCISE

This exercise illustrates the difficulty of marginal cost pricing when average cost is declining.

Imagine that the efficient provision of telephone calls in a medium-sized city involves an initial investment of $50 million financed by borrowing at 12 percent and variable cost of 5 cents a phone call. The phone company's annual fixed cost would be around $6 million (12 percent of $50 million).

1. Use this information about costs to plot short-run marginal cost and average total cost in Figure 30-1. (Use the $6 million figure for annual fixed cost.)
2. Assume that regulators set price at 5 cents, the level of marginal cost. What is the firm's profit position if 30 million calls a year are demanded at that price? 60 million? 120 million?
3. Is setting price equal to marginal cost a viable option in this case? Why or why not?

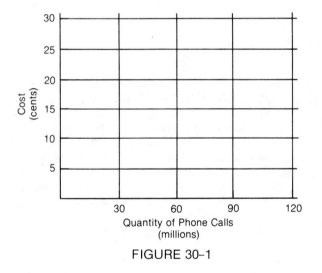

FIGURE 30-1

SELF-TESTS FOR UNDERSTANDING

Test A

Circle the correct answer.

1. Proponents of regulation would disagree with which one of the following?
   a. The public needs to be protected from the potential abuses of natural monopolies.
   b. The public needs fair public rationing of limited public resources that are used by certain industries, such as radio and television stations.
   c. "Caveat emptor" is an appropriate principle for the marketplace.
   d. In the absence of regulation many isolated communities might find themselves without vital services.
2. Which of the following is an example of economies of scale?
   a. Anna finds her costs increasing as she tries to increase the production of her custom-designed clothes.
   b. Jim discovers that a 15 percent reduction in price leads to a 30 percent increase in sales.
   c. Sarah realizes that the expertise and experience of her firm in producing specialized medical equipment will be useful in the production of testing equipment for physicists.
   d. IBM is able to reduce unit costs when it doubles the production of the IBM PC.
3. Which of the following is an example of economies of scope?
   a. An increase in circulation for the *Daily Planet* would involve only printing costs and require no increase in the editorial staff.
   b. Ramona and Ricardo have invested their wealth in stocks, bonds, and real estate.
   c. In an effort to keep production lines busy all year, Arctic Enterprises produces a variety of small-engine home and garden tools in addition to its successful line of snowblowers.
   d. Ma Bell used to use profits from long-distance calls to reduce monthly charges for local phone service.
4. The term *cross subsidy* refers to
   a. an angry firm that does not receive a subsidy.
   b. higher prices on some products that help to cover costs on other products.
   c. post office profits that help to keep the price of mailing a letter low.
   d. the financing of Christian churches.
5. Prices based on fully distributed costs
   a. would be identical to those based on long-run marginal costs.
   b. would be identical to Ramsey prices.
   c. have been proposed as a way of ensuring that prices on all lines of business are fair to both customers and competitors.
   d. provide strong incentives for increased efficiency.
6. Which one of the following is not among the alternatives that have been proposed to the present system of regulation?
   a. Deregulation of industries where there appears to be sufficient competition.
   b. The use of explicit performance criteria where feasible.
   c. An institutionalized regulatory lag in an effort to promote efficiency.
   d. More extensive use of fully distributed costs.
7. The term *regulatory lag* refers to
   a. the time it takes people to respond to a change in prices.

b. the long time it may take for a change in regulated prices to be approved.

c. the slowness of moves to deregulation.

d. the delay that occurs on many long-distance phone calls.

8. Which of the following does *not* provide a strong incentive for increased efficiency on the part of regulated firms?

a. Regulating profits so they equal the opportunity cost of capital.

b. Deregulation.

c. Performance criteria.

d. Regulatory lag.

9. In Canada and the United States natural monopolies tend to be regulated while in Europe they tend to be

a. nationalized.

b. privatized.

c. revitalized.

d. capitalized.

Test B

Circle T or F for True or False as appropriate.

1. There is overwhelming evidence that the rulings of regulatory agencies have generally resulted in lower prices for consumers than would otherwise have been charged.   T F

2. The term *economies of scope* refers to the reduction in average costs that result from large-scale production.   T F

3. Fair-rate-of-return regulations—that is, price controls that allow firms in an industry to earn profits sufficient to cover the opportunity cost of their capital—offer strong incentives for efficiency and innovation.   T F

4. The term *regulatory lag* refers to the lag between actual regulatory practice and the conventional wisdom as to the best practice.   T F

5. In the absence of regulation, firms that are required to provide service to isolated communities at high cost might find their more profitable low-cost markets taken over by competitors through a process called cream-skimming.   T F

6. Self-destructive competition is often used as an argument in favour of regulation.   T F

7. Having firms bid dollars for the right to use limited public resources, such as airwaves, has been proposed as an alternative to direct regulation. T F

8. Non-economists who talk about fully distributed costs and economists who talk about long-run marginal costs are using different language to describe the same thing.   T F

9. A major problem with nationalization as a solution to the problem of natural monopolies is that there are few systematic mechanisms to promote efficiency in nationalized industries.   T F

10. Nationalized industries in all countries are terribly inefficient.   T F

SUPPLEMENTARY EXERCISE

Pick your favourite regulatory agency, then go to the library and look up the appropriate annual reports to find out who has served on the regulatory commission recently. Use biographical information, such as is found in *Who's Who in Canada*, to trace the careers of these individuals. Did these commissioners come from the industry they regulated? After leaving the government did they take a job with the industry they regulated? Who is regulating whom?

Limiting Market Power: Competition Policy

LEARNING OBJECTIVES

After completing the material in this chapter you should be able to:

- define, understand, and use correctly the terms and concepts listed below.
- explain the major features of the Combines Investigation Act.
- describe the difference between conduct and structure as grounds for identifying illegal monopolies.
- describe the evidence about changes in concentration in Canada.
- explain the differences between vertical, horizontal, and conglomerate mergers.
- discuss the major arguments in favour of and opposed to bigness per se.
- describe how concentration may or may not be related to market power.
- evaluate arguments in favour of price discrimination.

IMPORTANT TERMS AND CONCEPTS

Competition policy
Combines Investigation Act
Price discrimination
Resale price maintenance
Predatory pricing
Structure versus conduct
Horizontal merger
Vertical merger
Conglomerate merger
Concentration of industry
Concentration ratio
Patent
Market power

CHAPTER REVIEW

This chapter discusses competition policy, which is designed to control the growth of monopolies and prevent undesirable behaviour on the part of powerful firms. The history of competition policy in Canada

starts with the Act for the Prevention and Suppression of Combinations in Restraint of

(1) _____ , passed in 1889. This act declared illegal actions in restraint of trade and attempts to monopolize trade. Vigorous legal action (*was*/*was not*) immediately adopted.

(2) Later, this original legislation was replaced by the _____

_____ Act. However, the government remained dissatisfied with the legislation because the rules relied on (*criminal*/*civil*) law. This meant that the government had to prove beyond any reasonable doubt that various acts by companies had not only lessened competition, but had done so to the obvious detriment of the public. Legal interpretation has established that this requires proving the existence of essentially a total monopoly (with respect to merger cases). Regarding agreements to restrict trade, it is not sufficient to prove that an agreement did formally exist; the government must prove that the agreement's purpose was to

_____ _____ .

Numerous unfair practices are ruled out under the Combines Investigation Act, such as resale price maintenance, predatory pricing, tied selling schemes, and misleading advertising. However numerous activities are currently exempt from the act including: the formation of unions, agreements among the banks and the professions, and the activities of regulated firms and crown corporations. Major changes in this legislation may occur soon, since

(3) extensive revisions were proposed in Parliament in _____ .

A firm can grow bigger by expanding its own factories or building new ones. A firm can also become

(4) bigger by buying up other firms. The combination of two firms into one is a _____ . When two companies, one of which sells inputs to the other, merge it is called a (*vertical*/*horizontal*) merger. Mergers

between competitors are called _____ mergers. The merger of two unrelated firms is

called a _____ merger.

Economists and others have long argued the question of whether bigness per se is good or bad. Opponents of bigness argue that the flow of wealth to firms with significant market power should be restrained

(5) because profit-maximizing monopolists are likely to produce (*more*/*less*) output than is socially desirable and

because large firms with significant market power have little inducement for _____ .

Those in favour of bigness argue that large firms are necessary for successful innovation. Further, they

(6) maintain that many big firms, because of (*increasing*/*decreasing*) returns to scale, can yield benefits to the public as a result of the associated (*reduction*/*increase*) in unit cost that goes along with large-scale production. To break up these firms into smaller units would (*increase*/*decrease*) costs.

There is no perfect measure of how concentrated an industry is. One widely used measure looks at the percent of industry output accounted for by the four largest firms. This measure is called a four-firm

(7) _____ ratio. International comparisons suggest that Canadian industry is (*more*/*less*) concentrated than those of other industrialized countries. Over time, concentration ratios in Canada have shown (*much*/*little*) change.

BASIC EXERCISE

This exercise illustrates how a monopolist may be able to increase her profits by engaging in price discrimination. Table 31-1 contains data on the demand for snow tires in two cities, Centerville and Middletown. Centerville does not get much snow, and the demand for snow tires is quite elastic. Middletown is smaller. And, since it gets more snow, it should not be surprising that the demand for snow tires in Middletown is less elastic than is the demand in

Centerville. Snow tires are supplied to both Centerville and Middletown by a monopolist who can produce tires with a fixed cost of $2,500,000 and a constant marginal cost of $10 a tire.

1. Assume that the monopolist charges the same price in both towns. Use the data on total demand to compute the monopolist's profit-maximizing level of output and price. First compute total revenue in order to compute marginal revenue by dividing the change in total revenue by the change in output.

TABLE 31-1

Price	Quantity Demanded Centerville	Middletown	Total Demand	Total Revenue	Marginal Revenue
48	10,000	40,000	50,000	_____	_____
45	25,000	43,750	68,750	_____	_____
42	40,000	47,500	87,500	_____	_____
39	55,000	51,250	106,250	_____	_____
36	70,000	55,000	125,000	_____	_____
33	85,000	58,750	143,750	_____	_____
30	100,000	62,500	162,500	_____	_____
27	115,000	66,250	181,250	_____	_____

Then compare marginal revenue to the monopolist's marginal cost of $10 to determine the profit-maximizing level of output.

Price? $_____

Output? _____

Profits? $_____

2. Assume now that the monopolist can charge different prices in the two towns; that is, the monopolist is a price discriminator. Can the monopolist increase her profits by charging different prices? Complete Table 31-2 to answer this question.

Profit-maximizing price in Centerville: $ _____

Profit-maximizing price in Middletown: $ _____

Quantity of snow tires in Centerville: _____

Quantity of snow tires in Middletown: _____

Total Profits: $ _____

3. In which town did the monopolist raise the price? In which town did she lower the price? The monopolist should charge a higher price in the town with the lower elasticity of demand. Can you explain why? Is that the case here?

SELF-TESTS FOR UNDERSTANDING

Test A

Circle the correct answer.

TABLE 31-2

| | Centerville | | Middletown | |
Price	Total Revenue	Marginal Revenue	Total Revenue	Marginal Revenue
48	_____		_____	
		_____		_____
45	_____		_____	
		_____		_____
42	_____		_____	
		_____		_____
39	_____		_____	
		_____		_____
36	_____		_____	
		_____		_____
33	_____		_____	
		_____		_____
30	_____		_____	
		_____		_____
27	_____		_____	

1. In regard to the Combines Investigation Act, which of the following is *not* true?
   a. It prohibited contracts, combinations, and conspiracies in restraint of trade.
   b. It prohibited acts that attempt monopolization of trade.
   c. It declared any firm with 80 percent of an industry's output to be an illegal monopoly.
   d. It contained no mechanism for enforcement.

2. The Combines Investigation Act subjects all but which one of the following to possible investigation:
   a. The direct purchase of a competitor's assets.
   b. Tying contracts.
   c. Price discrimination.
   d. Interlocking directorates.

3. Which of the following would constitute a vertical merger?
   a. A grocery chain merges with the bakery that supplies it with bread.
   b. Two television manufacturers merge.
   c. Esso buys Sears.
   d. Stelco buys Dofasco.

4. Which of the following would be a horizontal merger?
   a. Eaton's buys RCA Victor
   b. General Electric merges with *The New York Times*.
   c. Ford Motor Company merges with Goodyear Tire.
   d. CP Air merges with Pacific Western.

5. Which of the following would be a conglomerate merger?
   a. Ford merges with Goodyear.
   b. General Electric merges with *The New York Times*.
   c. Nordair merges with CP Air.
   d. Apple buys IBM.

6. If an industry is composed of 10 firms, each the same size, then the 4-firm concentration ratio would be
   a. 0.04
   b. 0.1
   c. 0.4
   d. 1.0

7. Data for Canada suggest that industrial concentration
   a. has declined significantly since the passage of the Combines Investigation Act.
   b. has shown little trend during the past 80 years.
   c. has increased dramatically since World War II.

8. Proponents of vigorous competition policy argue that bigness per se is bad for all but which one of the following reasons?
   a. Bigness may lead to undesirable concentrations of political and economic power.
   b. Monopolies may not feel competitive pressures to be innovative.
   c. Monopolies, in the pursuit of maximum profits, will usually restrict output below socially desirable levels.
   d. Large-scale firms may imply significant economies of scale.

9. Which of the following penalties is *not* provided for in the Combines Investigation Act?
   a. Fines on the company.
   b. Fines on individual company executives.
   c. Imprisonment of individual company executives.
   d. Withdrawing of patents and trademarks.
   e. Forced shut down of the company.

Test B

Circle T or F for True or False as appropriate.

1. A government combines investigation usually imposes a large financial burden on a company whether it has engaged in illegal actions or not.　　　　　　　　　　　　　　　　T F

2. Laws against monopoly are part of the criminal law (not civil law).　　　　　　　　　T F

3. Agreements among Canadian banks are exempt from the Combines Investigation Act.　　T F

4. If a manufacturing firm merges with its supplier, it is engaging in a horizontal merger.　T F

5. A four-firm concentration ratio is the percentage of industry output produced by the four largest firms.　　　　　　　　　　　　　　　　　T F

6. If concentration ratios for Canada showed no increase over a long period of time, we would be safe in concluding that the government's competition policies had been a success.　T F

7. Actual evidence on four-firm concentration ratios indicates a significant increase in concentration of Canadian business over the last 15 years.　T F

8. A technological innovation that favours large-scale production will always increase concentration in an industry.　　　　　　　　　　　　　　　T F

9. Research by economists suggests that only the largest firms can afford to engage in research and development.　　　　　　　　　　　　　T F

10. Price discrimination is always unfair.　　T F

Limiting Market Power: Tariff Policy

32

LEARNING OBJECTIVES

After completing the material in this chapter you should be able to:

- define, understand, and use correctly the terms and concepts listed below.
- list the important factors that lead countries to trade with one another.
- explain how trade, even if it does not increase total production, can be mutually beneficial to the trading partners.
- distinguish between absolute and comparative advantage.
- explain how absolute advantage and comparative advantage are related to the location and slope of a country's production possibilities frontier.
- explain how trade means that a country's consumption possibilities can exceed its production possibilities.
- explain how specialization, consistent with the law of comparative advantage, can increase total world output.
- contrast the efficiency and distribution effects of tariffs and quotas.

- analyse the arguments used to advocate trade restrictions.
- explain the role of adjustment assistance in a country favouring free trade.
- explain the fallacy in the "cheap foreign labour" argument.

IMPORTANT TERMS AND CONCEPTS

Imports
Exports
Specialization
Mutual gains from trade
Absolute advantage
Comparative advantage
"Cheap foreign labour" argument
Tariff
Non-tariff barriers
Quota
Export subsidy
Trade adjustment assistance
Infant-industry argument
Dumping

CHAPTER REVIEW

The material in this chapter discusses the basic economic forces that influence the international division of labour in the production of goods and the resulting pattern of international trade. The basic economic principle

(1) underlying an efficient international distribution of production is the *law of* _____ *advantage.* It is also important to remember that actual production and trade decisions are also affected by important policy interventions such as tariffs, quotas, and export subsidies.

Exchange rates—that is, the number of units of one country's currency that are changeable for another country's currency—are an important determinant of international trade and they were discussed in chapters 13 and 16. However, the real terms of trade—that is, how many import goods a country can get indirectly through export production rather than through direct domestic production—are the important measure of the benefits of trade, and they are considered here in some detail.

Individual countries can try to meet the consumption needs of their citizens without trade by producing everything their populations need. Alternatively, they can specialize in the production of a few commodities and trade for commodities they do not produce. Even if there were no differences between countries, specializing

(2) and trading would still make sense if there were important economies of _____ in production.

The most important reason for trade is that differences in oil deposits, fertile soil, and other natural resources, as well as differences in labour inputs and productive capital, will affect the efficiency with which

(3) countries can produce different goods. It is the law of (**absolute/comparative**) advantage that then indicates where countries should concentrate their production to maximize the potential gains from trade.

If country A must give up 200 tonnes of wheat in order to produce one car while country B must give up only 120 tonnes of wheat, then, for the same world production of cars, world production of wheat will

(4) increase if country (*A/B*) produces 10 fewer cars and country _____ produces 10 more cars. (World wheat production would increase by _____ tonnes.) In this case country A has a comparative advantage in producing _____ .

Looking only at its own domestic production opportunities, the opportunity cost of one more car in

(5) country A is _____ tonnes of wheat. Country B can produce one more car by giving up only _____ tonnes of wheat. Thus it should not be surprising if country A concentrates on the production of _____ and trades with country B, which concentrates on the production of _____ .[1]

As countries concentrate production on those goods in which they have a comparative advantage, equilibrium world prices and trade flows—that is, exports and imports—will be determined at the point where

(6) world _____ equals world _____ . This price is not at the intersection of domestic demand and supply curves; instead, it occurs at a point where the excess supply from (*importing/exporting*) countries (domestic supply minus domestic demand) equals the excess demand by

_____ countries (domestic demand minus domestic supply).

Just as Chapter 26 discussed the efficiency of competitive markets for self-contained economies, advanced courses in international trade show how prices derived under conditions of free trade will lead profit-maximizing firms to exploit the comparative advantage of individual countries. Most countries do not have unrestricted free

(7) trade. Rather, imports are often restricted by the use of _____ and _____ , and exports are often promoted through the use of export _____ . Tariffs reduce the quantity of imports by raising their _____ while quotas raise the price of imports by restricting their

---

[1] Does the law of comparative advantage imply that all countries should completely specialize in the production of just a few commodities? No, it does not, for several reasons. One important reason is that production possibility frontiers are likely to be curved rather than straight lines. The implication of the curved frontier is that the opportunity cost of cars in terms of wheat for country B will rise as B produces more cars. Simultaneously, the opportunity cost of cars in terms of wheat for country A will fall as A concentrates on wheat. In equilibrium, the opportunity cost, or slope of the production opportunity frontier, in both countries will be equal. At this point neither country has a comparative advantage for further specialization. Exactly where this point will occur will be determined by world demand and supply for cars and wheat.

_____ . Either a tariff or a quota could be used to achieve the same reduction in imports, but the choice between the two does have other consequences.

(8)   Tariff revenues accrue directly to the _____ , while the benefits of higher prices under a quota are likely to accrue to private producers, both foreign and domestic. (The government might be able to capture some of these profits by auctioning a limited number of import licences, but this is not usually done.)

Tariffs still require foreign suppliers to compete among themselves. This competition will favour the survival

(9)   of (*high/low*)-cost foreign suppliers. (What about domestic firms? They (*do/do not*) have to pay the tariff and so high-cost domestic suppliers (*can/can not*) continue in business.) Quotas are apt to be distributed on almost any grounds except efficiency, and thus have no mechanism that works in favour of low-cost foreign suppliers.

Why do countries impose tariffs and quotas? Many trade restrictions reflect the successful pleadings of high-cost domestic suppliers. Free trade and the associated reallocation of productive resources in line with the law of comparative advantage would call for the elimination of these firms in their traditional lines of business. It is not surprising that managers and workers resist these changes. Since the attempts to limit the market power of domestic firms by regulation or competition policy have not been particularly successful, many economists argue that we should force a drive for efficiency by these firms by reducing their protective tariffs.

If everyone is to benefit from the increased output opportunities offered by free trade, then a program of trade

(10)   _____ assistance will be necessary to help those most affected by the realignment of productive activities.

(11)   Other traditional justifications for trade restriction include the national _____

argument and the _____-industries argument. In both cases it is extremely difficult to separate firms with legitimate claims from those that are looking for a public handout. Recently some have argued that the threat of trade restrictions should be used in an attempt to convince others not to impose restrictions.

BASIC EXERCISES

1. This exercise is designed to review the law of comparative advantage.
   a. Assume that the following hours of labour are the only input necessary to produce hand calculators and backpacks in Canada and Japan.

	Calculators	Backpacks
Canada	6	4
Japan	2	3

   Which country has an absolute advantage in the

   production of hand calculators? _____
   Which country has an absolute advantage in the production of backpacks?

   _____

   b. If labour in Canada is reallocated from the production of calculators to the production of backpacks, how many calculators must be given up in order to produce one more backpack?

   _____

   What about Japan? How many calculators must it give up in order to produce one more

   backpack? _____
   Which country has a comparative advantage in

   the production of backpacks? _____
   Which country has a comparative advantage in

   the production of calculators? _____
   According to the law of comparative advantage,

   _____ should
   concentrate on the production of backpacks

   while _____
   concentrates on the production of calculators.

   c. Assume each country has 12 million hours of labour input that initially is evenly distributed in both countries between the production of backpacks and calculators: 6 million for each. Fill in the following table of outputs.

	Output of Calculators	Output of Backpacks
Canada	_____	_____
Japan	_____	_____
Total	_____	_____

   d. Assume that Canada now reallocates 1.8 million labour hours away from the production of calculators and into the production of backpacks. The change in Canadian calculator output is

   - _____ .

   The change in Canadian backpack output is

   + _____ .

   e. What reallocation of labour in Japan is necessary to be sure that world output of calculators (Japan plus Canada) remains unchanged?

_____ labour hours. What are the changes in Japanese output from this reallocation? The change in Japanese calculator output is

+ _____ .

The change in Japanese backpack output is

- _____ .

f. By assumption, the world output of calculators has not changed, but the net change in the world output of backpacks is a(n) (*increase/decrease*)

of _____ backpacks.

g. Questions c through f showed how specialization according to the law of comparative advantage could increase the output of backpacks without decreasing the output of calculators. Adjustments in line with the law of comparative advantage could alternatively increase the output of both goods. Suppose Japan had reallocated 900,000 labour hours to the production of calculators. Fill in the following table, and compare total outputs with your answers in Question f.

Calculators

	Labour input (millions of hours)	Output
Canada	4.2	_____
Japan	6.9	_____
Total		_____

Backpacks

	Labour input (millions of hours)	Output
Canada	7.8	_____
Japan	5.1	_____
Total		_____

h. (Optional) Work through Questions d and e again, but assume this time that the initial reallocation of 1.8 million labour hours in Canada is away from backpacks and to the production of calculators. Calculate the reallocation in Japan necessary to maintain world backpacks output. What happens to the total output of calculators? Why?

i. (Optional) Assume that the production of backpacks in Canada requires 9 hours rather than 4 hours. Work through the original output levels in Question c and the reallocation of labour in Questions d and e to see what now happens to total output of calculators and backpacks. Does your answer to Question f differ from your original answer? Why?

2. This exercise illustrates some of the effects of tariffs and quotas. Figure 32-1 shows domestic demand

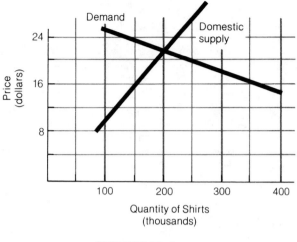

FIGURE 32-1

and supply for shirts in Autarkia, a small economy. In the absence of foreign trade, equilibrium price and quantity would be $22 and 200,000 shirts. Since Autarkia is small it can import as many shirts as it wants without affecting the world price, which is $16. (The assumptions for a small country are similar to the horizontal demand curve that faces a firm under perfect competition.) At any price below the world price, low-cost domestic suppliers can undersell importers, but in the absence of trade restrictions, the world price will put a limit on the domestic price, as importers can undersell high-cost domestic suppliers. In Figure 32-2 the heavy line shows effective supply in the absence of trade restrictions.

a. Under free trade, equilibrium price is

$_____ and equilibrium quantity is

_____ . As compared with the no-trade equilibrium illustrated in Figure 32-1, domestic production of shirts would decline by

_____ shirts.

b. Assume now that domestic shirt manufacturers and workers are able to persuade the government to implement a $4-per-shirt tariff. Draw the new supply curve reflecting the tariff in Figure 32-2. As compared with free-trade equilibrium, the equilibrium with the tariff shows consumer prices to be (*higher/lower*); domestic purchases of shirts to be (*higher/lower*); and domestic production of shirts to be (*higher/lower*). Note that the reduction in imports is (*greater/less*) than the decline in purchases.

c. What quota would have the same impact on price, consumption, and domestic production as

the $4 tariff? _____ . Are there other

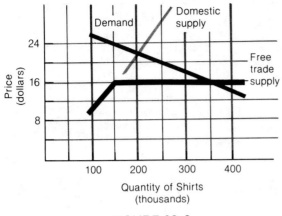

FIGURE 32-2

reasons for choosing between a tariff and a quota?

SELF-TESTS FOR UNDERSTANDING

Test A

Circle the correct answer.

1. Which of the following is an example of comparative advantage?
   a. Wages of textile workers are lower in India than in Canada.
   b. The slope of the production possibilities frontier between tomatoes and tables differs for Mexico and Canada.
   c. Canadian workers must work an average of only 800 hours to purchase a car, while Soviet workers must work 1600 hours.
   d. In recent years Swedish income per capita has exceeded that of Canada.

2. Economists argue that
   a. efficiency in international trade requires countries to produce those goods in which they have an absolute advantage.
   b. efficiency in international trade requires countries to produce those goods in which they have a comparative advantage.
   c. efficiency in international trade requires countries that have an absolute advantage in the production of all goods to become self-sufficient.
   d. countries with export surpluses will have a comparative advantage in the production of all goods.

3. Under free trade, world prices for exports and imports would be such that

   a. countries would specialize production along lines of absolute advantage.
   b. all countries would show a slight export surplus.
   c. the quantity supplied by exporters would just equal the quantity demanded by importers.
   d. every country would be self-sufficient in all goods.

4. If shoes can be produced with two hours of labour input in Italy and three hours of labour input in the United States, then it is correct to say that
   a. Italy has an absolute advantage in the production of shoes.
   b. Italy has a comparative advantage in the production of shoes.
   c. the United States has an absolute advantage in the production of shoes.
   d. the United States has a comparative advantage in the production of shoes.

5. Assuming that shoes are produced as in Question 4 and shirts can be produced with four hours of labour in both countries, then it is correct to say that
   a. the United States has a comparative advantage in the production of shirts.
   b. Italy has a comparative advantage in the production of shirts.
   c. Italy has an absolute advantage in the production of shirts.
   d. the United States has an absolute advantage in the production of shirts.

6. All but which one of the following have been used to restrict trade?
   a. Import subsidies.
   b. Tariffs.
   c. Quotas.
   d. "Voluntary" export agreements.

7. Which of the following is an example of a tariff?
   a. Japanese car manufacturers agree to limit exports to Canada.
   b. Canadian law limits the imports of cotton shirts to 3 million.
   c. Television manufacturers outside of Great Britain must pay a 5 percent duty on each set they ship to Great Britain.
   d. Foreign bicycle manufacturers receive a rebate of taxes from their own government for each bicycle they export.

8. One economic advantage of tariffs over quotas is that tariffs
   a. typically give preferential treatment to long-term suppliers.
   b. expose high-cost domestic producers to competition.
   c. allow low-cost foreign suppliers to compete.
   d. help avoid destructive price wars.

9. The imposition of a tariff on steel will lead to all but which one of the following?

a. A lower volume of steel imports.
b. Higher domestic steel prices.
c. Reduced domestic demand for steel.
d. Reduced domestic production of steel as higher steel prices reduce demand.

10. Which one of the following is not a justification for trade restrictions?
   a. Some industries would be so vital in times of war that we cannot rely on foreign suppliers.
   b. Competition from foreign suppliers will help keep prices to consumers low.
   c. The threat of trade restrictions may prevent the adoption of restrictions by others.
   d. A temporary period of protection is necessary until an industry matures and is able to compete with foreign suppliers.

Test B

Circle T or F for True or False as appropriate.

1. A country with a comparative advantage in producing all goods is better off being self-sufficient than engaging in trade.　　　T F

2. Countries gain from trade only when it allows them to adjust productive resources to take advantage of economies of scale.　　　T F

3. A country with an absolute advantage in the production of all goods will only export commodities.　　　T F

4. The unequal distribution of natural resources among countries is one important reason why countries trade.　　　T F

5. Which of two countries has a comparative advantage in the production of wine rather than cloth can be determined by comparing the slopes of the production possibility frontiers of both countries.　　　T F

6. It is not possible for all countries to simultaneously expand exports and reduce imports.　　　T F

7. A quota on shirts would reduce the volume of imported shirts by specifying the quantity of shirts that can be imported.　　　T F

8. The infant-industry argument is used to justify protection for industries that are vital in times of war.　　　T F

9. Dumping of goods by Canada on Japanese markets would necessarily reduce the Japanese standard of living.　　　T F

10. If foreign labour is paid less, foreign producers will always be able to undersell Canadian producers.　　　T F

SUPPLEMENTARY EXERCISES

1. Demand and supply for widgets in Baulmovia and Bilandia are as given below.

   Baulmovia
   　Demand: $Q = 156 - 7P$
   　Supply: $Q = -44 + 18P$
   Bilandia
   　Demand: $Q = 320 - 10P$
   　Supply: $Q = -20 + 10P$

   a. In the absence of trade, what is the price of widgets in Baulmovia? In Bilandia? What quantity is produced in Baulmovia? In Bilandia?
   b. With free trade what is the one common world price for widgets? Which country exports widgets? Which country imports widgets? What is the volume of exports and imports?
   c. Manufacturers in the importing country have convinced the government to impose a tariff on widget imports of $4.50 a widget. What will happen to trade and the price of widgets in the two countries?
   d. What quota would have the same impact on trade?
   e. What factors might lead one to prefer a tariff over a quota?

2. Ricardia is a small country that produces wine and cloth. The production possibilities frontier for Ricardia is

   $$W = \sqrt{324 - C^2}$$

   where W = millions of bottles of wine and C = millions of bolts of cloth.

   a. Use a piece of graph paper. Label the vertical axis "wine" and the horizontal axis "cloth." Draw the production possibilities frontier.
   b. Since Ricardia is a small country, it can export or import cloth or wine without affecting world prices. World prices are such that Ricardia can export one million bottles of wine for 750,000 bolts of cloth or it can export 750,000 bolts of cloth for one million bottles of wine. The government's chief economist argues that regardless of consumption preferences, Ricardia should produce 14.4 million bolts of cloth and 10.8 million bottles of wine. Do you agree with her? Why? (Hint: Consider what the consumption possibilities look like. For any production combination of wine and cloth, Ricardia's consumption possibilities are given by a negatively sloped straight line through the production point. The slope of the consumption possibilities line reflects world prices. A movement up the straight line to the left of the production point would imply exporting cloth in

order to consume more wine. A movement down the straight line to the right would reflect exporting wine in order to consume more cloth. Exactly what Ricardia chooses to consume is a matter of preferences, but its choice is constrained by its consumption possibilities line, which, in turn, is determined by Ricardia's production choice and world prices for cloth and wine. Why does the production point 10.8 million bottles of wine and 14.4 million bolts of cloth offer the greatest consumption possibilities?)

Taxation, Government Spending, and Resource Allocation

33

LEARNING OBJECTIVES

After completing the material in this chapter you should be able to:

- define, understand, and use correctly the terms and concepts listed below.
- distinguish between progressive, proportional, and regressive tax systems.
- describe the major taxes levied by the federal, provincial, and municipal governments.
- explain the concept of fiscal federalism.
- contrast various concepts of fair or equitable taxation.
- explain the difference between the burden and the excess burden of a tax.
- explain how changes in economic behaviour can enable individuals to shift the burden of a tax; that is, explain what is wrong with the flypaper theory of tax incidence.
- explain what factors influence how the burden of a tax will be shared by consumers and suppliers.
- explain the incidence of taxes levied on labour and capital.

IMPORTANT TERMS AND CONCEPTS

Progressive, proportional, and regressive taxes
Corporate profits tax
Excise tax
Direct and indirect taxes
Personal income tax
Payroll tax
Average and marginal tax rates
Tax shelters
Capital gain
Property tax
Fiscal federalism
Horizontal and vertical equity
Ability-to-pay principle
Benefits principle of taxation
Burden of a tax
Excess burden
Incidence of a tax
Flypaper theory of tax incidence
Tax shifting

CHAPTER REVIEW

This chapter concentrates on taxes: What sorts of taxes are collected in Canada and what economic effects they have. Few people like paying taxes. In fact, many people make adjustments in their behaviour to reduce the taxes they must pay. It is these adjustments that are the important measure of the economic effects of taxes, a part that is often overlooked in popular discussions.

(1) Taxes are levied by federal, provincial, and municipal units of government. For the most part, federal taxes tend to be (*direct/indirect*) taxes, while provincial and municipal governments rely more on

_____ taxes. The largest revenue raiser for the federal government is the

_____ _____ tax.

(2) When talking about income tax systems it is important to distinguish between *average* and *marginal* tax rates. The fraction of total income paid as income taxes is the (*average/marginal*) tax rate, while the fraction of

each additional dollar of income paid as taxes is the _____ tax rate. If the average tax

rate increases, the resulting tax system is called _____ . If the average tax rate is

constant for all levels of income, the tax system is said to be _____ , while if the average tax rate

falls as income increases, the result is a _____ tax system.

(3) Under the Canadian federal personal income tax system, both marginal and average tax rates (*increase/decrease*). However, the progressivity of the federal income tax is (*more/less*) than it appears on paper because wealthier taxpayers are able to reduce their taxes by taking legal advantage of various tax

_____ .

(4) Economists use their dual criteria of equity and efficiency to judge taxes. When talking about the fairness of a particular tax, one is talking about _____ . Various criteria have been advanced to judge the fairness of a particular tax. The principle that equally situated individuals should pay equal taxes is

referred to as _____ _____ . The principle that differentially situated individuals

should be taxed in ways that society deems fair is referred to as _____ . The ability-to-pay principle

is an example of _____ equity.

(5) Rather than looking at the income and wealth of families, there is an alternative approach to taxation that says people should pay in proportion to what they get from public services. This principle for taxation is

called the _____ principle. User fees for a variety of public services, such as garbage

collection, the use of parks, street cleaning, and so on, are an example of the _____ principle.

(6) Efficiency is the other criterion that economists use to judge taxes. Almost all taxes cause some inefficiency. The amount of money that would make an individual as well off with a tax as he was without the

tax is called the _____ of the tax. Sometimes it is just equal to the tax payment an individual makes, but more generally it is (*greater/less*) than an individual's tax payment. The difference between

the total burden and tax payments is called the _____ _____ . The reason that tax payments typically understate the total burden of a tax is that the existence of the tax will often induce a change in behaviour. Measuring only the taxes paid (*does/does not*) take account of the loss of satisfaction resulting from the induced change in behaviour. The excess burden is the measure of the inefficiency of a particular tax. Thus the principle of efficiency in taxation calls for using taxes that raise the same revenue but with the smallest

_____ burden, or using taxes that induce the least important changes in behaviour.

Often taxes will affect even those people who do not pay the tax. Imagine, for example, that the government imposes a $50 excise tax on bicycles, paid for by consumers at the time of purchase. Even though paid for by consumers, it may be easiest to examine the impact of this tax by viewing it as a shift in the supply curve, as illustrated in Figure 33-1. Consumers do not care why the price of bicycles has increased; there is no reason for their demand curve to shift. Suppliers collect the tax for the government and are concerned with what is left over after taxes in order to pay their suppliers and cover both their labour cost and the opportunity cost of their capital. How suppliers will respond to the after-tax price is given by the original supply curve. The before-tax supply curve comes from adding the excise tax onto the original supply curve and is given by the dashed line in Figure 33-1.

Looking at Figure 33-1 we see that compared with the original equilibrium, the new equilibrium involves a

(7) (*higher/lower*) price to consumers, a (*higher/lower*) price to suppliers, and a (*larger/smaller*) quantity of bicycles produced. It would not be surprising if the change in supply resulted in some or all of the following: some unemployed bicycle workers, lower wages for employed bicycle workers, and fewer bicycle firms. None of these workers or firms paid the tax, yet all were affected by it.

In the bicycle example, as consumers adjusted to the new tax, they shifted part of the burden of the tax onto others. The question of how the burden of taxes is divided up among different groups is the question of tax

(8) _____. At first glance it might appear that the burden of the tax is borne entirely by consumers who pay the tax at the time of sale. The notion that the burden of the tax rests with those who pay the

tax is called the _____ theory of tax incidence. As the bicycle example makes clear, if

consumers change their behaviour as a result of the tax, they may succeed in _____ part of the burden of the tax.

The study of tax incidence suggests that the incidence of excise or sales taxes depends on the slopes of

(9) both the _____ and _____ curves. Payroll taxes, such as contributions to the Canada Pension Plan and the unemployment insurance program, are like an excise tax on labour services. Statistical work suggests that for most workers the supply of labour services is relatively (*elastic/inelastic*) with respect to wage rates, which in turn suggests that (*workers/firms*) rather than

_____ bear most of the burden of the payroll tax. In many ways, profits taxation can be treated as an excise tax on capital services. Since the supply of capital to the Canadian economy is almost perfectly (*elastic/inelastic*) at the rate of return that is available in the rest of the world, firms' owners bear (*most/little*) of the burden of the tax on capital.

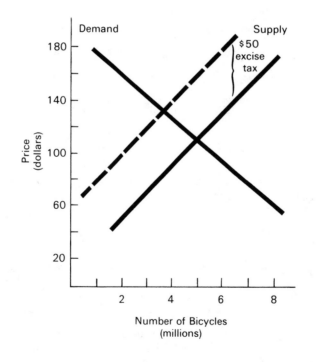

FIGURE 33-1

DEMAND FOR AND SUPPLY OF BICYCLES

BASIC EXERCISE

This exercise is designed to illustrate how the incidence of an excise tax depends on the elasticity (slope) of the demand and supply curves.

1. Table 33-1 has data on the demand and supply of running shoes. Plot the demand curve from column 1 and the supply curve from column 3 in Figure 33-2.
2. Determine the initial equilibrium price and quantity of running shoes.

     Price $ _____

     Quantity _____
3. Now assume that in a fit of pique, non-running Parliamentarians impose a fitness tax of $10 on each pair of shoes. Draw the new supply curve by shifting the original supply curve by the magnitude of the excise tax. The new equilibrium price is

     $_____ , and the new equilibrium

     quantity is _____ .
4. How much more do consumers, who continue to

     buy running shoes, pay? $_____
     How does this increase in price compare with the excise tax of $10?
5. What is likely to happen to employment, wages, and profits in the running-shoe industry?
6. On Figure 33-3, plot the demand curve from column 2 and supply curve from column 3 of Table 33-1. Comparing Figures 33-2 and 33-3, we have the same supply curve but different demand curves. Both figures should show the same initial equilibrium price and quantity.
7. At the initial equilibrium price and quantity, which

     demand curve is more elastic? _____
     (Review the appropriate material in Chapter 21 if you do not remember how to compute the price elasticity of a demand curve.) Remember this distinction when it comes to comparing results.
8. Now analyse the impact of the imposition of the same excise tax of $10 per pair of running shoes using Figure 33-3. The new equilibrium price is

     $_____ and the new equilibrium

     quantity is _____ . In which case, Figure 33-2 or Figure 33-3, does the equilibrium price of running shoes rise the most?

     _____ . In which case are the volume of employment and the level of wages likely

     to fall the least? _____ From this comparison we can conclude that the more inelastic the demand curve, the more the burden of an

excise tax will be borne by _____ .
9. (Optional) Use information on demand from either column 1 or 2 and the two supply curves in columns 3 and 4 to analyse the incidence of the tax as the elasticity of supply changes.

TABLE 33-1

DEMAND FOR AND SUPPLY OF RUNNING SHOES

(1)	(2)		(3)	(4)
Demand				Supply
(millions		Price		(millions
of pairs)		(dollars)		of pairs)
68	53.0	30	38	48.00
65	52.5	32	40	48.33
62	52.0	34	42	48.67
59	51.5	36	44	49.00
56	51.0	38	46	49.33
53	50.5	40	48	49.67
50	50.0	42	50	50.00
47	49.5	44	52	50.33
44	49.0	46	54	50.67
41	48.5	48	56	51.00
38	48.0	50	58	51.33
35	47.5	52	60	51.67
32	47.0	54	62	52.00

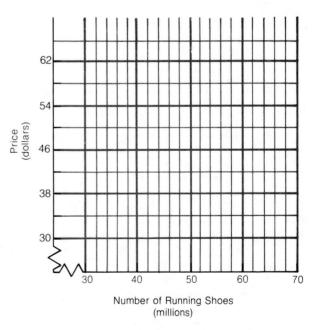

FIGURE 33-2

DEMAND FOR AND SUPPLY OF RUNNING SHOES

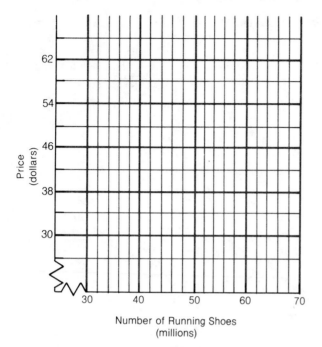

FIGURE 33-3

DEMAND FOR AND SUPPLY OF RUNNING SHOES

SELF-TESTS FOR UNDERSTANDING

Test A

Circle the correct answer.

1. The facts about tax collection show that in Canada since 1950 federal taxes as a proportion of GNP have
   a. declined.
   b. fluctuated but shown little trend.
   c. increased dramatically.
2. The facts about tax collection show that in Canada provincial and municipal taxes as a percentage of GNP have
   a. declined since 1960.
   b. shown virtually no change over the last 30 years.
   c. increased since 1950
3. The facts about tax collection show that as compared with other industrialized countries, total tax collections in Canada are
   a. higher than in any other country.
   b. lower than in many other countries.
   c. higher than in the US and UK.
   d. lower than in the US and UK.

4. Which of the following is an example of an indirect tax?
   a. Income taxes.
   b. Inheritance taxes.
   c. Head taxes.
   d. Sales taxes.
5. The Abbotts have an income of $20,000 a year and pay $2000 a year in income taxes. The Beards have an income of $40,000 a year and pay $5000 a year in income taxes. From this information we can conclude that this tax system
   a. is regressive.
   b. is proportional.
   c. is progressive.
   d. satisfies the benefits principle of taxation.
6. The ability-to-pay principle of taxation is an example of
   a. horizontal equity.
   b. vertical equity.
   c. the benefits principle.
   d. fiscal federalism.
7. If two families are identical in all respects, the principle of horizontal equity says that
   a. both families should pay more income taxes than other families with less income.
   b. both families should pay the same income tax.
   c. both families should have a lower average tax rate than a richer family.
   d. income taxes are, from a social viewpoint, a more appropriate form of taxation than are payroll taxes.
8. Which of the following are examples of the benefits principle of taxation?
   a. Excise taxes on cigarettes.
   b. Higher property taxes as a percent of market value for more expensive homes.
   c. Special assessments on homeowners in proportion to their street frontage to help pay for repairs to curbs and gutters.
   d. Medicare.
9. A sales tax on which of the following will involve a small excess burden?
   a. A tax on a commodity with a zero price elasticity of demand.
   b. A tax on a commodity with a very high elasticity of demand.
   c. A tax on a commodity that is consumed primarily by poor families.
   d. A tax on a commodity that is consumed primarily by rich families.
10. The flypaper theory of tax incidence
    a. is a shorthand reference to such sticky issues as the appropriate degree of progressivity in the personal income tax.
    b. implies that if a tax induces changes in economic behaviour, part of the burden of the tax may be shifted to other economic agents.

c. is usually right regarding who bears the burden of a tax.

d. says that the burden of a tax is borne by those who pay the tax.

8. If a tax does not induce a change in economic behaviour, then there is no excess burden. **T F**

9. The concept of excess burden proves that taxes can never improve efficiency. **T F**

Test B

Circle T or F for True or False as appropriate.

1. Over the past 35 years federal government taxes have been taking an ever-increasing share of the GNP. **T F**

2. Despite tax shelters, the federal personal income tax is more progressive than the statutory rates imply. **T F**

3. Federal payroll taxes are a less important source of revenue than either the federal personal income tax or the federal corporate income tax. **T F**

4. Provincial personal income taxes are an example of a direct, as opposed to indirect, tax. **T F**

5. The principle of horizontal equity says that equally situated individuals should be taxed equally. **T F**

6. The ability-to-pay principle says that people who derive benefits from a particular public service should pay the taxes to finance it. **T F**

7. The burden of a tax is normally less than the revenue raised by the tax. **T F**

SUPPLEMENTARY EXERCISE

Table 33-2 reproduces the federal income tax rates for single taxpayers in 1984. For simplicity we consider an individual whose only deduction from gross income is the basic personal exemption, which was $3960 in 1984. Thus, taxable income is gross income minus this exemption. Assume the individual lives in Ontario. The Ontario income tax is 48 percent of the federal income tax. With this information you can complete Table 33-3.

As of this writing, there was speculation that the government might move toward removal of some indexing features of the personal income tax system. To get some idea of the implications of such a move, consider what would have happened in 1984 if there had been 10 percent inflation, but the basic personal exemption had not been indexed. Instead of being $3960 as it was, the basic personal exemption would have been $3564 (90 percent of $3960). Derive a second version of Table 33-3, with the basic exemption being $3564 instead of $3960. Who is hurt more by the reduction in the exemption that occurs when inflation occurs without indexation? Those earning low incomes or those earning high incomes?

TABLE 33-2

1984 RATES OF FEDERAL INCOME TAX

Taxable Income	Tax	Taxable Income	Tax
$1238 or less	6%	$12 380	$ 2080 + 20% on next $ 4952
1238	$ 74 + 16% on next $1238	17 332	3070 + 23% on next 4952
2476	272 + 17% on next 2476	22 284	4209 + 25% on next 12 380
4952	693 + 18% on next 2476	34 664	7304 + 30% on next 24 760
7428	1139 + 19% on next 4952	59 424	14 732 + 34% on remainder

TABLE 33-3

TAX RATES FOR ONTARIO INDIVIDUALS-1984

Total Gross Income	Total Taxes (Federal plus Ontario)	Average Tax Rate	Marginal Tax Rate
$ 5000	$_____	_____	_____
$10 000	$_____	_____	_____
$20 000	$_____	_____	_____
$50 000	$_____	_____	_____
$80 000	$_____	_____	_____

The Economics of Environmental Protection

34

LEARNING OBJECTIVES

After completing the material in this chapter you should be able to:

- define, understand, and use correctly the terms and concepts listed below.
- describe the three major sources of environmental damage.
- explain why, in most cases, it is undesirable to reduce pollution to zero.
- explain why it is unlikely that profit-maximizing private firms can be expected to clean up the environment.

- describe the many alternative approaches to limiting pollution.
- compare the advantages and disadvantages of using taxes, subsidies, and permits to control pollution.

IMPORTANT TERMS AND CONCEPTS

Externality
Direct controls
Pollution charges (taxes on emissions)
Subsidies for reduced emissions
Emissions permits

CHAPTER REVIEW

This chapter explores the economics of environmental protection, with special emphasis on the use of financial incentives as a device to limit pollution.

Pollution is one example of instances in which unregulated markets will fail to achieve an efficient allocation of resources. Typically, pollution imposes little or no cost for the polluter, yet it imposes costs on others. In the

(1) language of economists, pollution is an example of a detrimental _____ . Pollution happens because individuals, firms, and government agencies use the air, land, and waterways as free dumping grounds for their waste products. Economists believe that if there is a high cost to using these public resources, then the

volume of pollution will (*increase/decrease*) because people will be more careful about producing wastes and/or choose less costly alternatives for waste disposal. One way to make the use of public resources costly is to impose (*taxes/subsidies*) in direct proportion to the volume of pollution emitted. This is an example of using the price system to clean up the environment.

However, most government policies have relied on other approaches, voluntarism and direct

(2)   _____ . Both of these policies have their place in a co-ordinated attempt to clean up the environment. Economists, though, are skeptical of relying on voluntary co-operation as a general long-range solution. Cleaning up the environment is costly, and firms that voluntarily incur these costs are likely to be undersold by less public-spirited competitors.

A government ruling that mandates an equal percentage reduction in pollution activity by all polluters is an example of a direct control. Economists argue that since the costs of reducing pollution are apt to vary among

(3)   polluters, an equal percentage reduction by all polluters is likely to be (*efficient/inefficient*) compared with other alternatives, such as emissions taxes. From a social viewpoint, unequal reductions in pollution will be more

_____ , as it is likely to cost less for some firms to reduce pollution. Faced with an emissions tax, firms will reduce pollution until the (*marginal/average*) cost of further reductions exceeds the tax. Firms that continue to pollute will pay the tax; other firms will pay for pollution-control devices. All firms will choose the least costly alternative.

Other financial schemes to clean up the environment include the use of subsidies and the sale of

(4)   emissions permits, Compared with the use of emissions taxes, subsidies may actually (*decrease/increase*) pollution because consumers will have little financial incentive to reduce their use of the polluting commodity. Emissions permits allow for more precise control of the volume of emissions, but quantity limits that are too strict may only lead to the destruction of the system of control rather than to a reduction in pollution.

BASIC EXERCISE

This exercise examines the implications of alternative pollution taxes.

Assume that plastic trash bags are produced in a market that is best characterized as one of perfect competition. All manufacturers have long used local rivers as convenient, free dumping grounds for their industrial wastes. Figure 34–1 plots the average cost of producing trash bags. These data are applicable for each firm.

1. In the absence of any pollution-control measures, what is the long-run equilibrium price of plastic

   bags? $ _____ . What is the long-run equilibrium level of output for each firm?

   _____ (To answer this question you may want to review the material in Chapter 25 about long-run equilibrium under perfect competition.)

2. The amount of pollution discharge is directly proportional to the number of bags produced. Assume that the government imposes a pollution charge of 5 cents per bag. Draw in the new average-cost curve on Figure 34–1. Will there be an increase, a decrease, or no change in each of the following as a result of the pollution charge? (Assume for now that there is no pollution-control technology, that each firm must pay the tax, and that the demand for plastic bags declines as price rises.)

   Industry output   _____

Price	_____
Number of firms in industry	_____
Average-cost curve for each firm	_____
Output level of each firm	_____
Total pollution	_____

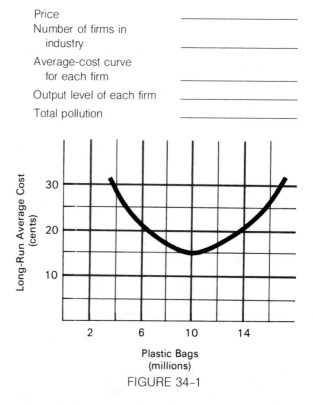

Plastic Bags
(millions)

FIGURE 34–1

3. Assume now that pollution-control equipment becomes available. This equipment will eliminate 75 percent of pollution at an average cost of 4 cents

per bag. Explain why no firm will adopt the pollution-control equipment if the pollution charge is unchanged at 5 cents a bag. (Assume that the cost of control equipment is all variable cost at 4 cents per bag and that there is no fixed-cost component.)

4. Assume now that the tax is shifted to the volume of emissions, not to the number of bags produced, and that it is equivalent to 5 cents a bag if no pollution-control equipment is installed. Will any firm purchase the pollution-control equipment?

5. With the emissions tax at a rate of 5 cents per bag, to what rate must the cost of pollution control decline before firms will use it? If the cost of pollution control is constant at 4 cents, to what rate must the tax increase to induce firms to install the pollution-control equipment?

6. (Optional) Assume now that the costs of reducing pollution are not identical for all firms. For simplicity, assume that there are two types of firms, low-cost pollution-control firms and high-cost pollution-control firms. The low-cost firms can eliminate pollution at costs lower than the emissions tax but the high-cost firms cannot. What is the result of the imposition of an emissions tax? What will happen to total industry output? Will any firms leave the industry? If so, which ones, the high-cost or the low-cost firms? Why?

SELF-TESTS FOR UNDERSTANDING

Test A

Circle the correct answer.

1. Which of the following suggests that, except for recycling, all economic activity results in a disposal problem?
   a. The edifice complex.
   b. The law of conservation of energy and matter.
   c. Emissions permits.
   d. Externalities.

2. The fact that pollution is often a detrimental externality suggests that
   a. cleaning up the environment must be done by direct government expenditures.
   b. without government intervention, profit-maximizing private firms cannot be expected to clean up the environment.
   c. public agencies have been responsible for most pollution.
   d. direct controls are superior to other forms of government intervention.

3. Which of the following is not an example of using financial incentives to clean up the environment?
   a. Mandated pollution-control equipment in an

attempt to reduce automobile emissions.
   b. A graduated tax that increases with the polluting characteristics of each automobile engine.
   c. The sale of a limited number of permits to control emissions into Lake Erie.
   d. Allowing firms to buy and sell emission rights originally assigned under a program of direct controls.

4. The use of pollution charges as a means of cleaning up the environment
   a. is the predominant form of pollution control in Canada.
   b. is likely to be more efficient than a system of direct controls.
   c. would be most appropriate in situations calling for sudden action, such as a serious smog condition.
   d. would have exactly the same effects on the volume of pollution as do subsidies for pollution-control equipment.

5. Compared with a system of direct controls, pollution charges
   a. are basically a "carrot" approach, relying on everyone's voluntary co-operation.
   b. are likely to lead to an equal percentage reduction in emissions from all pollution sources.
   c. will not reduce pollution, as firms will simply pass on these costs to their consumers with no impact on output levels.
   d. offer an incentive for continually reducing emissions, rather than reducing them just to some mandated level.

Test B

Circle T or F for True or False as appropriate.

1. Pollution has become a serious problem only since World War II.   T F

2. Only rivers in capitalist economies catch fire.   T F

3. Pollution is an example of a detrimental externality.   T F

4. Most public policies to control pollution in Canada have taken the form of direct controls rather than financial incentives   T F

5. When considering public policies to limit discharges of wastes into a river basin, an equal percentage reduction by all polluters is likely to be the most economically efficient policy.   T F

6. Emissions charges to limit pollution are a practical alternative, appropriate for all situations.   T F

7. Pollution charges imposed on monopolist firms will have no effect on the volume of their polluting activity, because they will simply pass on the higher costs in the form of higher prices.   T F

8. Auctioning off emissions permits is an example of using the price system to clean up the environment.   T F

9. Subsidies and taxes are likely to have the same effect on the volume of pollution.   T F

10. Efficiency considerations strongly suggest that society should spend enough to reduce all pollution to zero.   T F

SUPPLEMENTARY EXERCISES

1. The Great California Drought

During 1976 and 1977, northern California suffered from below-normal rainfall. The effects of the water shortage became progressively more severe, leading to the widespread adoption of various schemes for water rationing.

   Throughout 1976 many public and private agencies joined together in a campaign to encourage voluntary reduction in water usage. As the drought persisted, many areas established quotas for water usage, based usually on family size, with stiff increases in price for water consumption in excess of the quota. (The dashed line in Figure 34-2 illustrates such a quota–high-price scheme. The dashed line indicates the total water bill. The price per gallon is given by the slope of the line.)

a. The quota–high-price scheme offers a strong incentive to limit water consumption to the basic quota, but there is little monetary incentive to reduce water consumption below the quota. Economist Milton Friedman suggested that rather than impose quotas with high prices for excess consumption, water districts should charge a very high price for *all* water consumption, with a rebate to consumers with especially low water consumption. (See *Newsweek*, March 21, 1977.) The solid line in Figure 34-2 illustrates a possible high-price-rebate scheme. To ensure that a water district has enough money to cover its fixed costs, the position and/or slope of the solid line could be adjusted. Parallel shifts of the solid line would affect the maximum rebate and the no-charge point, but not the price of a gallon of water. Shifts in the slope would change the price. For example, pivoting the solid line on point A would change both the price and the maximum rebate, while leaving the cost of the basic quota unchanged.

   Which pricing scheme has the greater incentive for conserving water? Which scheme is the most equitable?

b. Ross and Judy live in San Francisco. During 1976, in response to the growing concern about

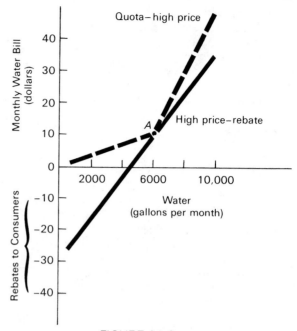

FIGURE 34-2

water conservation, they voluntarily cut their water consumption significantly below the quotas established by other water districts. The San Francisco rationing scheme, adopted in early 1977, mandated that all San Francisco residents reduce their consumption below 1976 levels by the same percentage. How equitable is such a system? What incentives do Ross and Judy have for future voluntary co-operation?

c. In 1965, New York City suffered from a severe drought. Residents of New York City pay for water through city taxes. Individual usage is not metered. What options would be available to reduce water usage in a city like New York that does not meter individual usage? How effective are these options likely to be compared with the options available to a city that does meter water usage?

2. Pollution and Prices

Can any producer simply pass on to his customers any pollution charge imposed on him? Consider the production of gizmos, which cause pollution in direct proportion to the volume of production. The demand for gizmos is given by

$$Q = 180,000 - 10,000 \times P.$$

a. Assume that gizmos are produced by a monopolist with total costs given by

$$TC = 6 \times Q.$$

Plot the demand, marginal-revenue, average-cost,

and marginal-cost curves on a piece of graph paper. What is the monopolist's profit-maximizing level of output, the associated price, and the monopolist's profits?

b. The government now imposes a pollution tax on the monopolist of $2 a gizmo. What happens to output, prices, and profits if the monopolist simply raises his price by $2? Can he do better by charging a different price? What is the new profit-maximizing level of output, price, and the associated profits?

c. Assume now that gizmos are produced by identical small firms under conditions of perfect competition. Each firm produces gizmos with average costs given by

$$AC = 0.00004 \, (Q - 500)^2 + 6.$$

What is the long-run market equilibrium price and quantity? How many firms are in the industry? How many gizmos does each firm produce?

d. Now the government imposes a pollution tax of $2 a gizmo on each producer. What happens in the short run when there are still the same number of firms in the industry? What is the new long-run market equilibrium price and quantity? How many firms will be producing gizmos? How many gizmos does each firm produce?

The Economics of Energy and Natural Resources

LEARNING OBJECTIVES

After completing the material in this chapter you should be able to:

- define, understand, and use correctly the terms and concepts listed below.
- explain why, under perfect competition and in the absence of any increase in the cost of extraction, the price of depletable resources must rise at the rate of interest.
- explain how and why actual prices of depletable resources have behaved differently over most of the twentieth century.

- explain why known reserves for many resources have not tended to fall over time.
- describe the three virtues of rising prices for scarce resources.

IMPORTANT TERMS AND CONCEPTS

Known reserves
Organization of Petroleum Exporting Countries (OPEC)
Rationing
Paradox of growing reserves of finite resources

CHAPTER REVIEW

This chapter discusses the economics of natural resources, with special attention given to the case of oil and energy. Some resources, such as trees and fish, continue to reproduce themselves every year. These resources are called renewable resources. This chapter concentrates on non-renewable or depletable resources such as minerals and oil. In this case there is no reproduction, although in some cases there may be recycling.

Many observers have voiced concern that the world is running out of natural resources. They allege that soon the quantity of resources supplied will not be able to keep up with the quantity of resources demanded and that the result will be massive shortages and chaos. Yet, in a free market we know that the quantity

(1) demanded (*can/can never*) exceed the quantity supplied, because demand and supply will always be brought into equilibrium by adjustments in _____ . This fundamental mechanism of free markets, first discussed in Chapter 4, is as applicable to the supply and demand of scarce resources as it is to any other commodity.

Harold Hotelling first described the special behaviour of the prices of depletable resources in free markets. He discovered that even if the costs of extraction are constant, the price of depletable resources

(2) must rise at a rate equal to the rate of _____ . This result follows from relatively simple considerations. Assets held in the form of bank deposits or bonds earn interest for their owners. Owners of natural-resource reserves expect their asset—the reserves—to earn a similar risk-adjusted return. If increases in the price of future resources offer a less attractive return than do interest rates, resource owners will sell their resources and put the money in the bank. This action decreases the current price of resources. There will be a continuing incentive to sell, with downward pressure on current resource prices, until the return from holding resources again provides a return competitive with interest rates. Similarly, if the future return from holding resources is expected to be extremely high, more investors will want to buy resource inventories, thereby depressing current supply and

_____ current prices. These pressures will continue until holding resource inventories again offers a risk-adjusted return comparable to that of investments in the bank.

The theory sketched above suggests that the prices of depletable resources should show a rising trend

(3) at a rate equal to the rate of _____ . But actual data are quite different. For much of the twentieth century the prices of many resources have been essentially steady and some have shown slight declines. Government subsidies, price controls, or the formation of effective producer cartels can make the actual behaviour of prices different from theoretical expectations, especially over short periods of time. Two other factors have been of more long-run importance: (1) the unexpected discovery of resource reserves that were previously not known, and (2) technological progress that has reduced the cost of extraction. Data on known reserves, rather than declining as implied in the literal interpretation of a non-renewable resource, have typically shown slight increases. These increases in reserves reflect the workings of the price system as the pressure for higher prices has induced new exploration. It is the results of new exploration that help to explain actual price behaviour. It is less clear how long one can expect continuing new discoveries. At some time market pressures for increasing resource prices must prevail. However, it is important to remember that this pressure for higher prices is what equates demand and supply, avoids chaos, and facilitates the adjustment to alternative technologies.

Many economists see increasing prices for depletable resources as an important virtue of free markets. Increasing prices help to deal with the problem of declining reserves in three important ways:

(4) 1. Increasing prices (*encourage/discourage*) consumption and waste and provide a(n) (*disincentive/incentive*) for conservation on the part of consumers.

2. Increasing prices (*encourage/discourage*) more efficient use of scarce resources by industry in the production of commodities and provide a(n) (*disincentive/incentive*) for technical innovation and the use of substitutes.

3. Increasing prices (*encourage/discourage*) additional exploration and the exploitation of high-cost sources of supply.

It is after considering these beneficial effects of higher prices that economists are therefore generally mistrustful of the use of price controls to "contain" rising resource prices, although concerns about income distribution and the impact of sudden, large price increases may call for limited forms of intervention. Adjustments in consumption, production, and exploration usually take some time. Thus, the long-run responses to higher prices are likely to be larger than short-run responses. In technical terms, the long-run price elasticities of demand and supply are

(5) (*greater/smaller*) than the short-run elasticities.

The 1974–84 controversy over Canadian oil prices stemmed from four main factors: consumers felt that

(6) (*high/low*) world oil prices were artificial; many workers feared that an oil-price increase would cause

_____ in Canadian manufacturing industries; the federal and provincial governments

were disputing which level of government should get _____ revenues; and the federal

government was concerned that the high degree of _____ ownership would mean that increasing oil-prices would transfer a large amount of income from Canadians to foreigners. Among the problems that resulted from the lag in oil-price increases were cutbacks in oil development, delays in moving to less energy-intensive production methods, and the deterioration in federal/provincial relations.

BASIC EXERCISES

1. Table 35-1 contains data on gross national expenditure and energy consumption for the Canadian economy. Use these data to compute the use of energy and petroleum per thousand dollars of GNE. What has happened to the energy intensity and petroleum intensity of GNE? What factor(s) do you think explain(s) the changes you have computed?
2. Table 35-2 contains a sampling of data on U.S. mineral prices extending over the past century. The top portion of the table contains data on actual prices. Divide each entry by the wholesale price index for the corresponding year to correct for general inflationary trends. What has happened to the real prices of these resources over the past century? When were real prices highest?

SELF-TESTS FOR UNDERSTANDING

Test A

Circle the correct answer.

1. Harold Hotelling argued that, in competitive markets, even if extraction costs are constant the price of depletable resources will rise at a rate equal to the rate of
   a. inflation.
   b. unemployment.
   c. interest.
   d. growth of real income.
2. Which one of the following would be expected to reduce the price of a natural resource?
   a. A change in interest rates.
   b. The discovery of an effective and less costly substitute.
   c. An increase in the rate of inflation.
   d. An increase in GNP.
3. Which one of the following is a likely response to higher prices for natural resources?
   a. Decreased attention given to the search for lower-cost substitutes.
   b. More current consumption as individuals become concerned about the availability of future supplies.
   c. Decreased exploration for new resource deposits.
   d. The use of higher-cost extraction technology to get at previously uneconomic sources of supply.
4. Rising resource prices can be a virtue as they lead to all but which one of the following?
   a. Increased conservation.
   b. Increased use of substitutes.
   c. Increased waste.
   d. Increased innovation.
5. Data for the twentieth century suggest that, when measured in relation to current consumption, the known reserves of some natural resources

TABLE 35-1

Year	Real GNE *(billions of 1971 $)	Energy Consumption (petajoules)		Energy Consumption (petajoules per thousand dollars of GNE)	
		All Energy	Petroleum	All Energy	Petroleum
1962	58	4045	1824	_____	_____
1970	88	7069	3301	_____	_____
1971	94	7390	3414	_____	_____
1972	100	7845	3624	_____	_____
1973	108	8262	3776	_____	_____
1974	112	8634	3877	_____	_____
1975	113	8412	3785	_____	_____
1976	120	8728	3867	_____	_____
1977	122	9009	3928	_____	_____
1978	126	9336	4005	_____	_____
1979	130	9658	4153	_____	_____
1980	132	9808	4070	_____	_____
1981	136	9627	3832	_____	_____
1982	130	9223	3403	_____	_____

Sources: Bank of Canada *Review*; Canadian Petroleum Association *Statistical Handbook.*

TABLE 35-2

U.S. RESOURCE PRICES

	1880	1890	1900	1910	1920	1930	1940	1950	1960	1970	1981
Copper[b]	17.7	15.2	16.0	12.7	17.5	13.0	11.3	21.2	32.1	57.7	85.1
Bauxite[c]		3.26	3.87	4.81	6.23	5.83	5.93	6.78	11.20	13.09	13.87
Manganese[a]					114.6	55.4	65.2	102.2	149.4	110.1	256.7
Chromite[c]			10.01	13.31	17.97	23.80	10.84	45.20	35.64	45.52	55.00
Tungsten[d]		0.20	0.38	0.38	0.60	1.03	1.41	1.12	2.03	6.46
Molybdenum[d]				0.49	0.55	0.68	0.85	1.25	1.72	7.48
Wholesale prices[a]	33.6	29.0	29.0	36.3	79.7	44.5	40.5	79.0	93.7	110.3	269.81
Copper	___	___	___	___	___	___	___	___	___	___	___
Bauxite		___	___	___	___	___	___	___	___	___	___
Manganese					___	___	___	___	___	___	___
Chromite			___	___	___	___	___	___	___	___	___
Tungsten		___	___	___	___	___	___	___	___	___	___
Molybdenum				___	___	___	___	___	___	___	___

[a] price index, 1967 = 100
[b] cents per pound
[c] dollars per ton
[d] dollars per pound

Source: 1880–1970: *Natural Resource Commodities: A Century of Statistics*, Robert S. Manthy, published for Resources for the Future by the Johns Hopkins University Press, 1978; 1981: *Minerals Yearbook*, Vol. 1, *Metals and Minerals*, Bureau of Mines, Department of the Interior, U.S. GPO.

a. have declined.
b. have remained roughly constant.
c. have increased.

6. Data for the twentieth century suggest that the real price of natural resources has
   a. corresponded closely to the Hotelling principle.
   b. declined continuously.
   c. been affected by a variety of other influences.

7. Effective price ceilings for natural resources are likely to
   a. provide an increased incentive for further exploration.
   b. shift the demand curve to the left.
   c. induce consumers to conserve.
   d. lead to resource shortages.

8. Over a long period of time, as compared to a short period of time, the demand for oil and other natural resources is probably
   a. less price elastic.
   b. more price elastic.
   c. of similar price elasticity.

9. The best measure of the scarcity of a particular resource is
   a. its price.
   b. the volume of known reserves.
   c. the ratio of reserves to current consumption.

d. the difference between the quantity demanded and the quantity supplied.

Test B

Circle T or F for True or False as appropriate.

1. If left unchecked, the free-market mechanism will cause the demand for natural resources to exceed supply.   T F

2. For much of the twentieth century the relative prices for most natural resources have shown dramatic increases.   T F

3. Hotelling argued that, in free markets and with constant extraction costs, the price of natural resources will rise at the rate of inflation.   T F

4. The unexpected discovery of new resource deposits would reduce prices and delay the onset of the Hotelling pricing principle.   T F

5. Rising prices can help control resource depletion as they induce firms and households to conserve.   T F

6. By effectively shifting the supply curve to the right, government subsidies can delay the depletion of natural resources forever.   **T F**

7. Higher resource prices will discourage the use of substitutes.   **T F**

8. Evidence to date suggests that higher energy prices have not reduced energy consumption. **T F**

9. Since OPEC first flexed its muscles in 1973, the real price of oil has only increased.   **T F**

10. When measured against current consumption, the reserves of some resources have actually shown slight increases since 1960.   **T F**

SUPPLEMENTARY READING

You might enjoy reading any of the following:
Robert M. Solow, "The Economics of Resources or the Resources of Economics," *American Economic Review*, May 1974, pp. 1–14. A non-technical discussion of the implications of the Hotelling pricing principle.

William J. Baumol and Sue Ann Batey Blackman, "Unprofitable Energy Is Squandered Energy," *Challenge, the Magazine of Economic Affairs*, July/August 1980, pp. 28–35. A non-technical discussion of why alternative technologies involving subsidies may actually use more energy than they save.

You might enjoy the following exchange about limits to growth:

Council on Environmental Quality and the Department of State (Gerald O. Barney, study director). *Global 2000 Report to the President of the U.S., Entering the 21st Century* (U.S. GPO, 1980–1981); also (Pergamon Press, 1980–1981).

Herman Kahn and Julian L. Simon, editors, *The Resourceful Earth: A Response to 'Global 2000'* (Basil Blackwell, 1984).

VII

The Distribution and Growth of Income

Input Prices: Interest, Rent, and Profits

36

LEARNING OBJECTIVES

After completing the material in this chapter you should be able to:

- define, understand, and use correctly the terms and concepts listed below.
- explain why the demand curve for a factor of production is the downward-sloping portion of its marginal revenue product curve.
- explain why the demand for inputs is a derived demand.
- distinguish between investment and capital.
- explain how changes in interest rates may affect the profitability of specific investment decisions and hence the demand for funds.
- distinguish between land rents and economic rents.
- identify input units that receive economic rent, given supply curves of various slopes.
- explain why the fact that apartment buildings need to be maintained and that they can be reproduced at close to constant cost implies that, in the long

run, rent-control measures will be self-defeating.
- explain why, in the real world, profits are likely to offer returns in excess of the rate of interest.

IMPORTANT TERMS AND CONCEPTS

Factors of production
Entrepreneurship
Marginal productivity principle
Marginal physical product
Marginal revenue product
Derived demand
Investment
Capital
Interest
Discounting
Marginal land
Economic rent
Entrepreneurs
Risk bearing
Invention versus innovation

CHAPTER REVIEW

The material in this chapter initiates the discussion of input prices by considering what determines the rental price of land, the rental price of money, and the income of entrepreneurs. If this material is combined with the material in Chapter 37 on wages—or the rental price for labour services—and material in Chapter 35 on the price of natural resources, one has a complete theory of income distribution based on marginal

(1) _____ . The material in this chapter and in Chapter 37 builds upon our earlier discussion of optimal input use by firms. In Chapter 22 we saw that the demand for factors of production can be derived from profit-maximizing considerations. A firm is willing to pay for labour, land, natural resources, and so forth because it can use these factors to produce and sell output. In Chapter 22 we also learned that the demand curve for a particular factor of production is simply the downward-sloping portion of the marginal

_____ product curve.

Interest rates adjust to balance the demand for funds by borrowers and the supply of funds from lenders.
(2) The demand curve for funds has a (*negative/positive*) slope, indicating that at a lower rate of interest people will want to borrow (*less/more*). The supply curve of funds will have a (*negative/positive*) slope, indicating that a (*higher/lower*) interest rate is necessary to induce lenders to increase the supply of loans. An effective usury ceiling would impose an interest rate (*above/below*) the market clearing rate as determined by the intersection of

the _____ and _____ curves.

The demand for funds for business borrowing derives from a consideration of the profitability of investment projects. In earlier chapters we talked about capital and labour as factors of production. Investment projects add to the stock of capital. The profitability of investment projects is another way of referring to the marginal revenue product of more capital. The profitability of investment projects is complicated because most projects require dollar outlays immediately while offering returns sometime in the future. To evaluate the profitability of an investment project we need some way of comparing dollars now with dollars in the future. Economists and

(3) business people compare future and present dollars through a process called _____ .
As explained in an appendix to this chapter, this process relies on interest-rate calculations, Higher interest rates will mean that (*fewer/more*) investment projects will be profitable. Thus higher interest rates will be associated with a (*higher/lower*) quantity of funds demanded and imply a (*negatively/positively*) sloped demand curve for business borrowing. (Remember the distinction between real and nominal interest rates first introduced in Chapter 6. Conclusions here about the impact of interest rates on the demand for funds refer primarily to the impact of real interest rates.)

The first thing to remember when considering the notion of *rent* is that economists use this term in a very special way that is different from everyday usage. Most of the rent that you may pay for an apartment
(4) (*is/is not*) economic rent. Economic rent refers to the earnings of a factor of production that exceed the minimum amount necessary to induce the desired quantity of that factor to be supplied.

If the supply curve of some factor, like land, is really vertical, it means that the factor would be willing to work for as little as nothing. It also means that it is impossible to duplicate this factor at any cost; otherwise a high enough price would induce an increase in supply and the supply curve would not be vertical. In the case
(5) of a vertical supply curve, (*some/all*) of any market price would be economic rent. If the supply curve of some factor is a horizontal line, the market price will reflect exactly what is necessary to induce any supply. An economist

would say that the factor receives _____ economic rent.
An upward-sloping supply curve means that higher prices will induce an increase in supply, but there will
(6) be some units of supply that would have been present at lower prices. In this case (*most/all*) units of the factor will receive economic rent. In fact, it is only the marginal unit, the unit on the supply curve at the market equilibrium price, that earns no economic rent. The market price is as high as it is to induce this last unit to supply itself. All other units would have been available at a lower price and thus (*part/all*) of their earnings are economic rent. Land is a traditional input to use when talking about rent, but remember that land is not the only factor to earn economic rent. Anyone who would stay in a particular job for less pay, because he or she likes the work or the location, or for any other reason (*is/is not*) earning some economic rent.

When considering land rentals it is clear that not all land is the same: some parcels are more productive or better located than others. Economists would expect that land rentals, the price for using a piece of land for a period of time, will adjust to reflect these differences. More productive land that produces the same
(7) output at lower cost will receive a (*higher/lower*) land rent. In equilibrium, rents should adjust so that the total cost

of producing the same quantity of output, including land rents, will be _____ on all parcels of land. If not, there is a clear incentive to use the land with lower total cost. This incentive to switch parcels increases the rent on the originally (*low/high*)-cost piece of land and decreases rent on the other pieces of land. The process stops only when land rentals have adjusted to again equate total cost.

(8)　　As with any other productive factor, an increase in the demand for goods produced with land will (*decrease/increase*) the demand for land. Poor-quality land, whose use was unprofitable at lower output prices, will now become profitable to use. Thus, more land will be used, and land rents will again adjust to equalize the costs of production on all parcels. As a result, the rent on previously used, higher-quality land will (*increase/decrease*). An additional part of the response to an increased demand for land is likely to be (*more/less*) intensive use of existing land.

　　Profits are a residual item after revenues have been used to pay other costs: labour, material inputs, interest on borrowed funds, and taxes. Profits also represent the return on equity investments in a firm.[1] In a world of perfect certainty, capitalists should expect that the profits on their investments will offer them a return that is just equal to the rate of interest. The rate of interest would be the opportunity cost of their equity investment in the firm. Any higher return would be competed away. Any lower return would lead some funds to be invested elsewhere in the pursuit of returns at least equal to the rate of interest. (Remember that in competitive markets, economic profits are equal to zero in long-run equilibrium.)

　　In the real world, investments are not certain. Many business investments look like uncertain gambles. If entrepreneurs dislike taking risks, then profits will have to offer them the expectation of returns that are

(9) (*greater/less*) than the rate of interest. Profits that are the result of monopoly power would be (*greater/less*) than the rate of interest. Finally, successful (*innovation/invention*) will often give an entrepreneur temporary monopoly profits and will also lead to a rate of profit that is (*greater/less*) than the rate of interest. The effects of taxing profits will depend upon whether profits are mostly economic rents or mostly a necessary return to attract entrepreneurial talent.

BASIC EXERCISE

This exercise is designed to illustrate how differences in land rents reflect differences in land productivity.

　　Dionne is considering her summer employment opportunities. She can work as a checker at the local grocery store for as many hours as she wants, earning $7.50 an hour. Dionne is also considering raising flowers on one of several plots of land. She figures that she must spend at least 20 hours a week on her flowers—weeding, watering, etc. If she spends more time, she will get more flowers and earn more money, but at a diminishing rate. Dionne has decided that she will spend time growing flowers as long as she earns at least $7.50 an hour.

1. Table 36-1 has information on projected weekly total revenue and hours worked for plot A. Fill in column 3 of Table 36-1 to determine how many hours Dionne should spend gardening. Dionne

   should spend _____ hours a week gardening.

2. Complete Table 36-2 to compute Dionne's projected weekly profit. (Note that when figuring her profit, Dionne appropriately views her wage of $7.50 an hour as a cost. It is the opportunity cost of her time.)

[1]Equity refers here to the amount of their own money the owners have tied up in the firm. Specifically, if they sold the firm and paid off their creditors, the amount left over is their equity.

TABLE 36-1

PROJECTED REVENUE FROM USING PLOT A

Hours Worked	Total Revenue	Marginal Revenue
20	$220	
25	265	_____
30	305	_____
35	340	_____
40	370	_____

TABLE 36-2

PROJECTED PROFIT

1. Total revenue	_____
2. Land rent	$30
3. Labour cost*	_____
4. Projected profit (1) − (2) − (3)	_____

*Labour cost = $7.50 per hour times the optimal number of hours.

TABLE 36-3

PROJECTED REVENUE
FROM USING PLOT B

Hours Worked	Total Revenue	Marginal Revenue
20	$200	
25	245	_____
30	285	_____
35	320	_____
40	350	_____

TABLE 36-4

MAXIMUM LAND RENT FOR PLOT B

1. Total revenue	_____
2. Labour cost	_____
3. Profit from plot A	_____
4. Maximum land rent	
(1) − (2) − (3)	_____

3. Plot B is less productive; the soil is not quite as good. As a result, total revenue from using plot B is $20 less than the comparable figure for Table 36-1. See Table 36-3. If Dionne uses plot B, how many

hours should she work? _____
hours.

4. Complete Table 36-4 to determine the maximum rent Dionne would be willing to pay for the use of plot B, given that she can use plot A for $30 a week. How does the difference in land rents relate to the differences in land productivity?

SELF-TESTS FOR UNDERSTANDING

Test A

Circle the correct answer.

1. The demand curve for productive factors is the downward-sloping portion of the relevant
   a. marginal physical product curve.
   b. marginal-cost curve.
   c. marginal revenue product curve.
   d. average-cost curve.

2. Profit-maximizing firms will use more of a productive factor as long as the price of the factor

is less than its
   a. marginal physical product.
   b. marginal cost.
   c. marginal revenue product.
   d. average product.

3. The concept of discounting suggests that when compared with a dollar next year, a dollar today is worth
   a. less.
   b. more.
   c. the same.

4. Which of the following is an example of investment as opposed to capital?
   a. The fleet of 747s owned by Air Canada.
   b. Julia's purchase of 100 shares of Xerox stock.
   c. The five apartment buildings owned by Ralph.
   d. The expanded warehouse facilities that Norma will have built this year.

5. Parcel of land B can be used to raise corn at a cost of $50,000. The same amount of corn can be raised on parcel P for $75,000. An economist would expect the rent on parcel B to exceed that on parcel P by
   a. $25,000.
   b. $50,000.
   c. $75,000.
   d. $125,000.

6. Marginal land refers to land that
   a. is most productive for growing any given crop.
   b. is on the borderline of being used in productive activity.
   c. earns economic rent.
   d. borders highways and rural areas.

7. An input will earn pure economic rent if the supply curve for the input is
   a. horizontal.
   b. upward sloping.
   c. vertical.

8. Which of the following individuals are earning economic rent?
   a. Ruth, who says, "If this job paid any less I'd quit; it wouldn't be worth the hassle."
   b. Sergio, who says, "This job is so interesting I'd work here even for a lot less."
   c. Nick, whose purchase of an apartment building should bring him a return equal to the rate of interest.
   d. Sophia, who is expecting a substantial profit from her investment in the manufacture of solar-energy panels to compensate her for the risks she is taking.

9. Which of the following is not a reason why, in the long run, profits might be greater than the rate of interest?
   a. Monopolies will earn profits in excess of the opportunity cost of capital.
   b. Nominal profits must be greater than the

nominal rate of interest to allow for the loss of purchasing power from inflation.

  c. Risk-bearing, safety-conscious entrepreneurs often demand that they earn profits greater than what they could get from relatively safe investments at the rate of interest.

  d. Innovation is a relatively risky undertaking and, if successful, often results in a temporary period of monopoly power.

10. Higher taxes on profits will have little impact if
  a. profits are mostly economic rent.
  b. profits are equal to nominal interest rates.
  c. profits are growing.
  d. the supply curve for entrepreneurial talent is horizontal.

Test B

Circle T of F for True or False as appropriate.

1. The demand curve for a factor of production is identical to its curve of marginal physical productivity.　　　　　　　　　　　T F

2. Interest rates represent the market price for the use of funds.　　　　　　　　　　　T F

3. Discounting means using the rate of interest to compare future and present dollars.　　　T F

4. The factories that the Ford Motor Company uses to produce cars are an example of investment rather than capital.　　　　　　　　　　　T F

5. According to economists, only land earns economic rent.　　　　　　　　　　　T F

6. Inputs available in perfectly elastic supply will earn no economic rent.　　　　　　　　T F

7. The rent on any piece of land will equal the difference between production costs on that piece of land and production costs on the next-best available piece of land.　　　　　　　T F

8. The law of diminishing returns implies that an increase in the demand for land will actually reduce the rent paid on most parcels of land. T F

9. The reason that most rent-control laws have adverse effects in the long run is that the long-run supply of structures, as opposed to land, is likely to be quite elastic.　　　　　　　　　T F

10. Economic theory proves that the rate of profits must equal the rate of interest.　　　　T F

Appendix A: Discounting and Present Value

LEARNING OBJECTIVE

After completing this exercise you should be able to use discounting, or present-value, calculations when considering investment decisions.

IMPORTANT TERMS AND CONCEPTS

Discounting
Present value

BASIC EXERCISE

Eric has an opportunity to purchase a machine to make gyros. The machine costs $4000 now and is expected to last for two years. After other expenses, Eric expects to net $2000 next year and $2500 in the following year. Assume that Eric has the $4000 to buy the machine now. Is it a good investment?

1. Fill in the column of Table 36–5 to compute the present value of costs and returns on the assumption that the rate of interest is 10 percent.

2. Add up the present value of the returns and compare this sum with the present value of the cost.

   Which is greater? _____ . Should Eric purchase the machine?

   _____

3. Assume now that the rate of interest is 5 percent. Fill in the relevant column of the table to compute the present value of the returns at a rate of interest of 5 percent.

4. Sum the present value of the returns and compare this sum with the present value of the cost. Which is

   greater? _____ Should Eric

   purchase the machine? _____

5. (Optional) Your responses to Questions 1 through 4 were based on the assumption that Eric had the $4000 initially. If the present value of the returns

TABLE 36-5

ERIC'S GYRO MACHINE

Time	Item	Amount	Present Value* $i = 5$ percent	Present Value* $i = 10$ percent
Now	Cost	$4000	_____	_____
One year	Return	2000	_____	_____
Two years	Return	2500	_____	_____
	Present value of all returns		_____	_____
	Net present value of project		_____	_____

*Present value $= \dfrac{\text{dollars in } n \text{ years}}{(1 + i)^n}$

= (dollars in the nth year) divided by (1 plus the rate of interest multiplied by itself n times)

TABLE 36-6

CAN ERIC DO AS WELL BY INVESTING $4000 AT THE RATE OF INTEREST?

	Interest Rate	
	5 percent	10 percent
1. Initial deposit	$4000	$4000
2. Interest after one year (5 percent and 10 percent of line 1)	_____	_____
3. Balance after one year (line 1 plus line 2)	_____	_____
4. Withdrawal after one year*	$2000	$2000
5. New balance (line 3 minus line 4)	_____	_____
6. Interest during second year (5 percent and 10 percent of line 5)	_____	_____
7. Balance after second year (line 5 plus line 6)	_____	_____

Compare line 7 with the $2500 Eric would have received in the second year if he had bought the gyro machine. Line 7 should be greater (less) if the net present value of the project in Table 36-5 is negative (positive). That is, if the net present value of the project is negative, Eric will do better by making a financial investment at the given rate of interest.

*This $2000 matches the return after one year from the gyro investment.

exceeds the present value of the cost, it means that Eric can do better by undertaking the investment than by investing in financial assets that yield the rate of interest we used to compute the present values. If the present value of the returns is less than the present value of the cost, it means that Eric would do better with a financial investment. You can verify that this is the case by filling in the missing parts of Table 36-6 for interest rates of 5 and 10 percent.

6. (Optional) What if Eric had to borrow the money? Would the same sorts of calculations be sufficient to help you decide whether or not he should borrow the money? The answer is yes. The reason is that while figuring the present value of the returns, you are accounting for appropriate interest payments whether Eric has the money or not. If Eric does not have the money, he will need to pay a lender. Even if he does have the money he will need to "pay" himself as much as he might have earned in some other investment. That is, he will need to meet the opportunity cost of his own money. Fill in the missing parts of Table 36-7, which has been constructed to illustrate just this point.

Table 36–7

WHAT IF ERIC HAD TO BORROW THE $4000?

	Interest Rate	
	5 percent	10 percent
1. Amount borrowed	$4000	$4000
2. Interest due at end of first year	$ 200	$ 400
3. Cash flow from investment	$2000	$2000
4. Net cash flow after interest payment (line 3 minus line 2)	_____	_____
5. Interest earned during second year by investing net cash flow (5 percent and 10 percent of line 4)	_____	_____
6. Cash flow from investment	$2500	$2500
7. Total at end of second year (line 4 plus line 5 plus line 6)	_____	_____
8. Interest due at end of second year	$ 200	$ 400
9. Loan repayment	$4000	$4000
10. Net (line 7 minus line 8 and line 9)	_____	_____

The crucial question is whether the gyro investment offers any return after paying back the loan with interest. Any dollars left over are pure profit for Eric since he did not invest any of his own money. It should be true that Eric will have a positive (negative) net if the present value of returns is greater (less) than the present value of costs. Is it?

(The entries on line 10 are dollars in the second year. What is the present value of these dollars? How do these present values compare with the net present values calculated in Table 36–5 above?)

To summarize

a. Present-value calculations use interest rates to transform dollars in the future into their equivalent today.

b. Comparing the present value of returns and cost is a good way to evaluate investment opportunities.

c. Comparing present value of returns and cost is a good procedure whether you have to borrow the money or not, assuming that you can borrow or lend at the same rate of interest you are using in your present-value calculations.

d. If the present value of returns equals the present value of cost, an investment opportunity offers the same return as investing at the rate of interest.

SUPPLEMENTARY EXERCISE

Can You Share in Monopoly Profits?
Assume for the moment that the major oil companies are able to exercise considerable monopoly power and, as a result, earn substantial monopoly profits on their investments, far in excess of the rate of interest. Can you share these profits and earn the same high rate of return by buying oil company stocks?

What determines the price of oil company stocks? An economist would expect the market price to be close to the present value of the future returns from owning the stock, that is, close to the present value of expected future dividends and capital gains. Thus if dividends are high because of huge monopoly profits, the price of the stock will be _____ . If huge monopoly profits and the resulting future dividends were known for sure, what rate of return do you think you could earn by buying oil company stocks? Just who does earn those monopoly profits?

The Labour Market and Wages

37

LEARNING OBJECTIVES

After completing the material in this chapter you should be able to:
- define, understand, and use correctly the terms and concepts listed below.
- explain how income and substitution effects influence the slope of the supply curve of labour.
- explain how the demand for labour is derived from a firm's profit-maximizing decisions about the use of factors of production.
- use demand and supply curves to determine the equilibrium wage and employment in a competitive labour market.
- explain why wages for some individuals contain substantial economic rent.
- discuss how human-capital theory explains the observed correlation between more education and higher wages.
- discuss some of the alternative views of the role of education.
- use demand and supply curves to analyse the impact of minimum-wage legislation.
- describe the history of unions in Canada.
- use demand and supply curves to describe the alternative goals that labour unions might follow.

- distinguish between a monopsonist and a monopolist.
- describe the important differences between public and private sector strikes.
- describe the proposals called corporatism and industrial democracy.

IMPORTANT TERMS AND CONCEPTS

Minimum-wage law
Income and substitution effects
Backward-bending supply curve
Economic rent
Investments in human capital
Human-capital theory
Dual labour markets
Union
Industrial and craft unions
Closed shop
Union shop
Monopsony
Bilateral monopoly
Collective bargaining
Mediation
Arbitration
Public-sector bargaining

CHAPTER REVIEW

In a competitive market without minimum wages or unions, wages and employment—the price and quantity of labour services—will be determined by the interaction of the demand for and the supply of labour services and can be analysed with tools that should now be familiar—demand and supply curves.

The supply of labour comes from individual decisions to work. Individual decisions to supply work are simultaneously decisions to forgo leisure. Thus, a decision to supply less labour is simultaneously a decision to

(1) demand _____ . At higher wages, the same number of working hours will mean a larger income. If leisure is not an inferior good, people are apt to demand (*more/less*) leisure as their income increases. This suggests that the supply of labour might (*increase/decrease*) as wages increase. This is called the (*income/substitution*) effect of higher wages but it is only part of the story.

Higher wages do increase the opportunity cost of an hour of leisure. As a result we expect that as wages

(2) increase the substitution effect will lead people to work (*more/less*). The ultimate effect of increased wages comes from the sum of the income and substitution effects. Statistical evidence suggests that at low wages the

_____ effect predominates and labour supply (*increases/decreases*) with an increase in

wages, while at high wages the _____ effect is stronger and labour supply may

_____ with an increase in wages. The response of individuals to a change in wages, the income and substitution effects, helps to determine the (*slope/position*) of the supply curve of labour. Other factors, such as the size of the available working population and nonmonetary aspects of any jobs, help to determine the

_____ of the labour-supply curve.

The demand for labour comes from the decisions of firms to use labour as one of many factors of production. Labour services are valuable to a firm because they add to output and, it is hoped, to profits. Thus the demand for labour is a derived demand. Chapter 22's discussion of how a profit-maximizing firm makes optimal decisions about the use of factors of production showed us that a firm should use more of any factor as long as the addition to revenue exceeds the addition to cost or, in technical terms, as long as the marginal revenue product of the factor is greater than the marginal cost of the factor. The demand curve for labour is derived from the marginal revenue product curve. The curve has a negative slope because of the law of diminishing marginal returns.

In competitive markets, equilibrium wages and employment are determined by the intersection of the

(3) market demand and supply curves, which come from the horizontal summation of firms' (*demand/supply*) curves

and individuals' _____ curves. Any factor that causes a shift in either curve will change equilibrium wages and employment. For example, an increase in the demand for a firm's output or a technological innovation that increases the productivity of labour will shift the (*demand/supply*) curve and lead to (*higher/lower*) wages, employment, or both.

Observations from the real world show that education and wages are positively correlated. That is, people with more education typically earn higher wages. Human-capital theory views these higher wages as the return to higher productivity from investments in human capital—that is, the time, money, and effort spent on schooling. Other theories of the effects of education on earnings offer alternative viewpoints to explain the correlation of education and earnings.

In some cases the market determination of wages and employment is interfered with by mandating a

(4) legal floor on wage rates, or a(n) _____ wage. Chapter 4 discussed the effects of price floors. One should expect similar results from minimum wages. To be effective the minimum wage must be higher than the market wage. The imposition of a minimum wage will (*increase/decrease*) the volume of employment as firms move backward and to the left along their demand curves for labour. At the same time the promise of higher wages is apt to increase the (*demand/supply*) of labour. The net result will be higher wages and income for those lucky enough to have jobs, but only frustration for many others who are seeking work.

(5) Minimum-wage laws affect primarily (*skilled/unskilled*) labour markets. A major noncompetitive feature in

many skilled labour markets is the existence of labour _____ . Currently, about 40 percent of Canadian workers belong to a union. The development of unions in Canada can be traced back to the small craft unions in the early 1800s. The first widely successful confederation of labour in Canada was formed about 100 years ago. Significant growth in union membership occurred during the 1940s, after developments such as a law in 1939 that made firing pro-union employees illegal.

In some labour markets, unions are the only supplier of labour services; that is, they are a

(6) (*monopolist/monopsonist*). As such, they face a trade-off between wages and employment just as a monopoly supplier of widgets faces a trade-off between price and output. Geometrically, a union, as a monopolist, can choose

any point on the relevant _____ curve for labour. The trade-off between wages and employment comes because the demand curve for labour has a negative slope. A union might be able to raise both wages and employment if it can shift the demand curve for labour to the (*right/left*). Feather-bedding and other restrictive work practices are examples of such attempts. (In terms of efforts to increase wages and income, do not limit your conception of unions to the Canadian Labour Congress. Many professional organizations, such as the Canadian Medical Association, also attempt to limit supply. When effective, these organizations will raise the wages and incomes of their members.)

Sometimes a union, as a monopolistic supplier of labour, faces a single buyer of labour services. When

(7) one buyer constitutes the entire market demand, the buyer is called a _____ . Both monopolists and monopsonists realize that their decisions about quantity must at the same time affect

_____ . Monopolists who want to sell more must accept a (*higher/lower*) price and

monopsonists who want to buy more must pay a _____ price. If a monopsonist faces a

monopolist, then the whole market has only _____ participants. The technical term for

this situation is _____ monopoly. Each will consider the actions of the other, and, as for oligopoly, the outcome is difficult to predict.

When union and management sit down to decide on the terms and conditions of employment, they are

(8) engaging in _____ _____ . This process will decide not only wages but also fringe benefits, overtime premiums, grievance procedures, and a host of other details. If both sides cannot come to an

agreement and wish to avoid a strike they may agree to _____ or _____ . If the middleman only helps labour and management to reach an agreement but has no power to enforce a

settlement, he is called a(n) _____ If the middleman listens to the arguments of both

sides and then also makes the final decisions, he is called a(n) _____ .

In most cases a strike against a private firm involves only workers and management of the company concerned, with little adverse effects on the general public. A strike by public employees, however, may affect the general population. Because of possible impacts on the public interest, the right to strike by public employees is

(9) often _____ .

BASIC EXERCISE

This problem illustrates the determination of wages and employment in both a competitive market and a market monopolized by a labour union.

Tony runs a small company, Bearpaw Boots, that manufactures hiking boots. Table 37-1 shows the total output of boots per month for different quantities of labour.
1. Fill in column 3 by using the data in column 2 to compute the marginal physical product of each additional worker.
2. Tony can sell boots for $60 a pair. Each boot contains $20 worth of leather, leaving $40 for wages or profits. As Tony has a small firm, the price is unaffected by the quantity that he sells. Fill in column 4 by computing the marginal revenue product of each worker. Be sure to use the $40 net figure rather than the $60 gross.
3. Tony is interested in maximizing profits. How many workers should he employ if monthly wages are

    $1100? _____

TABLE 37-1

OUTPUT FIGURES FOR BEARPAW BOOTS

Number of Bootmakers	Total Number of Pairs of Boots per Month	Marginal Physical Product (boots)	Marginal Revenue Product (dollars)
1	60	_____	_____
2	115	_____	_____
3	165	_____	_____
4	210	_____	_____
5	250	_____	_____
6	285	_____	_____
7	315	_____	_____
8	340	_____	_____
9	360	_____	_____
10	375	_____	_____

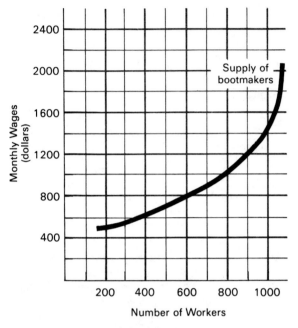

FIGURE 37-1

INDUSTRY DEMAND FOR AND SUPPLY OF BOOTMAKERS

4. Show that your answer to Question 3 maximizes profits by computing total profits for one more and for one less worker.
5. Figure 37-1 shows the supply of bootmakers for the entire industry. Assume that there are 100 competitive firms just like Tony's. Using your data on the marginal revenue product for a typical firm, plot the market demand for bootmakers. What is the equilibrium market wage and employment?

_____ How many workers should

Tony employ? _____ What are

Tony's profits?_____
6. Assume now that the International Association of Bootmakers has been successful in unionizing all bootmakers. In order to evaluate possible alternative goals, the union has asked you to use your knowledge of the industry demand curve to answer the following questions:
   a. If union membership is limited to 400 persons, what is the maximum monthly wage the union

   can get from employers? _____
   b. If the union wage is set at $700 a month, what is the maximum amount of employment?

   _____
   c. (Harder) What wage and employment combination will maximize total wage payments?

   _____

Test A

Circle the correct answer.

1. A change in which of the following will affect the slope of the labour-supply curve?
   a. An increase in the working-age population.
   b. A technological innovation that increases labour productivity.
   c. An increase in the price of a competitive firm's output.
   d. An increase in the willingness of people to trade higher money incomes for more leisure.
2. A change in which of the following will affect the demand for labour by affecting the marginal physical product of labour?
   a. The demand for a firm's output.
   b. The amount of other factors of production per worker.
   c. The supply of labour.
   d. The minimum wage.
3. A change in which of the following will affect the demand for labour by affecting the marginal revenue product of labour?
   a. The demand for a firm's output.
   b. Union militancy.
   c. The supply of labour.
   d. The minimum wage.
4. Historical data that show a declining work week along with rising real wages are probably reflecting
   a. minimum-wage laws.
   b. the income effect of higher wages.
   c. the substitution effect of higher wages.
   d. the Rand Formula.
5. The supply curve for schmoos is upward sloping. An increase in the demand for schmoos (the demand curve shifts to the right) will lead to all but which one of the following?
   a. The price of schmoos increases.
   b. The marginal physical product of labour schedule shifts upward.
   c. The marginal revenue product of labour schedule shifts upward.
   d. The demand curve for labour to produce schmoos shifts upward.
   e. More employment and/or higher wages in the schmoo industry.
6. The theory of human capital says that
   a. individuals can repair their own bodies with artificial parts, just like machines.
   b. soon all work will be done by computer-operated robots.
   c. Individual decisions to seek training and new skills can be modelled in the same way as

ordinary investment decisions, involving present costs in the expectation of future returns.

d. slavery is doomed to fail because it is uneconomical.

7. In contrast with unions in Europe, unions in Canada
   a. are much more political.
   b. have resulted in almost twice the level of strike activity found in any other country.
   c. currently involve a smaller percentage of the labour force than do most European unions.

8. A single union that controls the supply of labour to many small firms is a
   a. socialist.
   b. monopsonist.
   c. oligopolist.
   d. monopolist.

9. Which of the following are examples of

   mediation   _____

   arbitration   _____

   strike   _____

   feather-bedding   _____

   work slowdown   _____

   union shop   _____

   closed shop   _____

   a. Public school teachers and the local school board, who have been unable to reach agreement, agree to accept the determination of a three-person board.
   b. Plane schedules are delayed as air traffic controllers "do it by the book" in their handling of planes.
   c. Anyone may seek work at the local meat-packing plant, but once employed they must join the union.
   d. In an attempt to avert a steel strike, the Minister of Labour helps the steelworkers and the steel companies to resolve their differences.
   e. Mine workers start picketing after contract negotiations fail.
   f. none.

Test B

Circle T or F for True or False as appropriate.

1. Information on the marginal revenue product of labour can be used to derive a firm's demand for labour.   T F

2. The "law" of diminishing returns implies that the demand curve for labour will have a negative slope.   T F

3. The income effect of higher wages suggests that the supply of labour schedule may have a positively sloped portion.   T F

4. An increase in wages that increases the quantity of labour supplied is represented as a movement along the supply curve.   T F

5. Raising the minimum wage will raise the income of all people currently earning less than the minimum wage.   T F

6. If a labour union has complete control over the supply of a particular type of labour, it is a monopsonist.   T F

7. A market with a single buyer and a single seller is called an oligopoly.   T F

8. In general there is no conflict between union attempts to maximize wages for current union members and attempts to provide employment for the largest possible number of workers.   T F

9. Statistical evidence suggests that unions have been successful in raising wages by 50 to 100 percent above their competitive level.   T F

10. If a union and employer, unable to reach agreement on a new contract, agree to accept the decision of an impartial third party, they have agreed to settle their differences by arbitration.   T F

11. The Rand Formula made it illegal for workers to be forced to join a union.   T F

Appendix:
The Effects of Union and Minimum Wages Under Monopsony

LEARNING OBJECTIVE

The exercise below is designed to increase your understanding of the material in the appendix to Chapter 37.

IMPORTANT TERMS AND CONCEPTS

Marginal labour costs

BASIC EXERCISE

This problem illustrates what can happen when unorganized workers face a monopsonistic employer.

Assume that Bearpaw Boots (the subject of the Basic Exercise for the chapter) is located in a small, isolated town in New Brunswick and is the sole employer of bootmakers. Tony still sells his boots in a competitive market for a net price of $40. Table 37-2 contains data on what wages Tony must pay to get various numbers of employees.

1. Use the data in columns 1 and 2 of Table 37-2 to plot the supply curve of labour in Figure 37-2. Use the data on the marginal revenue product computed in Table 37-1 to plot the demand curve for labour in Figure 37-2. These curves intersect where wages

   are $_____ and the number of employees

   is _____. Will Tony pay this wage and employ this many workers? (yes/no) Why?

2. Remember, Tony is the only employer of bootmakers in town. As he employs additional workers, he must pay a higher wage not only to each new employee but also to all existing employees. Thus the marginal labour cost of an additional worker is (greater/less) than the wage. Fill in the remaining columns of Table 37-2 to compute Tony's marginal labour costs.

3. Plot the figures on marginal labour costs in Figure 37-2.

4. Tony's profit-maximizing level of employment is

   _____ .

5. What is the lowest wage that Tony must offer in order to attract the profit-maximizing number of

   workers? $_____

6. What are Tony's profits (net revenue minus total

   wages?) $_____

7. If Tony were forced to pay a minimum wage of $1100 a month, what would happen to wages and employment as compared with your answers to

   Questions 4 and 5? _____

8. Would a union necessarily force the minimum-wage solution to Question 7 on Tony? Why or why not?

TABLE 37-2

SUPPLY OF BOOTMAKERS IN A
SMALL ISOLATED TOWN

Number of Bootmakers	Monthly Wage (dollars)	Total Labour Cost (dollars)	Marginal Labour Costs (dollars)
1	300	_____	_____
2	400	_____	_____
3	500	_____	_____
4	600	_____	_____
5	700	_____	_____
6	800	_____	_____
7	900	_____	_____
8	1000	_____	_____
9	1100	_____	_____
10	1200	_____	_____

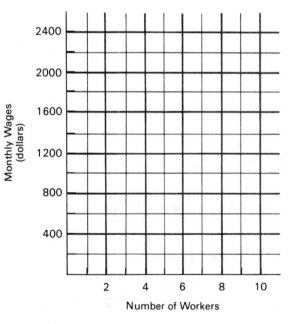

FIGURE 37-2

DEMAND FOR AND SUPPLY OF BOOTMAKERS

Poverty and Inequality 38

CHAPTER REVIEW

The material in this chapter discusses a number of topics concerned with the distribution of income: poverty, inequality in the distribution of income, and discrimination, as it contributes to poverty and inequality.

Discussions of poverty in Canada usually focus on the number of families below the poverty line. In 1983 this dividing line was about $14,000 a year for a family of four living outside a major city. The poverty line is a(n)

(1) (*absolute/relative*) concept of poverty rather than a(n) _____ concept, since it is defined as the level of income at which the average person spends about three-fifths of his or her income on the essentials of life (food, clothing and shelter). About 13.5 percent of families were poor by this definition in 1983.

The facts about the distribution of income can be presented in a number of different ways. Economists

(2) often use a particular form of graphical representation called a(n) _____ curve. To construct such a curve, one first orders families or individuals by income, lowest to highest. Then the cumulative percentage of total income is plotted against the cumulative percentage of families (or individuals). The Lorenz

curve starts at the origin, where zero percent of families have _____ percent of income.

Perfect equality in the distribution of income would result in a Lorenz curve that coincided with the _____ line.

In real economies, with inequality in the distribution of income, the Lorenz curve has a _____ slope and lies (*above/below*) the 45° line. (Can you convince yourself why the Lorenz curve never has a negative slope and why it never crosses the 45° line?) In fact, some researchers measure the degree of inequality by the area between the Lorenz curve and the 45° line as a proportion of the total area under the 45° line. Over the last 20 years this measure shows (*no/very little/significant*) change in the inequality of the distribution of income in Canada.

Canadian income data show that in 1982, families with incomes above $50,000 were in the top 20 percent of the income distribution, while families with incomes below approximately $15,000 were in the bottom 20 percent.

(3) The top 20 percent of families received _____ percent of income while the bottom 20

percent received _____ percent.

Why do incomes differ? The list of reasons is long and includes differences in abilities, intensity of work, risk taking, schooling and training, wage differentials for unpleasant or hazardous work, inherited wealth, luck, and discrimination. Some of the reasons for differences in incomes represent voluntary choices by individuals to work harder, take more risks, or accept unpleasant work. Some people work hard to earn higher incomes. Measures to equalize incomes may adversely affect the work effort of these individuals. In more technical terms, efforts for

(4) greater equality may mean reduced _____ . This important trade-off does not mean that all efforts to increase equality should be abandoned. It does mean that efforts to increase equality have a price and should not be pushed beyond the point where the marginal gains from further equality are worth less than the marginal loss from reduced efficiency. Exactly where this point is reached is the subject of controversy and continuing political debate.

The trade-off between equality and efficiency also suggests that in the fight for greater equality one should choose policies with small rather than large effects on efficiency. Economists would argue that many current welfare programs are inefficient. One important reason is the relatively large reduction in benefits for each additional

(5) dollar of earned income. These high implicit (*marginal/average*) tax rates (*increase/decrease*) the incentive for increased work effort on the part of welfare recipients who are able to work.

Many economists favour replacing the current welfare system with a negative income tax; that is, a system of direct cash grants tied to income levels and linked to the tax system. These schemes usually start with a

(6) minimum guaranteed level of income and a tax rate that specifies the (*increase/decrease*) in the cash grant for every dollar increase in income. A low tax rate will retain significant work incentives; however, a low tax rate also means that grants continue until income is quite high. The point where payments from the government stop and

payments to the government start is called the _____ — _____ level of income. A negative income tax with a low marginal tax rate can offer significantly better work incentives to those currently receiving welfare, but there will be (*positive/negative*) work incentives for those not now on welfare. Recent negative income tax experiments have investigated the size of these negative work incentives and found them to be (*large/small*).

Economic discrimination is defined as a situation in which equal factors of production receive

(7) _____ payments for equal contributions to output. Average differences in income between large social groups, such as men and women or blacks and whites, (*are/are not*) sufficient proof of economic discrimination. These averaged differences tend to (*overstate/understate*) the amount of economic discrimination. To accurately measure the impact of possible discrimination, one needs first to correct for the factors listed above that could create differences in income without implying economic discrimination. Some factors, such as schooling, are tricky to handle. For instance, differences in schooling do cause differences in wages without implying any discrimination if everyone has had an equal opportunity for the same amount of schooling. But it is unclear whether observed differences in schooling represent voluntary choices or another form of discrimination. Public policy makes it illegal to discriminate, but the evidence as to what constitutes discrimination is often subject to much dispute. Competitive markets can work to decrease some forms of discrimination, especially discrimination by (*employers/employees*).

BASIC EXERCISE

This problem illustrates the high marginal tax rates that often result from combining several welfare programs. The numbers in this problem do not come from any specific welfare program but are illustrative of many. (Recall the actual example on page 765 in the text.)

   Imagine a welfare system that offers a family of four the following forms of public support.

- *Basic welfare* in the form of a grant of $200 a month. The first $50 of earned income every month is assumed to be for work-related expenses and does not reduce benefits. After that, benefits are reduced by 67 cents for every dollar of earned income.

- *Food and medical expenses benefit* of $1200 a year. The family is assumed to receive these benefits as long as it is eligible for basic welfare.

- *Housing subsidy* that gives the family an apartment

worth $3,000 a year in rent. The family must pay rent equal to 30 percent of its net income, which is determined as gross wage earnings plus basic welfare minus $500 for each dependant.

1. Fill in column 6 of Table 38-1 by computing net income after taxes and after welfare payments for the different levels of earned income.

2. Use the data in columns 1 and 6 to plot net income against earned income in Figure 38-1. Plot each pair of points and then connect successive pairs with a straight line. What does the graph suggest about work incentives under these programs?

3. Use the data in Table 38-1 to complete Table 38-2, computing the implicit marginal tax rates that this family faces as it earns income. What is the relationship between the implicit marginal tax rates you computed in Table 38-2 and the slope of the graph in Figure 38-1? (How do these marginal rates compare with marginal rates under the positive portion of federal income taxes?)

TABLE 38-1

(1) Earned Income (dollars)	(2) Income Taxes (dollars)	(3) Basic Welfare (dollars)	(4) Food and Medical Expenses Subsidy (dollars)	(5) Housing Subsidy (dollars)	(6) Net Income (1) + (2) + (3) + (4) + (5) (dollars)
0	0	2400	1200	2880	_____
600*	0	2400	1200	2700	_____
4200	0	0	1200	2340	_____
4201	0	0	0	2340	_____
5000	0	0	0	2100	_____
6000	0	0	0	1800	_____
6400	– 20	0	0	1680	_____
10,000	–670	0	0	600	_____
10,800	–725	0	0	360	_____
12,000	–940	0	0	0	_____

*Assumed to be $50 a month.

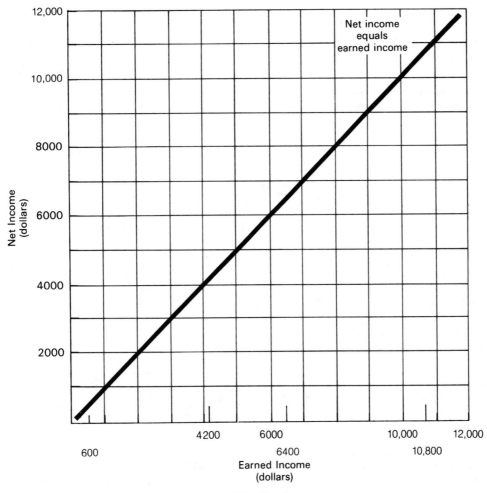

FIGURE 38-1

4. (Optional) One could reduce the implicit marginal tax rate by lowering the rate at which benefits are reduced under any of the programs. To investigate the impact of such reductions, construct a new version of Table 38-1 in which general assistance payments are reduced by only 25 cents for every dollar reduction in earned income. What happens to the magnitude of the subsidy payments at each level of income? What happens to the break-even levels of income for each program, that is, to the level of income when a family is no longer eligible? What would happen to total public outlays for these programs?

SELF-TESTS FOR UNDERSTANDING

Test A

Circle the correct answer.

1. Defining poor people as those who fall in the bottom 20 percent of the income distribution
   a. is an absolute concept of poverty.
   b. is a relative concept of poverty.
   c. means that continued economic growth will eliminate poverty.
   d. implies that the Lorenz curve is a straight line.

2. The facts on income distribution in Canada show
   a. a substantial move toward equality over the last 15 years.
   b. that the richest 20 percent of families receive about 80 percent of the total income.
   c. that the poorest 20 percent of families receive less than 2 percent of income.
   d. a Lorenz curve that sags below the 45° line.

3. Compared with other industrial countries, data on the distribution of income in Canada show
   a. rather more inequality than most other countries.
   b. about the same degree of inequality.
   c. much more equality.

4. Which of the following statements about the Lorenz curve is false?

239

TABLE 38-2

(1) Earned Income (dollars)	(2) Change in Earned Income (dollars)	(3) Net Income (Table 38-1, column 6) (dollars)	(4) Change in Net Income (dollars)	(5) "Implicit Taxes" (2) − (4) (dollars)	(6) Implicit Marginal Tax Rate (5) ÷ (2) (percent)
0					
	600				
600					
	3600				
4200					
	1				
4201					
	799				
5000					
	1000				
6000					
	400				
6400					
	3600				
10,000					
	800				
10,800					
	1200				
12,000					

a. It is a graph of the cumulative percentage of families (or persons) and the associated cumulative percentage of total income they receive.

b. It has a positive slope.

c. It would be a straight line if there were no economic discrimination.

d. For Canada it has not shifted much in the last 20 years.

5. Between 1981 and 1983, the proportion of families with incomes below the poverty line
   a. continued to decrease.
   b. stayed about the same.
   c. rose somewhat.
   d. rose to its highest point ever.

6. Consider a negative income tax scheme with a guaranteed minimum-income level of $5000 for a family of four and a tax rate of 50 percent. Which of the following statements is false?
   a. The break-even level of income will be $10,000.
   b. Reducing the tax rate below 50 percent will increase work incentives and increase the break-even level of income.
   c. Increasing the minimum guarantee without changing the tax rate increases the break-even level of income.
   d. If the Uptons earn $4000 in wages, their total income (earnings plus negative tax payment) will be $9000.

7. If a negative income tax system is to be financed within a given budget, then a reduction in the negative tax rate to increase work incentives
   a. can be offset by a reduction in the minimum guaranteed level of income.
   b. needs no change in the minimum guaranteed level of income.
   c. can be offset by an increase in the minimum guaranteed level of income.

8. Which of the following would be an example of economic discrimination?
   a. Census data showing that, on average, women earn less than men.
   b. Nurses earn less than doctors.
   c. Between 1970 and 1984 plumbers and electricians received larger percentage wage increases than did college professors.
   d. A careful study showing that among blacks and whites with identical education, work experience, productivity, and motivation, blacks earn less than whites.

9. All but which one of the following could give rise to differences in income without implying discrimination?
   a. Schooling.

b. Ability.
c. Compensating wage differential for night work.
d. Intensity of work effort.

10. The income-tax system in Canada has a smaller impact on the distribution of income than one might imagine for all but which *one* of the following reasons?
    a. Rich people use tax shelters to avoid paying taxes.
    b. Taxes and transfers can induce greater inequality in before-tax income.
    c. Sales taxes fall more heavily on the rich.
    d. Other taxes have a regressive impact.

Test B

Circle T or F for True or False as appropriate.

1. Continued economic growth is capable of eliminating poverty as measured by an absolute standard, but not as measured by a relative standard.   T F

2. Canadian data show almost no decline in poverty since 1960 as measured by the number of families below the poverty line.   T F

3. In Canada the 20 percent of families that are poorest receive about 20 percent of total income.   T F

4. Perfect equality in the distribution of income would result in a Lorenz curve that lies on top of the 45° line.   T F

5. Data for the last 20 years show almost no change in the Lorenz curve for Canada.   T F

6. The fact that women have lower average incomes than men is sufficient proof of economic discrimination.   T F

7. Competitive markets can help to eliminate discrimination by employers.   T F

8. In the absence of monopolies, unregulated markets would result in an equal distribution of income.   T F

9. Some differences in income reflect voluntary choices, such as decisions to work more hours or to take early retirement.   T F

10. The federal personal income-tax system has substantially reduced the degree of income inequality in Canada.   T F

SUPPLEMENTARY EXERCISES

1. Table 38-3 shows data on the distribution of income for 12 Organization for Economic Co-operation and Development (OECD) countries. Which countries have the greatest equality in the distribution of income? You might try drawing a Lorenz curve for several countries to help you decide. For example, consider Japan and Sweden. Use one large piece of graph paper to draw a Lorenz curve for both countries. In which country is income distributed more equally?

TABLE 38-3

PERCENTAGE OF POST-TAX INCOME RECEIVED BY POPULATION DECILES

		Population Deciles									
	Year	1	2	3	4	5	6	7	8	9	10
Australia	1966-67	2.1	4.5	6.2	7.3	8.3	9.5	10.9	12.5	15.1	23.7
Canada	1969	1.5	3.5	5.1	6.7	8.2	9.7	11.2	13.1	15.9	25.1
France	1970	1.4	2.9	4.2	5.6	7.4	8.9	9.7	13.0	16.5	30.4
Germany	1973	2.8	3.7	4.6	5.7	6.8	8.2	9.8	12.1	15.8	30.3
Italy	1969	1.7	3.4	4.7	5.8	7.0	9.2	9.8	11.9	15.6	30.9
Japan	1969	3.0	4.9	6.1	7.0	7.9	8.9	9.9	11.3	13.8	27.2
Netherlands	1967	2.6	3.9	5.2	6.4	7.6	8.8	10.3	12.4	15.2	27.7
Norway	1970	2.3	4.0	5.6	7.3	8.6	10.2	11.7	13.0	15.1	22.2
Spain	1973-74	2.1	3.9	5.3	6.5	7.8	9.1	10.6	12.5	15.6	26.7
Sweden	1972	2.2	4.4	5.9	7.2	8.5	10.0	11.5	13.3	15.7	21.3
United Kingdom	1973	2.5	3.8	5.5	7.1	8.5	9.9	11.1	12.8	15.2	23.5
United States	1972	1.5	3.0	4.5	6.2	7.8	9.5	11.3	13.4	16.3	26.5

Source: Malcolm Sawyer, "Income Distribution in OECD Countries," *OECD Occasional Studies*, July 1978, Table 4, p. 14. Reprinted by permission.

Compare these data on income distribution for industrialized countries with similar data for lower-income developing countries. *World Development Report, 1983*, published by Oxford University Press for the World Bank, reports data on income distribution for 40 countries.

2. Following is a suggested list of additional readings on three important topics covered in this chapter.

On the general issue of trade-offs between increased equality and reduced efficiency, read Arthur Okun's *Equity and Efficiency: The Big Trade-off*, published by the Brookings Institution, 1975. This important book is the source of the "leaky bucket" analogy used in the text.

For part of the story on how an income-tax system that starts with a highly progressive structure of income-tax rates can end up with very little effect on the distribution of income, read the chapter on the individual income tax in the latest edition of *Federal Tax Policy* by Joseph Pechman, published by the Brookings Institution, 1977.

For an excellent discussion of how existing welfare schemes confront poor people with "economic choices no rational person would want to make," read *Why Is Welfare So Hard to Reform?* by Henry J. Aaron, published by the Brookings Institution, 1973.

3. Investigate the details of welfare programs where you live. Use this information to construct your own version of Table 38-1.

Productivity Problems

39

LEARNING OBJECTIVES

After completing the material in this chapter you should be able to:

- define, understand, and use correctly the terms and concepts listed below.
- explain why productivity growth is the major determinant of living standards.
- distinguish between the problem of the recent slowdown in productivity growth in Canada and the productivity gap that exists vis-à-vis other countries.
- discuss and evaluate arguments about the cause of both the productivity slowdown and the productivity gap.
- discuss the crucial role that savings and investment play in both understanding productivity problems and their solutions.
- explain the difference between taxation of real capital gains and taxation of nominal capital gains and how a policy of taxing real capital gains could help encourage increased productivity growth.

- discuss and evaluate other measures proposed to increase productivity.

IMPORTANT TERMS AND CONCEPTS

Compounding of productivity gains
Labour productivity
Productivity growth
Research and development (R and D)
Service industries
Lifetime employment
Quality circles
Entrepreneurship
Capital gain
Real capital gain
Nominal capital gain
Basic and applied research
Free-rider problem
Supply-side economics
Industrial strategy

CHAPTER REVIEW

The growth in labour productivity is the major long-run determinant of living standards. Growth in labour productivity explains why, on the average, your parents are wealthier than their parents and their parents' parents. Continued growth in labour productivity will mean that your children and their children will be wealthier than you. For these and other reasons, growth in labour productivity is of fundamental importance to an economy.

Discussions of productivity usually focus on labour productivity, which is defined as the amount of output per unit of labour input. For a firm producing a single output, measuring labour productivity is a simple matter of dividing output by total labour hours. For the Canadian economy, output is usually measured in terms of real GNP, and labour input is preferably measured in terms of total labour hours. An increase in labour productivity means that

(1) the same number of labour hours can produce (*more/less*). If aggregate output were unchanged, an increase in labour productivity would mean (*more/less*) unemployment. But remember the unemployment rate is determined by

the intersection of the aggregate _____ and _____ curves. An increase in productivity means that the production possibilities frontier has shifted (*out/in*). Appropriate macroeconomic policy determines whether we take advantage of new possibilities.

Economists are concerned about two productivity problems. The first refers to the slowdown in the rate of growth of productivity since the mid-sixties. The second refers to the gap that exists between the rate of growth of productivity in Canada and other countries. After the late 1960s the growth of productivity declined dramatically in all industrialized economies. While no one is completely sure why the growth of productivity declined so drastically, there is agreement about a number of major contributing factors. Workers are more productive when they are able to work with the latest equipment and machinery. Reductions in investment in plant and equipment are believed to be a major factor contributing to the decline in productivity growth. New machines and new ways of making products require thought and experimentation. Research to solve practical problems in the development of new

(2) machines and products is called _____ research. This type of research depends on a flow of new

ideas that come from _____ research. In recent years there has been a decline in the proportion of GNP that has been directed to both types of research. The production of goods is amenable to automation with resulting increases in productivity. Services, on the other hand, with their large personnel component, offer less opportunity for increased productivity. (Remember the discussion of the cost disease of personal services in Chapter 29.) Changes in the composition of output away from goods and toward services will (*increase/reduce*) overall productivity growth.

The dramatic increase in energy prices probably had a greater impact on productivity than conventional measurement would suggest. The design of new equipment and factories—as well as the retrofitting and adjustment of existing buildings and machines—to take account of new, higher energy prices adds to costs without adding to output. There will be a clear reduction in productivity during the period of transition to higher energy prices. It is still an open question as to whether higher energy prices also reduce the rate of growth of productivity on a permanent basis.

The slowdown in productivity growth in Canada was matched by a similar slowdown in virtually all industrialized economies. While misery may love company and similar factors might have been at work in other countries, it is also true that productivity growth in Canada remains substantially below that of other industrialized countries. Again,

(3) a lower level of savings and _____ is a major factor contributing to the lower relative growth of productivity in Canada. A decline in the ability and willingness of Canadians to take risks and try

new ideas, that is, a decline in _____ , is another important factor that has been cited to explain relative productivity experience. Differences in foreign institutions and cultural practices may also be important here. We can learn much from labour and management practices abroad, but the transfer of foreign practices may be more difficult than many realize. Finally, many analysts argue that Canadian tariffs have caused many firms to operate within Canada to service only the domestic market, and so they operate relatively short production runs. As a result they cannot take full advantage of technological improvements that tend to reduce variable costs more than fixed costs.

Some have argued that higher rates of productivity growth are easier for foreign countries, because they can simply borrow advanced technology from the United States. Such an explanation was probably valid for much of the post-World War II period. It can explain catch up, but it cannot explain cases where foreign productivity is now ahead of American technology.

Why should one worry about either a slowdown in productivity growth or a productivity gap vis-à-vis other countries? A higher rate of productivity growth would mean larger increases in our standard of living. It would

(4) make it easier to address pressing social problems, and it would make it (*easier/harder*) to reduce the rate of inflation. When compared with other countries, lower rates of productivity growth need not mean massive unemployment and an inability to compete on world markets, but they do entail other significant costs. Supply curves shift to the right with either an increase in productivity or a reduction in the cost of major inputs such as labour. Canada can compete with other countries through higher productivity or (*higher/lower*) wages. We saw in

Chapter 32 that a country's exports are determined by (*absolute/comparative*) advantage, not by _____ advantage. Higher productivity growth abroad is likely to erode the comparative advantage of traditional Canadian exports. Having to continually develop new export industries to exploit changes in comparative advantage imposes heavy adjustment costs on an economy.

(5) Proposed changes in tax policy to increase savings and _____ include taxation of

(*nominal/real*) capital gains instead of _____ gains and reduced taxation of savings. Other proposals to increase productivity growth include government support of (*applied/basic*) research to

overcome the free-rider problems of _____ research and changes in competition policy

laws to facilitate co-operative arrangements between firms engaged in _____ research.

It is inevitable that increases in productivity will require increased levels of savings and investment, and perhaps the reallocation of some current investment activity away from things such as homebuilding and toward the construction of new plant and equipment to take advantage of innovations. As first discussed in Chapter 3, this change in the composition of current output is a direct measure of the cost of higher growth.

Supply-side economics and industrial strategy have been much in the news as additional solutions to our productivity problems. Supply-side tax policies are often criticized as just being tax giveaways, instead of tax reductions that are conditional on actions that would enhance productivity. As for industrial strategy, many are concerned that a program designed to pick winners not be subverted into a program that subsidizes losers.

BASIC EXERCISES

1. Productivity growth compounds like interest. Over appropriate periods of time small differences in the growth of productivity compound to quite substantial differences in the level of income. This exercise is designed to illustrate precisely this point.

Since 1961, output per person employed in the nonfarm sectors of the economy has increased by 41.1 percent. Over the same period of time, real compensation per person, that is, wages plus fringe benefits adjusted for any inflation, has increased 41.5 percent. The closeness of these two figures is not accidental. It reflects the fact that productivity growth is the fundamental long-run determinant of increases in real income and standards of living. (You might want to look at the Basic Exercise in Chapter 19.)

Imagine that you have just graduated from university at age 23 and are starting to work for $18,000 a year. What will happen to your real income if it only matches increases in the economy-wide rate of productivity growth? Complete Table 39-1 to find out. Are the increases with 3 percent growth three times those with 1 percent growth? Why?

TABLE 39-1

REAL INCOME ASSUMPTIONS ABOUT
ALTERNATIVE GROWTH IN PRODUCTIVITY

	Rate of Productivity Growth per Year			
Age	0	1%	2%	3%
23	$18,000	$18,000	$18,000	$18,000
25	18,000	_____	_____	_____
30	18,000	_____	_____	_____
40	18,000	_____	_____	_____
50	18,000	_____	_____	_____
60	18,000	_____	_____	_____

TABLE 39-2

	Index of Real Output			Index of Persons Employed			Index of Output per Worker		
	1962	1972	1982	1962	1972	1982	1962	1972	1982
Produced goods	60.0	106.7	120.1	85.3	102.5	107.1			
Services	60.5	108.0	163.6	71.7	105.3	153.1			

Source: Department of Finance, Canada, *Economic Review*, April 1984, pp. 169-70. The base for the indexes is 1971=100.

TABLE 39-3

PERCENTAGE CHANGE IN INDEX OF OUTPUT
PER WORKER*

	1972-1962	1982-1972
Produced goods	_____	_____
Services	_____	_____

*(change ÷ initial value) × 100

2. Which sector of the Canadian economy has experienced the fastest growth in productivity? Which decade showed the largest growth in productivity? Complete Tables 39-2 and 39-3 to find out. Are your results consistent with the discussion of the cost disease of personal services in Chapter 29?

SELF-TESTS FOR UNDERSTANDING

Test A

Circle the correct answer.

1. When compared with other countries, the growth of productivity in Canada has been
   a. higher than any other country.
   b. about the average of other countries.
   c. lower than most other countries.
2. Which period showed the highest growth of productivity in Canada?
   a. 1945-1965.
   b. 1965-1972.
   c. 1972-1982.
3. Which period showed the lowest growth of productivity?
   a. 1945-1965.
   b. 1965-1972.
   c. 1972-1982.
4. Productivity growth during the period 1972-1982

was approximately what proportion of its value during the period 1945-1965?
   a. They were about equal.
   b. 2/3
   c. 1/2
   d. 1/3
5. Which of the following is probably the most important factor explaining both the slowdown in productivity and the productivity gap?
   a. Declines in entrepreneurship.
   b. Low rates of investment.
   c. A lack of government-sponsored industrial strategy.
   d. A lack of quality circles.
6. Those in favour of higher productivity growth argue that it can have all but which one of the following effects?
   a. Help increase living standards.
   b. Help contribute to reducing inflation.
   c. Help finance expansions of important social expenditures.
   d. Have little impact on aggregate GNP.
7. Which of the following has been offered as a reason why productivity growth in other countries has exceeded that of Canada?
   a. Higher rates of savings and investment in Canada.
   b. A decline in entrepreneurship in other countries.
   c. Higher rates of inflation.
   d. Programs abroad to assist industrial growth.
8. If a $100,000 machine in 1975 would sell for $175,000 in 1985, there would be

a. a nominal capital gain of $75,000.
b. a real capital gain of $75,000.
c. a nominal capital gain of $175,000.
d. a real capital gain of $175,000.

9. If from 1975 to 1985 prices doubled, the machine in question would show
a. a real capital gain of $75,000.
b. no real capital gain or loss.
c. a real capital loss of $25,000.

10. In the absence of increases in productivity, Canadian goods can be competitive in international trade if
a. there is a reduction in relative real wages of Canadian workers.
b. inflation increases.
c. inflation slows down.
d. foreign currencies becomes cheaper in terms of Canadian dollars.

Test B

Circle T or F for True or False as appropriate.

1. In the long run it makes little difference whether productivity grows at 1 percent per year or at 3 percent per year.　　　T F

2. Although productivity growth has slowed in Canada, it still remains higher than in most other industrialized countries.　　　T F

3. Basic research suffers from the free-rider problem.　　　T F

4. During a period of inflation, real capital gains will be less than nominal capital gains.　　　T F

5. If productivity growth in Canada is lower than that of our major international competitors, there will be no gains from international trade as foreigners can undersell us in everything.　　　T F

6. From 1972 to 1982 the growth in productivity in Canada was about three times what it was right after World War II.　　　T F

7. Economists are in general agreement that productivity growth is unaffected by the level of investment in plant and equipment.　　　T F

8. Changes in the composition of output, especially growth in services as compared with manufacturing, are likely to reduce productivity growth.　　　T F

9. As compared with Canada, many of the industrialized countries with higher productivity growth rates devote a larger proportion of their GNP to investment.　　　T F

10. The experience of Great Britain at the beginning of the 20th century suggests that excessive government regulation lies at the heart of productivity problems.　　　T F

SUPPLEMENTARY EXERCISE

There has been much written about the wonders of recent Japanese economic performance. You might enjoy reading "Industry Policy: A Dissent," Charles L. Schultze, *The Brookings Review*, Fall 1983, pp. 3–12, and *Can America Compete?*, Robert Z. Lawrence (The Brookings Institution, 1984).

Growth in Developed and Developing Countries

LEARNING OBJECTIVES

After completing the material in this chapter you should be able to:

- define, understand, and use correctly the terms and concepts listed below.
- describe what exponential growth is and explain why it cannot continue forever.
- describe the arguments for and against continued growth.
- explain why the composition of aggregate demand is an important determinant of the rate of economic growth.
- describe other factors that are important in determining an economy's rate of growth.
- distinguish between embodied and disembodied growth.
- explain why, even if growth rates of income per capita in LDCs exceed those of developed countries, absolute income differentials will still increase for a number of years.
- discuss some of the important factors that impede the growth of incomes in LDCs.

- discuss what things LDCs can do for themselves to increase their growth.
- describe what role developed countries can play in assisting LDCs.
- explain what the World Bank and CIDA are and what they do.

IMPORTANT TERMS AND CONCEPTS

Output per capita
Exponential growth
Social infrastructure
Exchange between present and future consumption
Embodied growth
Disembodied growth
Less developed countries (LDCs)
Growth rate in GNP
Growth rate in per-capita income
Multinational corporations
Disguised unemployment
Entrepreneurship
Brain drain
World Bank
CIDA

CHAPTER REVIEW

This chapter discusses some of the general issues concerned with economic growth: Can it continue forever? Is it desirable? What actions can countries take to influence their rates of growth? Economics cannot always offer definitive answers to these questions, but it can help you to sort out and to think about the issues in a systematic fashion.

(1) Growth that occurs at a constant percentage rate for a number of years is called _____ growth. This "snowballing" effect, when projected into the future, seems to suggest doom for the human race. Simple extrapolations of population at current rates of growth lead to ridiculous conclusions. The clear implication is that growth (*can/cannot*) continue at current rates forever.

Many factors are clearly important for growth that are not well understood by economists or by anyone

(2) else. Examples include _____ , _____ , and the _____ _____ . Other factors that influence growth rates, and that countries *can* do something about, include accumulating more capital by higher levels of

(*consumption/investment*) and devoting more resources to _____ and

_____ . Some new ideas and inventions require new machines before they can help increase output. Growth from these sorts of inventions is called (*disembodied/embodied*) economic growth. If new

ideas permit more output from existing resources, the resulting growth is called _____ growth.

In a full-employment economy, more of anything, including investment spending or research and development, requires less of something else. This reduction, which is necessary to release resources for an increase in

(3) investment, is the _____ cost of increased investment. In a full-employment economy, resources for more investment would be available if consumers decided to decrease the amount of their

(*consumption/savings*) and increase the amount of their _____ .

The tools of economics cannot help you determine whether an economy should grow faster or slower; they can, however, identify the sources of growth and the consequences of more or less growth. In particular, a number of economists oppose zero economic growth on the grounds that a move in this direction may seriously hamper efforts to eliminate poverty and to protect the environment. Solutions to these problems are likely to require more rather than fewer resources. Many feel that it is easier to reach a political agreement to devote resources to problems of poverty and the environment if total output is expanding rather than if it is not growing.

Concerns about economic growth are an everyday reality for citizens in developing countries. While one inevitably ends up making lists of "the problems" of developing countries, it is important to remember that there is much diversity among these countries and that their problems are not all alike. For example, Nigeria, Mexico, and Indonesia have significant oil reserves while most other less developed countries do not. Also, the growth and density of population show a wide diversity among LDCs, as do recent gains in per-capita incomes.

Three-quarters of the world's population lives in countries with a per capita GNP of $750 or less per year. During the decade of the 1970s, real GNP in these countries increased at an average rate of more than 5

(4) percent a year, while population increased less rapidly. As a result, GNP per capita has (*increased/decreased*) on average. While this change in income is good news, there are other developments that are less optimistic.

Some observers believe that the recent increase in income in LDCs has been associated with increasing

(5) (*equality/inequality*) in the distribution of income, although detailed statistics on this trend are not available. Further, all LDCs (*have/have not*) shared equally in the increases in per-capita income. In many countries the rate of population growth is still high in comparison with developed countries. And future shocks, such as dramatic changes in oil prices, could have an adverse impact on many LDCs.

As for narrowing the income gap with the developed countries, it should be remembered that growth in

(6) the developed countries (*has/has not*) stopped. Even if developed countries and LDCs show the same percentage growth in income, the absolute differences in incomes will (*increase/decrease*) due to the (*higher/lower*) base of the developed countries.

LDCs face many problems in their quest for higher incomes. A fundamental problem is the lack of physical capital. More capital would help to increase labour productivity. LDCs can accumulate more capital in either of two ways: They can try to get it either from domestic sources or from foreign sources. The first option, domestic

(7) sources, would require (*more/less*) consumption in order to increase savings and investment.[1] This option will be (*easy/difficult*) for many countries because of their current extremely low levels of income. The second option, foreign sources, is not without its own risks. Profit-maximizing private businesses will clearly want as good a deal for themselves as possible. Mutual gain is still possible, however, especially if the LDCs insist upon the training of native workers for positions of responsibility and the development of social infrastructures, such as transportation and communication systems.

Population growth continues to be high for many LDCs primarily because of recent dramatic declines in

(8) (*birth/death*) rates. These declines appear to be the result of relative (*inexpensive/expensive*) public health measures rather than the result of advancements in medical technology. High rates of population growth result in tremendous demands on a country in terms of ensuring that people do not starve. Recent advances in agricultural productivity offer some hope along these lines. The experience of advanced economies also suggests that birthrates are likely to (*increase/decrease*) as income rises. A lack of trained technical workers, extensive unemployment—especially disguised unemployment—a lack of entrepreneurship, and other social impediments to business activity, as well as extensive government interferences in markets, are additional problems facing LDCs.

What can the LDCs do to help themselves? Economists, betting on the efficiency of markets, argue that LDCs should work to eliminate red tape in the regulation of business. Price controls, which destroy the incentive for

(9) economic activity, should be eliminated as should (*undervalued/overvalued*) exchange rates, which only (*raise/lower*) the price of a country's exports on world markets. Education, especially (*general/technical*) training, should be given high priority. Finally, any increase in domestic savings and investment will help by adding to the amount of physical capital available for increased production.

What can the advanced economies do for the LDCs? They can help them accumulate both technical skills and physical capital. Training individuals from LDCs will add to the pool of technical skills for these countries if those receiving education return to their native countries. The fact that many of these individuals have not returned is

(10) referred to as the _____ _____. Aid in acquiring physical capital can be provided

by long-term loans at preferential terms or by direct _____ that never have to be repaid. Aid can be given by individual countries or through international organizations, drawing on the resources of many

countries, such as the _____ Bank.

BASIC EXERCISES

1. Investment Expenditures and Growth

Table 40-1 presents data on the growth in per-capita income and total domestic investment expenditures (public and private) for a sample of 15 countries. Data on the growth in income are for the period 1970 to 1981. Data on investment expenditures are for the year 1981 and are in general representative of experience over the whole period.

a. Plot these data in Figure 40-1.
b. What does Figure 40-1 imply for countries that want to increase their rate of growth of income per capita?

2. Comparative Economic Growth

GNP per capita in a number of developed countries in 1980 was about $8000, while in a number of less developed countries it was around $700. It is a matter of mathematics, not economics, that if GNP per capita in LDCs grows at a more rapid rate than in the developed countries, incomes in the LDCs must eventually catch up with those of the developed countries. At the same time it should be emphasized that "eventually" may be a very long time, best measured in centuries rather than years; and even then one will need higher rates of growth in the LDCs over the entire interval. The determination of growth rates is a matter of economics, not mathematics. The following questions are designed to illustrate just how long this whole process may take.

a. Assume that income per capita in the developed countries does not increase from a level of $8000, while income per capita in the LDCs grows at 2.5 percent a year. How many years will it take for income per capita in the LDCs to reach $8000 if it starts at an initial level of $700?

_____ years. (You

---

[1] We have seen earlier that $Y = C + I + G + X - IM$. If one wants to increase I and maintain a balance of trade, reductions in either C or G will do. In an analysis of opportunities for growth, it is often useful to reclassify elements of G as either C or I.

Highways and dams would be _____, while bureaucrats and paper clips would be

_____. With this reclassification, the only way to increase I is to reduce

_____.

TABLE 40-1

INVESTMENT EXPENDITURES
AND THE GROWTH IN INCOME PER CAPITA
FOR SELECTED COUNTRIES

Country	Gross Domestic Investment as a Percent of Gross Domestic Product* 1981 (in percent)	Average Annual Growth Rate of Real Gross Domestic Product* Per Capita, 1970-1981 (in percent)
Canada	25	2.6
Colombia	31	3.8
Ethiopia	10	0.2
France	21	2.8
Germany	23	2.6
Haiti	13	1.7
India	23	1.5
Israel	20	1.4
Japan	31	3.4
Kenya	25	1.8
Pakistan	17	1.8
Sweden	19	1.5
United Kingdom	17	1.6
United States	19	1.9
Yugoslavia	32	4.8

*Gross domestic product is similar to gross national product.

Source: Compiled from data in *World Development Report*, 1983, published for the World Bank by the Johns Hopkins University Press. Data for column 1 from Table 5, pp. 156-57; data for column 2 from Table 2, pp. 150-51, and Table 19, pp. 184-85.

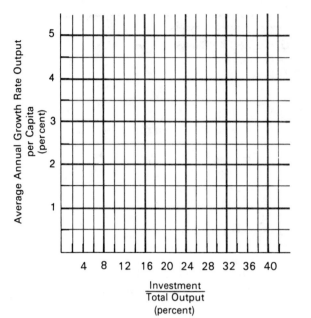

FIGURE 40-1

TABLE 40-2

Year	Income in LDCs	Income in Developed Countries	Difference (2) – (1)	Ratio (1) ÷ (2)
1985	$700	$8000	$7300	0.0875
1990	$ _____	$ _____	$ _____	$ _____
2000	$ _____	$ _____	$ _____	$ _____
2085	$ _____	$ _____	$ _____	$ _____
2100	$ _____	$ _____	$ _____	$ _____

can compute the number of years directly by the use of logarithms, or you can use a hand calculator or microcomputer to start with $700 and multiply by 1.025 until you get to $8000.)

b. Assume that income per capita in the LDCs grows at an annual rate of 2.5 percent, while in the developed countries it grows at an annual rate of 1.5 percent. Compute per-capita income and income differentials for the years listed in Table 40-2. Can you explain the seemingly contradictory behaviour of the "difference" and "ratio"?

c. (Optional) How many years will it take for income per capita in LDCs to catch up with income per

capita in developed countries if growth continues as assumed in Question b?

_____ years. What would GNP per capita be in both countries at that time?

$ _____

d. (Optional) In Question b you may have noticed that while the ratio of income in LDCs to income in developed countries is rising continuously, the absolute difference increases enormously over the first 100 years. How many years will it take for the absolute difference to stop increasing and start decreasing? _____ years.

SELF-TESTS FOR UNDERSTANDING

Test A

Circle the correct answer.

1. If the objective of economic growth is an increase in individual material welfare, which of the following is an appropriate indicator?
   a. Growth in total output.
   b. Growth in inflation.
   c. Growth in inventiveness.
   d. Growth in output per capita

2. Exponential growth
   a. in human population can be expected to continue at current rates forever.
   b. can prove that economic growth must come to an end within the next 200 years.
   c. means that the absolute amount of successive increases is the same, and thus the percentage increase becomes smaller over time.
   d. means that the percentage increase is the same, and thus the absolute increase becomes larger and larger.

3. Which of the following is *not* an example of investment in social infrastructure?
   a. The construction of the trans-Amazon highway in Brazil.
   b. Substantial investments in public education in Canada.
   c. The development of Indonesian oil fields by American oil companies.
   d. Investments in public health to reduce the incidence of infant mortality.

4. Which of the following is the appropriate measure of the opportunity cost of increased investment undertaken to raise the rate of growth?
   a. The resulting increase in future consumption.
   b. The rate of interest.
   c. The present consumption goods that could have been produced with the resources used to produce the investment goods.
   d. Zero, because economic growth is really costless.

5. Disembodied economic growth
   a. refers to increased output from better ways of using existing resources.
   b. has a zero opportunity cost because it requires only new ideas.
   c. has never been important in the real world.
   d. is likely to mean more resource depletion than embodied growth.

6. The recent record of economic growth in LDCs shows
   a. no growth in either GNP or GNP per capita.
   b. increases in GNP but not in GNP per capita.
   c. substantial increases in both GNP and GNP per capita for all LDCs.
   d. an uneven distribution of increases in GNP per capita.

7. High rates of population growth in many developing countries are the result of
   a. recent dramatic increases in birthrates.
   b. recent dramatic increases in death rates.
   c. the application of advanced medical technology.
   d. the success of compulsory programs of birth control.

8. Which of the following is *not* among the obstacles to high levels of income in the LDCs?
   a. Large rural–urban migration with dramatic increases in urban unemployment.
   b. Domestic savings rates that are so high they depress aggregate demand.
   c. A lack of entrepreneurial talent.
   d. Numerous well-intentioned government interventions that discourage the efficiency of private business.

9. Which one of the following is *not* likely to help LDCs achieve higher levels of income?
   a. Any increase in savings and investment that can be squeezed out of existing low levels of income.
   b. Expanded programs of technical trainings.
   c. Exchange rates fixed at even higher levels to encourage exports.
   d. Removal of impediments to innovation and entrepreneurial talent.

10. Which one of the following has *not* been an important source of loans and grants for development projects in LDCs?
   a. The World Bank.
   b. The International Monetary Fund.
   c. The United States.
   d. The Soviet Union.

Test B

Circle T or F for True or False as appropriate.

1. Even if total GNP increases, it is possible that GNP per capita might decline if population growth is sufficiently high. T F

2. The fact that population growth has recently been exponential is a good reason to believe that it will continue that way forever. T F

3. Zero economic growth would be easy to achieve and an unambiguous gain for the fight to clean up the environment. T F

4. Increased investment spending leading to more capital accumulation is likely to increase the rate of economic growth. T F

5. Embodied economic growth refers to ideas and inventories that require new machinery. **T F**

6. Disembodied economic growth means that an economy can have higher rates of growth without having to sacrifice any current consumption. **T F**

7. For any year that the growth rate of income per capita in the LDCs matches that of the developed countries, the absolute difference in income will decrease. **T F**

8. The recent increases in income per capita in the LDCs have been evenly shared by all LDCs. **T F**

9. Statistical evidence from both the developed and underdeveloped countries refutes the Malthusian law of population growth. **T F**

10. Research suggests that expenditures on technical training rather than general education are likely to have a greater impact on the rate of economic growth in LDCs. **T F**

11. Disguised unemployment is only a problem for developed economies and has little relevance for LDCs. **T F**

12. Unlike Canada, LDCs have not experienced any substantial rural-urban migration. **T F**

13. The only real constraint to growth in the LDC's is a lack of entrepreneurship. **T F**

14. In order to avoid the problem of default on loans, the World Bank makes loans only to developed countries, such as Britain and France. **T F**

SUPPLEMENTARY EXERCISES

1. Select one of the developing countries as a subject for research, and go to the library to find out about its recent economic developments. Has population growth been rising or falling? Why? What percentage of GNP is used for investment? How does this percentage compare with other countries? Has the growth in GNP per capita been rising or falling? Compared with Canada, what proportion of GNP is derived from agriculture? Does this country rely on one or two major exports? If so, what are they and what has recently happened to world prices for these commodities? How large a percentage of the country's GNP are exports and imports? How does this percent compare with Canada, the United States, Japan, and the countries of Western Europe? How equal or unequal is the distribution of income? To what extent does the country rely on markets or planning? On capitalism or socialism? (See Chapter 41 for a discussion of these alternatives.) A good initial data source is *World Development Report*, prepared each year by the World Bank. The United Nations and the International Monetary Fund are also good sources for data.

2. The volume of U.S. aid to developing countries dwarfs that from all other sources. However, the U.S. economy also dwarfs that of all other countries. How does U.S. commitment to development assistance compare to Canada and other developed countries when measured as a percent of GNP? Has the volume of aid from all developed economies, both in total and as a percent of GNP, been increasing or decreasing? What about OPEC countries? A good place to start to answer these questions is the library. *World Development Report* typically contains data on official development assistance from major industrialized countries and OPEC countries. *The United Nations Statistical Yearbook* is another source of data.

3. In 1950, the world's population was estimated to be 2.501 billion. From 1950 to 1984 it grew at an average annual rate of 1.94% to 4.8 billion. Assume that population has always grown at an annual rate of 1.94%. If we started with a population of two, how many years would it take for the world population to reach 4.8 billion?

VIII

Alternative Economic Systems

Comparative Economic Systems: What Are the Choices?

LEARNING OBJECTIVES

After completing the material in this chapter you should be able to:

- define, understand, and use correctly the terms and concepts listed below.
- describe how in theory and practice the decisions about economic co-ordination and ownership—markets or planning; capitalism or socialism—are distinct choices.
- evaluate the record of market and planned economies regarding the choice of goods to produce, the efficiency of production, the distribution of income, economic growth, and fluctuations in economic activity.
- describe the role of the "profit motive" in capitalism and the implications of its absence under socialism.
- briefly describe the choices as to ownership and co-ordination and the experiences with these choices in Sweden, France, Yugoslavia, and China.
- explain why the Soviet Union was able to achieve high rates of economic growth in the face of substantial inefficiencies of production.
- describe the Soviet planning process: who makes the decisions, the role of Five-Year and One-Year Plans, and the meaning of material balance.

IMPORTANT TERMS AND CONCEPTS

Capitalism
Socialism
Planning
Free markets
Consumer sovereignty
Welfare state
Indicative planning
Workers' management
Soviet Five-Year and One-Year Plans
Material balance
Material incentives
Great Leap Forward
Great Proletarian Cultural Revolution

257

CHAPTER REVIEW

Countries must make choices about how to organize their economies. The discussion in this chapter looks at two crucial decisions: How should economic activity be co-ordinated? And who should own the means of production? The alternatives are compared using indicators of both equity and efficiency, and the experiences of five countries—Sweden, France, Yugoslavia, the Soviet Union, and China—are considered in terms of the above issues.

When considering how to co-ordinate economic activity, economies can choose to emphasize

(1) _____ or _____ . These options are not simple all-or-nothing alternatives. For most countries the choice is a matter of emphasis and degree. That is, market economies allow for government intervention in many areas, and most planned economies rely on market forces in several areas.

When considering ownership of the means of production, economies can choose to emphasize private

(2) ownership, that is, _____ , or public ownership, that is, _____ . Again, most countries do not choose one to the exclusion of the other. Most countries have some of both.

Are socialism/planning and capitalism/markets the only feasible combinations? Both theory and real-world

(3) examples suggest that this pairing (*is/is not*) inevitable. Yugoslavia is an example of a (*socialist/capitalist*) country that relies heavily on (*markets/planning*) for the co-ordination of economic activity.

What difference does it make whether a country emphasizes markets or planning? We can keep score on the following five issues:

(4) 1. *What goods to produce.* Market economies respond to the preferences of _____ , and

planned economies respond to the preferences of _____ . Which option one values

depends, in part, on how much one values individual _____ .

2. *Production efficiency.* Here _____ economies have a clear advantage over

_____ economies. The _____ motive is a powerful device for promoting efficiency. Planned economies have not yet found an alternative incentive scheme that consistently works as well.

3. *The distribution of income.* When considering the distribution of labour income, market and planned economies show (*a significantly different/about the same*) degree of inequality. If planning is associated with socialism, there is apt to be (*more/less*) equality in the overall distribution of income. But remember planning need not be associated with socialism.

4. *Growth.* One can find examples of planned economies that have grown faster than market economies and vice versa. Different countries will probably continue to make different choices based on different political systems, value judgments, traditions, and aspirations.

5. *Business fluctuations.* Here _____ economies clearly have the better track record.

How one strikes the final balance on these five issues is a matter of trade-offs, the basic stuff of economics. But remember again that one does not need make all-or-nothing decisions. As the experiences of our five countries illustrate, there is a wide variety of alternatives.

(5) Sweden is a (*capitalist/socialist*) economy, as more than 90 percent of industry is (*privately/publicly*) owned. At the same time Sweden relies on government intervention to maintain full employment and to effect the distribution of income. Direct intervention in labour markets has succeeded in keeping the unemployment rate consistently lower than in Canada. The distribution of income in Sweden is more (*equal/unequal*) than in Canada

because of an extensive and comprehensive _____ system.

(6) The French experience of _____ planning produced almost continuous full employment from the late 1950s until recently, when economic growth slowed significantly. French planning relies on voluntary co-operation, but the government can still affect aggregate demand by influencing

_____ spending, both directly and indirectly. Indicative planning as practised in France (*would/would not*) be a violation of Canadian anti-combines laws.

As mentioned above, Yugoslavia is a socialist economy with extensive reliance on markets. In

(7) Yugoslavia (*central planners/individual firms*) make decisions about what to produce and how to produce it. The managers of firms are chosen by _____ and act to _____

_____ . Individual firms can decide how to use their own profits, whether for expansion or

for higher _____ .

(8)   The Soviet Union is an example of a (*capitalist/socialist*) economy with comprehensive, centralized planning.

The broad objectives of Soviet policy are set forth in the _____-Year Plans, while more

detail for implementation is provided in _____-Year Plans. Soviet planning relies

extensively on targets and _____ .

Because of the complexity of the Soviet economy, it is quite a problem to ensure that all the quantity

(9)   targets are mutually consistent. The Soviets refer to consistency as achieving _____
balance. Input-output analysis could be used here, but the enormity of the information requirements make it
infeasible for detailed planning. (You might refer back to the Supplementary Exercise to Chapter 26 in this book.)
The Soviets attempt to solve this problem by trying as best they can and by establishing priority sectors that will be
favoured when problems arise.

(10)   The Soviet Union form of central planning, where (*data/orders*) flow down from the top and

_____ flow up from the bottom, places a tremendous burden on the transmission of
information. The result is, almost of necessity, a considerable amount of inefficiency. Because rewards are based on
achieving one's quota, plant managers have an incentive to (*be truthful/deceive*). There is (*strong/little*) incentive
for innovation. Compared with Western experience, inventories of strategic materials are often excessively
(*high/low*). Many consumer goods are of (*high/low*) quality.

(11)   Until recently the Soviet economy experienced (*higher/lower*) rates of growth than the United States.
Economic growth depends on growth in inputs and advances in technology. Often in the past the Soviet Union

simply borrowed existing advanced _____ from the West. An increased industrial labour

force came from a reduced _____ labour force. A rapidly growing capital stock came
from adjusting the composition of output to favour the production of (*consumption/investment*) goods over

_____ goods. These three factors are no longer able to contribute to Soviet economic
growth. In addition, the inefficiencies of the Soviet central planning system appear to be taking an increasing toll on
the economy.

(12)   China is a (*planned/market*) economy with extensive (*private/state*) ownership. Chinese planning and
economic growth have moved in fits and starts related to domestic ideological struggles. Chinese planning is
patterned after Soviet planning, but the Chinese version is (*more/less*) centralized. Recent decisions in China imply
a significant increase in the role of markets.

SELF-TESTS FOR UNDERSTANDING

Test A

Circle the correct answer.

1. The form of economic organization in which the
   state owns the means of production is called
   a. capitalism.
   b. consumer sovereignty.
   c. socialism.
   d. laissez faire.
2. Market economies clearly do much worse than
   planned economies in which of the following
   areas?
   a. Avoiding business fluctuations.
   b. Fostering a high rate of growth.
   c. Achieving efficiency in the production of goods
   and services.

d. Achieving equality in the distribution of labour
   income.
3. Match each of the following with the appropriate
   country.
   Sweden _____ a. indicative planning
   France _____ b. material balance
   Yugoslavia _____ c. workers'
                            management
   Soviet Union _____ d. welfare state
4. The historical record shows that compared with
   Canada, Sweden has achieved which of the
   following?
   a. A lower unemployment rate on average.
   b. A lower average rate of inflation.
   c. Less equal distribution of income.
   d. Lower taxes.
5. Which one of the following is *not* true of the French
   system of indicative planning?
   a. It calls for voluntary co-operation between

government, industry, and labour over the volume and composition of national output.

b. It would likely violate Canadian anti-combines laws.

c. It has been associated with almost continuous full employment from 1958 until the mid-1970s.

d. It is a direct copy of planning in the Soviet Union.

6. The Yugoslav system of economic organization

a. is one of worker-determined management of firms.

b. has resulted in almost complete equality in the distribution of wage income.

c. is essentially the same as that of the Soviet Union.

d. has eliminated business cycles.

7. The Soviet planning system

a. makes extensive use of input–output analysis to ensure that each One-Year Plan has internal consistency.

b. saves on information requirements by having plant managers maximize profits.

c. is one of consumer sovereignty, since Soviet citizens are free to buy consumer goods of their own choosing.

d. creates incentives for plant managers to deceive in order to establish easy quotas.

8. The record of the Soviet economy shows all but which one of the following?

a. Low agricultural productivity.

b. High levels of efficiency associated with centralized planning.

c. Substantial amounts of low-quality consumer goods.

d. Extensive use of wages, rather than quotas, in the allocation of labour.

9. The term "material balance" refers to

a. inventories at the end of each planning period.

b. consistency in plans so that the quantity demanded and the quantity supplied of each commodity are equal.

c. the wealth of Kremlin leaders.

d. the choices planners must make as they balance competing claims for consumption and investment goods.

10. In China, the record of the economy shows

a. a consistent and unwavering commitment to highly centralized planning.

b. extensive use of material incentives to motivate workers.

c. successful use of indicative planning.

d. the recent introduction of aspects of a market economy.

Test B

Circle T or F for True or False as appropriate.

1. Socialism must be accompanied by central planning.   T F

2. Consumer sovereignty is the term used for the form of economic organization in which private individuals own the means of production.   T F

3. Planned economies have done a better job in terms of avoiding business cycles than have market economies.   T F

4. Market economies are clearly superior to planned economies in terms of the efficiency of production.   T F

5. A major problem with planned economies is devising an incentive mechanism for managers that works to promote efficiency.   T F

6. In Sweden more than half of industry is owned by the state.   T F

7. France is an example of a basically capitalistic economy that relies heavily on planning.   T F

8. Yugoslavia has avoided serious business cycles through the use of centralized planning.   T F

9. In the Soviet Union One-Year Plans set broad objectives while Five-Year Plans contain the details of implementation.   T F

10. The Chinese system of planning is a direct copy of Soviet planning.   T F

Dissenting Opinions: Conservative, Moderate, and Radical

42

LEARNING OBJECTIVES

After completing the material in this chapter you should be able to:

- define, understand, and use correctly the terms and concepts listed below.
- critically evaluate the libertarian dissent from mainstream economics and current public policy.
- critically evaluate Galbraith's criticisms of mainstream economic theory and the Canadian and U.S. economies.
- critically evaluate the New Left criticisms of mainstream economic theory and the Canadian and U.S. economies.

- understand that critical evaluation does not imply that one must completely reject a particular viewpoint.

IMPORTANT TERMS AND CONCEPTS

Libertarianism
Economic power
Technostructure
New Left economics
Manipulation of the consumer
Alienation
Liberal versus radical views of the state

CHAPTER REVIEW

Not many would argue that mainstream economics is above criticism. Most economists, however, would argue for marginal changes, a shift of emphasis here or there. This chapter discusses three major dissenting views that call for more fundamental and far-reaching changes in analysis.

Libertarianism

(1)   Libertarianism is more a _____ than a system of economic thought. The

fundamental goal of libertarians is a maximum amount of individual _____ in both economic and social relations. Libertarians think their goal is best achieved by (*more*/*less*) government intervention. Among economists, Milton Friedman is perhaps the most effective spokesperson for the libertarian viewpoint.

(2) Friedman argues that political freedom and _____ economies go hand in hand. He also argues for a (*larger*/*smaller*) role for government. He sees a need for government to fulfill three limited roles: to serve as umpire, that is, to enforce contracts, to control natural _____ , and to correct for market failure in the case of _____ . In Friedman's view these legitimate roles for government (*are often*/*have never been*) used to expand the role of government into inappropriate areas.

The Liberal Viewpoint of John Kenneth Galbraith

According to Galbraith, mainstream economics is especially deficient in its failure to consider how the use of

(3) economic _____ has subverted the idealized workings of market processes as described in introductory economics textbooks. According to Galbraith, corporations (*do*/*do not*) compete to meet the independent desires of consumers. Rather corporations use their power to manipulate demand and control markets. Galbraith sees the economy as essentially a _____ system, run by _____ who are guided by _____ _____ . These technocrats work to maximize (*profits*/*growth*), which in turn maximizes _____ _____ .

When looking at the Canadian and U.S. economies, Galbraith is distressed by the relative abundance of

(4) (*public*/*private*) goods and the relative scarcity of _____ goods. Galbraith also argues that the U.S. economy shows a shocking disregard for the _____ of life.

While many economists agree with some of Galbraith's personal evaluations of our North American economies,

(5) most (*agree*/*disagree*) with Galbraith's analysis of the reasons why things have turned out this way. Galbraith argues that profit maximization (*is*/*is not*) the motivating factor of the planning system. Mainstream economists (*agree*/*disagree*). They see profit maximization as a workable approximation yielding useful results. Galbraith argues that the volume of internally generated funds of large corporations gives them freedom to do as they please and to avoid any market discipline. Others point out that even internally generated funds have a(n) _____ _____ , and any corporation that neglects its profits may be vulnerable to a(n) _____ .

Radical Economists of the New Left

Radical economics is the most recent challenge to mainstream economics. The text discusses five major radical criticisms of mainstream economics.

1. Radicals charge that modern economics is too narrow. Accepting institutions as given and immutable, it is

(6) _____ . As a result, mainstream economists end up, either implicitly or explicitly, as apologists for the present system.

2. Radicals charge that mainstream economics accepts tastes and motivation as _____ . Galbraith would agree with this charge. But the radical criticism is broader, extending beyond the modern corporation to argue that social institutions, such as schools, only mold tastes and behaviour to serve the purposes of the _____ _____ .

3. Radicals charge that mainstream economics is too heavily concerned with (*efficiency*/*equality*) and too little concerned with _____ . They argue that _____ rather than marginal productivity is the better explanation of distribution of income.

4. Radicals argue that mainstream economics seems more concerned with quantity than with

_____. In the radical view, a larger GNP is apt to despoil the environment and

increase the _____ of workers.

5. Finally, radicals charge that many liberals have a (*naive/sophisticated*) theory of the state. Many liberals think that the state can be made to serve the broad public interest. Radicals believe instead that the state serves the

_____ _____ by helping them to maintain their

_____.[1] Government policies that appear to advance the interests of lower-income

groups are either shams or attempts to _____ the working class.

    Radical charges against mainstream economics have not gone unchallenged. As for the issue of narrowness, mainstream economists argue that radicals are so broad in their approach that they tend to be superficial.

(7) Mainstream economists argue that narrowness (*is/is not*) necessary for scientific progress. Many mainstream economists (*agree/disagree*) that modern economics seems overly concerned with efficiency. As to the issue of power, many economists are concerned that due to a lack of precision, one runs the risk of engaging in

_____ , not science. A similar concern arises in the use of concepts like alienation and dehumanization.

    Many radicals see themselves as the heirs of Marx. Like him, radicals have also concentrated on detailed criticisms of capitalism. To date there is no agreed-upon radical alternative. Two items that do seem to be

(8) elements of most radical alternatives are a _____ and _____ system rather than an authoritative, centralized system.

SELF-TESTS FOR UNDERSTANDING

Test A

Circle the correct answer.

1. Which of the following are likely to agree with the statements listed below?

    Libertarians   _____

    Galbraith   _____

    New Left   _____

    None   _____

  a. Modern corporations are above the discipline of the marketplace.
  b. There is an overabundance of private goods and a relative scarcity of public goods.
  c. We would be better off with an expanded role for markets and a restricted scope for government.
  d. Government actions are most likely to serve the purposes of the ruling classes rather than any broad social interest.
  e. By the use of modern advertising, corporations are able to manipulate demand for their output.
  f. Economic power is a more important determinant of prices than is supply and demand.

2. Milton Friedman would agree with which of the following government programs?

  a. Government licensing of economists to protect the public from charlatans.
  b. More extensive government regulation of important basic industries, such as steel.
  c. The court system to enforce contracts.
  d. Permanent wage-price controls.

3. Galbraith argues that
  a. modern corporations are inherently inefficient because they are so big.
  b. the technocrats who run corporations are primarily concerned with maximizing profits.
  c. permanent wage-price controls would improve the inflation-unemployment trade-off.
  d. expansion of the federal government has meant an overabundance of public goods.

4. For each of the following indicate whether Solow and Galbraith would agree or disagree.

	Solow	Galbraith
a. The modern corporation can safely ignore the market.	____	____
b. Profit maximization is useful as a description of firm behaviour.	____	____
c. Modern advertising means that there is no effective consumer choice	____	____

5. Which of the following is *not* a part of the radicals' charge that mainstream economics has too narrow a focus?

---

[1] A number of conservative economists also argue that liberals have a naive view of the state. Conservatives argue that rather than supporting a particular class, government bureaucrats work to advance their own interests in terms of bigger budgets and more influence, a viewpoint not unlike Galbraith's description of technocrats.

a. A preoccupation with marginal changes blinds one to important big changes.

b. Mainstream economics has spent too much time studying the evolution of modern institutions.

c. Mainstream economists have become apologists for the status quo.

d. Modern economics is ahistorical.

6. Which of the following is *not* a part of the radicals' critique of modern economics?

a. Mainstream economists are naive if they believe that the government is a consistent defender of the public interest.

b. Alienation and dehumanization are fundamental defects of capitalism.

c. Most social institutions, such as schools, serve the purposes of capitalists.

d. Modern economics concentrates too much on equality while ignoring important questions of efficiency.

7. Most radical economists would prefer to see which one of the following?

a. Rigidly centralized government planning.

b. A participatory system for organizing firms and other institutions.

c. A larger reliance on unfettered and unlimited competition.

d. More government-industry co-operation, similar to the recent government guarantee of loans to Dome Petroleum.

Test B

Circle T or F for True or False as appropriate.

1. Laissez faire means minimal government interference in economic matters.   T F

2. Libertarians argue that free markets, rather than the state, are the best bet for preserving freedom.   T F

3. According to Galbraith, the Canadian economy is best described as a planning system rather than a market economy.   T F

4. Being concerned with profit maximization, the Galbraithian technocrat who runs the modern corporation is fundamentally different from the planners who run the socialist economies of eastern Europe.   T F

5. Galbraith argues that the market economy places little emphasis on the quality of life.   T F

6. Radical economists of the New Left view themselves as direct intellectual descendants of Adam Smith.   T F

7. According to radical economists, private ownership and free markets are fundamental causes of much of what is wrong today.   T F

8. Radical economists accept the marginal productivity theory of income distribution of mainstream economics.   T F

9. In contrast to Marx, radical economists have offered a detailed description of alternatives to the existing market economy.   T F

10. The only way the government can expand aggregate demand to ensure full employment is by increased military spending.   T F

SUPPLEMENTARY READING

To learn more about each of the three alternative viewpoints discussed in this chapter, read one or more of the following:

Free to Choose by Milton and Rose Friedman. This book comes from the PBS TV series of the same name and is published by Harcourt Brace Jovanovich, Inc.

The New Industrial State by John Kenneth Galbraith. This book is available in paperback from the New American Library. After you have finished reading this book, go to the library and read Robert Solow's review of it and Galbraith's reply in *The Public Interest*, Fall 1967.

The Capitalist System: A Radical Analysis of the American Society, edited by Richard Edwards, Michael Reich, and Thomas Weisskopf. This book is available in paperback from Prentice-Hall, Inc.

The Political Economy of the New Left, by Assar Lindbeck, published by Harper & Row. A collection of essays about this book has been published in the *Quarterly Journal of Economics*, November 1972.

Answers

CHAPTER 1

Chapter Review

(1) means; ends
(2) information, value

Self-Test

1. F
2. F
3. T
4. T
5. T
6. F

CHAPTER 2

Chapter Review

(1) horizontal; vertical; origin
(2) time-series
(3) vertical; horizontal; constant; positive; up; negative; no
(4) ray; 45°
(5) tangent
(6) contour

Basic Exercises

1. a. 300
   b. increased; 500
   c. decreased; 200
2. a. No, increases in aggregate income due to inflation or population do not increase individual purchasing power.
   b. 8.3 times ($8046 ÷ $971); column 3; 971; 1486; 2523; 8046
   c. 2 times ($3619 ÷ $1772); column 5; 1772; 2061; 2604; 3619
3. a. Figure 2-4. Including the origin eliminates the illusion that inflation stopped.
   b. The use of data over 12 months eliminates the impact of short-term special factors.
      14.7; 14.7; 14.4; 14.3; 13.2; 12.8; 12.8; 12.6

Self-Tests

Test A

1. c, a, b, d
2. a, c, b, d
3. a
4. c
5. d

Test B

1. F	5. T	9. F
2. T	6. T	10. T
3. T	7. F	
4. F	8. T	

CHAPTER 3

Chapter Review

(1) scarce
(2) opportunity cost
(3) scarce; specialized; less; more; more; consumption
(4) slope
(5) increase; increasing; specialized
(6) inside; inefficient
(7) will

Basic Exercise

1. a. 56 000; 4000; rises; 12 000; continue to rise; specialized
   b. Point A is not feasible; point B is feasible; point C is feasible; on and inside
   c. Point B is inefficient.

Self-Tests

Test A

1. c	4. a	7. a
2. d	5. b	8. c
3. c	6. b	9. c

Test B

1. F	5. F	9. F
2. F	6. F	10. F
3. T	7. T	
4. T	8. T	

Supplementary Exercises

3. a. 300 000 cars; 1000 tanks
   b. yes, it bows out.
   c. 6 cars; 30 cars; 120 cars
   d. opportunity cost = (0.6)T; yes, opportunity cost increases as T increases.

CHAPTER 4

Chapter Review

(1) price, negative; more; movement along; shift in
(2) positive; more; shift in
(3) demand

(4) $200; 4000; less; 6000; 2000; surplus; reduction; shortage; demanded; supplied; increase
(5) intersection; equilibrium
(6) demand; supply; movement along; supply; demand; demand
(7) hard; auxiliary restrictions
(8) high

Basic Exercises

1. b. 30; 1100
   c. increased; 40; increased; 1200
   d. increase; decrease; 45; 1100
2. a. demand; rise; rise
   b. supply; fall; rise
   c. supply; rise; fall
   d. demand; fall; fall

Self-Tests

Test A

1. a	4. a	7. b
2. a	5. b	8. d
3. b	6. b	9. b

Test B

1. F	6. T	11. F
2. T	7. T	12. T
3. T	8. F	13. F
4. F	9. F	14. F
5. F	10. T	

Supplementary Exercises

1. a. domestic demand; 38; domestic supply; 31 imports; 7
   b. Quantity demanded would have declined to 34.8; domestic supply would have increased to 33.25; imports would have declined to 1.55.
   c. price = $13.75; quantity = 33.9
2. Price and quantity should approach $3 and 650.

CHAPTER 5

Chapter Review

(1) microeconomics; macroeconomics
(2) price; quantity; national product
(3) inflation; deflation; recessions; higher; higher; inflation; left; decrease; stagflation
(4) money; final; nominal; real; real; nominal; real
(5) up; depends; risen
(6) inflation; stabilization; recession; inflation

Basic Exercises

1. a. c; d
   b. b; yes, 1930-1933
   c. a
   d. c
2. a. left
   b. right
   c. Real GNP will fall; prices will rise.

Self-Tests

Test A

1. a	5. c
2. d	6. d
3. b, d, a, c, f	7. b
4. a	8. d

Test B

1. F	4. T	7. F
2. T	5. F	8. T
3. F	6. F	9. F

CHAPTER 6

Chapter Review

(1) more; more
(2) cannot; partial; some
(3) potential; actual GNP
(4) is not; frictional; cyclical; structural
(5) discouraged, decrease; understate
(6) frictional
(7) real; the same; as
(8) different; less; more
(9) higher; nominal; real; inflation
(10) will; be unchanged
(11) creeping; galloping

Basic Exercises

1. a. 1955: 0.228; 0.141; 0.631
      1982: 0.228; 0.302; 0.470
   b. increase: females
      decrease: males
   c. $(0.228 \times 11.8) + (0.141 \times 8.8) + (0.631 \times 8.1) =$
      9.04;
      0.16 percentage-points lower than the actual
      1982 unemployment rate;
      1955 proportions give less weight to
      unemployment rates for females.
   d. 1982 saw the economy in a major recession;
      1955 was a recovery year.
   e. There are many possible reasons. The most

probable is that this is a reflection of the methods
of measuring the number of women in the
workforce at that time. It is unlikely that the low
unemployment rate meant that it was easier for
women to find employment than for men.

   f. As teenagers and young adults become a
      relatively smaller proportion of the labour force,
      and if full-employment unemployment rates for
      adults do not rise, the overall full-employment
      unemployment rate should fall.

2. a. $250,000; $5,250,000; $4,772,727; $5,750,000;
      $5,227,272. Borrowers gain at expense of
      lenders.
   b. $775,000; $5,775,000; $5,250,000; $5,225,000;
      $4,750,000. Both are treated equally.
   c. $1,000,000; $6,000,000; $5,454,545; $5,000,000;
      $4,545,455. Lenders gain at expense of
      borrowers.

Self-Tests

Test A

1. c	5. a	9. c
2. b	6. c	10. d
3. a	7. a	
4. b	8. a	

Test B

1. F	5. F	9. F
2. F	6. F	10. T
3. F	7. F	
4. F	8. F	

APPENDIX

Basic Exercises: Appendix

I. 1. a. 2500; 400
      b. $16,500
      c. 110
      e. 10 percent
      f. $15,771; 5.1 percent
   2. 1984 index, using 1985 base, 91.1. 1985 base
      implies inflation of 9.8 percent. The slightly lower
      rate of inflation reflects a larger weight on more
      slowly rising clothing prices when using the 1985
      expenditure pattern.
II. 1 and 2 Insufficient information; for example, the
            price index for Canada for 1960 shows how
            1960 Canadian prices compare to 1967
            Canadian prices, not how Canadian prices
            compare to those in other countries.
   3. Italy; West Germany

CHAPTER 7

Chapter Review

(1) demand; consumption; investment; government; exports

(2) before; after

(3) more; movement along; shift in

(4) C; I; G; X–IM; less; decrease

(5) increase; marginal; larger; more; smaller

Basic Exercises

1. a. change in consumption; 1600; 1600; 1600; 1,600 MPC; 0.8; 0.8; 0.8; 0.8
   b. 0.92; 0.90; 0.89; 0.88; 0.87
   c. APC and MPC differ.
   e. slope of the consumption function
   f. Rays become less steep; their slope declines.
2. a. $11 000; $17 400; $2 840 000
   b. 0.87; 0.92
   c. $12 600; $15 800; $2 840 000
   d. In the example, MPC is the same for rich and poor. The rich reduce their consumption by the same amount that the poor increase their consumption.
3. $C = 1400 + 0.8 \times DI$

Self-Tests

Test A

1. b	5. a	9. a
2. d	6. c	10. d
3. b	7. c	
4. c	8. c	

Test B

1. F	4. T	7. T
2. F	5. T	8. T
3. T	6. F	9. T

APPENDIX A

1. $1000; $1400; $1800; $2200; $2600
2. change in savings $400; $400; $400; $400
   MPS: 0.2; 0.2; 0.2; 0.2
4. APS: 0.08; 0.10; 0.11; 0.12; 0.13

APPENDIX B

Appendix Review

(1) produced

(2) income; do not; net; depreciation

(3) value added

Basic Exercises: Appendix B

1. $2200
2. $1700
3. $1700
4. $500
5. $1200
6. $1700
7. $1700
8. $1700

Self-Tests: Appendix B

Test A

1. a	4. d	6. c
2. c	5. d	7. b
3. d		

Test B

1. F	4. F	7. F
2. T	5. F	8. F
3. F	6. T	

Supplementary Exercise: Appendix B

1. $MPC = 50/\sqrt{(DI + 2500)}$; MPC declines as income rises. Total consumption spending rises following redistribution from rich to poor as decline in consumption by rich is less than increase in consumption by poor.
   MPC + MPS = 1 and APC + APS = 1

CHAPTER 8

(1) increase; increasing; decrease

(2) intersection

(3) less; downward; lower; more; higher

(4) inflationary; recessionary

Basic Exercises

1. b. Difference is investment spending of 30.
   d. $320
   e. 290; 300; 310; 320; 330
   f. Spending would be greater than output, inventories would decline, firms would increase output.
   g. Inflationary gap; $20; recessionary gap, $30
   h. Expenditure schedule shifts up; $340; $300; aggregate-demand curve shifts to right.
2. b. $300
   c. $340

d. aggregate-demand curve
e. negative

Self-Tests

Test A

1. c	5. b	9. c
2. a	6. a	10. c
3. c	7. b	
4. b	8. b	

Test B

1. F	5. T	9. F
2. T	6. F	10. T
3. F	7. T	
4. F	8. F	

APPENDIX A

Basic Exercises: Appendix A

1. 0; $10; $20; $30; $40
2. $320; the same
3. Investment; not equilibrium since total spending exceeds total output.
4. Saving; now total spending less than output
5. $340; the same
6. $I = S$

APPENDIX B

Basic Exercises: Appendix B

1. $C + I = Y$; $(130 + 0.5\ Y) + 30 = Y$;
   $Y = 160/(0.5) = 320$
2. $Y = 170/(0.5) = 340$
3. $(140 + 0.5Y) + 30 = Y$;
   $Y = 170/(0.5) = 340$

CHAPTER 9

Chapter Review

(1) more than
(2) MPC
(3) consumption spending
(4) income; MPC
(5) smaller; inflation; imports; interest rates; taxation; exchange rates
(6) do not; supply; autonomous; horizontal

Basic Exercises

1. a. 370; 385; 400; 415; 430; equilibrium: 400
   b. 440

c. 40
d. 4; equilibrium level; income; autonomous spending
e. 0.75
f. $1/(1 - 0.75) = 1/(0.25) = 4$
2. less; autonomous
   a. 420
   b. –20
   c. fall
   d. 20; 4
   e. the same
   f. It ignores effects of inflation, imports, interest rates, taxation, and exchange rates

Self-Tests

Test A

1. c	5. b	9. b
2. b	6. c	10. c
3. c	7. c	
4. a	8. b	

Test B

1. F	5. F	9. F
2. F	6. F	10. T
3. T	7. F	
4. T	8. T	

CHAPTER 10

Chapter Review

(1) increase; movement along; shift in
(2) steeper
(3) intersection; increases
(4) inflationary; is; up; movement along; higher; lower
(5) less
(6) inflationary; supply

Basic Exercises

1. a. $420
   e. 95; $410
   f. Inflationary gap; increasing production costs would shift aggregate-supply curve; 100 and $400
   g. no gaps
   h. recessionary gap; elimination of gap likely to be very slow; 90; $420
2. horizontal
   a. no
   b. At P* aggregate demand exceeds aggregate supply. Prices will rise. The increase in prices implies a movement along the dashed aggregate-demand curve to the equilibrium given

by the intersection of the dashed aggregate-demand curve and the solid aggregate-supply curve. The increase in prices will reduce the purchasing power of money fixed assets, leading to a downward shift in the expenditure schedule. It is the downward shift in the expenditure schedule that reconciles the analysis in the income - expenditure diagram with that of the aggregate-demand/aggregate-supply diagram.

3. s, m, -, -; m, s, -, +;
   m, s, +, -; s, m, +, +

Self-Tests

Test A

1. b	5. c	9. a
2. b	6. d	10. d
3. a	7. d	
4. a	8. c	

Test B

1. T	5. F	9. F
2. T	6. F	10. F
3. T	7. F	
4. F	8. T	

Supplementary Exercise

1. $C + I = 1500 + 0.75Y -5P$
2. $P = 300 - 0.05Y$ or $Y = 6000 - 20P$
3. $P = 95$; $Y = 4100$
4. New expenditure schedule

$$C + I = 1450 + 0.75Y -5P$$

New aggregate-demand schedule

$$P = 290 - 0.05Y$$

$P = 90$; $Y = 4000$

CHAPTER 11

Chapter Review

(1) expenditure; demand; supply
(2) up; 1; 1; equal to
(3) are not; higher; increase; increase; 1; less; propensity; less; investment
(4) less; less
(5) income; consumption
(6) up; down; less; smaller
(7) smaller
(8) increase; decrease; decrease; increase; tariffs
(9) supply; increase

Basic Exercise

1. $360
2. $330
3. 2
4. $360
5. 1.2
6. The multiplier for a change in taxes is less than the multiplier for a change in government purchases.
7. No. The $25 reduction in taxes raised the GNP from $330 to $360. The increase in GNP increased tax revenues by $5 for an overall decrease in tax revenues of $20.
8. 7.5; 12.5
9. $330; the multipliers are the same.
10. MPC = .6; tax rate = 1/6.
    G multiplier = $1/(1 - .6 (1 - 1/6)) = 2$;
    Tax multiplier = $.6/(1 - .6 (1 - 1/6)) = 1.2$
11. Initial equilibrium = $360; G multiplier = $1/(1 - .6)$ = 2.5, which exceeds previous multiplier of 2. New equilibrium = $322.5.

Self-Tests

Test A

1. c	4. d	7. b
2. b	5. c	8. a
3. b	6. b	9. b

Test B

1. F	5. F	9. F
2. T	6. F	10. F
3. F	7. T	
4. F	8. F	

Supplementary Exercise

1. Income taxes and imports are reasons why the multiplier is less than the oversimplified formula.

APPENDIX

Basic Exercises: Appendix

1. $Y = 360$; $C = 225$
2. No; Y declines by 4 to 356; $I = 75$;
   $G = 55$; $C = 226$; tax and spending multipliers differ.

CHAPTER 12

Chapter Review

(1) barter; harder
(2) money
(3) commodity; fiat

(4) M1; M2
(5) lending; 850; reserve requirement
(6) 1/(reserve requirement); less
(7) excess; smaller; smaller
(8) contraction; no

Basic Exercise

1. 1000; unchanged; col. 1; 250; 750
2. Col. 2; 250; 750; 1000; 250; 0
3. Col. 3; 750; 0; 750; 187.50; 562.50; 1750; 750
4. Col. 4; 187.50; 562.50; 750; 187.50; 0
5. Col. 5; 562.50; 0; 562.50; 140.63; 421.87; 2312.50; 1312.50
6. 750; 562.50; 421.87; 316.41; 0.25; 4000; required reserve fraction.

Self-Tests

Test A

1. b	5. a, 9000	9. a
2. c	6. a	10. b
3. c	7. a	
4. d	8. d	

Test B

1. T	5. F	9. F
2. F	6. F	10. F
3. F	7. T	11. T
4. T	8. F	

Supplementary Exercises

1. 2750; 1750
2. Change in deposits = $(1/(M + E + C)) \times$ (change in the monetary base)

CHAPTER 13

Chapter Review

(1) 1935; central; monetary
(2) excess
(3) securities; buy; increase; reduction; destruction
(4) Bank Rate
(5) more; fewer; larger
(6) right; demand
(7) decreases; increased; right; increased; left
(8) intersection; supply; right; increase; decrease; left; decrease; increase
(9) exchange; depreciated; appreciated
(10) demand; supply; exports; financial; physical; supply; demand
(11) demand; increase; appreciation; supply; depreciation; appreciation
(12) surplus; buy; risen; foreign-exchange; flexible

Basic Exercise

1. decrease; left; restrictive; fall; rise
2. increase; right; supply; depreciate; less; more; increased; increases; right

Self-Tests

Test A

1. c	4. c	6. b
2. c	5. b	7. d
3. a		

Test B

1. F	4. F	7. T
2. F	5. F	8. F
3. F	6. F	

CHAPTER 14

Chapter Review

(1) GNP; money
(2) nominal GNP; *M; V; P; Y;* velocity
(3) money; does not; nominal GNP; 100
(4) should not; opportunity cost
(5) velocity
(6) decline; increase; increase
(7) increased; rise; decline
(8) increase; increase
(9) monetary; fiscal
(10) output; prices; steep; flat; steep; monetarist; Keynesian

Basic Exercise

1. V_1: 10.80; 11.49; 12.11; 13.35; 13.93; 13.78
   V_2: 3.15; 3.11; 2.93; 2.91; 2.80; 2.88
2. Col. 3: 248.4; 281.5; 307.6; 341.8; 392.8
   Col. 5: 268.1; 315.0; 341.7; 371.0; 377.4
3. Not clear; errors of similar magnitude for M_1 and M_2.

Self-Tests

Test A

1. b	5. d	9. c
2. c	6. b	10. b
3. a	7. d	
4. b	8. b	

Answers

Test B

1. T	5. F	9. F
2. F	6. F	10. T
3. F	7. F	
4. T	8. T	

Supplementary Exercises

1. 2400
2. increases to 2480
3. 2400; 12; 480
4. $BR = 104$; $M = 540$

CHAPTER 15

Chapter Review

(1) goods; money; right; right; money supply
(2) foreign; differential
(3) float; money supply; fixed
(4) higher; appreciates; contraction; export
(5) fixed; Bank of Canada; money supply; reinforces
(6) lower; domestic; currency; counteracts
(7) floating; depreciates; stimulation; reinforces
(8) floating; costs

Basic Exercise

a. option one: buy the Canadian bond for 100 Canadian dollars and end up with 112 Canadian dollars.

option two: buy 100 American dollars for 100 Canadian dollars; buy the American bond; and end up with 110 American dollars, which can be converted then to 110 Canadian dollars.

Since interest earnings of $12 are preferred to earnings of $10, choose option one.

b. option one: buy the Canadian bond and end up with 112 Canadian dollars, as before.

option two: buy 100 American dollars for $(100/0.95) =$ 105.26 Canadian dollars; buy the American bond; and end up with 110 American dollars, which can be converted then to $(110)(1/0.95) = (110)(1.0526) = 115.79$ Canadian dollars. The interest earnings in Canadian dollars are $(115.79 - 105.26) = \$10.52$

Since interest earnings of $12 are preferred to earnings of $10.52, choose option one.

c. option one: buy the Canadian bond and end up with 112 Canadian dollars.

option two: buy 100 American dollars for 100 Canadian dollars; buy the American bond; and end up with 110 American dollars, which can be converted then to

$(110)(1.0526) = 115.79$ Canadian dollars. The interest earnings in Canadian dollars are $(115.79 - 100) =$ $15.79

Since interest earnings of $15.79 are preferred to earnings of $12, choose option two.

Self-Tests

Test A

1. a	5. b
2. a	6. c
3. d	7. a
4. b	8. c

Test B

1. T	5. F
2. F	6. F
3. F	7. T
4. T	8. F

CHAPTER 16

Chapter Review

(1) purchasing power parity; depreciate; depreciating; appreciating
(2) Bretton
(3) deficit; demand; supply; surplus
(4) buy; increasing
(5) deficit; increase; decrease; contraction
(6) disliked
(7) speculators
(8) less; more; increase; decrease

Basic Exercise

I. 30
a. $4.80; Sales of French wine would increase. Sales of California wines would decrease. The U.S. balance of payments would show a deficit.
b. 15 cents
c. United States
d. deficit
e. depreciating

Self-Tests

Test A

1. b	4. c	7. c
2. b	5. d	8. b
3. b	6. c	9. b

Test B

1. T	5. F	9. T
2. F	6. F	10. F
3. T	7. F	
4. T	8. F	

Supplementary Exercises

1. Col. 1: $14,000,000; £5,000,000
   Col. 2: $14,000,000; £5,384,615
   Col. 3: $14,000,000; £5,833,333

CHAPTER 17

Chapter Review

(1) spending; revenue; revenue; spending; deficit; surplus
(2) down; demand; left; decline; decline; deficit; increase; decrease; accentuate
(3) will; will not
(4) small; small; large
(5) monetized
(6) foreigners
(7) investment; out

Basic Exercise

1. Col. 7: 364; 376; 388; 400; 412; 400
2. 0
3. surplus; 5
4. 380; deficit increased to 5; no change
5. raise; lower equilibrium level of income
6. lower; lower equilibrium level of income
7. 10; 360
8. –13.33; 3,46.67

Self-Tests

Test A

1. d	4. d	7. a
2. c	5. c	8. d
3. c	6. c	9. b

Test B

1. F	4. T	7. T
2. F	5. F	8. T
3. F	6. F	9. T

Supplementary Exercises

2. g. The ratio of debt to GNP should approach 0.7333.
   h. As long as g is greater than τ and λ is greater than R, the ratio of debt to GNP tends toward $(1 +$ $\lambda) (g - \tau) (\lambda - R)$. If g is less than τ, the government runs surpluses that eventually pay off the debt. If R is greater than λ, then interest payments on the debt are sufficient to make the national debt grow faster than GNP, and the ratio of debt to income grows without limit.

   Is recent experience a case of adjusting to a lower value for τ and hence a larger, but stable, ratio of debt to GNP or is it a case of interest rates exceeding the growth of GNP ($R > \lambda$), in which case there may be no limit to the ratio of debt to GNP? What is likely to happen if the ratio of national debt to GNP rises continuously?

CHAPTER 18

Chapter Review

(1) higher; negatively; Phillips; negative
(2) incorrect; inflationary; natural; vertical
(3) smaller; larger; higher; steeper
(4) vertical
(5) steep; fast; conflict
(6) lower; positive

Basic Exercise

1. purchase; decrease; increase; increase
2. 103
3. No; aggregate-supply curve will shift up as long as output exceeds full-employment level of output; prices will rise faster and faster, implying a vertical Phillips curve.
4. a. 370; 106
   b. expansionary; 109
   c. restrictive; 360

Self-Tests

Test A

1. d	5. d	9. c
2. a	6. a	10. d
3. c	7. d	
4. d	8. b	

Test B

1. F	5. T	9. F
2. F	6. F	10. F
3. T	7. T	
4. T	8. F	

CHAPTER 19

Chapter Review

(1) demand

(2) jawboning; 5
(3) expectations; is not; Anti-Inflation Board
(4) indexing
(5) increase
(6) more
(7) more; more; less; automatic
(8) are not

Basic Exercises

1. a. 440,000; $2,200,000; $440,000; 10%; yes
   b. 440,000; $2,200,000; $480,000; 7.5%; 20%; no;
      yes;
   c. 440,000; $2,310,000; $462,000; both wages and
      profits increase by 15.5%.
   d. What happens if inflation turns out to be different
      from the target rate?
2. Col. 3: 11.9%; 12.1%; 9.3%; 4.5%; 3.8%
   Col. 5: 13.9%; 14.1%; 11.3%; 6.5%; 5.8%

Self-Tests

Test A

1. b	4. b	7. c
2. b	5. c	8. c
3. a	6. d	

Test B

1. F	4. T	7. F
2. T	5. F	8. T
3. T	6. T	

CHAPTER 20

Chapter Review

(1) marginal; will; decrease
(2) price; greater; increase
(3) greater; price; marginal; more; up; negative
(4) demand; utility; inferior
(5) substitution; income; fewer; substitution; income

Basic Exercise

1. 55; 50; 40; 35; 25; 15; 10
2. 2; 4; 5
3. Col. 3: 10; 15; 10; 0; –20; –50, –85;
   Col. 5: 25; 45; 55; 60; 55; 40; 20;
   Col. 7: 35; 65; 85; 100; 105; 100; 90;

Self-Tests

Test A

1. b	5. b	9. b

2. a	6. d	10. a
3. d	7. d	
4. c	8. c	

Test B

1. T	5. T	9. F
2. F	6. T	10. T
3. F	7. F	
4. T	8. T	

APPENDIX

Appendix Review

(1) straight; negative; intercept; slope
(2) indifference; indifferent; are; negative
(3) in; more; substitution; decreases
(4) budget; indifference; highest; budget line
(5) budget line

Basic Exercise: Appendix

2. 20; 10
3. 3; 2
5. equals the slope of the budget line

Self-Tests: Appendix

Test A

1. c	3. b	5. a
2. d	4. c	

Test B

1. F	4. F	7. F
2. F	5. F	8. T
3. F	6. T	9. T

Supplementary Exercises: Appendix

2. $F = 114$; $C = 43$
3. $F = 84$; $C = 44$
4. $F = 124$; $C = 48$; no
5. $F = (Y + 20P_C - 12P_F)/2P_F$
   $C = (Y - 20P_C + 12P_F)/2P_C$
   where P_F = price of food, P_C = price of clothing and
   Y = income. The demand curves come from solving
   the following two equations for F and C:

   At tangency

   $$(F + 12)/(C + 20) = P_C/P_F$$

Budget constraint

   $$F \bullet P_F + C \bullet P_C = Y$$

CHAPTER 21

Chapter Review

(1) horizontal
(2) negative; negative; law
(3) shift in
(4) elasticity; demand
(5) zero; infinite; changes
(6) elastic; inelastic; unit elastic
(7) will not; 1.0
(8) greater; increase; decrease
(9) cross
(10) complements, negative; substitutes; positive

Basic Exercises

1. b. 1.0
   c. 1.0
   d. 1.0
2. straight
   a. 1.57; 1.0; 0.64; decreases
   b. $486,000; $540,000; $540,000; $486,000.
   Total revenue increases (decreases) as price
   declines if the elasticity of demand is greater
   (less) than 1.0. Total revenue increases
   (decreases) as prices increases if the elasticity of
   demand is less (greater) than 1.0.

Self-Tests

Test A

1. b	5. a	9. c
2. c	6. b	10. d
3. b	7. b	
4. a	8. a	

Test B

1. T	5. T	9. T
2. T	6. F	10. F
3. F	7. T	
4. F	8. F	

Supplementary Exercises

1. Not much; plotting historical data is an inappropriate
   way to estimate a demand curve.
2. a. $Q = 600 - 20P$
   b. flatter
   c. 3.0; equal
   d. $Q = 600 - 18P$; flatter; elasticity of market curve
   in between individual elasticities;
   Angela 3.0; Dan 1.50; market 2.08

CHAPTER 22

Chapter Review

(1) increase; physical; revenue
(2) marginal revenue; price
(3) reduce; less; more
(4) production; increasing; decreasing; constant
(5) short run
(6) output; total
(7) long run; lower
(8) is unchanged; less; fall; more; rises

Basic Exercise

1. 100 hectares; increasing returns; 0 to 2 workers;
   decreasing returns; 2 to 4 workers; negative returns;
   4 to 6 workers
2. 200 hectares; increasing returns; 0 to 2 workers;
   decreasing returns; 2 to 5 workers; negative returns;
   5 to 6 workers
   300 acres; increasing returns; 0 to 2 workers;
   decreasing returns; 2 to 6 workers
   The output-labour curve shifts up as land increases.
3. 100: 1; 3; 2; 1; –1; –2
   200: 2; 4; 3.5; 2.5; 1; –1
   300: 3; 4.5; 3.5; 3; 2; 1
4. Marginal returns to land generally decline.
5. increasing; constant; increasing; decreasing
6. $10 000; $20 000; $17 500; $12 500; $5 000; –$5 000
   Hire 4 workers; $28 000 = (12 000 × $5) - ($8 000 ×
   4)

Self-Tests

Test A

1. d	5. d	9. a
2. b	6. c	10. c
3. b	7. d	
4. c	8. b	

Test B

1. F	5. T	9. T
2. T	6. F	10. F
3. F	7. T	
4. F	8. F	

APPENDIX

Appendix Review

(1) production-indifference; more
(2) negative; will; diminishing marginal
(3) straight; horizontal

(4) lowest
(5) expansion

Basic Exercise: Appendix

1. 200; 2; 100; 3. The lowest budget line has both *x* and *y* axis intercepts that are closest to the origin.
2. $80

Self-Tests: Appendix

Test A

1. b   3. d
2. c

Test B

1. F   4. F   6. F
2. T   5. F   7. T
3. T

Supplementary Exercise: Appendix

2. 250,000 machines hours; 1,000,000 labour hours
3. b. MPP of labour = $250/\sqrt{L}$; the MPP of labour is the slope of the total product curve.
   c. MPP of labour declines continuously, but is never negative.
   d. 1,085,069.45 labour hours; (Find the quantity of labour such that the MPR of labour is equal to the price of labour. $(250/\sqrt{L}) \times 50 = 12$.) Output = 520,833.33 widgets.

CHAPTER 23

Chapter Review

(1) average; marginal
(2) marginal; marginal; profits; revenue; cost
(3) total
(4) marginal; marginal; positive; equals
(5) fixed; variable; variable; will not

Basic Exercises

1. a. Marginal cost: $1900; $1800; $1700; $1600; $1500; $2100; $2600; $2800; $3000
   Total revenue: $3500; $6800; $9900; $12 800; $15 500; $18 000; $20 300; $22 400; $24 300; $26 000
   Marginal revenue: $3300; $3100; $2900; $2700; $2500; $2300; $2100; $1900; $1700
   b. 7
   c. 7 widgets. Increasing output to 8 entails negative marginal profits as marginal cost exceeds marginal revenue;

   d. $7700
   e. average cost: $2000; $1950; $1900; $1850; $1800; $1750; $1800; $1900; $2000; $2100
   f. profits; does not (in this case)
   g. marginal cost same as in a; average costs increase; 7; $6700
2. is not; horizontal; vertical; horizontal

Self-Tests

Test A

1. b   5. c   9. c
2. b   6. c   10. a
3. d   7. c
4. a   8. b

Test B

1. F   5. F   9. F
2. F   6. T   10. F
3. F   7. T
4. F   8. F

APPENDIX

Basic Exercise: Appendix

1. a. The marginal-profit curve should equal zero where total profits are maximized.
   b. The marginal-cost curve should go through the minimum of the average-cost curve.

Supplementary Exercises: Appendix

1. a. $16 000
   b. Average cost = $16 000/Q + 120 − 0.4Q + 0.002Q^2$
      Marginal cost = $120 − 0.8Q + 0.006Q^2$
   c. It should.
   d. Marginal revenue = $300 − 0.5Q$
   f. Q = 200
   g. Find the positive value of *Q* such that marginal cost = marginal revenue
      $120 − 0.8Q + 0.006Q^2 = 300 − 0.5Q$
      Q = 200
   h. Price = $250; total revenue = $50 000; total cost = $40 000; total profits = $10 000
   j. Average cost = $20 000/Q + 120 − 0.4Q + 0.002Q^2$
      No change in profit maximizing level of output; total profits = $6000
2. Demand is elastic up to the point of 600 stereo sets and $150. Demand is inelastic beyond that point. The profit-maximizing level of output in Question 1, 200 sets and $250, is in the elastic portion of the demand curve.

CHAPTER 24

Chapter Review

(1) proprietorship; partnership; corporation; limited
(2) stock; bonds; ploughback
(3) are not; more; bonds; meet bond payments
(4) falls; loss; increase; gain
(5) riskiness
(6) higher; lower; insurance
(7) random walk; today

Basic Exercise

1. a. 16%; 10%; 6.25%; 4%
   b. 40
   c. Stock price will fall to $25; stock price will rise to $64.
   d. At the previous price of $40; a dividend of $8 offers a 20 percent return, twice that available on corporate bonds. The increased demand for ABC stock will increase its price now.
   e. $80; an $80 stock price and $8 dividend imply a 10 percent return.

Self-Tests

Test A

1. b	4. a	7. d
2. d	5. d	8. a
3. c	6. b	9. b

Test B

1. T	4. F	7. F
2. F	5. F	8. F
3. F	6. F	9. F

CHAPTER 25

Chapter Review

(1) Many; Identical; Easy; Perfect; do not; zero
(2) horizontal; marginal
(3) marginal; losses; variable; fixed
(4) horizontal; demand; supply
(5) loss, three; better; opportunity
(6) profits; (shaded rectangle should go from the y axis to a quantity of 1450 and from 20 to 14, the difference between the market price and the firm's average cost when producing 1450 units of output); enter; right; fall; $13.70 (minimum average cost; see the Basic Exercise); average

Basic Exercise

1. 1400; $5544 = (P − AC)Q; $5310; $5330

2. 1200; −$4380 = (P − AC)Q; −$4550; −$4532; −$10 140 (fixed costs)
3. 0; price does not cover average variable cost.
4. $13.70; 1300

Self-Tests

Test A

1. b	5. b	9. c
2. c	6. b	10. d
3. d	7. c	
4. c	8. c	

Test B

1. F	5. F	9. F
2. F	6. F	10. F
3. F	7. F	
4. F	8. T	

Supplementary Exercise

1. a. Average Cost = $10 140/Q + 0.00001Q^2 − 0.02Q + 15$
   b. Average variable cost = $0.00001Q^2 − 0.02Q + 15$
   c. Marginal cost = $0.00003Q^2 − 0.04Q + 15$
3. To find the minimum of either cost curve set its derivative equal to zero.
   For AC, Q = 1300; AC = 13.70;
   for Q = 1300, MC = 13.70
   For AVC, Q = 1000; AVC = 5;
   for Q = 1000, MC = 5
4. Supply = 0 if P<5

$$\text{Supply} = \frac{0.04 + \sqrt{-0.0002 + 0.00012P}}{0.00006} \quad if \ P>5$$

CHAPTER 26

Chapter Review

(1) are not
(2) selection; planning; distribution
(3) was not; efficient
(4) efficient; decreasing
(5) utility; cost
(6) increase; cost; greater; is not; equals
(7) price; marginal cost; price; price
(8) utility; cost; equals
(9) input-output

Basic Exercise

1. 7; 5
2. 2; more
3. decrease; 2; fewer
4. 5

Answers

Self-Tests

Test A

1. d	5. b	9. a
2. b	6. c	10. a
3. b	7. b	
4. a	8. c	

Test B

1. T	5. F	9. F
2. F	6. F	10. T
3. F	7. T	
4. T	8. T	

APPENDIX

Basic Exercises: Appendix

1. every consumer must have the same marginal utility for every commodity.
   a. No
   b. increase; 1; increase; 2; inefficient
   c. All consumers respond to the same set of prices and consume so that marginal utility equals price.
2. marginal revenue product of any input is the same in every industry.
   a. 120; 1200; marginal physical product; the price of output; 120; 600; zero; +600

CHAPTER 27

Chapter Review

(1) one; no
(2) natural; barriers; entry
(3) negative; lower
(4) marginal; marginal revenue; price; is not
(5) average; less; below; above
(6) demand; greater; less; less; will not; higher; lower
(7) price; price; marginal revenue; less; greater; greater
(8) up; down
(9) will not; does not; maker

Basic Exercise

1. Total revenue: $114 000; $120 900; $127 400; $133 500; $139 200
   Total cost: $84 816; $90 441; $96 516; $103 041; $110 016
   Marginal revenue: $6900; $6500, $6100; $5700
   Marginal cost: $5625; $6075; $6525; $6975
   a. 14
   b. revenue; cost; 14
   c. $9100
   d. $30 884

2. Total revenue: $114 000; $120 900; $127 400; $133 500; $139 200
   Marginal revenue: $6900; $6500; $6100; $5700
   Total cost: $96 816; $103 441; $110 516; $118 041; $126 016
   Marginal cost: $6625; $7075; $7525; $7975
   a. 13 widgets; $9300; $13 000; $200
   b. $17 459
3. No change in output = 14 widgets; no change in price = $9100; profits down $30 884 to $17 884. No change in pollution as output is unchanged. The differences between Questions 2 and 3 reflect the differences between the effects of a change in marginal and fixed costs. Note that in Question 2 marginal cost changed as the tax was imposed on each widget produced. In Question 3 marginal cost in unchanged as the pollution charge in independent of the number of widgets produced.

Self-Tests

Test A

1. d	5. a	9. b
2. c	6. c	10. a
3. b	7. b	
4. c	8. b	

Test B

1. F	5. T	9. F
2. T	6. F	10. F
3. F	7. T	
4. F	8. F	

Supplementary Exercise

a. Total revenue = $11\,900Q - 200Q^2$
   Marginal revenue = $11\,900 - 400Q$
   Average cost = $225Q + 52\,416/Q$
   Marginal cost = $450Q$
c. $11\,900 - 400Q = 450Q$; $850Q = 11\,900$; $Q = 14$
d. Per-unit charge:
   TC = $52\,416 + 225Q^2 + 1000Q$
   AC = $225Q + 52\,416/Q + 1000$
   MC = $450Q + 1000$
   Fixed charge:
   TC = $65\,416 + 225Q^2$
   AC = $225Q + 65\,416/Q$
   MC = $450Q$
   Note that the addition of a fixed cost element does not change marginal cost.

CHAPTER 28

Chapter Review

(1) monopolistic; negative; marginal revenue; marginal cost; zero; entry; tangent; average

(2) oligopoly; cartel; price leadership

(3) zero; lower; larger

(4) payoff; strategy; zero-sum

(5) will; will not; revenue; cost

(6) entry; exit; opportunity cost; capital

Basic Exercises

1. a. Total revenue: $11 400; $13 600; $15 000;
   $15 600; $15 400
   Total cost: $13 002; $14 000; $15 000; $15 996;
   $16 996
   Total profit: -$1602; -$400; 0; -$396; -$1596
   Profit-maximizing level of output = 1000 meals
   b. Marginal revenue: $2200; $1400; $600; -$200
   Marginal cost: $998; $1000; $996; $1000
   Profit-maximizing level of output = 1000 meals
   MC is less than MR at less than 1000 meals
   MC exceeds MR at more than 1000 meals.
   See also the Supplementary Exercise to this
   chapter.
2. a. Strategy C
   b. Strategy V
   c. Each firm gets 50 percent of the market.
   d. Strategy B
   e. Strategy U
   f. The series of alternative adjustments continues
      forever; C, V, B, U, A, W, C, V, B. . .
   g. Neither firm has an incentive to change its
      strategy.

Self-Tests

Test A

1. b	5. c	9. c
2. d	6. c	10. b
3. a	7. b	
4. d	8. c	

Test B

1. T	5. F	9. T
2. T	6. T	10. F
3. F	7. T	
4. F	8. F	

Supplementary Exercise

Total Revenue = $25 Q - Q^2/100$
Marginal Revenue = $25 - Q/50$
Average Cost = $10 000/Q + 5$
Marginal Cost = 5
Profit-maximizing level of output: $25 - Q/50 = 5$;
$Q = 1000$

CHAPTER 29

Chapter Review

(1) opportunity

(2) marginal cost; marginal utility; on

(3) little

(4) externalities; detrimental; beneficial externalities

(5) higher; higher

(6) private; inefficient; much; less

(7) excludability; depletability; public

(8) difficult; rider

(9) zero; zero

(10) limited

(11) does not; less

(12) irreversible

Basic Exercise

1. Col. 1: 125; $2 640 000; $11; 100; $2 112 000; $10.56
2. 4.17; Col. 2: 120; $2 640 000; $11; 100; $2 200 000;
   $11; cost of producing widgets unchanged; cost per
   hour of police service up 4.17 percent.
3. Col. 3: 80; $2 640 000; $11; 100; 3 300 000; $16.50;
   cost of producing widgets unchanged; cost per hour
   of police service up 56 percent over 11 years.

Self-Tests

Test A

1. c	5. a	9. d
2. d (possibly b)	6. b	10. b
3. b	7. b	
4. a	8. b	

Test B

1. F	5. F	9. T
2. F	6. F	10. F
3. T	7. T	
4. F	8. T	

Supplementary Exercises

1. b. Widgets: MP(L) = 33.33   AP(L) = 66.67
      Recitals: MP(L) = 50   AP(L) = 50
   c. Widgets: MP(L) = 36.67   AP(L) = 73.33
      Recitals: MP(L) = 50   AP(L) = 50
   d. Opportunity cost of recitals has increased 10
      percent from 0.67 widgets to 0.73 widgets:
      PPF: $M = 50 [10 000 - W^2/(3600 K)]$
   e. The new production possibilities frontier is never
      inside the original frontier.

CHAPTER 30

Chapter Review

(1) regulate; nationalize
(2) scale; scope; is not; below; above; fixed; variable
(3) high
(4) fully distributed
(5) marginal; lower; less; demand
(6) less; incentive
(7) regulatory; inefficiency; efficiency

Basic Exercise

2. $6 million loss; $6 million loss; $6 million loss
3. No; fixed costs are never covered.

Self-Tests

Test A

1. c	4. b	7. b
2. d	5. c	8. a
3. c	6. d	9. a

Test B

1. F	5. T	9. T
2. F	6. T	10. F
3. F	7. T	
4. F	8. F	

CHAPTER 31

Chapter Review

(1) Trade; was not
(2) Combines Investigation; criminal; limit competition
(3) 1984
(4) merger; vertical; horizontal; conglomerate
(5) less; efficiency
(6) increasing; reduction; increase
(7) concentration; more; little

Basic Exercise

1. Total Revenue: $2 400 000; $3 093 750; $3 675 000;
   $4 143 750; $4 500 000; $4 743 750; $4 875 000;
   $4 893 750
   Marginal Revenue: $37; $31; $25; $19; $13; $7; $1
   Price $33; Output 143 750; Profits $806 250
2. Centerville; Total Revenue: $480 000; $1 125 000;
   $1 680 000; $2 145 000; $2 520 000; $2 805 000;
   $3 000 000; $3 105 000
   Marginal Revenue: $43; $37; $31; $25; $19; $13; $7
   Price $30; Quantity 100 000

Middletown: Total Revenue: $1 920 000; $1 968 750;
$1 995 000; $1 998 750; $1 980 000; $1 938 750;
$1 875 000; $1 788 750
Marginal Revenue: $13; $7; $1; –$5; –$11 –$17;
–$23
Price $45; Quantity 43 750
Profits: $1 031 250
3. Middletown; Centerville

Self-Tests

Test A

1. c	4. d	7. b
2. a	5. b	8. d
3. a	6. c	9. e

Test B

1. T	5. T	9. F
2. T	6. F	10. F
3. T	7. F	
4. F	8. F	

CHAPTER 32

Chapter Review

(1) comparative
(2) scale
(3) comparative
(4) A; B; 800; wheat
(5) 200; 120; wheat; cars
(6) demand; supply; exporting; importing
(7) tariffs; quotas; subsidies; price; quantity
(8) government
(9) low; do not; can
(10) adjustment
(11) defense; infant

Basic Exercise

1. a. Japan; Japan
   b. ⅔; 1½; Canada; Japan; Canada; Japan
   c. Calculators: 1 000 000; 3 000 000; 4 000 000
      Backpacks: 1 500 000; 2 000 000; 3 500 000
   d. 300 000; 450 000
   e. 600 000 hours; 300 000 calculators; 200 000
      backpacks
   f. increase; 250 000
   g. Calculators: 700 000; 3 450 000; 4 150 000
      Backpacks: 1 950 000; 1 700 000; 3 650 000
      The output of both calculators and backpacks
      has increased as compared to Question c.
   h. Canadian backpack output would fall to
      1 050 000. Japan would need to reallocate
      1 350 000 labour hours. Total calculator output

would fall to 3 625 000. This reallocation is not in line with the principle of comparative advantage. The opportunity cost of backpacks in terms of calculators is greater in Japan than in Canada.

   i. There will be no change in total world output. Neither country has a comparative advantage. The opportunity cost of increased calculator or backpack production is the same in both countries.

2. a. $16; 350 000; 50 000

   b. higher; lower; higher; greater

   c. quota of 75 000 shirts; yes, incentives for efficiency; government revenue

Self-Tests

Test A

1. b	5. a	9. d
2. b	6. a	10. b
3. c	7. c	
4. a	8. c	

Test B

1. F	5. T	9. F
2. F	6. T	10. F
3. F	7. T	
4. T	8. F	

Supplementary Exercises

1. a. Baulmovia: 8, 100; Bilandia: 17, 150
   b. 12; Baulmovia; Bilandia; 100
   c. Baulmovia: price = 10;
     Bilandia: price = 14.5;
     Trade = 50.
   d. 50
   e. Tariff revenues accrue to the government. Tariffs do not protect high-cost foreign producers.

2. Production of 14.4 million bolts of cloth and 10.8 million bottles of wine allows Ricardia to choose from the outermost consumption possibilities line. Note that to be on the outermost consumption possibilities line Ricardia must choose to produce at the point where the slope of the production possibilities frontier equals the ratio of world prices.

CHAPTER 33

Chapter Review

(1) direct; indirect; personal income

(2) average; marginal; progressive; proportional; regressive

(3) increase; less; shelters

(4) equity; horizontal equity; vertical equity; vertical

(5) benefits; benefits

(6) burden; greater; excess burden; does not; excess

(7) higher; lower; smaller

(8) incidence; flypaper; shifting

(9) demand; supply; inelastic; workers; firms; elastic; little

Basic Exercise

2. $42; 50 million

3. $46; 44 million

4. $4; it is less than increase in tax.

5. All are likely to decline.

7. The first demand curve.

8. $50; 48 million; Figure 33-3; Figure 33-3; consumers

Self-Tests

Test A

1. b	5. c	9. a
2. c	6. b	10. d
3. c	7. b	
4. d	8. c	

Test B

1. F	4. T	7. F
2. F	5. T	8. T
3. T	6. F	9. F

Supplementary Exercise

Total taxes: $92; $1315; $4424; $15 861; $30 165
Average tax rate: 1.8%; 13.2%; 22.1%; 31.7%; 37.7%
Marginal tax rate: 8.9%; 26.7%; 29.6%; 44.4%; 50.3%

CHAPTER 34

Chapter Review

(1) externality; decrease; taxes

(2) controls

(3) inefficient; efficient; marginal

(4) increase

Basic Exercise

1. 15 cents; 10 million

2. falls; rises; no change in short run, declines in long run; shifts up by 5 cents; short run—declines; long run—no change or falls to zero; declines

3. Since the tax is per bag, not per unit of pollution, the pollution control equipment will not reduce a firm's pollution tax.

4. No. Since the equipment is only 75 percent effective,

the total cost of using the equipment (4 cents plus the 1.25-cent tax per bag) is greater than the tax of 5 cents per bag.

5. less than 3.75 cents; more than 5.33 cents

6. Price rises and industry output declines as at least some high-cost firms leave the industry.

Self-Tests

Test A

1. b   4. b
2. b   5. d
3. a

Test B

1. F   5. F   9. F
2. F   6. F   10. F
3. T   7. F
4. T   8. T

Supplementary Exercises

2. a. 60 000; $12; $360 000
   b. 40 000; $14; $240 000; yes
      50 000; $13; $250 000
   c. market; 120 000; $6, 240 firms each producing 500 gizmos
   d. Now AC = 0.00004 $(Q -500)^2$ + 8
      Short run: Each firm produces 466 gizmos.
      Long run: Market 100 000; $8; 200 firms each producing 500 gizmos.

CHAPTER 35

Chapter Review

(1) can never; price
(2) interest; increasing
(3) interest
(4) discourage; incentive; encourage; incentive; encourage
(5) greater
(6) high; unemployment; tax; foreign

Basic Exercises

1. Energy: 69.7; 80.3; 78.6; 78.5; 76.5; 77.1; 74.4; 72.7; 73.8; 74.1; 74.3; 74.3; 70.8; 70.9
   Petroleum: 31.4; 37.5; 36.3; 36.2; 35.0; 34.6; 33.5; 32.2; 32.2; 31.8; 31.9; 30.8; 28.2; 26.2
   Energy and petroleum intensities in the early 1970s exceeded those in 1962. After the early 1970s, both energy and petroleum intensities declined significantly in response to higher prices. Energy intensity in 1982 was approximately equal to that in

1962, while petroleum intensity in 1982 was significantly lower than in 1962.

2. Copper: 52.7¢; 52.4¢; 55.2¢; 35.0¢; 22.0¢; 29.2¢; 27.9¢; 26.8¢; 34.3¢; 52.3¢; 31.5¢
   Bauxite: $11.24; $13.34; $13.25; $7.82; $13.10; $14.64; $8.58; $11.95; $11.87; $5.14
   Manganese: 143.8; 124.5; 161.0; 129.4; 159.4; 99.8; 95.1
   Chromite: $34.52; $36.67; $22.25; $53.48; $26.77; $57.22; $38.04; $41.27; $20.38
   Tungsten: $0.69; $1.05; $0.48; $1.35; $2.54; $1.78; $1.20; $1.84; $2.39;
   Molybdenum: $.61; $1.24; $1.68; $1.08; $1.33; $1.56; $2.77
   Copper 1900: Bauxite 1940; Manganese 1940; Chromite 1950; Tungsten 1940; Molybdenum 1981
   Remember that eventually something akin to the Hotelling effect must come to dominate resource prices.

Self-Tests

Test A

1. c   4. c   7. d
2. b   5. c   8. b
3. d   6. c   9. a

Test B

1. F   5. T   9. F
2. F   6. F   10. T
3. F   7. F
4. T   8. F

CHAPTER 36

Chapter Review

(1) productivity; revenue
(2) negative; more; positive; higher; below; demand; supply
(3) discounting; fewer; lower; negatively
(4) is not
(5) all; no
(6) most; part; is
(7) higher; equal; low
(8) increase; increase; more
(9) greater; greater; innovation; greater

Basic Exercise

1. Marginal revenue; $45; $40; $35; $30
   30 hours; At $7.50 per hour, Dionne must earn at least $37.50 for five hours.
2. $305; $225; $50

3. Marginal revenue; $45; $40; $35; $30
   30 hours
4. $285; $225; $50; $10
   The differences in land rents equal the difference in productivity.

Self-Tests

Test A

1. c	5. a	9. b
2. c	6. b	10. a
3. b	7. c	
4. d	8. b	

Test B

1. F	5. F	9. T
2. T	6. T	10. F
3. T	7. F	
4. F	8. F	

APPENDIX

Basic Exercise: Appendix

1. $4000; $1818.18; $2066.12; 3884.30; –$115.70
2. cost; no
3. $4000; $1904.76; $2267.57; $4172.33; $172.33
4. present value of returns; yes
5. 5 percent: $200; $4200; $2200; $110; $2310
   10 percent: $400; $4400; $2400; $240; $2640
6. 5 percent: $1800; $90; $4390; $190
   10 percent: $1600; $160; $4260; –$140

CHAPTER 37

Chapter Review

(1) leisure; more; decrease; income
(2) more; substitution; increases; income; decrease; slope; position
(3) demand, supply; demand; higher
(4) minimum; decrease; supply
(5) unskilled; unions
(6) monopolistic; demand; right
(7) monopsonist; price; lower; higher; two; bilateral
(8) collective bargaining; mediation; arbitration; mediator; arbitrator
(9) restricted

Basic Exercise

1. 60; 55; 50; 45; 40; 35; 30; 25; 20; 15

2. $2400; $2200; $2000; $1800; $1600; $1400; $1200; $1000; $800; 600
3. 7
4. Total profits with 7 workers: $4900
   (315 × $40) – (7 × $1100)
   Total profits with 6 workers: $4800
   (285 × $40) – (6 × $1100)
   Total profits with 8 workers: $4800
   (340 × $40) – (8 × $1100)
5. $1000; 800; 8; $5600
6. a. $1800
   b. 900 workers
   c. $1400 and 600 workers, or $1200 and 700 workers

Self-Tests

Test A

1. d	4. b	7. c
2. b	5. b	8. d
3. a	6. c	9. d; a; e; f; b; c; f

Test B

1. T	5. F	9. F
2. T	6. F	10. T
3. F	7. F	11. T
4. T	8. F	

APPENDIX

Basic Exercise: Appendix

1. $1000; 8; no; Tony is a monopsonist; Price is less than marginal cost of labour for a monopsonist.
2. greater
   Total labour cost: $300; $800; $1500; $2400; $3500; $4800; $6300; $8000; $9900; $12 000
   Marginal labour cost: $300; $500; $700; $900; $1100; $1300; $1500; $1700; $1900; $2100
4. 6 workers
5. $800
6. $6600 ($40 × 285 – 6 × $800)
7. Both wages and employment would increase. Tony would hire 7 workers at $1100 a month. The "high" minimum wage increases employment because Tony is a monopsonist. The minimum wage changes Tony's marginal cost of labour schedule.
8. No. If the union had more than 7 workers, it might want a lower wage to increase employment. If the union had 7 or fewer workers, it might be able to extract a higher wage.

CHAPTER 38

Chapter Review

(1) absolute; relative
(2) Lorenz, zero; 45°; positive; below; very little
(3) 38.9; 6.3
(4) efficiency
(5) marginal; decrease
(6) decrease; break-even; negative; small
(7) different; are not; overstate; employers

Basic Exercise

1. 6480; 6900; 7740; 6541; 7100; 7800; 8060; 9930;
   10 435; 11 060
3. Col. (4) 420; 840; –1199; 559; 700; 260; 1870; 505;
   625
   Col. (5) 180; 2760; –1200; 240; 300; 140; 1730; 295;
   575
   Col. (6) 30; 77; 120 000; 30; 30; 35; 48; 37; 5

   The implicit marginal-tax rate is the slope of the
   schedule you graphed in Figure 38-1. These
   marginal rates are not equaled under the positive
   portion of the federal income-tax system until very
   high income levels.

Self-Tests

Test A

1. b	5. c	9. a
2. d	6. d	10. c
3. a	7. a	
4. c	8. d	

Test B

1. T	5. T	9. T
2. F	6. F	10. F
3. F	7. T	
4. T	8. F	

CHAPTER 39

Chapter Review

(1) more; more; demand; supply; out
(2) applied; basic; reduce
(3) investment; entrepreneurship
(4) easier; lower; comparative; absolute
(5) investment; real; nominal; basic; basic; applied

Basic Exercises

1. 1%; $18 362; $19 298; $21 317; $23 548; $26 011
   2%; $18 727; $20 676; $25 204; $30 724; $37 452

3%; $19 096; $22 138; $29 751; $39 983; $53 734
No; because productivity growth compounds, the
advantages of higher rates of productivity growth
over lower rates continue to grow.
2. Table 38-2
   1962: 70.3; 84.4
   1972: 104.1; 102.6
   1982: 112.1; 106.9
   Table 38-3
   1972-1962: 48.1; 21.6
   1982-1972: 7.7; 4.2

Self-Tests

Test A

1. c	5. b	9. c
2. a	6. d	10. a
3. c	7. d	
4. d	8. a	

Test B

1. F	5. F	9. T
2. F	6. F	10. F
3. T	7. F	
4. T	8. T	

CHAPTER 40

Chapter Review

(1) exponential; cannot
(2) inventiveness; entrepreneurship; work ethic;
investment; research; development; embodied;
disembodied
(3) opportunity; consumption; saving
(4) increased
(5) inequality; have not
(6) has not; increase; higher
(7) less (footnote: I; C; C) difficult
(8) death; inexpensive; decrease
(9) overvalued; raise; technical
(10) brain drain; grants; World

Basic Exercise

1. b. Figure 40-1 shows a clear, positive relationship
      between more investment and higher rates of
      growth. However, be careful of oversimplified
      generalizations based on these data. This is only
      a sample of countries, and, as explained in the
      text, many other factors also influence the growth
      rate of income. Still, investment—that is, the
      accumulation of capital—is clearly a very
      important factor.

2. a. 98 years, 8 months
   b. LDCs: $792; $1014; $8270; $11 977
      DCs: $8618; $10 002; $35 456; $44 329
      Difference: $7826; $8988; $27 186; $32 352
      Ratio: .0919; .1014; .2332; .2702
      The difference between the "difference" and
      "ratio" reflects the much higher initial base for
      developed countries.
   c. 248 years, 6 months; $323 433
   d. 198 years

Self-Tests

Test A

1. d	5. a	9. c
2. d	6. d	10. b
3. c	7. b	
4. c	8. b	

Test B

1. T	6. F	11. F
2. F	7. F	12. F
3. F	8. F	13. F
4. T	9. T	14. F
5. T	10. T	

Supplementary Exercises

3. 1 124 years, 1 month, 7 days

CHAPTER 41

Chapter Review

(1) markets; planning
(2) capitalism; socialism
(3) is not; socialist; markets
(4) consumers; planners; freedom; market; planned; profit; about the same; more; planned
(5) capitalist; privately; equal; welfare
(6) indicative; investment; would
(7) individual firms; workers; maximize profits; wages
(8) socialist; Five; One; quotas
(9) material
(10) orders; data; deceive; little; high; low
(11) higher; technology; agricultural; investment; consumption
(12) planned; state; less

Self-Tests

Test A

1. c	5. d	9. b
2. a	6. a	10. d
3. d; a; c; b	7. d	
4. a	8. b	

Test B

1. F	5. T	9. F
2. F	6. F	10. F
3. T	7. T	
4. T	8. F	

CHAPTER 42

Chapter Review

(1) philosophy; freedom; less
(2) laissez-faire; smaller; monopolies; externalities; are often
(3) power; do not; planning; technocrats; their own self-interest; growth; opportunities for their own advancement
(4) private; public; quality
(5) disagree; is not; disagree; opportunity cost; takeover
(6) ahistorical; given; ruling (capitalist) classes; efficiency; equality; power; quality; alienation; naive; ruling classes; power; bribe
(7) is; agree; rhetoric
(8) participatory; decentralized

Self-Tests

Test A

1. libertarians; c; Galbraith; a, b, e, f; New Left; a, b, d, e, f
2. c
3. c
4. Solow; disagree, agree, disagree; Galbraith; agree, disagree, agree
5. b
6. d
7. b

Test B

1. T	5. T	9. F
2. T	6. F	10. F
3. T	7. T	
4. F	8. F	

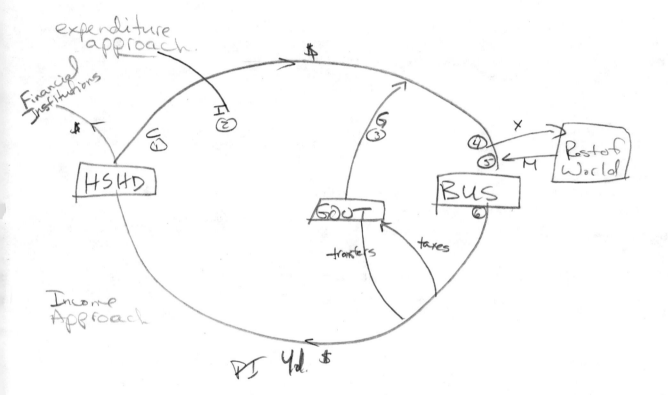

expenditure
approach.

Financial
Institutions

Income
Approach

HSHD

GOVT

BUS

Rest of
World

transfers   taxes

PI Yd. $

X

M

①

②

③

④

⑤

⑥

$